Sphere of Influence

Sphere of Influence
Writings on cricket and its discontents

GIDEON HAIGH

SIMON &
SCHUSTER

London · New York · Sydney · Toronto · New Delhi

A CBS COMPANY

First published by Victory Books,
an imprint of Melbourne University Publishing, in 2010
First published in Great Britain in 2011 by Simon & Schuster UK Ltd
A CBS COMPANY

1 3 5 7 9 10 8 6 4 2

Simon & Schuster UK Ltd
1st Floor
222 Gray's Inn Road
London
WC1X 8HB

www.simonandschuster.co.uk

Simon & Schuster Australia, Sydney
Simon & Schuster India, New Delhi

The publishers have made every effort to contact those holding rights in
the material reproduced in this book. Where this has not been possible, the
publishers will be glad to hear from those who recognise their material.

A CIP catalogue copy for this book
is available from the British Library.

ISBN: 978-0-85720-684-8

Design and typography © Melbourne University Publishing Limited, 2010
Printed in the UK by CPI Cox & Wyman, Reading, Berkshire RG1 8EX

Contents

INTRODUCTION

A World of Worry

> *The British 'Sphere of Influence'*—the cricket ball.
> Anonymous, Mr Punch's Book of Sport (1907)

> *In the Victorian era, cricket was an Anglo-Saxon political tool*
> *to civilise the world. Today is an Eastern economic imperialism rooted*
> *in cricket about to commence?*
> Boria Majumdar, *An Illustrated History of Indian Cricket* (2007)

Does any game worry more than cricket? There are the on-field frictions: sledging, appealing, chucking, cheating. There are off-field fixations: administrative lapses, player peccadillos. The one-time game of Empire sinks readily into postcolonial brooding on nation, race, religion, sovereignty, security. Each of the three forms of international competition has become freighted with concerns. Is Test cricket too old-fashioned? Is one-day cricket too formulaic? Is Twenty20 cricket too successful, and might it eclipse either of the others, or both?

For all that, cricket is a micro-worrier. Its Laws are voluminous, its codes of conduct and definitions of fair play constantly expanding, its systems of adjudication neurotic in their sophistication. Yet to truly big issues, like its governance structure and global economy, there is a kind of studied indifference. The International Cricket Council? Beyond redemption. The Board of Control for Cricket in India? Beyond restriction. The players? Too greedy. The media? Too cynical. Can we just watch, please? We'll be good, really we will—just don't let them take our lovely game away.

What constitutes cricket's welfare, meanwhile, is seldom addressed in other than banal terms. Cricket must grow. Cricket must change with the times. Cricket must expand its audience. Because, you know, lots of people are running around saying that cricket must shrink, must turn back the clock and reduce its audience, aren't there? As one modern expert puts it:

The game is definitely at the coalface of anticipated change. What I can bring to the table is a real currency and a slightly more contemporary style of looking at the way cricket and the business of cricket is managed and maintained. Strategically it's really important to recognise that iconic series such as the Ashes can never be removed, and in fact need to be protected and maintained, throughout the cricketing landscape. At a time when the market is looking to find new ways to engage our sport I think it's also really important to go on a journey and go on a debate and recognise that we have got something very special in the creation of franchise cricket and the globalisation of those brands.

The qualifications for this speaker are not, surprisingly, an MBA and a decade at McKinsey, but 8625 Test runs at 50.7. Matthew Hayden, for it is he, joined the Cricket Australia board a year ago, seamlessly swapping a bat for a Blackberry, already as fluent in jargon as he was through the covers. And when the cricketers already sound like marketing wise-guys, just imagine what the marketing wise-guys sound like ...

Ostensibly, authority for global cricket is vested in the ICC, with its ten full (Test-playing) members, and thirty-four associate and sixty affiliate members. In reality, such a large proportion of the game's commercial activity and fans are located in India that nothing happens without the say-so of the mahouts aboard the thirty-one-member elephant that is the BCCI, whose annual revenues for 2010–11 were set to exceed US$400 million. And modern cricket's lucrative instability stems from nowhere but the BCCI's creation of supranational Twenty20 attractions beyond the jurisdiction of the ICC, offering rewards by comparison with which those in the established international game pale.

Arguably, no single game is bigger in any single country: the dynamism of India's economy, growing between 4 per cent and 10 per cent annually during the twenty-first century, and the size and shape of India's population, 1.2 billion people, half of them under twenty-five, make it so. India is also, of course, a bafflingly diverse and contradictory country, containing four of the world's eight richest men and 40 per cent of its chronically malnourished children, possessed of a world-class information technology industry while two-thirds of its people remain dependent on agriculture and half have no electricity, proud to espouse free-market turbocapitalism while ranking 133rd out of 183 countries in 'ease of doing business' according to the World Bank's 2010 *Doing Business Report*. But its people, for all their huge and minute differences of ethnicity, religion, caste, wealth and education, share an incandescent passion for cricket—which makes cricket a key means of exploiting its new prosperity.

What follows are my own attempts at intervals over the last two years to make sense of cricket's new order: the spread of Twenty20 and of private ownership, the eclipse of international cricket's other formats and of the ICC, the rise of India, the tribulations of Pakistan, the prodigies of Lalit Modi, the false promise of Allen Stanford. My background in journalism is in business. At times, it feels like I have come full circle. Historically, cricket has been the most traditional of games; it has developed a taste for change bordering on compulsive. Prognostication is perilous under such circumstances; on the other hand, like going for a catch maybe slightly out of your reach, there's no harm trying.

Sphere of Influence begins with a detailed recapitulation of the key events in the emergence of India as cricket's unipolar super-power—so often experienced today as a fact of life rather than what it is: the product of cultural, political and economic forces. It also contains reviews of the on-field fortunes of Australia and the Subcontinent in this era, plus a look at some of their recent past masters, and some rueful reflections on the recent spot-fixing saga. Fortunately for me, enough things have not changed that I can still find good editors to rely on, content to indulge my gropings towards an understanding of the shape of cricket now: Sambit Bal, Scyld Berry, Suresh Menon, Boria Majumdar, Sally Warhaft, Seamus Bradley, Tim Blair, Tom Switzer, and the late, lamented Vinay Verma. I thank them all. *Sphere of Influence* has been experienced by my wife, Charlotte, and daughter, Cecilia, meanwhile, as a sequence of all-too-frequent vanishing acts. I dedicate it to them with love and apology.

Gideon Haigh
May 2011

Part I
A Brief History of Now

THE BCCI, THE IPL AND THE RISE OF TWENTY20

What Just Happened

It was a big game at the time. Since then it has only grown in significance. India entered the 1983 World Cup as 66–1 outsiders, having won only one game in two previous tournaments, and that against East Africa. One-day cricket had yet to take root in India; the previous year, the BCCI's chairman of selectors, Raj Singh Dungarpur, had scorned it as 'artificial' and 'irrelevant'. But in the Lord's final, India overthrew the West Indies, hitherto undefeated in the competition. The result was extraordinary, the ramifications even more so. 'My slogan is India can do it', read the telegram from their prime minister, Indira Gandhi. 'Thank you for living up to it.' BCCI president NKP Salve, a member of Gandhi's Congress Party, decided that the next step would be for India to stage cricket's quadrennial one-day jamboree. It was a drive with a personal edge: Salve's request for extra tickets to the 1983 final, legend has it, had been brusquely turned down by the Marylebone Cricket Club.

The BCCI was at the time the dowdiest and dustiest of bureaucracies. Created under the *Societies Registration Act of 1940*, its secretariat was located in drab quarters at Mumbai's Wankhede Stadium, while its logo was a derivation of the Order of the Star of India, India's highest order of chivalry during the days of the Raj. Administrative expertise was at a premium, cricket competence almost non-existent. As Dilip Doshi wrote in his memoir *Spin Punch* (1991):

What is the background of the gentlemen who run cricket in India? It is a sad fact of life that not even a small percentage of them are cricketers of any stature. In fact, I would like to go to the other extreme and say that some of them have not even played cricket at school level. There is a sort of closed shop at the top, perpetuated by a system of self-preservation, where it is not possible for outsiders to crash into the establishment ... There are thirty-odd members who vote for each other and elect the president, the secretary, the treasurer and the other minor functionaries. On many an occasion, such elections are known to have slipped totally out of control and been scenes for shameless horse trading to ensure continuance in power.

The BCCI was also almost permanently poor, its exchequer at the time of the World Cup containing barely Rs200 000. The night of India's triumph at Lord's, team members dined in a Wimpy Bar in Piccadilly. To reward Kapil Dev's triumphant eleven, Salve had to ask Lata Mangeshkar, legendary singer of Bollywood themes, to stage a benefit concert at Delhi's Indraprastha Stadium. But that storied day at Lord's turned the BCCI into a bigger one-day cricket fan than Kerry Packer. In April 1984, India won the Rothmans Asia Cup against Pakistan and Sri Lanka, the inaugural tournament staged at the Sharjah Cricket Association Stadium in the United Arab Emirates. Over the next twenty years, this brainchild of a cricket-crazy construction magnate, Abdulrahman Bukhatir, would host more than 200 one-day internationals before audiences chiefly composed of expatriate Indian, Pakistani and Sri Lankan remittance workers.

One-day cricket's eastward shift was confirmed in July 1984 at a meeting of the ICC when a handsome bid from PILCOM, a consortium representing India, Pakistan and Sri Lanka and bankrolled mainly by Dhirajlal Ambani's textile giant, Reliance Industries, wrested from England the right to hold the World Cup. In financial terms, this was not a Herculean effort: the inaugural World Cup had reaped just £100 000 in toto from media rights, sponsorship and ticket sales. But as a geopolitical shift, it was profound. Although Salve received much of the credit, rising shortly to become Gandhi's minister for power, the bid's real mastermind was his companion Jagmohan Dalmiya, secretary of the Cricket Association of Bengal. A Marwari from Calcutta who had taken over his family's construction business at the age of nineteen, he was a disciple of the free market in a country still mired in Gandhian socialism, protectionism and the so-called 'Licence Raj'; Bengal's chief minister, Jyoti Basu, was then an unreconstructed communist. Dalmiya was no less scornful of the ICC, as he later told Nalin Mehta: 'They were a corrupt kind of a set-up ... basically it was England, Australia and New Zealand. India and Pakistan were just two members. South Africa was in exile at that time. It was more a colony or more a small kind of a club, and we felt it was necessary to change all that'.

TV or Not TV

The Cup was a triumph, played out in September 1987 before capacity crowds. One-day cricket's conquest of India was complete. When the world-champion West Indies commenced a five-Test series in India soon after, the BCCI unilaterally reduced the series to four, in order to add two further one-day internationals to a previously arranged five: India has not staged a five-Test series since.

Yet the real money—television money—remained out of reach. For India's airwaves were ruled by the national broadcaster, Doordarshan, which did not merely pay nothing for its antiquated coverage of international cricket but actually charged for its services under antique legislation: the Indian Telegraph Act of 1885, granting India's government 'the exclusive privilege of establishing, maintaining and working telegraphs'.

As had players in other countries in the late 1970s, precipitating Kerry Packer's insurgency, Indian players were growing restless. Kapil Dev's team had worn the logos of their own sponsors during the World Cup, rather than that of Reliance; five wore the logo of the tobacco giant Wills, while others advertised soft drink companies and television manufacturers. The embarrassed BCCI cracked down on logos after the tournament ended, then in August 1989 tried imposing a year's suspension on the country's six best players—Kapil Dev, Dilip Vengsarkar, Ravi Shastri, Mohammed Azharuddin, Arun Lal and Kiran More—for the misdemeanour of playing some exhibition matches in North America while returning from a Caribbean tour. Like the boards of England and Australia faced by Packer, the BCCI could not make the ban stick, and a public relations fiasco ensued: the draconian punishment was successfully challenged in the Supreme Court, having already failed in the court of public opinion.

Worst of all, the country was in financial turmoil. As 1990 unfolded, India's fixed exchange-rate regime, high taxes and high tariffs precipitated a balance of payments blow-out. After intervention by the International Monetary Fund, the chastened Congress Party government of PV Narasimha Rao mandated a technocrat, Manmohan Singh, to liberalise aspects of the economy, simplifying foreign direct investment, privatising state-owned enterprises and generally ensuring against repetition of the humiliation. Dalmiya, now the BCCI's secretary, with support from allies like Inderjit Singh Bindra from the Punjab Cricket Association and Niranjan Shah of the Saurashtra Cricket Association, won a parallel mandate from BCCI president Madhavrao Scindia: to break Doordarshan's feudal control over cricket broadcasting.

First, taking advantage of the new foreign investment dispensations, the BCCI sold television rights to the 1992–93 England tour of India to a foreigner: Trans World International, a subsidiary of IMG. To fulfil its charter, Doordarshan actually had to pay TWI US$1 million. Given the telephone number figures now commonplace in Indian cricket, the US$600 000 benefit to the BCCI seems tiny, but Dalmiya used it as a springboard for another Subcontinental bid for the World Cup, with revenue forecasts predicated on a substantial sum from television. After a thirteen-hour battle royale at Lord's, the ICC consented, England giving way. India, in fact, achieved even more than it bargained for, because Dalmiya's campaign for change at the ICC was likewise promoted: it was as a result of this showdown that the body was provided with its first full-time secretariat, specifically chairman Sir Clyde Walcott of the West Indies and chief executive David Richards of Australia.

The role of television in this second evincing of Eastern power made it more significant than the first. Western journalists began writing for the first time of an 'Asian bloc' involving India, Pakistan, Sri Lanka and later Bangladesh—they formed a force within a force, the Asian Cricket Council. But the results for television would be as far-reaching as they were for cricket.

Initially it was thought that TWI would be PILCOM's television partner. Symbolically, however, the successful bidder was a Connecticut-based Indian expatriate, Mark Mascarenhas, who had left Bangalore in 1976 to study, but whose patriotism had been wakened by the signs of economic reform in his homeland. His production company, WorldTel, offered a knockout US$10 million in August 1993, planning to offset the costs by breaking the rights up and onselling them to other offshore broadcasters. He had obtained a bargain, almost making his money back with his first two sales, to TVNZ and British cable consortium CPP-I. But Mascarenhas still had a gauntlet to run.

In November 1993, Dalmiya's Cricket Association of Bengal was to celebrate its diamond jubilee by hosting a one-day tournament involving India, Pakistan, Sri Lanka and South Africa called the Hero Cup. Emulating the BCCI, it had sold the rights to TWI, which agreed to provide coverage for Rupert Murdoch's newly acquired Hong Kong–based Star TV. Suddenly, Doordarshan's director-general, Rathikant Basu, barged into Calcutta's Supreme Court brandishing the 109-year-old *Telegraph Act*. Basu, with the backing of the information and broadcasting minister, KP Singh Deo, argued that the uplink of a video signal to a foreign organisation jeopardised national security, apprehensions having been inflamed by an angry phase in India's perennial wranglings with Pakistan over Kashmir: Indian troops were at the time laying bloody siege to Hazratbal, the disputed territory's holiest Muslim shrine.

It was a clash between Indias old and new. Old India used methods crude but effective. Doordarshan imposed a radio and television blackout on the Hero Cup; customs officials impounded TWI's equipment on arrival. New India placed the burden on government to walk its talk. CR Irani of the Statesman commented acidly: 'The next time Mr Narasimha Rao and Mr Jyoti Basu go round the world seeking investments and much else besides, they must expect to be asked some searching questions'. Actually, it didn't take that long. Some of the most insistent inquiries came from the South Africans, recently rehabilitated in international cricket but now deprived of watching their team on television, and wondering aloud whether they had been mistaken to support the BCCI's World Cup bid: even Nelson Mandela took an interest. In a letter, Mascarenhas advised board president Bindra of the stakes: 'In my opinion irreversible damage has already been done. We look to the Board to take all steps necessary to rectify the situation before it jeopardises the 1996 World Cup and the investments of all involved, and does lasting harm to India as a sponsor of major sporting events'. Bindra acknowledged: 'If there is no worldwide television coverage [of the World Cup] ... the BCCI will go bankrupt'.

Indian cricket has a flair for both labyrinthine controversies and supple solutions. Satisfying both the economic rationalists and the economic nationalists, Mascarenhas did a deal with Doordarshan's Basu. Reassured, networks all round the globe signed up to WorldTel's feed: Pakistan's PTV, South Africa's SABC, Bangladesh's BTV, Murdoch's Star TV through Hong Kong and Packer's newly reacquired Nine Network in Australia. Yet the battle was only half-won, for Bindra shortly further incurred Doordarshan's ire by negotiating a US$30 million, five-year deal for the rights to broadcast Indian cricket with TWI and a new player, ESPN, the sports cable arm of Capital Cities/ABC of the United States—another controversial foreign incursion.

'Who created Sunil Gavaskar and Kapil Dev?' Basu fumed. 'Doordarshan has been in the forefront of telecasting cricket Tests and one-day internationals.' So BCCI's TWI/ESPN deal also ended up in the Supreme Court, with momentous results in February 1995 when Justices Sawant, Mohan and Reddy established three landmark principles: that India's airwaves were public property; that the right to impart and receive information was a species of freedom of expression guaranteed by the constitution; and that the government should set up an independent public authority to control Indian broadcasting: what became Prasar Bharti, or the Broadcasting Corporation of India, created in November 1997. Doordarshan responded petulantly, so uncooperative as a partner during the World Cup that it was also sued by WorldTel in the Delhi High Court. But long before an out-of-court settlement was reached a week before the World Cup's first match, it was clear that Doordarshan had sustained an innings defeat, as Basu himself recognised a few months later when he joined Star TV.

In the second half of the 1990s, satellite television swept India, the landscape stomped by overlapping footprints of the likes of ESPN, Star TV, Subhash Chandra Goel's Zee Television, Abdulrahman Bukhatir's Ten Sports and Harish Thiwani's Nimbus Communications. It was a combination of high technology and low: the satellite far above, and below, the foot-slogging local cable operator who set up a dish and distributed the satellite signals for a fee. Television audiences, of course, grew massively, if never precisely, because the ramshackle terrestrial arrangements militated against exact ratings figures.

It was a revolution—and it was cricket's doing. What the government had failed to bring about, despite all its reformist rhetoric, the game had helped accomplish. As Boria Majumdar notes in *Twenty-Two Yards to Freedom* (2004), liberalisation of the Indian broadcast media 'will forever remain a gift of Indian cricket to the Indian nation'—a gift, moreover, that keeps on giving, for India now has 125 24-hour television news services and more than 1100 TV channels, not to mention a staggering 68 000 newspapers.

All the same, it could hardly be described as an open-handed gift, being, as it increasingly was, a gift of itself. One-day internationals in India, massively popular, reaching audiences of up to 400 million, and hugely profitable, with the capacity to expose a corporate name up to 350 times, went forth and multiplied. In 1980s America, Bruce Springsteen sang famously of '57 Channels (And Nothin' On)'; in 1990s India, this was varied to '57 Channels and Nothin' On but Cricket'.

Boss of Bosses

The BCCI-led PILCOM faced one more challenge in hosting the 1996 World Cup. During the summer of 1995–96, Australia had received Cup co-host Sri Lanka and played them in an ill-tempered series, ending with the visitors publicly refusing to congratulate members of the home side. Days later, Tamil Tiger guerrillas drove a truck filled with explosives through the entrance of the Central Bank building in downtown Colombo, killing eighty-one and injuring 1000—a block from the Taj Sumadra Hotel, where the Australian team were due to stay during the opening match of the tournament. The players, who had already received threats from irate Sri Lankans, agreed with the Australian Cricket Board that security assurances were insufficient and forfeited the game. Former board chairman Malcolm Gray was sent to an ICC meeting at Calcutta's Taj Bengal Hotel to defend the decision, a move with profound implications.

> Anyway they [Dalmiya and Bindra] just shouted at us all morning. Called us cowards, called us racists. Threatened us with everything they could think of. We broke for lunch and hadn't moved an inch. After lunch they started again. Bindra had this incredibly loud voice and he just yelled. I finally said: 'Bindra. I'm sick of you yelling. I can yell too and I'm going to yell now'. So I did.

The tournament was a turning point in cricket's economics. For one thing, it was a huge financial success: the naming rights alone, sold to tobacco giant Wills, were worth US$12 million. For another, it was organised and won by the Subcontinent: in the final at Lahore's Gaddafi Stadium, the Australians slumped to an apparently karmic defeat against their recent nemesis Sri Lanka. Cricket's geopolitics were also further changed, for Dalmiya emerged with a sense of manifest destiny. He soon made clear his aspirations to succeed Walcott as chairman of the ICC, in opposition to the candidate favoured by England, Australia and New Zealand: Malcolm Gray.

The patrician Gray, long groomed for high cricket office, arrived in London with colleagues Denis Rogers and Graham Halbish in July 1996 to find his candidacy in unexpected turmoil, the ICC's then nine full and twenty-two associate members exquisitely split. The vote was thrown into further disarray by the sudden candidature of South Africa's Krish Mackerdhuj, and again when he withdrew by the imprecision of the ICC's constitution and the enigmatic personality of Mackerdhuj's countryman Ali Bacher. The scenario that unfolded is related by Bacher's biographer Rodney Hartman.

On the basis of a simple majority, Dalmiya would have won because he had the support of the smaller associate members of the ICC. What he did not have was majority support of the Test-playing nations, many of whom were nervous of this ambitious and dogmatic man heading up world cricket at a time when east-west relations were clearly strained. Amazingly, the rules of the ICC were unclear on the actual voting process but Dalmiya, who had enlisted a team of lawyers to assist him in his bid, insisted that a simple majority was the only requirement. Walcott, however, had the final say when he ruled that a two-thirds majority of the nine Test-playing nations was needed ...

When Mackerdhuj withdrew from the ballot, Gray was confident that South Africa's vote would gain him the presidency [sic]. He needed six votes and he was already assured of four from West Indies, England, New Zealand and Australia. He believed that South Africa ... would go with him and take Zimbabwe with them. Dalmiya had the votes of Pakistan, Sri Lanka and India so, even if South Africa and Zimbabwe sided with him, he still would not have the required six votes. He simply could not win. Ali recalls the tense meeting: 'The mood in world cricket at that time just wasn't right to have a winner. There were concerns about an east-west split in the game.'

South Africa abstained, deadlocking the vote. To undo this Gordian knot, Sir John Anderson of New Zealand Cricket was commissioned to devise a new constitution involving a three-year presidency assigned to a member country on a rotating basis, with policy and direction vested in an executive board including representatives of all nine Test nations and three associates. Denis Rogers sealed the deal at the ICC's special meeting in Kuala Lumpur in March 1997 with a tactful concession, agreeing that Dalmiya could take first turn at the presidency if Gray was guaranteed the second, 'because we were never going to get Gray through the first time'.

Bringing to the ICC his successful BCCI formula, Dalmiya did indeed bring about a financial revolution, taking over as president of an entity with barely US$30 000 in the bank, and plenishing its coffers with US$20 million from a knockout tournament, the Wills International Cup, staged in Dhaka in October 1998.

Attending the event, Wisden editor Matthew Engel noted the tightening knit of cricket and celebrity on the Subcontinent: 'Sachin Tendulkar seemed ubiquitous: on the field he played the innings of the week ... and purveyed his mixed-up offies and leggies with growing confidence; off the field, he seemed to be smiling winsomely in every TV advert'. That was the work of Dalmiya's confederate at WorldTel—burly, bearded Mascarenhas. Glimpsing Tendulkar first during the Hero Cup, he had induced Indian cricket's wunderkind to become his client in a five-year deal worth about US$6 million. When Tendulkar appeared in Pepsi commercials alongside Bollywood luminaries like Shah Rukh Khan and Amitabh Bachhan, it confirmed what was becoming a commonplace sentiment: that cricket knew no Indian rival as a star vehicle.

Dalmiya's big-money plans now fructified. In June 1999, the BCCI signed a five-year deal with Doordarshan worth almost US$60 million. A year later, the ICC voted to appoint World Sport Group as vendor of commercial rights to its next two World Cups, three other international one-day tournaments and sundry other events. The minimum guarantee was an extraordinary US$550 million. Even more extraordinarily, it was, for the first time, divided equitably: full members who had received about US$500 000 for playing the 1996 World Cup would each receive about US$10 million for playing the 2007 World Cup.

Dalmiya, however, also brought to the ICC a BCCI modus operandi, more politics than diplomacy, more deal-doing than actual administration, inevitably riling conservative peers from England and Australia by seeming preoccupied with the bottom line. Then there were the rumours around Dalmiya himself, and his relationship with Mascarenhas: the deal between the BCCI, WorldTel and Doordarshan on the Wills International Cup was subjected to one of Prasar Bharti's first investigations.

Worst of all, Dalmiya was slow to grasp the enormity of match-fixing, demanding that journalists cease efforts to 'malign the name of Indian cricket for the sake of a juicy story', perhaps loath to admit that the surfeit of one-day cricket for which he was partly responsible had been a precondition of corruption. The BCCI had received a steady stream of intelligence about match-fixing during Dalmiya's secretaryship. Suspicion fell in particular on India's captain, Mohammed Azharuddin, who had embraced cricket celebrity by leaving his wife for Bollywood star Sangeeta Bijlani, and chased the lifestyle to go with it: in the course of two years, it transpired, he had been paid almost US$300 000 by bookmaker Mukesh Gupta for various services rendered.

Bindra's persistent questioning about match-fixing enraged Dalmiya, and annoyed his colleagues also—they withheld grants to the Punjab Cricket Association in retaliation for his outspokenness. In the celebrated secret tapes compiled by Tehelka, the antagonists were captured in full spate. Dalmiya complained of no respect:

> I have served cricket at the cost of my family. At the cost of my business. Let anybody in this world come out and say, 'Bloody, you are a culprit!' God has given me enough. After sacrificing so much for the game, what return am I getting? ... When the elections happened [at the ICC], I had to fight to be elected. Now the entire ICC is giving me respect. But I don't get any support here in my country.

Bindra complained of no action: 'We just have to take them on ... I am going the whole hog. I am not going to spare them ... Obviously Dalmiya is mixed up because he never brought it to my notice at all'.

In April 2000, India's Central Bureau of Investigation stumbled on a telephone conversation between South African captain Hansie Cronje and bookmaker Sanjay Chawla. The lid was off. When the CBI presented its report, it was scathing about the BCCI:

> The BCCI has been the single biggest beneficiary of the enormous commercial success of the sport. It is a matter of record that the BCCI earns substantial sums from media exposure of the game—which media exposure is in fact responsible for the qualitative change that has come about in the entire scenario. It would be the elementary duty of anyone purporting to be the apex regulatory body of the sport, to keep a close watch on the performance of the team and to thoroughly investigate into the slightest gossip, leave alone suspicion, of any malpractice.

For the ICC's erstwhile president, however, the consequences were minimal. The BCCI haughtily dismissed the CBI's report as reflecting 'their disregard for the glorious history of the board and its excellent work over the years'. In September 2001, Dalmiya smoothly displaced the locum he had left in charge of the BCCI, Chennai-based industrialist AC Muthiah, with the help of a new ally, Ranbir Singh Mahendra of the Haryana Cricket Association, thereby also sidelining his former friend Bindra. He then set about applying the BCCI's growing financial heft for political advantage, a strategy gilded by India's on-field successes under captain Sourav Ganguly and coach John Wright. It was a future into which the BCCI marched briskly backwards.

Pawar without Glory

Wright's *Indian Summers* (2006) is an invaluable glimpse of the BCCI at work, in the cramped quarters at Wankhede Stadium that then lurked behind an antique tin sign.

The BCCI is an extraordinary organization. It's run by a handful of people who often make bewildering decisions and don't give a hoot what the outside world thinks of them. The staff are delightful and amazingly loyal—one of them told a local paper he hadn't had a raise for 35 years. Although the BCCI generates a major proportion of cricket's total revenues, its office in Mumbai has concrete floors and a toilet that requires key access. I reckon those ramshackle surroundings are the greatest feat of camouflage since a wolf put on sheep's clothing.

At the time Wright took over, the BCCI's inventory of team gear featured three baseball mitts, thirty cones and three crooked blue plastic stumps. He had no bowling coach, no fitness trainer and at first not even a team manager: Wright was expected to do that job, to handle travel arrangements and organise team appearances, himself. The selection process was hopelessly politicised. There were five selectors, each representing a geographic zone, each doing his best to serve that zone's interest. 'If their boys weren't picked,' Wright noted, 'they tended to cross their arms, clam up and take no further part in the meeting'. The scheduling followed a strict rotation process among nine test and twenty-four one-day international venues, so that travel arrangements were chaotic. The BCCI functionaries appointed to accompany the team on the Buggins' Turn principle were, according to Wright, time servers and worse.

The worst was the bloke who had a misguided confidence in his understanding of the game and was itching to get involved in the coaching. There was Colonel Sharma, who waved his handkerchief every time we got a wicket and considered himself a yoga expert, so much that we once had to let him take the warm-up. There was a gentleman who handed out the meal allowance in the dark so that it was hard to count, and another who nicked the players' official shirts. There was the manager who unilaterally changed the departure time for what would be a full day's traveling, with the upshot that half the team was on the bus and the rest were still in bed ... and at the end of the series he made me return all the white practice balls. One guy used to slip a sheet listing the scores of players from his region under my door and another managed to lose the entire party's meal allowance money for the last two days of a tour. Just as well aircraft meals are free.

Dalmiya was also a micro-manager, happy to dish out advice based on a minimum of cricket knowledge. He essentially ran the BCCI from the office of his construction company in Calcutta with the help of two personal assistants, without reference to board secretary Niranjan Shah. Fortunately for Wright, Dalmiya was more concerned with India's rivals off the field than on, acting to strengthen the BCCI's bilateral ties and weaken its multilateral ones. Cricket relations were restored with Pakistan five years after the Kargil War, while Dalmiya also conceived the Afro-Asia Cup, a three-stage competition between an Asian XI (chosen from India, Pakistan and Sri Lanka) and an African XI (South Africa, Zimbabwe and Kenya), as a means of spreading Indian television largesse, the rights to the event being bought by another new player, Nimbus Communications. At the same time, he baited the ICC's new chief executive, Malcolm Speed from Australia, at every opportunity, whether in response to referee Mike Denness' disciplinarianism in South Africa, or commercial restrictions placed on Indian players at the 2002 Champions Trophy and 2003 World Cup.

In the eyes of England and Australia especially, Dalmiya had become a veritable hobgoblin of mischief: Wright heard another administrator describe him as 'a cricket terrorist'. In fact, he had also been using up the residue of goodwill towards him in India, and the death of Mascarenhas in a car accident in January 2002 cost him a close friend and important ally. As Tendulkar's agent, Mascarenhas had provided Dalmiya with a link to India's greatest player, and richest media property. Now there loomed formidable new political presences in the 2001 elections of two former chief ministers of their states: Lalu Prasad Yadav at the Bihar Cricket Association and Sharad Pawar at the Mumbai Cricket Association.

Pawar, formerly defence minister to Narasimha Rao, was especially formidable. The so-called 'King of Maharashtra' was no respecter of persons, having been expelled from the Congress Party for disputing the succession to leadership of Rajiv Gandhi's Italian-born widow Sonia, and having usurped widely respected former Test captain Ajit Wadekar to take cricket power in Mumbai. Four months after his so-called Nationalist Congress Party was welcomed into Manmohan Singh's coalition administration, the so-called United Progressive Alliance, he forged a cricket alliance with Bindra. Dalmiya was seeking the role of the BCCI's patron-in-chief and to install Mahendra as president; against Pawar, their ticket barely survived. Pawar's Maharashtra loyalists exacted revenge by having a pitch prepared in Nagpur to favour the visiting Australian seamers, who took sixteen wickets in routing the home side.

Indian cricket's headline story in 2005 was the feud between captain Ganguly and new coach Greg Chappell; it was echoed by the leadership struggle between Dalmiya and Pawar, who couched his bid for the presidency in terms of India's new *Right to Information Act*. While Chappell v Ganguly had a couple of years to run, Dalmiya v Pawar was resolved more quickly. Despite Mahendra's best efforts to defer the BCCI elections, Pawar won them comfortably, promising a new broom at the BCCI in a 'vision statement':

> Never, perhaps, in the history of the Indian cricket board an election has aroused so much interest and expectation from the vast majority of the game's fans in the country as the recent one has. Some of the happenings during the last few years have grievously dented the board's image. Our first priority should be to restore its pristine glory by creating confidence among the followers of the game that the board is indeed a sincere custodian of Indian cricket. Frankly the question being asked is, as the richest body in world cricket, has it fulfilled its obligations towards the players and paying public? For that we all need to introspect and touch our hearts before saying 'yes, we have'.

As a premier national sports body, the board had been a model for all others sports organizations, but of late it has invited scorn from the public. In a fast paced world driven by market forces, we have to gear up to meet the ever increasing challenges and aspirations of a cricket-crazy nation. When the country is getting excited about the *Right to Information Act*, the Board is being ridiculed for its lack of transparency. Unless we believe in the free flow of information, particularly when millions and millions of rupees are involved, we are bound to be misunderstood. There can't be a better start to the new-look board than resolve that everything we do from hereon will be transparent and in the game's and public interest, be it election or allotting television rights or the team selection. The buzz word should be 'Transparency'.

A buzzword is exactly what 'transparency' proved merely to be.

Twenty20 Hindsight

The BCCI devoted so much time to internecine blood-letting in the first five years of the new century that it nearly missed two developments fundamental to its market. The first was the shift on Indian television from cricket as game to cricket as lifestyle. Big as cricket had been in India in the twentieth century, its coverage had revolved principally around the telecasting of matches. You'd seen cricketers playing; you'd seen them in advertisements; you'd seen the odd one on the movie screen. This changed in 2000 with the coming of Sony Entertainment, which sought to leverage Indian rights it had acquired from WSG by basing a series of programmes on its new cricket-only SET Max channel around 'brand ambassador' Kapil Dev, who became in retirement even more ubiquitous than he had been on the cricket field. To host their coverage of the 2003 World Cup, Sony then hired Mandira Bedi, sudsiest of soap stars. The short-term result was a surge in female viewership: by the second week of the tournament, women accounted for 46 per cent of the audience. The long-term result was many more job opportunities for India's soap stars.

By mid-decade, every news channel had at least one show devoted entirely to cricket, most of them several. Star News' biggest show, for example, was the weekly *Wah Cricket* (*Wow Cricket*), while its most controversial, shown each evening during Pakistan's tour of India in early 2005, was *Match ke Mujrim* (*Criminal of the Match*), where a kangaroo court presided over by Bishen Bedi (for the prosecution) and Syed Kirmani (for the defence) argued out the day's worst player. The greatest star the trend made was Navjot Sidhu, who rode his celebrity from big-hitting batsman to motor-mouth pundit all the way to India's Lower House (Lok Sabha), where he became the Bharatiya Janata Party member for Amritsar after the July 2004 general election. Around the Indian team, the atmosphere was one of constant adulation, temptation, demand and distraction. 'Sometimes,' noted Wright, 'I felt trapped in a bubble of bullshit, where media and public perception, public relations, commercial imperatives and board politics seemed to matter more than actual performance'.

The other shift was in cricket itself, and began far away, in a realm from which Indians thought they had nothing further to learn. Forty years after England had introduced its counties to one-day cricket, it sold them on an even-briefer version of the game. Where other efforts to winnow cricket away, like Super 8s in Australia and Cricket Max in New Zealand, had petered out, Twenty20 caught on within weeks of the competition's unsuperstitious unveiling on Friday 13 June 2003: sixteen of the forty-six matches were sellouts, and counties obtained their biggest crowds at Lord's and Old Trafford in fifty years.

The tournament was the brainchild of Stuart Robertson, the England Cricket Board's marketing director, who had persuaded Channel 4 to bankroll £250 000 of market research on cricket crowds, which over the preceding five years had declined 17 per cent. Robertson found that cricket's audience at domestic level had dwindled to a core of white, middle-aged males. Twenty20 was designed specifically to entice cricket 'tolerators', amid an atmosphere of non-stop carnival, including live bands and children's entertainment; it struck, to quote Matthew Engel, 'the motherlode of public affection for cricket that runs just below the surface crust of apparent indifference'.

At around the same time, an apparently munificent Texan entrepreneur, Allen Stanford, was mutually mourning Caribbean cricket with West Indian past master Michael Holding. What could they do? 'My initial thought was just to do anything to give the West Indies a shot in the arm', Stanford recalled. 'But this thing was a lot more successful than we thought.' This 'thing' was a domestic Twenty20 tournament in July 2006, again involving eye-catching entertainments, with an emphasis, as Tony Cozier noted, on the sponsor:

> It was staged entirely in Antigua, where part of Stanford's global financial operations is based, at the manicured, purpose-built Stanford Cricket Ground in the Stanford Complex, adjacent to the airport, amid Stanford banks, offices, restaurants and a newspaper plant. The advertising boards proclaimed only Stanford's diverse empire, including two airlines which transported players and officials. Cheerful, flag-waving children turned out under the lights; the majority were women and children, a new fan base.

Among those who quickly intuited that the exercise was more about Stanford than cricket was Holding: 'I am not going to be involved in a farce. He is telling people in the Caribbean that he wants to revive West Indian cricket but how is a week of Twenty20 cricket in Antigua going to do that?' The real resistance to Twenty20 at this stage, however, was not from purists, but from the guardians of the status quo ante, chief among them BCCI president Pawar, who argued that Twenty20 'dilutes the importance of international cricket'; it might also, of course, dilute the money to be earned from domestic television rights, for which through 2005 and 2006 the BCCI was holding another typically unruly but potentially lucrative auction. 'Twenty20?' Niranjan Shah was heard to ask at an ICC executive board meeting. 'Why not ten-ten or five-five or one-one?'

Because of the BCCI's ambivalence, the ICC hastened slowly: the first Twenty20 international was not held until February 2005; the first in Australia not until January 2006. And rather than throw in their lot with the new format, the BCCI pressed the ICC to tinker with fifty-over cricket, introducing new rules and new gimmicks, although without shortening the game and thereby reducing its naturally occurring advertising opportunities. The ICC itself was absorbed in the effort, initiated by its Pakistani chairman Ehsan Mani, of removing itself to Dubai in the United Arab Emirates as a tax minimisation measure, a relocation that finally took place in August 2005. The BCCI's conservatism, meanwhile, was indicative of an inner malaise.

The year 2006 began with an incident almost comical. Pawar and his new colleagues caucused in New Delhi with representatives of the boards of Pakistan, Sri Lanka and Bangladesh to finalise their bid for the 2011 World Cup, due to be presented to the ICC in Dubai the following week. Only, there was no bid. As the Pakistan Cricket Board's Sharayar Khan recalls in his *Shadows across the Playing Field* (2009):

> To my horror, the BCCI had not completed its preparations for our joint bid which entailed filing detailed and copious forms that ICC had sent out to all the countries bidding for the World Cup. There was consternation in the ranks when we—Sri Lanka, Bangladesh and Pakistan—pointed out that our joint bid was bound to hit the rocks because India had not remotely completed the data provided by the ICC. Sharad Pawar was naturally deeply upset to learn of this potential disaster and ordered his secretary Niranjan Shah to sit up all night with his South Asian colleagues to complete the data.
>
> Next morning I saw a bleary-eyed Salim Altaf, my chief executive, at breakfast. I enquired from him the results of the night vigil. He said, 'I'm afraid the task could not be completed. We sat up with Niranjan Shah until 3am but then the effort collapsed because the Indian board simply did not have the factual data. I'm afraid our bid will be found to be non-compliant in Dubai'.

So much for 'transparency'; opacity was now the order of the day. At the ICC executive board meeting in Dubai on 20 and 21 March, Pawar filibustered for all he was worth, pleading for an extension of time to finalise the bid on grounds that the Dalmiya regime had not surrendered the requisite information. To smooth ruffled feathers, Pawar promised Ray Mali of South Africa and Peter Chingoka of Zimbabwe that the Afro-Asia Cup, which he had wanted to kill, would continue; he also offered financial assistance to the permanently impecunious West Indies Cricket Board. Cricket Australia and New Zealand Cricket made a joint presentation generally agreed to be outstanding, but the BCCI and its partners obtained their month's grace.

The other item for discussion was a mooted Twenty20 World Championship in South Africa the following year. India, still without a domestic Twenty20 competition, was reluctant to participate; Pakistan, having just held its first, was similarly hesitant. But the tournament badly needed their television audiences; as badly, indeed, as the BCCI-led consortium craved the 2011 World Cup. In a quid pro quo the following month, India and Pakistan agreed to grapple with Twenty20, and the other ICC members to award the World Cup to the Subcontinent. In truth, the commercial logic was compelling: the disparity between the value of television rights centred on India and on anywhere else was shortly emphasised by the resolution of the protracted BCCI auction, the result a five-year deal with Nimbus Communications worth US$612 million. Cricket also began hearing for the first time of the suave but searingly ambitious BCCI vice-president, Lalit Modi.

Cricket à la Modi

Lalit Modi grew up around money, from a family tobacco business, and power, from political connections. His grandfather, Rai Bahadur Gujarmal Modi, was close to Jawaharlal Nehru; his father, Krishna Kumar Modi, was a confidante of Rajiv Gandhi. He is a Marwari, like Dalmiya, like Lakshmi Mittal, the Indian steel magnate who has become Britain's richest man, and like Harshad Mehta, the 'Big Bull' of the Bombay bourse, jailed for suckering the Indian elite in various stock market scams in the early 1990s: one panoramically offensive ethnic jest says that a Marwari can buy from a Jew and sell to a Scot and still make a margin.

Like Mascarenhas, Modi furthered his business education in the United States, at Duke University; he also broadened his life experiences in a brush with cocaine, narrowly escaping jail for being found in possession of 400 grams. On returning to India, he worked for subsidiaries of Philip Morris and Estée Lauder, then set about building the Modi Entertainment Network by distributing channels for Disney, then its associate ESPN, then Dubai-based Ten Sports and finally Paris-based Fashion TV. The pattern to these ventures was big plans, initial success, and usually a conclusion in court. More a serial entrepreneur than an industrialist, he also dabbled in property, state lotteries ... and cricket.

Modi wasn't much of a cricketer. 'I was a batsman', he once explained. 'I wasn't very good at it.' But he understood cricket as the *passé partout* to India's circles of influence. As early as 1995, a Modi Entertainment Network associate, Home Communication Network Ltd, registered seven city-based companies using the template 'Indian Cricket League'— ICL-Bombay, ICL-Delhi, ICL-Calcutta, ICL-Bangalore, ICL-Hyderabad, ICL-Madras and ICL-Gwalior. The BCCI was not interested in the schemes of an upstart 31 year old.

Modi might now be identified with cricket's shortest game, but he knew how to play a long one. The way to be heard, he reasoned, was to be an insider. His first attempt failed. He won election to the cricket association of the wealthy northern state of Himachal Pradesh in 1999, but resigned after a year, apparently at the request of the local chief minister, Prem Kumar Dhumal. Lesson learned, he arrived in Jaipur in October 2004 to oust the family oligarchy in charge of the Rajasthan Cricket Association led by construction magnate Kishore Rungta.

By this stage, according to an investigation by the *Indian Express*, Modi Entertainment Network was in straitened circumstances. 'Employees in various offices, including Delhi, wouldn't get their salaries for months on end', a former employee told journalist

Archna Shukla. 'Most offices, except for the one in Mumbai, shut down eventually.' You would not have known it: Modi based himself in the Prince's Suite at the opulent Rambagh Palace Hotel. For in Jaipur, Modi had an advantage: Rajasthan's chief minister, Vasundhara Raje Scindia of the BJP, was actually an old family friend. In building a substantial portfolio of local property interests, Modi seemed to enjoy an uncommonly smooth ride with government. Raje's most important favour to Modi, however, was to push through a new statute, the *Rajasthan Sports Act*, whose effect was to dilute the Rungta voting base at the RCA. Modi campaigned stealthily; according to *Outlook* magazine, he caught opponents napping by initially using a false name, purporting to be 'Lalit Kumar' of Nagpur. It paid off: with assistance from an influential member of the Indian Administrative Service, Sanjay Dixit, Modi was elected in February 2005.

Now he was on the inside, Modi sought a patron at the BCCI, and found one in Bindra, who saw this quicksilver commercial mind as strengthening his anti-Dalmiya forces. Bindra took the unusual step of introducing his new protégé to local cricket media at a press conference during India's Mohali Test against Pakistan in March 2005. 'Cricket in India is a $2 billion a year market', Modi told a bemused audience. 'We are sitting on a gold mine. Our players should be paid on par with international footballers and NBA stars, in millions of dollars and not in measly rupees.' Modi was duly on the right side of the barricades when Pawar finally bested Dalmiya, and carved out a niche as a corporate go-getter by selling the team sponsorship and apparel rights to Subrata Roy's Sahara Group and Nike respectively for more than US$150 million. He endeared himself further to the new regime by denigrating the old: '[Under Dalmiya] there was no professionalism, they were not doing enough, there was no transparency. It was always ad-hocism ... He [Dalmiya] had the golden opportunity to make a difference to Indian cricket and it's amazing that a man of his calibre didn't do anything that we are now'. Soon after, Dalmiya went from being merely patronised to actively persecuted: determined to extirpate his influence root and branch, the BCCI egged on challengers to him in his own stronghold.

Few events, in fact, have better demonstrated the twenty-first-century politicising of Indian cricket than the elections at the Cricket Association of Bengal in July 2006, when Bengal's communist chief minister Buddadeb Bhattacharya, backed by Pawar, supported the campaign of local police commissioner Prasun Mukherjee against Dalmiya, who attracted the support of Bhattacharya's predecessor, former mentor now antagonist Jyoti Basu, in cahoots with Congress Party enemies of Pawar. In a fascinating commentary on the election, Nalin Mehta notes:

> All channels covered the polling live through the day and, at least three commissioned exit polls with professional agencies: Times Now with A.C. Nielson, Star Anando/Anand Bazar Patrika with MODE and Kolkata TV with IMG-MARG. All this, for a regional sports management association with a grand total of 120 voters. All national channels also conducted popular opinion polls, asking viewers to vote for their preferred victors through SMS messages. It had only been two weeks since India's biggest single terrorist attack in two decades, the Mumbai train blasts on July 11 which claimed more than 200 lives but judging by the television coverage, it seemed as if the only thing that mattered that day was the president-ship of the Cricket Association of Bengal.

Historically, India's cricket has never been so radically politicised as Pakistan's. But Dalmiya's fight for survival was only the most visible manifestation of changing times, brought about by cricket's new prestige and wealth. By decade's end, two-thirds of state associations were ruled by politicians, like BJP general secretary Arun Jaitley, who also runs the Delhi & District Cricket Association, and his colleague and friend Narendra Modi, chief minister of Gujarat, who also runs the Gujarat Cricket Association or their proxies; the secretary of the governing council of the Congress Party, Rajeev Shukla, also became the BCCI's vice-president and chief spokesman. The reasons were not far to seek. There's no doubt that Pawar's popularity as a man of cricket enabled him to brazen out two corruption scandals in his food and agriculture portfolio—the so-called stamp paper scam and the wheat import tender controversy. Nor is he the only Indian politician who has felt himself in need of favour-able publicity. In India's Lok Sabha after the elections of May 2009, according to the service National Election Watch, there were '150 newly elected MPs who had criminal cases pending against them'.

This did not always suit Modi, a man with big plans whose aims were chiefly commercial: even now he was inside the BCCI rather than outside, progress was slow. Fascinated by the franchise-based ownerships structures popular in American sport, he revived his plan for a city-based fifty-over premier league in India. Interestingly, Mascarenhas had floated such an idea five years earlier: 'I think if cricket really has to become a professional sport then it has to go in ... the direction of the Premier League and be backed up by international competitions like the European Championships and the World Cup'. Bindra acted as an advocate for the scheme, stating publicly and prophetically: 'We should start a league like the European soccer leagues. Build it around cities or states, and a fierce local following will develop. Invite international players. With the audiences in India, it can reach the level of European soccer. It can be bigger than international cricket'. But the state associations were averse to anything that might undermine their authority, and their capacity to distribute patronage. Foreign players? Private ownership? It all seemed rather racy.

Biding his time, Modi reverted to the issue of ICC commercial rights for 2007 to 2015, due to be sold in December 2006. He proposed a revolutionary idea: the BCCI would acquire the rights. 'We are ready to pay top dollar for it', he boasted. 'Our money is as good as anybody else's.' This time the political obstacles were global. The ICC's other members looked askance. Would Manchester United be an acceptable owner of the English Premier League's commercial rights? Crisis portended until the ICC tabled legal opinions suggesting an irrevocable conflict of interest and, perhaps more importantly, ESPN-Star agreed to pay just over US$1 billion.

Nevertheless, Modi's gambit won him golden opinions in India. Earlier in the year, Lakshmi Mittal's eponymous steel giant had bid for Europe's premier steelmaker, Arcelor. Arcelor's haughty French chief executive, Guy Dolle, had caused outrage by dismissing Mittal Steel as 'a company of Indians' paying 'monkey money'. India's commerce and industry minster, Kamal Nath, had written a furious protest to the European Union's trade commissioner, Peter Mandelson, complaining that investors should not be 'judged by the colour of their skin' in 'an era of globalisation, cross-border investment and liberalisation'; a humiliating climbdown was necessary.

The debate about the ICC's commercial rights contained a similar dynamic. Speed gravely offended the BCCI by casting aspersions on its record. 'I have an old-fashioned view', he said. 'I judge sports organisations on the basis of three things: one, how the team performs; two, how the board looks after its stakeholders in terms of facilities on the grounds; and three, how well they use resources like population to produce great cricketers'. Modi's retort that you might not respect us but you must respect our money was timely and popular. 'India has been subservient for 100 years', he stated. 'People are used to dictating terms to us. We're just evening the playing field. And if it's our turn to have some glory, so much the better.'

Modi's dormant premier league plan was also about to gain an ally as vital as it was unintended: the conglomerate Essel Group, which had rushed to take advantage of the deregulation of Indian television after the BCCI's showdown with Doordarshan, and whose Zee Television had become the first Indian-language satellite channel. Essel's founder, Subhash Chandra Goel, was a perennially thwarted pursuer of broadcast rights to cricket, beaten for the ICC rights by WSG in 2000 and the BCCI rights by Nimbus in 2006. Now, like Kerry Packer in 1977, he envisioned a DIY solution, a cricket circuit made for a new Zee Television sports channel. Like Packer, too, he saw the future in an underexploited variant of the game: where Packer had been the first to glimpse cricket's one-day future, Chandra was as much a fan of Twenty20 as the BCCI was not.

Challenges to official cricket's monopoly are rare because the barriers to entry are so high—and such was Chandra's experience after foreshadowing his plans in March 2007. The BCCI waged a scorched earth policy at home and abroad: local players were intimidated with talk of life bans; foreign players were discouraged by overseas boards on notice that the competition was actively disapproved of by India's powers-that-be, and only superannuants like Brian Lara, Chris Cairns and Jason Gillespie were prepared to sign on; one of its chief recruiting agents, Kapil Dev, was sacked from his post at the National Cricket Academy in August 2007.

Nonetheless, a player pool of 135 was assembled, and the city-based clubs were rolled out: the Chandigarh Lions, Chennai Superstars, Delhi Giants, Hyderabad Heroes, Kolkata Tigers and Mumbai Champs. And although these entities were not franchises, the structure bore an eerie resemblance to Modi's own premier league brainchild. Chandra even used the same rubric: Indian Cricket League. No incentive could have been more effective in promoting Modi's vision than the possibility of someone else implementing it.

By the time the first ICL took place in December 2007, the Indian landscape had been transformed by two other events, both deeply ironic. In the World Cup in March 2007 in the West Indies, India, led by the self-effacing veteran Rahul Dravid, lost in short order to Bangladesh and then to Sri Lanka and left early; Pakistan joined them by the wayside, Ireland their improbable conquerors. One-day cricket was suddenly discredited, at least in the eyes of those broadcasters, sponsors and advertisers on the Subcontinent who had simply assumed the teams' passage through to the Super Eights, but whose profits now disappeared, as it were, in the Bermuda Triangle. Indians turn cricket on with glee, but are apt to turn it off in disgust. The only beneficiary of India's failure in the Caribbean was Lalit Modi, an important advantage of whose premier league idea was now seen more clearly. How do you ensure Indian participation all the way through a tournament? Compose it of only Indian sides.

It was in July that Modi had his famous 'chat over a cup of tea' at Wimbledon with Andrew Wildblood, senior vice-president of

IMG, about reviving his premier league idea. Within a month, IMG had produced the outline of a competition between eight city-based franchises involving fifty-nine Twenty20 matches all taking place during primetime evening viewing hours. Because the services of international players would be sought, the scheme was introduced to representatives of Cricket Australia and Cricket South Africa. In fact, Cricket Australia had had its own brainwave of brevity: a championship involving the winners of the different domestic Twenty20 tournaments, which chief executive James Sutherland and chairman Creagh O'Connor introduced to Modi, Bindra and Pawar at the home of the last in Delhi.

A tide had come in the affairs of the BCCI. On 13 September, the BCCI foreshadowed not one but two Twenty20 tournaments: an Indian Premier League scheduled for April 2008 involving eight city-based franchise teams, and an International Champions League featuring the top three teams from this IPL and the top two from domestic Twenty20 tournaments in England, Pakistan, South Africa and Australia, scheduled for October 2008. Sachin Tendulkar, Rahul Dravid, Sourav Ganguly, Anil Kumble, Glenn McGrath and Stephen Fleming were all present for the press conference in Delhi, but they were essentially scenery. Modi was the star—and also, of course, the potential scapegoat if matters went awry. But he was about to have a stroke of luck—six strokes, to be exact. Six days later, Yuvraj Singh hit Stuart Broad for six sixes in the nineteenth over of India's game against England in Durban in the World Twenty20. These were shots that echoed round the world: the tournament in which the BCCI had been such a reluctant participant suddenly became a national obsession. India, led now by latter-day matinee idol MS Dhoni, had a few days earlier beaten Pakistan in a bowl-out on the same ground to resolve a tie; within five days they would beat favourite Australia, then Pakistan again to take the trophy. The final at Wanderers was comparable in historical significance to the World Cup final twenty-four years earlier. Now the televisions in India stayed on, and for weeks afterwards. Fifty-over cricket was suddenly passé and twenty-over cricket hot to the point of radioactivity, as India embraced the game of which it was now the unlikely world champion.

For his part, Modi has always objected to the idea that his was a response to Subhash Chandra's attraction: 'This is not a knee-jerk reaction to any tournament but a project we have been working on for two years'. But if the tournaments were not about reacting to ICL, they were certainly about obliterating it. When the inaugural ICL season of fifteen games in seventeen days began in December at Tau Devi Lal Stadium, a small ground in Chandigarh leased from the government of Haryana, it lacked everything the BCCI had, including India's new Twenty20 heroes. Certainly it was altogether overshadowed by events now threatening to rip the game apart.

Billion-Dollar Babies

When Australia hosted India at the Sydney Cricket Ground on 2 to 6 January 2008, all the preconditions existed of a serious skirmish. Anil Kumble's Indians were strung to concert pitch, having just successfully hosted Pakistan for the first time in almost thirty years. Ricky Ponting's Australians, irked by Indian Twenty20 triumphalism on their recent one-day tour of the country, had meted out a retaliatory thrashing in the Boxing Day Test. Poor umpiring, worse behaviour, inept refereeing and inflammatory coverage of events in both countries duly turned Bhajigate into one of the bitterest on-field controversies in recent memory.

Yet these were not the events rending cricket asunder. Rather were they two announcements passing, at least in Australia, almost without notice, as Bhajigate raged: the BCCI statement on 15 January 2008 that Sony Entertainment/WSG had acquired the rights to the IPL for more than US$1 billion, and the BCCI statement on 24 January that the winning bids for the league's eight city franchises had raised US$723.59 million. In a sense, the success of the IPL was already guaranteed: nothing succeeding like success, naming rights were sold soon after to real-estate firm DLF Universal for US$50 million over five years, and associate sponsorships worth US$120 million were agreed with Hero Honda, Citibank and Vodafone.

The broadcasting rights and franchise sales may be Modi's greatest coups, for the circumstances of neither were propitious.

As regards the former, several key players were out of the running: ESPN-Star had bought the ICC rights, Nimbus the Indian rights, and Zee was embroiled in ICL; Sony CEO Kunal Dasgupta came through for Modi, an old friend, just when he was needed. And where the franchises were concerned, big industrial presences like Tata, Hero and the Mittal group had held aloof from the untested concept. But Modi's search for franchisees, in cahoots with IMG and direct marketing firm Direxions Marketing Solutions, had turned up an impressive mix of blue-chip and blue-sky investors.

Five franchisees were chiefly commercial, albeit with strong sporting links. Mukesh Ambani of family-owned Reliance Industries, whose father had sponsored the 1987 World Cup, acquired the Mumbai Indians for US$111.9 million. Vijay Mallya of family-owned UB, whose Kingfisher beer empire already owned a Formula One team, football team and thoroughbred stable, acquired the Bangalore Royal Challengers for US$111.6 million. Media baron T Venkattram Reddy, who controls Deccan Chronicle Holdings, forked out US$107 million for the Deccan Chargers. Industrialist Narayanaswami Srinivasan led Indian Cements into the US$91.9 million purchase of the Chennai Super Kings. And GM Rao's infrastructure conglomerate GMR backed the US$84 million acquisition of the Delhi Daredevils.

Then came the glamour. GMR's bid was fronted by Bollywood star Akshay Kumar, and two other franchises laid it on even thicker. Bollywood starlet Preity Zinta fronted the US$76 million bid involving her businessman boyfriend, Ness Wadia, and investors Mohit Burman and Karan Paul, for Kings XI Punjab; Shah Rukh Khan, blockbuster maker extraordinaire, put his Red Chillies Entertainment on the line for US$75 million in buying the Kolkata Knight Riders. Perhaps most intriguing of all was Emerging Media, run from London by Manoj Badale and associated with Rupert Murdoch's son Lachlan, who under the name Investors in Cricket had promoted ventures like a reality television talent search called *Cricket Star* with actress Shilpa Shetty. The Rajasthan Royals were acquired for a cut-down US$67 million, and recruited the only foreign captain in Shane Warne; Shetty, brand ambassador for the franchise, was later announced to have acquired a minority stake with her husband, Raj Kundra.

For the last in particular but all in general, the business proposition was disarmingly attractive. The franchises stood to receive 60 per cent of the sponsorship revenues in the first ten years, and 80 per cent of the television revenues after production costs in the first two years, scaling down slightly thereafter. The advertising benefits were less quantifiable, but arguably no less real: Royal Challengers was named for UB's whisky brand in a country that forbids the advertisement of alcohol, the Super Kings for Indian Cements' flagship product Coromandel Super King. It's arguable, in fact, that the ensuing player auction on 20 February, devised by IMG in collaboration with Christie's and Sotheby's, was the most conspicuous but least financially significant event of the preliminaries to the league. The money was already in the pot; the players merely spiced the recipe.

Where the auction *was* significant was in a cricket sense. For while Modi was apt to present the IPL as involving 'more than cricket', insofar as it featured music, dancing and other entertainment, it also involved less than cricket, for the comprehensive skill base cricket has traditionally encouraged was in some respects almost a disadvantage for players. The auction prices players fetched were dictated by local marketability, momentary caprice and bidder's ego. Peripheral members of the Indian team were hyped up: Ishant Sharma cost US$950 000, Irfan Pathan US$925 000 and Robin Uthappa US$800 000. Warne, meanwhile, was valued at US$450 000, Ponting at US$400 000 and Chaminda Vaas at just US$200 000. Indian youngsters Suresh Raina, Mohammad Kaif and Manoj Tiwary fetched more than US$2 million between them; Glenn McGrath and Shivnarine Chanderpaul attracted no bids at their first offer, and were bought second time around at their base prices, respectively US$350 000 and US$200 000. Not that bias was wholly parochial. Brett Lee, singer of a self-penned Bollypop hit with Asha Bhose and poster boy in India for Timex, New Balance and TVS, cost Kings XI Punjab US$900 000; Wasim Jaffer, India's most consistent Test batsman of the previous twelve months, was a US$150 000 snip for the Bangalore

Royal Challengers. 'Obviously it hurts', he admitted. 'I have proved myself, and I have made runs in Test cricket, over 2000 of them.' But he was an orthodox, unflinching opening batsman—a type for which Twenty20 had no call. The auction was about value, the market's verdict and also values, which were not those of cricket as hitherto understood. The question unanswered to this day, how the latter will henceforward be shaped by the former, has been phrased best by another opening batsman Aakash Chopra, bought for a chump change of US$30 000 by the Kolkata Knight Riders. As he puts it in *Beyond the Blues* (2009):

> Not so long ago, playing first-class cricket was the only reason for our existence. Everything revolved around making it to the state team, doing well to secure a berth for the next level and eventually playing for your country. You would spend hours trying to hone the skills more likely to see you through in the longer format of the game ... Performing in the shorter format would take you only so far and as far as playing for the country was concerned ... It was your performance in the longer format that counted.
>
> Players now might get swayed by the rewards on offer in the Twenty20 format and hence ignore the importance of playing first-class cricket. Lasting five days on the field and performing at your peak not only needs skills but also a different level of mental and physical fitness. To maintain that level, you have to push yourself to the hilt ... On the other hand, Twenty20 matches last only a few hours, the tournament is scheduled to happen once a year over a period of forty-five days, and though they require a different set of skills and physical and mental attributes, you don't have to push yourself hard for the rest of the year ... I may be sounding like a cynic, but isn't there a potential threat to the way people approach the game?
>
> I've spoken to a lot of people who have played Twenty20 cricket at the highest level and their response is similar—there is

a lot of fun but no real cricket pleasure in the format. It's ideal for viewers, but for the cricketers it's more like a lottery … A lot of players involved in the IPL have, at some stage in their career, voiced their dislike for this format but are more than willing to take part in this mega event. No prizes for guessing what draws everyone to this billion-dollar baby of cricket.

A simplification of the game's evolution might now run like this: Test cricket was devised for nations; one-day cricket was devised for crowds; Twenty20 was devised for television, for the activities it emphasises are those most telegenic—the hitting of fours and sixes, the catching of blinders, the launching of appeals. Television's values had been impinging for some time on aspects of the game such as the size of playing fields, as John Wright noted:

> The TV companies know the public wants to see fours and sixes, so the ropes are coming in all over the world. I had many deep and meaningful pre-game discussions with Indian groundsmen, pointing out that we had two spinners, so would they please push the ropes back? Then the TV company would demand more space for the advertising hoardings, and when we arrived at the ground on match day the ropes would have come in again and I'd get dark looks from the spinners. Money talked a lot louder than I did.

In the IPL, skills are entirely posterior to the entertainment package. The opening match of the first tournament began twenty minutes late because of Salman Khan's prolonged advertisement for his new Sony Entertainment game show *Dus Ka Dum*. The most debated feature of the first couple of weeks was the team cheerleaders, including those from the Washington Redskins hired by the Bangalore Royal Challengers. An *Economic Times* survey after the first IPL concluded that more viewers had tuned in to watch Shah Rukh Khan and Preity Zinta than Sachin Tendulkar and Sourav Ganguly; of the top ten individuals recalled by viewers, only five were cricketers.

In the IPL, even the skill of commentary was subordinate to the goal of entertainment. In a revolutionary move, the BCCI originated the coverage itself, employing a production company and its own hand-picked commentators, including Modi's colleagues on the IPL's governing council, Sunil Gavaskar and Ravi Shastri. Shastri epitomised the propagandistic tone when he rechristened his boss 'Moses', for leading cricket into its promised land. Ashok Malik argued in a pithy commentary for Cricinfo that the transition beginning with the 'dumb belles' who followed Mandira Bedi's role for Sony at the 2003 World Cup was complete: the commentator was no longer a disinterested analyst of the play, but a straightforward handmaiden of commercial interests. 'The IPL has taken this process to its logical extreme', observed Malik. 'When a wicket falls the television audience is more inclined to watch the cheerleaders do their number than listen to the commentator, if he has anything to say at all.'

Conflict of interest in general, in fact, was not a concept of which the IPL showed a firm grasp, in spite of the BCCI's constitution, clause 6.2.4 of which states that 'no administrator shall have direct or indirect commercial interests in the matches or events conducted by the Board'; to the clause was airily appended 'excluding IPL, Champions League and Twenty20'. This enabled Srinivasan to continue running Chennai Super Kings despite being the BCCI's secretary and president of the Tamil Nadu Cricket Association, and to employ BCCI chairman of selectors Kris Srikkanth as the Super Kings' 'brand ambassador'. Bangalore Royal Challengers' owner Vijay Mallya joined the BCCI's marketing committee, while his Kingfisher Airlines became the IPL's official carrier and umpire partner. Rajasthan Royals' shareholders included Suresh Chellarum, the Nigeria-based husband of Modi's sister-in-law; likewise was Mohit Burman, investor in Kings XI Punjab, related to Modi by marriage. If anything, absence of interest was deemed more suspect. Cricinfo, a bastion of independent coverage of cricket, was shut out of the IPL because of its potential rivalry to the BCCI's own online content, ownership of which, it turned out, was also linked to Modi.

The cricket itself had its moments. There was breathtaking hitting: Gilchrist made a hundred from 42 balls, Brendon

McCullum 158 from 73 balls, and more than a quarter of the runs in the tournament accrued in sixes. There was amazing ineptitude: the Bangalore Royal Challengers sustained five ducks and three run outs against Kings XI Punjab, then were on the receiving end of Laskmipathy Balaji's hat-trick for Chennai Super Kings. The peaks and troughs seemed to occur partly because the teams were restricted to playing only four of their internationals at a time, leading to rather many catchweight contests, although it could be argued that this made for more dramatic fluctuations in the course of games. The crowds, as great as 87 000 at Eden Gardens when the Kolkata Knight Riders saw off the Deccan Chargers, had plenty to savour. With average attendances of 58 000, the IPL was second only to the National Football League in the United States among domestic sporting attractions. Ratings soared to twice those normally experienced by conventional programming; soap and serial audiences shrank in proportion. Losers reeled: Vijay Mallya sacked his coach and chief executive. Winners prospered: the Rajasthan Royals stuck to basics, worshipped their wily captain/coach Warne, and brought glory to none other than Modi's adopted state.

There was a non-stop cycle of issues and controversies, not least when Mumbai Indians' captain Harbhajan Singh was suspended for slapping his Indian teammate but Kings XI Punjab opponent Shantakumaran Sreesanth. A surprising feature of the first IPL, indeed, was how easily local rivalry coexisted with international. Despite 130 years in which the nation has been the standard unit of cricket rivalry, fans rallied free-flowingly behind new favourites: the Kolkata Knight Riders, whose host of glamorous stars included Sourav Ganguly and Shoaib Akhtar, but above all whose impresario was the ubiquitous Shah Rukh Khan, were comfortably the competition's most popular team despite being among the least successful. The IPL has 'little cricketing logic, but sound television logic', argue TR Vivek and Alam Srinivas in *IPL: Cricket & Commerce* (2009): 'The Indian youth wants to watch big names and celebrity parties, where the camera has an obsessive focus on the cleavage. They want a Bollywood awards show with a dash of instant-result cricket'.

It amounted, nonetheless, to a celebration. For a glorious six weeks, India was not just the centre of the cricket world, but the cricket world itself. The only news emanating from the ICC in this time was of the defenestration of its CEO, Malcolm Speed, often in his tenure at loggerheads with the BCCI, but who had finally fallen out with his South African president, Ray Mali, over the issue of Zimbabwe: they had had an 'angry and bitter exchange' over Mali's support, despite growing evidence of administrative corruption and government interference, for Zimbabwe's continued Test status. The forum of Speed's ouster had, in fact, been an informal 20 April meeting of ICC directors in Bangalore as the IPL opened at which Modi, with Niranjan Shah, had represented the BCCI, in the absence of Pawar and Bindra.

Thus were cricket's recent realities perfectly reflected: while the BCCI staged a billion-dollar party in its own honour, the ICC disintegrated over what by comparison were footling sums in the world's sorriest cricket state. That Speed was joining his old nemesis Dalmiya on the sidelines of this new cricket revolution was appropriate: their rivalry now seemed like the vestige of a former age. The ensuing shake-up at ICC better mirrored the emergent global order: Bindra, briefly touted as Speed's successor, took the new position of 'advisor' to incoming chief executive Haroon Lorgat; Pawar took the new position of vice-president to new president David Morgan of England, leaving in his stead at the BCCI a loyal locum, lawyer Shashank Manohar. With the IPL consolidating the BCCI's status as the de facto seat of global cricket power, the ICC effectively took on a new position too: that of an organisation to deal with whatever did not interest the BCCI.

Last Man Standing

For a year after the first IPL, cricket was altogether dwarfed by its commerce. Players played incessantly but as pointlessly as if they were batting for a declaration, so dwarfed were they by larger forces, greater agendas and a sneaking yet growing sense of unreality. For economic trends were newly bleak. In England, Northern Rock had failed, and massive write-downs were being revealed at

UBS, Barclays and the Royal Bank of Scotland. The last, a major benefactor of cricket through the NatWest Trophy, would shortly pledge to shrink its US$300 million sponsorship portfolio by half. Vodafone decided after twelve years not to renew its sponsorship of the national team. In Australia, ABC Learning, Allco, Opes Prime and Storm Financial were heading for the boneyard of the bourse. Even in India, the stock market was beating a headlong retreat, as foreign investors had second thoughts about the country's runaway growth.

That air of unreality was not dispelled at Lord's on 11 June 2008 when a helicopter in the gold-leaf livery of his financial services firm disgorged the gaudy Allen Stanford, who had agreed on terms with the ECB for five Twenty20 internationals between England and an all-star West Indian team with an unprecedented grubstake of US$100 million; Stanford had tried and failed to strike a similar deal with the ICC. Publicly, it was the ECB's initiative to keep faith with players who had been unable to participate in the IPL because of the clash of seasons; privately, it was an attempt to establish a sphere of influence to rival the BCCI's, using the advantages of England's season, time zone and advanced infrastructure.

It had not been the only proposal in the mix: England's counties had earlier rejected a discussion document prepared by two senior administrators, David Stewart of Surrey and Keith Bradshaw of the Marylebone Cricket Club, mooting a nine-team English Premier League comprising fifty-seven matches in twenty-five days. Ironically in hindsight, Stanford appealed more because it involved apparently less upheaval of the established order. But the counties in one respect were right to be wary of Twenty20's propensity to suck all the oxygen from its surroundings. In September, Australia arrived in India to play four Tests—a scenario that had provided unforgettable cricket in 2001 and 2004. Now the stadia were deserted and forlorn, despite the hosts' impressive form. After several variations, the biggest version of ICL yet commenced on 10 October, now lasting a month, involving thirty-six games on four grounds, and including three new teams: the Ahmedabad Rockets, Dhaka Warriors and Lahore Badshahs, the last two lending the tournament a pan-Asian impact by hailing from Bangladesh and Pakistan respectively. While the nearby Bangalore Test attracted only desultory interest, the opening game between the Badshahs and the Hyderabad Heroes drew 20 000.

Nor was the ECB alone in seeking strength through innovation. On 24 October, Cricket Australia, Cricket South Africa and New Zealand Cricket foreshadowed plans for a ten-team Southern Premier League to begin two years hence, the series rotating between the three participating countries. The only board not Twenty20 crazy was the Pakistan Cricket Board, devoured by internal politics as Musharraf fell, and with him his cricket stooge Naseem Ashraf. The PCB had spent much of Ashraf's reign persecuting the twenty players who had signed with the ICL, including the country's best batsman, Mohammad Yousuf—a craven effort to endear themselves to the BCCI, which events would shortly render entirely pointless.

On the eve of the Champions League, the second stage of Modi's grand plan, disaster struck: Pakistani terrorists trained by Kashmiri liberationists Lashkar-e-Taiba (Army of the Pure) laid bloody siege to Mumbai for sixty hours. Their locus was the Taj Mahal Hotel, Indian cricket's long-standing entrepot, where even then officials were forgathering to finalise the Champions League's details. This league had been a troubled venture—unlike the IPL, Indian participation could not be guaranteed for the duration. Television rights had been sold for US$975 million to ESPN-Star at the peak of IPL hype, but naming rights had proven impossible to sell, and scheduling almost impossible to nail down: Cricket Australia had finally consented to delaying their Perth Test in order to facilitate the participation of Australian players. With the attack, the tournament was again in limbo, as were Pakistan's relations with India, thanks to the involvement of its nationals in the bloodshed. Sports minister MS Gill ruled out an impending Indian tour of Pakistan with chilling emphasis: 'You can't have one team coming from Pakistan to kill people in our country, and another team going from India to play cricket there'.

No blow to Pakistani cricket could have been as grievous— and thus was the gesture intended. Because of concerns about the country's internal security, the PCB had not been able to host a Test since October 2007, and its television tie-up with PTV, predicated on the continuity of Pakistan's defining cricket rivalry, was unravelling: the financial losses suffered were in the order of US$40 million. Pakistan's almost unrivalled capacity to disappoint then took on epic proportions on 3 March 2009, when a bus carrying Mahela Jayawardena's Sri Lankans, who had filled the breach left by India, was ambushed by anonymous gunmen en route to Lahore's Gaddafi Stadium. The flimsy security disappeared; several players and officials were wounded. The PCB's desperate protestations, which involved making an official complaint to the ICC about referee Chris Broad's comment that 'security vanished and left us to be sitting ducks', then cost them much sympathy. 'Even in the history of this wretched board,' stated Cricinfo's Osman Samiuddin, 'nothing has been as shameful, not the match-fixing crisis, or any cock-up. Obviously none were sacked. Some got promoted'.

There being little around to damage, five-day cricket on the Subcontinent was hardly affected: England played Tests in Chennai and Mohali soon after. But fifty-over cricket sustained significant collateral damage: Pakistan's roles as host of the 2009 Champions Trophy and co-host of the 2011 World Cup were effectively doomed. Twenty20, meanwhile, suffered the most significant check. It emerged that the ten players from Pakistan who had played in the first IPL would not be welcome in the second; likewise the Pakistani teams lined up for the now-deferred Champions League. The format's headlong expansion seemed to be catching up with it: Allen Stanford's business empire crumbled after just one instalment of his Stanford Super Series on the businessman's picturesque ground in St John's. The ECB officials who had jostled for proximity to Stanford eight months earlier suddenly distanced themselves from the affair, seeking and attaining PCB standards of accountability. No suitable place in the cricket calendar being found, the Southern Premier League also gradually petered out.

Worst of all, the IPL itself was threatened by the coincidence of India's elections, whose official security needs were deemed greater even than cricket. The BCCI was actually chastised by external affairs minister Anand Sharma, who argued that catering for the IPL's security requirements would 'trivialise Indian democracy', and home minister Palaniappan Chidambaram, who said that 'too clever' Modi simply 'did not try to understand the compulsions and concerns of the Police force'. Other boards, however, sensed an opportunity to endear themselves to a powerful ally, and Modi accepted Cricket South Africa's offer to stage the tournament lock, stock and bail: he emerged from discussions with CSA on 24 March with a deal to preserve his venture's vital spark.

That spark guttered in South Africa: second time round, the novelty was diminished, the straining for effect was more obvious and the efflorescence was provided mainly by money. Most excitement attended a beauty pageant, Miss IPL Bollywood, involving forty-eight South African models, six representing each franchise. Most fun was provided by a blog, *Fake IPL Player*, which purported to provide scurrilous intelligence from inside the Kolkata Knight Riders camp. But Modi had pulled it off: just before the IPL, the precipitate global recession had induced the ICL to abandon its season. The audacity of Modi's scheme, creating a mini-India abroad for the sake of the country's televised amusement, preserved his aura of infallibility—perhaps in his own mind too. For like Dalmiya before him, a man who seemed to personify Indian cricket abroad had been accumulating enemies in his own household.

Modi at Bay

Modi was by now as recognisable a face in India as any of his cricketers, a celebrity in his own right who risked a mob at his every public appearance and who maintained a constant banter on Twitter. Although he ostensibly answered to the IPL governing council appointed by the BCCI, in reality Modi made all the running, with the assistance of a hand-picked CEO, Sundar Raman, a former executive with advertising giant WPP.

As a gesture of faith in his enterprise, Modi very publicly forewent all salary from the IPL—how he funded himself, in fact, was rather a mystery, heightening his mystique. Certainly, he was surrounded by the accoutrements of power: limousines, private jets et al. The national sports editor of the *Times of India*, Bobilli Vijay Kumar, described a visit to his lair on the thirty-third floor of Worli's five-star Four Seasons Hotel in terms akin to a call on Lord Copper in *Scoop*:

> If you really need to see his power ... you need to walk into his IPL headquarters in Mumbai; of course, that is easier said than done. Right at the entrance of the plush five-star hotel, there are close to 10 NSG-style commandos, all armed to their teeth. You walk through the gate at your own risk. There is an IPL help-desk, next to the reception. When you say you have an appointment with Modi, a call is quickly made; only on confirmation, the hotel staffer reveals the floor number. Another one steps forward and punches in the card that gives you access to the floor. When you step out of the lift, the corridor is eerily silent. In the far corner, you can see another bunch of armed guards; nobody is allowed here without valid IDs. One of them asks you to sit outside while a second one goes in to announce your arrival; the secretary comes out to do her bit of fact-finding. You are given an audience after another brief wait.

Although such arrangements could keep the hoi polloi at bay, they could not completely stave off reality. In Rajasthan, Modi had fallen out with an old crony, local bureaucrat Sanjay Dixit. India's elections had then proved doubly inconvenient when Vasundhara Raje lost her job as chief minister. Throughout the campaign, Raje's Congress Party challenger Ashok Gehlot had accused Modi of exercising 'extra constitutional authority', even of acting as a 'shadow chief minister'. Voters found the charges all too credible.

Now without political cover, Modi could boss round the cricket world but not the Rajasthan Cricket Association: he was twice beaten at elections in 2009, first by Dixit, then by CB Joshi, union minister of Panchayat Raj. As many as twenty court cases involving Modi as defendant in Rajasthan, concerning allegations of financial irregularities and tax evasion, were either initiated or resumed. Although long-time patron Bindra had installed him as vice-president of the Punjab Cricket Association, Modi was now without direct influence on the BCCI. His perceived eclipse emboldened other detractors, including the ubiquitous Srinivasan, boss of Indian Cements, monarch of the Chennai Super Kings and custodian of the BCCI exchequer.

With the power vacuum following Pawar's departure, Srinivasan had become perhaps the key string-puller at the BCCI. Shrewd enough to have unseated former board president AC Muthiah in coming to power at the Tamil Nadu Cricket Association, and wealthy enough not to care whom he offended, he detested Modi, whom he saw as a self-aggrandising dandy cultivating the IPL's independence from the BCCI. In particular, Srinivasan enlisted Manohar in a cause he believed in: IMG's rake-off from the IPL. There had been considerable dissatisfaction about the arrangement from the beginning, an anonymous board member complaining to *Mint*:

> Lalit (Modi) just signed that contract and then brought it to the finance committee meeting. The members felt 10% revenue share was too much. At that time he said he had consulted Mr Pawar and had signed it on his behalf. At the next meeting, Mr Pawar said he didn't know about it. Modi, then, said he had signed it himself.

Srinivasan and Manohar issued their ultimatum to IMG executives in London in June 2009: reduce the fee or face losing it altogether.

When IMG stood firm, sent their bill for about US$7 million, and were unilaterally sacked in August, Modi swung into action, persuading the other seven franchises to bombard the BCCI with protests. This enraged Srinivasan further: the franchises owed their existence to the BCCI; the BCCI was not about to accept them influencing the policies of Indian cricket. Modi then had a stroke of luck: ahead of elections in Maharashtra, Pawar was keen to bring about an *entente cordiale* with the industrialist Mukesh Ambani, owner of the Mumbai Indians. Pawar's covering note to Ambani's letter of complaint reprimanded his old BCCI colleagues: 'Not only will this lead to a prolonged legal battle but it will also show us in bad light in public'. Even so, when a settlement was brokered by Manohar whereby IMG agreed to reduce their fees by almost a fifth, Srinivasan could claim he had obtained a better deal for the league than had Modi.

A year after it had been scheduled, the Champions League finally unfolded, a lower-key event than the IPL, from which English teams were a last-minute withdrawal in a dispute over revenue sharing. It provided some pleasing cricket, especially from finalists New South Wales and Trinidad and Tobago, but petered out in public attention when the local teams dropped out early. ESPN's outlay for the rights now looked decidedly extravagant. Mystery also surrounded payments of US$5 million to the IPL franchises unable to contest the cancelled league—the Rajasthan Royals, connected with Modi's brother-in-law, and the Chennai Super Kings, Srinivasan's plaything; no other competitor had been so compensated. Whatever the objectives of the payment, Srinivasan showed no signs of placation, continuing to machinate so tirelessly that, in December 2009, Modi barely survived what was essentially a no-confidence motion at a meeting of the BCCI: he kept his job only on the proviso that he speak every day to Manohar. Modi still managed to make trouble for himself, threatening to ban from the IPL any Australian player who put his own country's domestic cricket before representing their franchise, and attracting a defamation action from Chris Cairns, whom he disbarred from the third IPL player auction on unsubstantiated grounds that the New Zealander had been embroiled in match-fixing during the ICL. His embarrassment might have been greater had the BCCI not at the same time faced a greater one, being forced to sack its own pitches committee after the abandonment of a one-day international in Delhi because of a surface deemed 'unfit' by the ICC referee. In any event, new alliances were forming. When Modi visited Eden Gardens for a routine inspection at the end of the year, he was reported to have met with Dalmiya, now restored as the pooh-bah of the Cricket Association of Bengal. The BCCI had expelled Dalmiya in December 2006 over alleged financial irregularities in the 1996 World Cup, Modi being among those who had jeered gleefully; having successfully challenged the ban in court, he was again a force to be reckoned with. Necessity, as they say, is the mother of strange bedfellows.

The Fifteen-Month Year

Calendar 2009 contained 150 one-day internationals; forty-eight Twenty20 internationals, including a world championship; and eighty-two games in the IPL and Champions League. Nobody could miss the inference: cricket was now a duopoly market in oversupply, the ICC providing international content, the BCCI its supranational competition. The ICC's Future Tours Programme was only three years old, but, agreed to before the irresistible rise of Twenty20, now looked as obsolete as the Julian calendar.

Something had to give, and that was Test cricket, of which there were merely thirty-eight matches despite the scheduling of marquee series like the Ashes and the Frank Worrell and Wisden Trophies. Of these thirty-eight, India played only six, including just two at home, preferring a number of instantly forgettable one-day series with traditional political allies Sri Lanka and Bangladesh. Nor was this because India was a poor team, but in spite of it being a good one: in December, MS Dhoni's eleven officially achieved the number one ranking on the ICC's World Test Championship. India's next international engagement at the time happened to be against South Africa, whom it had displaced from its perch, yet only five one-day internationals had been scheduled. Belatedly, the BCCI condescended to two Test matches: exciting games of high-quality cricket which ended one-all. But the likelihood remained that India would play too few matches in 2010 to defend its hard-won status, and Rahul Dravid was quoted as worrying that the next generation of Indian players did not actually care: 'There is no all-consuming desperation for them like there was for me or cricketers of my generation to do well in Tests'. The shift was on, too, at junior level, as Sunil Gavaskar noted from his vantage point as a member of the IPL's governing council:

Parents are encouraging their children to take up cricket as a career option because of the IPL and the amount of money it provides. But the worrying factor is far too many youngsters see the IPL as the be all and end all. A lot of players miss out on domestic cricket before the IPL to avoid injuries. That is what we have to be very careful about—the IPL being seen as the be all and end all, not the India cap. The other thing to guard against is players in the age group of 19–22 going the wrong way. Younger players get carried away by fame, publicity and success.

Sorrier still was the state of Pakistan, playing so little that its skills seemed to have atrophied, and the interest of vagrant key players waned. 'Twenty20 cricket is a virus', warned its foremost modern batsman, Javed Miandad. 'If the ICC doesn't restrict matches of this format it will finish Test cricket, as leading players will no longer want to play for their country.' Their captain, Mohammad Yousuf, whose team had nine Tests in 2009 after none at all the year before, went further, blaming his team's batting frailties on an infatuation with Twenty20 that followed their victory in that year's world championship:

> Because of Twenty20 cricket no player knows how to stay at the wicket anymore. Batsmen are finding it very difficult. I know the format has money, players get it and boards do but if Pakistan hypes up Twenty20 too much, Test and ODI cricket will really go down … Twenty20 is easy for Pakistanis because they know how to hit, nobody knows how to defend. Until players play with discipline and play ball to ball and leave balls they are supposed to we will struggle in ODIs, let alone Tests. If you see a ball, hit it because you have to score. But if you are going to slog all the time what is the point?

That Twenty20-centrism made the news of January 2010 even harder to bear: because of apprehensions about the security environment and doubts about their availability, Pakistan's players attracted not a single bid at the third IPL player auction. 'The way I see it, the IPL and India have made fun of us and our country', fumed Shahid Afridi, the star of Pakistan's earlier triumph. 'We are the Twenty20 world champions.' There were high-level complaints too, Pakistan sports minister Aijaz Hussain Jakhrani remonstrating with his Indian counterpart about 'the unjust and discriminatory treatment meted out to the Pakistani cricketers'; Geo Super, Pakistan's only local sports channel, declined to show the IPL after the country's cable operators threatened to boycott any channel showing it. But IPL franchises were also confirming their indifference to notions of diplomatic symbolism and sporting magnanimity. Pakistani players, Modi argued, were simply too hot to hold in a climate of global uncertainty. 'They [the franchises] are spending money', he said. 'And they want to get the results.'

The existence of the IPL, and the breakdown of official cricket's monopoly that it represented, was impacting everywhere. In the West Indies, whose captain, Chris Gayle, publicly opined that the end of Test cricket would not be a matter of regret to him, most of the leading players stood aloof from international cricket for much of the year in pursuit of a better deal from their board: the scattering of Stanford's billions had created expectations difficult to meet. In New Zealand, Daniel Vettori, Brendon McCullum, Jacob Oram, Ross Taylor, Jesse Ryder and Kyle Mills signed national contracts in July 2009 only after ensuring that they had preserved their right to play IPL. 'We realise that if these situations continue to come up, it will be difficult for players to continue to turn down the money', said Vettori. 'So we implore the powers that be to [find a solution] so we don't have to make these decisions every year.'

A particular bugaboo was the phenomenon of the 'freelance player': the gifted cricketer renouncing international cricket in favour of plying his trade with the worldwide network of Twenty20 events which didn't actually exist yet but which everyone somehow assumed soon would. This player, spared the obligation of providing the IPL with an NOC (no objection certificate) from his own board, would be attractive to franchises because of his unrestricted availability. There were prototypes, in particular two Andrews who had found cricket to be the curse of the drinking classes. Andrew Symonds, Australian cricket's number one management challenge, wearied of official inhibitions on his behaviour, and preferred the task of earning US$1.35 million for six weeks work with the Deccan Chargers. Andrew Flintoff, England's charismatic former captain, found that his body was no longer equipped to withstand Test cricket's rigours, and elected to confine himself to the more lucrative and time efficient option of earning his US$1.55 million fee for the Chennai Super Kings.

Whether an imminent profusion of freelance cricketers was a likelihood is debatable. Players associations played it up; cricket boards played it down. For players in their thirties with more cricket behind them than ahead, concentrating on big-money Twenty20 was certainly an enticement, and further opportunities for freedom of lance loomed when Australia's KFC Big Bash attracted overseas cricketers in 2009–10, including West Indians Dwayne Bravo, Chris Gayle and Dwayne Smith, and Pakistanis Shahid Afridi and Naved-ul-Hasan. But this was a greater cultural change than many grasped: the attitude of a player with a lifetime in a structured national environment does not naturally conduce to becoming a self-directed, self-organising, self-motivated, have-bat-will-travel type. The annual survey of Australian first-class players by the Australian Cricketers' Association found that two-thirds could foresee one of their peers declining a Cricket Australia contract in order to pursue a freelance career, but 98 per cent had 'never considered' doing so themselves.

The possibility of freelance cricketers denuding the international game of its talent further spurred plans for the rehabilitation of Test cricket, centring on a full-fledged world championship. On assignment for CA, Boston Consulting Group worked throughout 2008 on a structure for such a scheme, addressing both the status of five-day cricket and the growing inequalities between cricket's emergent 'big four'—India, England, Australia and South Africa—and the rest. BCG's package involved a conservative four-year cycle and a radical pooling of television monies, so that strong countries subsidised the weak. Predictably, the strong, particularly India and England, were having none of it.

The Marylebone Cricket Club, sticking its oar into the global game for the first time in nearly twenty years, then presented an alternative scheme. The work of the club's three-year-old World Cricket Committee, a think tank of past and present cricket eminences including Martin Crowe, Rahul Dravid, Steve Waugh, Mike Atherton and Geoff Boycott, it was a minimalist model, involving a two-year cycle and no revenue sharing. The MCC presented the proposal, buttressed by some rather flimsy market research, to the ICC's own cricket committee in Dubai in November 2009; the committee was to report to the executive board in February 2010 but, without an obvious champion, the proposal stood little chance of progress.

Stymied at the ICC, CA also experienced a worrying home summer, with crowds and viewing audiences sharply down. Like most forty-year-olds, one-day international cricket was looking increasingly flabby and unfashionable, especially compared to fun, footloose Twenty20. CA's directors took heart from the growing momentum of its KFC Big Bash, already the most lucrative tournament in Australia because finalists gained admission to India's Champions League. The tournament's next stage was foreshadowed: six city-based teams, each controlled by the relevant state association, plus two franchises based in regional centres. For Australian administrators, this mooted experiment with private ownership amounted to revolutionary thinking. By Indian standards, of course, it was a trifle. But everyone was about to have a lesson on the side effects of private ownership.

Triple Witching Hour

In the early days of Twenty20, cricket's gradualist governors had been loath to destabilise the game's established commercial and cultural structures. By 2010, they had shed all inhibitions. In the ten weeks from 12 March to 20 May, more than 100 games of elite Twenty20 were scheduled: IPL, another ICC World Twenty20, plus a women's event. A game that has traditionally walked backwards into the future was now running headlong with its eyes shut. Just as importantly, there were signs of shifting corporate priorities in

India. Brand Finance, a marketing consultancy, valued the IPL at US$4.13 billion. According to media buying agency GroupM India, the league now accounted for about 40 per cent of the national advertising spent on sport. The first IPL franchise to be onsold, Kings XI Punjab, was initially rumoured to be on the market for US$275 million—four times its original cost, despite having yet to earn a profit. This staggering market strength, however, held grave portents for cricket's other forms. As 2009 concluded, the BCCI revealed it had received not a single bid for sponsorship rights to the national team, which it had priced at about US$150 million; Srinivasan admitted that his colleagues had been poorly advised about the 'realistic value' of the rights. In fact, Subrata Roy's Sahara Group, the previous sponsor, had changed focus. On 21 March, two weeks after the first attempt at an auction had been mysteriously cancelled, it emerged as one of two successful bidders for new IPL franchises: Sahara, with the political patronage of civil aviation minister Praful Patel, paid US$370 million for the franchise for Pune, which would constitute the second IPL team in Maharashtra, while a consortium calling itself Rendezvous Sports World, under the aegis of fast-moving junior foreign minister Shashi Tharoor, paid US$333 million for the franchise in Kochi, in the state of Kerala.

Adding significantly to the paper fortunes already made, the successful bidders were paying more for two franchises than the first group of investors had two years earlier paid for eight. They were buying, moreover, nothing except rights: no players, no stadium, no infrastructure, nothing except a share of a pot of television monies. Nonetheless, they were expecting bang for their buck. Rendezvous, a coalition wrangled by private investors Shailendra Gaekwad and Pooja Gulati, had an eye on the wealthy expatriate Gulf community; they had, as yet, no home ground. Rendezvous' financiers, who included Harshad Mehta of Rosy Blue Diamond (owner of a popular jewellery brand), Mehul Shah of Anchor Switches (a real estate firm) and Mukul Patel and Vipul Shah of the Shree Ram Group (recyclers of ships), made no bones about being in it for the money. 'I'm just a businessman and have absolutely no interest in cricket', said Patel.

There was, it so happened, more money to share. A year earlier, Modi had terminated the IPL's original broadcasting contract with Sony/WSG after an ugly squabble in Bombay's High Court over Sony's purported failure to discharge its obligations, which cost CEO Kunal Dasgupta his job. It looked suspiciously like an attempt to sell the IPL rights again, and so effectively it proved: Multi-Screen Media, a new Sony entity, and WSG agreed to pay US$1.6 billion over the nine remaining years of the contract. The broadcasting rights holders in the United Kingdom, cable channel Setanta Sports, had gone into administration in June 2009, so Modi came up with the innovative solution of going to Google, who offered to stream games live on YouTube; Modi subsequently also sold British rights to ITV. The third IPL was projected to earn about US$160 million.

In fact, it was hard to avoid the sensation while watching the third IPL when it began on 12 March that what was happening off the field was far more significant and interesting than what was happening on. The sensations on the field were so fleeting, the forces at work off it so huge and game-altering. Shaun Tait bowled an excitingly fast over—then he came off. Yusuf Pathan made a hundred for the Rajasthan Royals against the Mumbai Indians—off a mediocre attack it took 37 balls, and afterwards he could hardly make a run. The coverage itself was more staccato for the innovation of advertisements in the *middle* of overs, sold at premium rates outside the agreement with MSM by Pioneer Diagsys, a new company controlled by none other than Kunal Dasgupta. The accent on spectacle rather than competition was more acute for the lavish nightly bacchanals, run by Colors, a general entertainment subsidiary of Viacom: IPL parties, where weary players mingled with perky Bollywood stars, businessmen, politicians and models, were a moveable feast of whatever took your fancy, with ticket prices more than ten times the cost of attending a game. For players, like one who spoke in confidence to Heena Zuni Pandit of the *Hindustan Times*, the novelty was steadily wearing off:

So you tell yourself, 'I'll go down for an hour', only, it's never an hour. Before you know it, it's 4am and you're heading back to your room, hurrying to pack up and head to another city, another game, another sponsor's commitment (which are endless), another shoot possibly and yes, another party. The problem is that you can never switch off mentally. Not on the field, not during the hours spent in airports when fans and the airport staff want an autograph, photograph or just a chat and not in the parties, where you'll be introduced to important people who will listen to you and perhaps, be important contacts who will make money for you. It's a choice and it's tiring but it's also business. You have to be switched on. It takes a toll, when you play a game, party till 4am, pack and grab an hour's sleep before heading for the airport and spend six to 12 hours travelling. Places like Jaipur and Chandigarh don't have direct connections to everywhere else. That's my most vivid memory of IPL, not the matches, not the parties but the endless travel and exhaustion — and next year, with 34 games more, it will only get worse.

The star was, again, undoubtedly Modi who, leaning on a bat and flanked by cheerleaders, hovered over the headline 'Billion Dollar Baby' on the cover of *India Today*, the country's biggest newsweekly. But amid the constant distraction, nobody noticed that the final agreement for Rendezvous' purchase of Kochi seemed to be taking rather a long time to finalise. Not until Manohar sent a BCCI lawyer to Bangalore to track Modi down on 10 April was progress made, and it wasn't until 2.30 a.m. the following morning that the document was actually signed. An hour later, Modi deviated from the usual hoopla and celebrity endearments on his Twitter account to compose four uncommonly detailed tweets about his league's newest franchise. 'Who are the shareholders of rendezvous', he began. 'And why have they been given this 100's of million dollar bonanza?' [sic] He listed first the acknowledged equity holders, then those who had been given 'free equity'— apparently rights convertible into shares. These included a name prompting a select few to instant recognition: Sunanda Pushkar. In response to an inquiry from 'xxxDEVxxx'—a Bangalore-based follower Roshan Dev—Modi then went a little further: 'a big? I was told by him [Tharoor] not to get into who owns rendezvous. Specially Sunanda Pushkar. Why? The same has been minuted in my records'. [sic]

Dubai-based Sunanda Pushkar, formerly sales manager of a company called Tecom, is best described as the significant other of Shashi Tharoor, the former under-secretary-general of the United Nations who had been political patron of the Kochi bid; Tharoor was at the time in the throes of divorcing his Canadian second wife, Christa Giles. Modi's inference was hard to avoid: that Tharoor had cut, literally, a sweetheart deal. Members of the BJP—with whom in Rajasthan, of course, Modi had been allied—did not miss the opportunity to embarrass a government minister. Members of the Communist Party were more extreme still, calling for the IPL to be 'banned'. 'Cricket is being maligned in the country', said MP Gurudas Dasgupta. 'Black money is coming from Mauritius and Dubai through dubious sources and betting is going on openly ... It is a only a game of gamble, an organised gamble.'

Modi's motivations were ambiguous. Mischief? Pique? Spite? According to Harshad Mehta, Modi had spent a good deal of the bid process trying to discourage the Rendezvous consortium. 'He told us that so many partners can't handle a team', Mehta complained to the *National*. 'We listened to whatever he had to say. He is the IPL chairman. We listened and we kept our cool.' Shantanu Guha Ray of *Tehelka* alleged that the success of the Kochi bid had been more than a surprise—it had been a deuced inconvenience. Modi had been carefully orchestrating the bid process to provide a franchise for Ahmedabad, bankrolled by the infrastructure magnate Gautam Adani and approved by the Gujarat Cricket Association, and also to deliver Pune to Venugopal Dhoot's Videocon Industries. The reason? Since his ousting in Rajasthan, Modi had been seeking a means of recovering his vote on the BCCI, and been promised same by the Gujarat association's boss, Narendra Modi, also the state's chief minister. Guha Ray spiced his story further with background on the tensions between Modi, Tharoor and Miss IPL Bollywood contestant Gabriella Demetriades:

A few days earlier, newspapers had carried front-page stories linking a beautiful South African model, Gabriella Demetriades, with Modi. It seems Modi no longer wanted the association and had requested Tharoor's office, as Minister of State for External Affairs, to deny Gabriella a visa. Piqued by the back-room pressure and anxiety Modi had been visiting on his boss and the Kochi team, Tharoor's aide Jacob Joseph refused to entertain the request and not only expedited the visa but apparently taunted Modi's aides about it. The story goes that when Modi found out, he called Tharoor in a rage at night and slammed the phone down, vowing vendetta.

Modi has consistently told the media that he does not know Gabriella and has nothing to do with her. Unfortunately for him, however, he seems to have left an e-mail trail when he wrote to Joseph for help about denying the visa. These emails contravene his claim about not knowing Gabriella because in his hurry to shunt her off, he apparently forgot to delete his chain-mail exchanges with her.

Whatever the case, Modi's tweets resounded like the crack of doom. BCCI president Manohar publicly upbraided the IPL's founder for making the ownership details public. Tharoor condemned it as an 'extraordinary breach of all propriety' designed to discredit the franchise; he also denied nest self-feathering: 'I have neither invested nor received a rupee for my mentorship of the team. Whatever my personal relationships with any of the consortium members, I do not intend to benefit in any way financially from my association with the team now or at a later stage'. Modi, who had never shown any interest in transparency, suddenly became a convert, calling on all the IPL franchises to divulge full ownership details. There was the sound of paper being shuffled awkwardly, and some intriguing disclosures. The register of the Rajasthan Royals was especially confused, shares having been transferred freely but without the approval of the Foreign Investment Promotion Board or the Reserve Bank of India; Shilpa Shetty and Raj Kundra, it emerged, had brought their glamour to the Royals, but not their money.

Members of the Rendezvous consortium, meanwhile, were confiding anonymously of extraordinary pressure brought on them to either quit the scene or offer equity to thwarted investors, including rich businessmen and senior politicians. According to Rediff.com, two consortium members became so concerned at the intimidation that they went direct to Congress Party boss Sonia Gandhi. Prime minister Manmohan Singh was in Washington for talks with Barack Obama about the Nuclear Liability Bill when the mother of all bombs detonated. Shailendra Gaekwad's brother Satyajit, a former Congress Party MP, told CNN-IBN that, a week after its success, Rendezvous had been offered US$50 million by Modi to 'just quit the game and get out'. Gaekwad went on:

> That is where the investors thought that since they had won the bid and had worked hard for the last six–seven months to get this bid, they did not agree. That's the reason there were some delaying tactics taking place and a confusion created by Mr. Lalit Modi that he didn't know who the owner was. In that case, if it was so, why would we have won the bid? That's the million-dollar question Modi needs to answer.

Modi, of course, was giving as good as he was getting, contending that Rendezvous had 'a lot to hide and as such have lied about who are the actual owners of the shares'. The day after, when income tax officials swooped on his suite at the Four Seasons Hotel seeking documents to do with the auction, he insisted that he welcomed investigation. He denied the bribe allegation, and Shailendra Gaekwad was subsequently replaced as Rendezvous' CEO by Harshad Mehta. The immediate casualties of the crossfire, in fact, were Pushkar, who chose to forgo her stake 'given the deeply unpleasant publicity surrounding my involvement', then Tharoor, who quit in order not to further 'embarrass the [Congress] Party'.

Modi still had strong relations with franchise owners like Vijay Mallya, and also obtained political support from India's energy minister, Farooq Abdullah, a member of the IPL governing council, who deplored the Indian equivalent of the tall poppy syndrome: 'It is an old Indian habit to try and pull down someone who is going up'. And the BCCI, at least initially, seemed to hope the whole affair would blow over. Manohar hesitated, foreshadowing a meeting of the IPL governing council 'within ten days', whose timing then slipped further. Income tax officials were now swooping left and right, on each of the franchises in turn, and also selected shareholders. There was widespread talk of ticket scams designed to evade entertainment tax, of monies routed through tax havens to avoid attracting levies in India, of restive state associations wondering why they lost money on the IPL while franchises benefited, of Air India flights rerouted for the IPL's convenience; the name of crime boss Dawood Ibrahim, the Subcontinent's Professor Moriarty, was being bandied freely. But what brought matters to a head was the publication on 19 April in the *Times of India* of the details of a confidential tax investigation presented to the Indian government *six months earlier*. 'Mr Lalit Modi', the report began, 'has had a trail of failed ventures and defaults till four years back but has a lifestyle now that includes a private jet, a luxury yacht and a fleet of Mercedes S class and BMW cars all acquired in the last three years'. The key to his fortunes, said the report, was equity held on his behalf in no fewer than three IPL teams: the three—Kolkata Knight Riders (Shah Rukh Khan), Kings XI Punjab (Preity Zinta) and Rajasthan Royals (Shilpa Shetty)—with glamorous Bollywood links.

If the allegations were substantiated, Modi was toast. He was said to have done his deals for television, mobile and digital rights in return for commercial favours; he was reported to be 'deeply embroiled in both generation of black money, money laundering, betting in cricket (match-fixing of certain IPL matches)'. The more interesting story, perhaps, was how such a report had come to be compiled and had then languished for six months before being leaked at this particular time—but on these issues, the *Times* was silent. But the issues for Modi to address were now multiplying daily, even if they sometimes seemed inconceivably involuted. There was, for instance, a 'facilitation fee' of US$80 million paid by MSM in order to rebid for the IPL broadcasting rights, US$25 million of which was alleged to have been routed to Modi. Then there were the IPL digital rights which four months earlier had found their way to Global Cricket Ventures, a Mauritius-registered company half-owned by UK-based Elephant Capital, whose principals included Modi's son-in-law, Gaurav Burman, brother of the co-owner of Kings XI Punjab. Even if above board, this *sounded* suspicious. The media tide was also turning. Three weeks after his appearance on the cover of *India Today*, Modi was back there; this time the headline read 'Run Out?' Editor Aroon Purie was unabashed:

> Rule No. 1 of journalism: there are no gods. And if they appear to be so they usually have feet of clay. So it was with a fast-talking dynamic 46-year-old man who came from nowhere three years ago and became the god of cricket in India ... It is rare for *India Today* to fete someone on the cover for spectacular achievement and then put them on it within the same month for being in trouble. It was, however, inevitable as the IPL is not only a phenomenon that has revolutionised cricket but last week shook the government and led to the exit of one of its ministers.

Attention also fell on Pawar, incoming president of the ICC, whose daughter turned out to be working for the IPL, and whose son-in-law emerged as a shareholder in MSM. He was already under political pressure after a precipitous rise in food prices, which in some centres had incited riots. The day after the revelations in the *Times of India*, the 'King of Maharashtra' met two key cabinet colleagues at Parliament House in New Delhi—home minister Palaniappan Chidambaram and finance minister Pranab Mukherjee—to discuss Modi's position. Pawar was apparently still inclined to defend him, as he had in the past, but incurring bad political blood as a result. Unsatisfied simply with Tharoor's scalp, BJP leader Yashwant Sinha, was pressing for a thorough government inquiry: 'A lot of people, including people in the government, are neck deep in this scam. IPL has turned out to be a huge scam. I think the worst ever, the biggest ever in this country and therefore there is a need for an impartial enquiry into this whole episode'. The Congress Party was countering with its own allegations, such as a call for investigation of the Himachal Pradesh Cricket Association, Modi's first stamping ground, now run by Anurag Thakur, a BJP member of parliament; the administration of Thakur's chief minister father, Prem Kumar Dhumal, had spent extensively on bringing two IPL matches to Dharmasala, including the provision of a helicopter for Modi's family. The atmosphere was confused, frenzied. Rajeev Shukla, it was reported, had twice provided detailed briefings to Manmohan Singh himself: the annual summit of the South Asian Association for Regional Cooperation in Kathmandu was delayed to allow the Indian prime minister's late arrival.

Dropping the Pilot

Modi was not going quietly. He challenged the validity of the calling of an IPL governing council meeting scheduled for 26 April because its agent was his adversary Srinivasan, whom he argued was only a council member because of his role as BCCI secretary. 'I do not propose to attend any unauthorised meeting', Modi wrote to Manohar. 'He is actually an *ex-officio* member of the GC as an office bearer of BCCI and as he is a conflicted party who owns an IPL team. He has never and can never call a GC meeting.' It was a technicality with a whiff of desperation from which he then backed off, issuing instead a challenge to the governing committee to put up or shut up by circulating his own agenda, requesting 'complaints in writing with the requisite supporting documents at the meeting … so they can be replied in full'. He revived, too, his dormant Twitter account, breathing defiance: 'People pressurising me to resign—I can tell you will not happen. Let them remove me then. Truth will prevail soon. Trial by media and no chance to present the facts is like the wild west'. Then: 'Wait for the IPL to finish. I will reveal the men who have tried to bring disrepute to the game and how we stopped them from doing it'.

The BCCI *did* wait for the IPL to finish on 25 April, but just a few minutes. Even as Lalit Modi was presenting the trophy to MS Dhoni of the Chennai Super Kings—ironically, the franchise run by Srinivasan—a show-cause notice was winging its way to his email account, giving him fifteen days to prove why disciplinary action should not be taken against him, as well as a 34-page document containing twenty-two issues for which his explanation was sought. In the meantime, he was suspended as the chairman of the governing council, which in his absence next morning promoted another member, Chirayu Amin, to replace him: executive chairman of Vadodara-based pharmaceutical company Alembic Ltd, Amin had spent twenty-two years as president of the Baroda Cricket Association.

The suspension—rather than a sacking—had been Bindra's suggestion. Modi's oldest ally, indeed, was the only individual to speak in his protégé's favour at the meeting, providing the saga with a sound bite to cherish: 'The media has been ready with the guillotine to hang the hero of the IPL'. Those who had basked in Modi's reflected glory, such as Gavaskar and Shastri, were reportedly silent; Abdullah did not turn up. Investigators, meanwhile, were beginning to feel like Old Mother Hubbard. As the income tax authorities had found before him, the BCCI's administrative officer, Professor Ratnakar Shetty, learned that the crucial documents had disappeared. So many gaps were there that the BCCI actually forbade employees taking work home with them.

Then, another shoe dropped, with ECB chairman Giles Clarke becoming involved. On 7 May, Clarke notified the BCCI of a 31 March lunch in Delhi between Modi, Yorkshire CCC chief executive Stewart Regan, Warwickshire CCC chief executive Colin Povey, Lancashire CCC treasurer David Hodgkiss, and IMG's Andrew Wildblood and Peter Griffiths. Five pages of minutes kept of the meeting by Regan for circulation among the bosses of counties staging Test matches adumbrated a plan for the IPL franchises to bid for franchises based around these grounds: the franchises would keep 80 per cent of gross revenue, the counties the balance, with a guarantee of US$3–5 million and an additional annual staging fee of US$1.5 million. The raison d'être, Regan explained, was the existing limits on the IPL season: 'The only way to leverage more value is to offer the existing franchises the chance to buy a second franchise in the Northern Hemisphere'. He also recorded Modi's expansive table talk:

> The IPL model relies heavily on 'star players' and this is why they have been so successful. They have taken TV and sponsorship monies from the film and soap opera categories and brought women into the game like never before. Matches include fashion shows, after-match parties and entertainment. They have launched the word 'CRICKETAINMENT' which I think is really innovative. Players are now the new 'idols' in India ... Going forward, availability will be key and Modi predicts a revolution among players if they are not allowed to get involved. Indeed, he will soon launch a new franchise rule stating that a player has to be available to be auctioned. Given the earning potential, he expects players to demand to be part of it. If governing bodies try to block the development of IPL20 then the franchisees could simply buy out the players and create their own structure. Modi believes that most star players would take the money rather than spend months playing county/state or indeed Test cricket. Indeed, if he wanted he could launch IPL Tests & ODIs!

Clarke's email to Manohar claimed that Modi's plan was 'to destroy world cricket's structure and especially that in England, and create a new rebel league', a plan that would eclipse boards of control altogether and 'involve players in a fashion unheard of'. The counties backpedalled hastily, Regan insisting that they had sought Modi's counsel in an 'educational' capacity: 'The success of the IPL proves that cricket is a product that people want to buy and that sponsors want to get involved with, and those were the key learning areas that we were interested in. It would not be appropriate to comment any further'. Given that this was belied by the content of his own notes, it's not surprising others begged to differ, including the BCCI, who issued Modi with another show-cause notice. If Clarke's allegations were true, it said, Modi's activities would amount to a blow to 'the very foundation of the way cricket is administered and played across the world', with governing authorities 'forced to watch helplessly while the game and the power of administration are hijacked'. Legal teeth were bared in London and Mumbai.

The IPL was now experiencing further and deeper criticisms as a result of the World Twenty20, won by England, but during which India and South Africa were conspicuous underachievers. With India's pampered batsmen all at sea on unexpectedly fast and bouncy Caribbean pitches, MS Dhoni commented on the gulf between the IPL and international cricket; with South Africa's players badly short of match practice, former chairman of selectors Craig Matthews complained: 'The IPL doesn't help other teams. The only South African who benefited from playing in the IPL was Jacques Kallis. The rest of them all sat on the sidelines'. Expansion of the IPL from sixty to ninety-four matches in 2011 no longer looked quite such an undiluted good, and governing council member MAK Pataudi confessed that he had already harboured misgivings:

> I can't exactly tell you what happened in the council meeting but it wasn't exactly a unanimous decision I assure you. A lot of people said there is too much cricket going on, but it was carried. It will be a long summer for cricket. Cricket is going to become more and more stressful as we continue, and people will have to be fitter and tougher mentally as well as physically.

A dispute that had begun with Twenty20-style pyrotechnics would now evidently resolve itself in Test match-tough attrition, with both sides acting to shore their positions up. On 17 May, Manohar and Srinivasan met Wildblood and two IMG colleagues, Paul Manning and John Lafflagen, to discuss their future role in the league; IMG was threatening to sue Clarke for his correspondence with BCCI. Modi's lawyers, meanwhile, had wheeled 15 000 pages of documentation into the BCCI headquarters in six large cardboard containers, his marquee lawyer Mehmood Abdi promising more if needs must: 'The BCCI President is a renowned lawyer and has the habit of reading 1,000 pages in a minute. So, I feel he should not take much time in reading our reply'. Modi's response to the BCCI charge sheet, a fourteen-page letter widely leaked on 25 May, was essentially to draft his own, accusing Manohar and Srinivasan of knowing more than they had let on, and demanding they both be rescued from the adjudication on his suspension, with Srinivasan himself suspended.

In a rather unconvincing 'in-sorrow-not-in-anger' tone, Modi insisted that Manohar's had been the hidden hand in the cancelled auction of the new franchises:

> The allegation that I tried to rig the bidding in favour of two bidders, namely Adani's and Videocon has caused me much anguish ... I had kept my peace in the larger interest of the Board but now that such an allegation has been made I am constrained to put the following facts on record.

Manohar, he claimed, had sought, at Tharoor's request, to accept the Kochi bid after the official 5 p.m. deadline:

> I declined to accept the same, saying it was beyond time. You [Manohar] however asked me to accept the bid. You advised me to anti time the bid to 12 noon for 6th March 2010 ... You seemed to be under extreme pressure to ensure that the late bid be included in the bidding process. Since you failed to ensure that the bid be included you then decided to ensure that the bid process itself is cancelled.

The wandering tenses were confusing; the inference was clear. Official grounds for the cancellation had been Modi's too-onerous demands of bidders' net worth; by Modi's account, terms had not been onerous enough. Srinivasan, meanwhile, was accused of a variety of misdeeds to advantage the Chennai Super Kings, including efforts to appoint local umpires to its games, hang on to key players, and a flouting of the board's constitution in holding on to his conflicted position. He had pressure from another legal quarter too. Slowly but steadily, his erstwhile rival in Tamil Nadu, AC Muthiah, had been working up a legal challenge to his dual hold on office at the BCCI and the Chennai Super Kings. Muthiah popped his head up amid the wranglings between the BCCI and Modi to remind both of that old clause 6.2.4 with its prohibition on 'direct or indirect commercial interests in the matches or events conducted by the Board'.

The BCCI, however, had by now closed ranks tightly. The facilitation fee was unravelled, the BCCI announcing that it rather than WSG Mauritius would now be the recipient; compensation payments to the Rajasthan Royals and the Chennai Super Kings for the cancellation of the inaugural Champions League were likewise rescinded. The BCCI terminated the relationship with Colors, killing the IPL parties, and even audited Modi's limousine and hotel bills, demanding repayment of private usages. The franchises, which had fallen in line behind Vijay Mallya, were prepared to do business with the BCCI—providing, of course, their needs were met. As Mallya said, they were 'in it [IPL] for business interest'.

With the abiding exception of Bindra, Modi had no public allies left. An earlier defender, Abdullah, was speaking darkly of his 'major irregularities'. The *Times of India* published another startling revelation: that, contrary to earlier denials, a company associated with Pawar, City Corporation, had been involved in an unsuccessful bid for the IPL franchise in Pune. The revelation was less significant than the strategy underlying its leakage: Manohar and Srinivasan were letting Pawar know that his defence of Modi was no longer acceptable. A BCCI source quoted in Calcutta's *Telegraph* laid the blame for Modi's indiscretion directly at Pawar's door:

> Once unlimited powers are given, officially or otherwise, it's next to impossible to withdraw them. It's because of the carte blanche given to Modi that he didn't bother to take the IPL's governing council into confidence ... Never bothered to consult it ... The council kept quiet because most, if not all, of its members knew of Modi's arrangement with Pawar.

Interestingly, when Modi leapt to Pawar's defence in the wake of the disclosure, Pawar did not reciprocate. At a special general meeting of the BCCI on 3 July, which referred Modi's case to a three-member disciplinary committee, not one delegate spoke in his favour: Bindra, one who might have, did not attend. Modi tweeted defiantly: 'Battle lines have been drawn. Agendas fixed. Timelines laid. Let's see who wins and who is guilty of what. Now truth will emerge. Wait watch'. But when he announced a Supreme Court challenge to the disciplinary process a week later, Modi, while never to be underestimated, was very much on his own.

Howard's End ... and Modi's

The ICC looked on throughout the foregoing without comment: over quite possibly the biggest cricket story in a decade, since match-fixing, it had no jurisdiction and no influence. Such marginalisation of the ostensible control body for global cricket had become such a routine feature as to pass unremarked, although not, at Cricket Australia, unnoticed: indeed, in about September 2009, it had been the impetus for an unusual initiative, with an approach to former prime minister John Howard to become involved. Under the latest iteration of the rotation policy for the ICC presidency, it was the turn of Australia and New Zealand to promote a vice-president to serve from July 2010, and succeed to the role of president two years later. Courted by CA chairman Jack Clarke, and former political ally Ian McLachlan, Howard agreed to put his name forward as Australia's candidate in a straight fight with New Zealand's Sir John Anderson. A lengthy and rather laborious selection process by a specially appointed committee ensued; that committee's chairman, businessman Rod Eddington, finally used his casting vote to choose Howard on 2 March.

On the eve of the IPL, and the travails therefrom, it was soon swallowed up by events. Murmurs of discontent took nearly seven weeks to emerge, at the ICC executive board meeting in Dubai on 19 and 20 April, which was nonetheless inconclusive, several nations being unable to attend because of the volcanic disruption of civil aviation. Agitator-in-chief was the dubious chairman of Zimbabwe Cricket, Peter Chingoka, whose country's pariahhood Howard had deepened by forbidding a 2007 visit by the Australian cricket team.

Whether directly or indirectly influenced by ZC's position, Cricket South Africa chairman Dr Mtutuzeli Nyoka sent a poisonous letter to ICC president David Morgan claiming that an 'overwhelming number of directors were opposed to Howard', even if he named none; in fact, as the BCCI, which nations financially dependent on tended naturally to follow, had yet to make any determination, no consensus was ascertainable. CA trusted in what it believed were good relations with the BCCI and CSA: they were, after all, among other things, CA's joint-venture partners in the Champions League. They were gratified when Pawar, shortly before his ascension to the ICC presidency, pronounced himself a supporter of the Howard nomination, while Jack Clarke emerged from a meeting between Howard and Chingoka in Harare confident that a rapprochement had been reached.

They may have deceived themselves; they were certainly deceived. Pawar was no longer indicative of the BCCI's views. Even as Clarke, his chief executive James Sutherland and NZC chairman Alan Isaac left for the ICC executive board meeting, representatives of the boards of South Africa, India, Pakistan, Sri Lanka, Bangladesh and, at the last moment, the West Indies were signing a letter announcing their unwillingness to support Howard. No reasons emerged. No precedent existed. Howard was not permitted to address the refuseniks. A rich variety of reasons were advanced by *bien-pensant* pundits, some writing in good faith, others not. For a four-term prime minister, it was an epic snub; for CA, it was, as clearly intended, a humiliation. Whether it meant the rise of an 'Afro-Asian bloc', as some described it, was another matter. Rather, because any protest would have vaporised without the BCCI's support, the gesture was a tacit admission of weakness, representing as much relevance as any of these increasingly beleaguered organisations had experienced in years. Faceless cricket administrators could suddenly feel like weighty men of affairs, through an act costing no time, no caste and, most importantly, no money. In very few other respects, one reflected, had they any significance at all.

The second half of 2010 was cast into darkness by the allegations of spot-fixing by Salman Butt, Mohammad Amir and

Mohammad Asif during the Lord's Test, first levelled by *News of the World*, then duly taken up by the ICC and the police. Pakistan's players, gradually precluded from sharing in the Twenty20 riches of their near-neighbours, had long been thought susceptible to corruption. At sight of the headline 'Caught!' there was a weary sense in cricket that this interlude had been a long time coming – the pity was that the malfeasance had been detected not by the ICC's own anti-corruption and security unit but a one-off investigation by a tabloid newspaper. The PCB's helplessness lay revealed; the suspension of the trio by an ICC judicial panel on 5 February 2011 after a week of hearings in Doha felt like a small mercy.

Less visibly, the BCCI was in court trying to make stick their announcement on 10 October 2010 that Rajasthan Royals and Kings XI Punjab, the two franchises closest to Modi, were to be turfed from the IPL on grounds of agreement violations and contract breaches – essentially unnotified changes of ownership. With the continuing misadventures of the Kochi franchise, there was fleetingly a threat that the envisaged ten-team competition for the fourth IPL would become a seven-team shadow of its former self. The franchises did rather better than the Pakistani trio: after several stays in the High Court in Mumbai and attempts at arbitration, the BCCI lost the stomach for the contest. All ten franchises, including the Kochi Kerala Tuskers and Pune Warriors, lined up for the new auction of 350 players at Bangalore's ITC Royal Gardenia on 8 and 9 January, spending freely up to their $9 million salary cap – if not, in a few cases, perhaps a mite beyond.

In a sense, the BCCI had accomplished its objective, by aggressive and ham-handed means, but always with an end in mind of extirpating Modi's influence in IPL. The IPL governing council was turned over, and reconstituted sans Gavaskar and Pataudi as essentially a board sub-committee. As for Modi, disciplinary forums set up to hear the allegations against him came and went. Hearings were held, challenges continued, but the wheels of BCCI justice ground so exceeding small that interest in the matter steadily faded. Modi, having retreated to London, was left with a defamation case to pursue alongside IMG against the ECB's Giles Clarke. A low-key website that pleaded his side of the story continued to describe him as the 'founder and architect of the successful Indian Premier League (IPL) of cricket', but the BCCI dogs had barked, and the Twenty20 caravan had moved on. Even a proposed Bollywood biopic, *The Commissioner*, was cancelled.

The BCCI also continued to brazen out Srinivasan's dual roles as board secretary and Chennai Super Kings boss, the subject of the long-wending legal complaint of A. C. Muthiah. At the end of April 2011, the Delhi High Court gave a split decision: Justice Gyan Sudha Misra agreed with Muthiah that the amendment to clause 6.2.4 had been 'an abuse of the amending power exercised by the BCCI' introduced 'not to promote the game of cricket but to promote the interest of Mr. N. Srinivasan'. Justice J. M. Panchal took the more robust attitude that there was no conflict of interest if nobody complained of one: 'The record does not indicate that any franchisee or any other member of the BCCI has complained of any alleged conflict of interest. Thus, the plea of conflict of interest is substance-less and is hereby rejected.' And so the challenge persisted, being referred up to India's chief justice, S. H. Kapadia for posting before a larger Bench.

On the field, it was actually as glorious a period as India has known. Having played just enough Test matches in 2010 to consolidate its number-one world ranking, M. S. Dhoni's team wrested the World Cup in front of their own crowds at Mumbai's Wankhede Stadium on 2 April 2011. This time victory was not the shock it had been twenty-eight years earlier. India were a formidable team, well-led, well-resourced, and well-rewarded. Interestingly, though, when the fourth IPL began less than a week later, with its new teams, new management and host of new allegiances, the ratings fluctuated, tapering off after a solid start. Without Modi, someone said, it was like 'chocolate without sugar'.

After disappointing recent crowds, the ECB had also announced plans to scale down its FP T20 competition, while Australia's Big Bash League was having teething troubles as well, with about the only details public being the names of the teams and their colours – private ownership was proving rather more complicated than simply a big payday for everyone. A tedious squib in its second outing in South Africa, the Champions League was struggling to find a constituency: as of May, no venue had been agreed for the third, scheduled just four months hence. Some levelling-off in Twenty20's heady growth was to be expected, although these were salutary warning signs that an undue dependence on the format could also be costly. Cricket has historically thrived on glorious uncertainty; not so much cricket administration.

Part II
Crisis? What Crisis?

THE FUTURE OF CRICKET

The Kravchuk Factor

The first president of Ukraine, Leonid Kravchuk, put it best. 'Yesterday the Ukraine stood poised on the brink of a great abyss', he said in his inaugural parliamentary address. 'Today we have taken a great step forward.' Thus the state of international cricket, poised to do away with structures a century and more in the making, but rendered helpless to do otherwise by the ineluctable momentums of commerce. Which is not to say that parts of that system aren't ripe for some creative destruction. But there are aspects of cricket's new dispensation which lie disconcertingly unexamined, in the excitements of the moment, and the confusions of personal and national ambitions.

Consider one modern lamentation common among traditionalists—of which, I might say, I am generally to be counted. It is: 'Cricket is run too much like a business'. This is misconceived. The International Cricket Council looks nothing like the standard organisation unit of modern business, the publicly listed corporation. Its shareholders are not dispersed and mainly voiceless; they are concentrated and inclined to vociferous rivalries. It has no power over who sits on its executive board, having to cop whomever is sent by the sovereign national associations that control it; its presidency rotates on a fixed-term basis, and incompetence is no bar to appointment.

The ICC's biggest and most historic enterprise, the Test match, generates losses for the majority of its shareholders. In return for absorbing these losses, those shareholders receive dividends derived from the ICC's other commercial properties, including World Cups and Champions Trophies. Over the use of these dividends, the ICC exerts no control, and nobody knows exactly how they are spent— whether they genuinely contribute to the beneficiation of the game, or of certain sticky-fingered individuals.

The shareholders are racked with their own problems. One, India, provides the lion's share of the cash, and others are loath to cross it. At least three, meanwhile, are on a Ukraine-style financial brink—Pakistan, Sri Lanka and the West Indies. But neither the ICC nor its member boards have any authority over the most lucrative properties so far conceived in global cricket, the ostensibly 'domestic' Twenty20 competitions conjured in India: the Indian Premier League and the Champions League. This is despite the players these boards have developed and groomed being the feature that makes those properties work.

I could go on, but you get the picture. You could argue that cricket's problem is not that it is run too much like a business, but that it isn't run like a business enough. There are sound cultural reasons for this, emanating from the way cricket control boards were originally structured to run domestic first-class competitions, with representation based on the local and regional teams composing them. But even at country level, those arrangements are looking anachronistic. Does anyone really understand how the Board of Control for Cricket in India is elected? Is anyone prepared to swear hand on heart that it is a transparent democratic process in which the ablest candidates are always chosen? Not that an Australian should necessarily point the finger, when Cricket Australia recently overlooked the obvious choice for its own chairmanship, Mark Taylor, in favour of an Adelaide solicitor Jack Clarke, for the sake of interstate harmony. Jack's a genial old hearty, but if ever there was a time when a smart ex-player with worldwide respect would have been useful as chairman, it is today.

In one respect, however, the traditionalists have it right. Cricket is tightly in the grip of commerce in the sense that it has lost the sense of existing for any other purpose. The priorities of business can be witnessed in the supersaturation point reached by international competition: television demands a constant supply of new, live product, good or not. Turn on your television, flick idly between the Test match here, the IPL game there and the one-day international everywhere, and one sees not competition but content, created simply to be sold to the highest bidder. 'Sport is business', warned Lamar Hunt, progenitor of World Championship Tennis. 'And business is business.'

This invites an always useful question: *cui bono*? To whose benefit? The answer has never been straightforward where cricket is concerned. For all that the game's past provided for the enjoyment of fans, the ambitions of players and the pride of patriots, it also shored up old imperial structures and political prejudices. But there is a sense that the game's present has become so thoroughly subverted by economic objectives, the interests of broadcasters, advertisers, corporate investors, a group of entrepreneurial administrators and an elite of international players, that the rest of us must accept our lot as simple customers at the end of the assembly line.

What we're watching, then, is akin to a process of privatisation—that is, we are being sold something we thought we owned. The game, which administrators once held in a kind of public trust, is becoming a private sector product—the same kind of transfiguration that occurs in the bottling of water. During the 2008 Boxing Day Test, I attended a lunch of Cricket Australia where the chief executive, James Sutherland, referred incessantly to me and others like me who love cricket, as 'cricket consumers'. Is that all we do? Consume it? We do, bollocks, I thought. It was then that I started thinking about Leonid Kravchuk.

Tehelka, July 2009

INDIA AND AUSTRALIA

Who's Afraid of the Big, Bad Indian?

Not long ago, I was writing a piece about the power and sway of the BCCI and decided to go and talk to Cricket Australia's James Sutherland on a not-for-publication, not-for-attribution, not-even-for-whispering-about-in-a-noisy-pub basis. Sometimes you'll come away from such a chat with an arresting thought or phrase that informs what you write. What I'll remember from this audience is James' candid and repeated reply: 'I don't know'. What about this, James? 'I don't know.' And how about that? 'I don't know either.' If this happens, what would you do? 'That's another good one. I don't know, and if you have any suggestions let me know.' I'm still not sure whether I was more worried before or after I arrived. He didn't provide ready answers, but clearly would have been pretending had he done so.

Things had changed. At the start of the year, I'd had a dinner conversation with a director of CA, who had muttered with chagrin of the repercussions of India's victory in the Twenty20 World Championship: 'Six months ago, the BCCI didn't want to know about Twenty20. Now they think they invented it'. The inference of my conversation with James was that the BCCI had now gone on to patent that invention, would brook no opposition, and that ICL stood not for Indian Cricket League but for Infidels Cluttering the Landscape.

I've chosen my title carefully, because my subject is not India per se but evolving Western impressions of Indian cricket. Normally for such an inquiry, I'd range more widely. I'd want to touch on Ranji, Duleep, Bedi, Gavaskar. But I'm not sure, beyond some prettifying decoration, that it serves much purpose here. When Greg Chappell, Dennis Lillee and Rod Marsh retired a quarter of a century ago, it was without a single Test in India between them. So I'll start in an uncompromisingly modern way with the autobiography of Adam Gilchrist, *True Colours*.

Extracts from this book concerning Harbhajan, Tendulkar and others would be familiar, the parts on which the media has focused with its unerring capacity for finding and hyping the least interesting aspect of everything. Instead, I've chosen four impressions of India accumulated over a decade on four tours, prefiguring the 2008 IPL.

In 1998, Gilchrist was mainly an onlooker, arriving to play one-dayers after a 1-2 Test defeat. He found the camp in demoralised condition, not just from the defeat, but the peculiar mixture of claustrophobia and paranoia that sets in when men are cooped up for too long. He says:

> That fatalistic pessimism can set in instantly in India. Guys would go into a kind of trance, just focusing on survival. In the hotels, because there were always so many people approaching you for an autograph or to ask for tickets, you'd shut yourself in your room and become a virtual prisoner ... Plenty of guys did genuinely hate being in India and that flowed through to on-field performances. As we'd learn in 2001 and 2004, it is one thing to make the right noises and say the right things, but another thing to do it repeatedly and consistently under the physical and mental stress of a long tour.

This is India as a kind of cricket heart of darkness: demoralising, decadent, even degenerate, for Gilchrist tells several tales of frustration, and also casual corruption. When Australia participated in the Pepsi Cup, for example, they could get no response from their hosts to persistent questions about prize money. The BCCI would promise to get back to them, but did not until Australia was ten minutes from winning the trophy—whereupon, you guessed it, they were told there was no prize money. When they participated soon after in the Coca-Cola Cup in Sharjah, they noted that India received a fat winner's cheque for their victory, and Sachin Tendulkar US$400 000 for his century in the final.

In 2001, of course, Gilchrist scored a dazzling hundred in Mumbai, but was then the middle man in a Harbhajan hat-trick in Kolkata and felt himself steadily overwhelmed. This is an unguarded book written by a sensitive and perceptive amanuensis, and describes the subject's fall graphically—Gilchrist describes watching himself, as though perched atop one of the Eden Gardens light towers.

> The never-ending sprawl of Kolkata, patterned with green treetops and the roofs of colonial buildings, the traffic at a standstill as groups of people excitedly gathered round radios and small black & white TVs, living and breathing every ball bowled. Within the ground I could see the fanatical crowd celebrating a wicket, the smoky haze as some of them lit newspapers and whatever else was in reach, and in the centre of the wicket, the unstoppable Indian team huddled tightly, plotting the next batsman's downfall. In amongst it all, I sensed the noise, the smells, the electric atmosphere. A tiny figure among the 100,000 people in the ground and the many hundred millions watching around the world, I could see myself making my slow way back to the pavilion, as lost and lonely as I had ever felt in my life ... My mindset by then was uncontrollably negative.

The 2001 Border–Gavaskar Trophy coincided with the launch of Aaj Tak (Till Today), the 24-hour cable news channel, which as a news source now outshines even Doordarshan. Part of its strategy was to aggressively own cricket, based around its nightly show *Who Will Become the World Champion?* Its news cycle was punctuated with cricket updates and reviews, and a text graphic of the live score at all times. No wonder it felt to Gilchrist like there was not a moment's respite, while acknowledging that his was a privileged vantage point:

You cannot escape cricket there. You come home, turn on the TV and the first thing you see is a replay of the entire day's play on one channel while another has highlights and yet another will have news. The country itself had got a hold of me. It was weird: I felt riven by anxiety, yet every day I saw what people lived with in India and it put my worries into perspective. I find that the more you think about your time in India, the more you realise it's the most valuable place you've ever been, although you don't know that at the time you're learning.

By the time he returned three years later, Gilchrist was Australia's locum as captain; more importantly, perhaps, he was a prior tourist. The pressure remained acute, but there was fun in fame too. He describes one extracurricular activity—the filming of a Castrol advertisement in Kolkata's Jobul markets. In it, Gilchrist, like the Beatles in *A Hard Day's Night*, has suddenly to flee a throng of well-wishers, but fails to make his escape when a cab won't start; the way Gilchrist describes it, the imagined scenario wasn't far from reality.

The crew said they were doing a documentary on Kolkata. They made a point of not mentioning me or any of the cricketers … We had one day to shoot it and I had to get there at 5.30am. So I got there, pulled around the corner and saw a massive sign: 'welcome to Jobul Markets, Adam Gilchrist'. There were several thousand people on the streets and the roofs, cheering as I got out of the car. I don't know who leaked it and how, but they sat there all day watching the filming. The crew had to call the police to keep them back. Whenever I wasn't required I'd be whisked away to a room, and when I'd come out they'd scream and cheer. I felt like a rock star but it was so funny. During the filming, I'd be standing waiting for the director to say 'Quiet on set'. The police would look around and the locals would fall silent. I'd look up and wave to them and they would erupt, screaming. The director would get stuck into me for wasting time … The important thing was I didn't have to tell

myself to 'embrace India'. I was loving it without any effort at
all. I wasn't a lost boy wandering around in the woods, as I'd
been in 2001. I was floating above it all.

Again, the metaphor of watching from altitude, this time in
peace rather than turmoil; he is floating rather than sitting; he is
making the television, not watching it. This is still an assimilative
process, because he is still ducking in and out, he is still dealing
with India as a crowd rather than on an individual basis. He has
found an angle of incision, and the angle, interestingly, is money:
the outcome is theatrical, but the theatre itself is commercial. The
forum for understanding is an advertisement for a multinational oil
company: oil implies grease, grease implies gears, and gears implies
the economic powerhouse of modern India. But oil, of course, with
water notoriously does not mix.

The last extract, from 2007, describes a meeting in a Mumbai
hotel during a one-day series, involving a group of Australian players
and Lalit Modi. Notice immediately the change in dynamics. Here
the Australians are the group, the audience; Modi is the individual,
the star. The Australians are no longer being importuned; they are
being invited, although with a hint of menace.

He was young, slick and charismatic, certainly not your
typical Indian cricket administrator. He outlined a vision
for a competition—the Indian Premier League. It was big, it
was imaginative and, he assured us, it was here for the long
term. Nothing, he said, was impossible. We believed him. He
presented it with an air of inevitability. 'It's going to happen,'
he said, 'so if you want to do it, this is what you have to do. If
you try to get funky, we'll just go on without you'.

'Get funky'? Where's that from? Here is modern, technocratic,
turbocapitalist India incarnate. Modi is young in an ancient culture,
slick in a landscape alternately rugged and exquisitely textured, and
charismatic in a country identified with the spiritual and eternal. He
speaks like a Westerner, but thinks bigger than the Western minds he
is opening. And, of course, he comes with the authority of millions.

What was a land rich, chaotic, alien, intractable, intimidating, he has harnessed, interpreted and monetised comprehensively. These, at least, are the perspectives of Gilchrist, collected over a decade, and they relate a little more about cultural difference than further debate about the Punjabi word for motherfucker.

The message of this last story has many echoes: if everyone wants to get rich, they will have to learn to take orders. Before going further, it might be worth commenting on the cast of mind that elides the BCCI, Indian cricket and indeed India. They are not the same thing; although it is not an assumption, of course, that the BCCI will ever do anything to discourage. It is extremely useful to be regarded as synonymous with a country, because one can then claim merely to be mobilised by its public opinion; when you seem to have a billion people at your back, you cast a long, long shadow. In truth, I suspect, Indian public opinion is far more atomised and chaotic than the BCCI is apt to pretend, and Australians are apt to assume: if there is one worn-out cliché it is time to retire, it is that of the effigy-burning Indian fan fomenting at some perceived Western slight; these days it is internet that is the echo chamber of indignation.

But I suspect it is here to stay because the authority of the BCCI is enhanced by invocation of a huge, passionate and volatile fan base, and because clichés offer Australian journalists the freedom from thought they so patently crave.

If everyone expects to get rich, furthermore, they will also have to pay homage. About this, there remains confusion. Matthew Hayden recently stirred a hornet's nest by referring to India as 'Third World'; he was evidently baffled by objections:

> The politics of cricket, I think, has gone mad. One of the things
> I love the most about India, is that you walk around the back
> of the hotel, and there's a man who's selling peanuts on the
> street for one cent a month, and he holds his head so high,
> and is so proud, as if he was making $2 million a month. It
> frustrates me that certain sections of humanity want to take
> someone like myself down, who is a really great admirer of the

country, and who has really built his career on the back of the country in a very proud and honoured way ... There is a large portion of India that is third world, that is below the poverty line. But from my experience, it is those people who I admire the most.

Heavens, what's the world coming to when you can't make a condescending comment about the poor but proud?

All Hayden proves is that he hasn't read CA's annual report. Cricket is a divided game. There are two streams. There is the stream when India plays and the stream when it does not. In- and outbound Indian tours are so much more lucrative than those of any other country that the economically rational behaviour for every sovereign board is to maximise them—thus the escalating rewards for Australian players over the last decade, as we have done so. In 2006–07, CA had what appeared objectively to be the most prosperous summer possible: an Ashes series sold out in advance, with handsome television and radio rights sales back to England, and a colossal payday from winning the World Cup. Yet they still made far more from four Tests and one-day internationals involving India here the following summer.

One often hears from the Subcontinent the sentiment: 'England and Australia ran cricket for 100-plus years; now it is our turn'. But this is more than a power shift; it is a change in the nature of power.

The Anglo-Australian axis exerted cultural suasion: England as the progenitor of the game, Australia as its oldest, most skilful and most sophisticated opponent. India exerts, chiefly, economic power. The old order involved spreading the game to instil imperial fealty, with the perverse outcome that it also fanned nationalist fantasies of independence; the new order seems to be about bringing existing markets into an Indian sphere of commercial influence, creating a world in which India wins, or is perceived to win, again and again. There is a wry passage in Andrew Symonds' book *Roy* about Neo Cricket, the 24-hour cricket pay channel run by Nimbus Communications, which shows the game's potential as grist for a propaganda mill:

Someone said to me while I was there, 'I've been watching the TV here a bit—has Australia ever beaten India?'

'Not if you watch Neo Cricket they haven't!' I replied. 'I've never hit a four on Neo Cricket, let alone been able to celebrate.'

Interestingly, I think the rise of the BCCI as the game's hegemon represents also a general twenty-first-century shift from soft power to hard. The Anglo-Australian alliance at the ICC represented their conception of cricket as involving diffused authority. Sovereign boards had unchallenged domestic powers; umpires were masters of the on-field domain; players were expected to follow unwritten and even unuttered codes; the ICC was a filing cabinet in the Marylebone Cricket Club secretary's office. In some respects, the Indian model is much more in tune with the times and habits. Sovereign boards are weaker; umpires are answerable to television and players to a voluminous Code of Conduct; and immense power emanates from a single central concentration.

So it is not a matter of turn, nor of wisdom or expertise. It is that God is on the side of the big battalions, and none have greater resources than the BCCI, with its mixture of feudalism and hyper-capitalism, vaulting domestic political ambition and postcolonial chippiness. The ICC is actually almost as nugatory as it always was: for decades a postbox at Lord's, it is these days more like the BCCI's waiting room.

In recent memory of these tensions, the incident that springs instantly to mind is Bhajigate. As a topic, I suspect it's probably near exhausted.

There's been much learned debate, and even more unlearned, about what this episode tells us about race in both countries, even if I'm not sure it's much, except that the minute race enters any discussion it becomes heir to centuries of accumulated bitternesses. But as an incident that has informed Australian views of Indian cricket, it has no rival. Here's the account of the incident in Gilchrist's memoir:

Harbhajan took a few lusty swings, when he got one away to fine leg off Brett Lee. As he jogged through for the single Harbhajan gave Brett a light, inoffensive pat on the backside. Brett looked over his shoulder and gave Harbhajan a rueful sort of half-smile.

The next thing I saw, Symo had come across the wicket while changing his position and said to Harbhajan something like, 'Don't touch him, you've got no friends here'.

Harbhajan never needed an invitation for a bit of banter, and Symo had given him one. So it was on again, the bickering between the two of them.

I'd gone back to my keeping spot and Brett finished the over. Then, at the change of ends, I heard Haydos and Harbhajan talking to each other. 'You've got a witness now', Haydos was saying. Ricky, Tendulkar and Harbhajan were standing on the wicket talking. I thought I'd go up to see what was going on, and I heard Harbhajan say to Ricky: 'I'm sorry, I apologise, it won't happen again'. The look on Harbhajan's face was very telling. He looked like he was thinking: 'Oh shit, what have I done here? They're all over me'.

Gilchrist recounts that the incident was discussed in the Australian dressing room, and Ricky Ponting's resolution to take the complaint that Harbhajan had used the word 'monkey' to Symonds to the match referee. Then, as Gilchrist says: 'The cricket community seemed to blow up around us'.

For an intelligent cricketer, this last seems a naive comment: of course it did; never was it likely to be otherwise. In all other respects, it sounds a pretty fair-minded and accurate summary, insofar as nobody emerges well. Symonds and Harbhajan both sound like idiots. The Australian players escalate the crisis out of sheer bloody-mindedness. The Indian players, irritated by the provocation, fib to evade the offence. We all know what happened next: the incompetent ICC referee got into the act—the same one who in Melbourne had let Yuvraj Singh stand there like a statue of himself getting out—and the BCCI raged incandescently.

Australians were sharply divided by this incident; or, to be more precise, this incident and its antecedents. For over the last few years, Australian cricketers have done rather less than endear themselves to some members of their public. They see a Harbhajan as getting his retaliation in first. When they hear an opposition captain invoke the spirit of cricket, they are instinctively in sympathy with the complainant.

There is an equally strident lobby that not only sees India as becoming too hot to handle, but perceives any gesture that might give aid and comfort to Australian cricket's critics as a form of Cliveden-like appeasement—political correctness gone mad, to use the tabloid phrase. There is no doubt that the possible punishment of an Indian cricketer for the use of a racist epithet struck them as deliciously ironic.

Neither of these positions, it seemed to me, had very much to do with the incident at all. Instead, events were reconstructed to cohere with a pre-existing set of prejudices, with the emphases varying according to the convictions held about Australian society. It is no fluke that the respective extremities of the debate were staked out by rival media organisations exactly as one would expect. In the wishy-washy Fairfax newspapers, Peter Roebuck almost called for a national sorry day. He placed great weight on Harbhajan becoming his family's breadwinner in his youth—an implicit criticism of prosperous, leisured Australians who could not understand the quotidian realities of the East. In the polemical News Ltd stable, Malcolm Conn became cricket's Keith Windschuttle; an Institute of Public Affairs fellow was even wheeled out to pronounce that Ricky Ponting's critics were members of the 'self-loathing left'. India, in these constructions of the controversy, barely came into focus at all, bulking distantly, as a mirror of our ill nature in the Fairfax press, and a dimly glimpsed nemesis in News Ltd. But in both cases, it instilled a certain dread: one camp worried about what sporting contact with India might illuminate about our own inner natures; the other fretted at Australia's waning autonomy, and that the world's best cricket team seemed on the point of eclipse by the world's richest.

What the BCCI was up to still puzzles me. Bestowing a racist epithet was not something any cricketer could lightly confess to; but the avowed explanation for their position, that they believed their man, does not really satisfy. Harbhajan has a record of indiscipline a yard long; when he had his cheeky exchange with Shantakumaran Sreesanth a few months later, the IPL promptly meted out exemplary justice. I suspect, in fact, that this betrayed a level of irritation. They expected some reciprocity from Harbhajan for turning him into the most improbable of martyrs in Sydney; he mistook their support for a certification of impunity.

Two explanations suggest themselves. The first is that the BCCI was experimenting with the extent of its suasion. A superpower is as a superpower does, and what is power if you do not use it? Another explanation, which smacks of post hoc rationalisation but might provide an insight into the BCCI's attitudes, appears in a *Wisden Cricketer* piece by Stephen Brenkley about Test cricket's malaise. When Brenkley sought the view of the BCCI regarding sparse crowds at international venues, he received a reply of what he called 'doom-laden acceptance'. Crowds are thin worldwide, said the board; the only hope, according to spokesman Javed Akhtar, was to engage interest for 'reasons other than cricket'.

> For example, the issue of racism raised its ugly head when Australia last visited India. Following this, when India went to Australia earlier this year the spat between Harbhajan Singh and Andrew Symonds and comments from Matthew Hayden and others created a hype around the series that resulted in the matches being followed with much greater interest.

So, there you have it: racism might be heinous, but it has its uses. And while my title is chiefly rhetorical, I might as well say that this, rather than the big or the bad, is the India I fear: the reckless, cynical and self-interested one.

For it is here, I suspect, that we can anticipate further frictions in the game, because dependent relationships, as Australia's now is with India, are capable of breeding resentment, both among players and administrators—as, indeed, was the case in the 1970s, 1980s and 1990s, when Australia had the most lucrative summer in the calendar, and somehow India could be accommodated only once a decade or so. At the recent news that the BCCI might smuggle the suspended Gautam Gambhir into its Test team for Nagpur, for example, James Sutherland, who publicly is circumspect and cryptic, gave an uncharacteristically terse speech along the lines: 'Great power must be matched with great responsibility'. Tobey Maguire utters the same piety at the end of *Spider-Man*, where it is an allusion to American unipolar power. Sutherland was referencing the similar power exerted by India, without countervailing force or cultural inhibition. Usually grievances are contained by the calming medium of cash. Here was a rare, and telling, moment of candour.

For all that they insist on understanding of their cultural differences in matters like Bhajigate, Indians are strangely incurious about those elsewhere: the charge of racism, brandished like an indelible proof of personal virtue, will suffice as an explanation for most anything. It's a charge that doesn't lack force in Australia; there is a lot to condemn. But it misses the countries' common bond of colonisation. For much of Australia's past, history has been something that occurs far away; or at least, if this is too sweeping a judgement, history has been set in motion by events elsewhere. One of the chief exceptions to this state of affairs, however, has been sport, where Australians have long outgrown any colonial inferiority complex; we might have tugged the forelock at the Privy Council, but never at Lord's. India's combination of economic heft and sporting clout, then, resonates with a residual disquiet about and resentment of Australia's frequent branch office status; it threatens us, moreover, in an area where we've become accustomed to ruling the roost. We are masters of our cricket destiny no more. Some of us will become a great deal richer in the process, like Adam Gilchrist. But not all of us will have the luxury of his privileged journey.

Pride, Prejudice, Power and Race in Cricket conference, November 2008

CHAMPIONS TROPHY 2008

Creeping Insecurities

In Western countries, no word has become such an excuse for the absurd in the last ten years as 'security'. Every politician is pledged to increase it; every general and police chief thinks this an excellent idea; every media organisation assents. Every airport is choked with dopy, leering layabouts in uniform forcing passengers to surrender their belts and shoes as they pass through X-ray machines—an annoyance about which there is a remarkable forbearance, even though the inattention is such that you could probably smuggle a howitzer through while these knuckleheads are scrutinising laptops.

One man's threat being another's opportunity, a flourishing class has emerged of high-end, hi-tech professionals to appease the post-9/11 conviction that too much security is never enough. And no member of this class ever got rich underplaying security risk, by saying: 'Stop being paranoid. What are you worried about?' If anything, the ability to identify small risks and perceive their potential for bigness is a badge of professional distinction. And their advice is readily accepted by administrations and organisations who wish to perceive themselves as doing the right thing by their representatives.

This template does not fit precisely the circumstances of the postponement of the Champions Trophy, which had been scheduled for October 2008 in Pakistan. A country where the Kalashnikov seems less a weapon than a fashion accessory is a potentially confronting environment at the best of times. Even now, the fear is not so much that players will be a specific target of violence; it is that they need only be in the wrong place at the wrong time to come to harm. But it is also true that the attitudes taken by Australia, England, South Africa and New Zealand reflect, above all, the huge modern Western discomfort with any semblance of insecurity—real, imagined and/or both.

Apprehensions have changed. Thirty years ago, England toured Pakistan in the wake of a military coup, and during the unruly trial of president Ali Bhutto; twenty years ago, Australia toured in the immediate aftermath of the fiery end of Bhutto's nemesis, General Zia ul-Haq. It is hard to believe that either tour would have taken place amid present perceptions, even with the rise to power of Bhutto's son-in-law.

It is also hard to believe that exactly those same concerns will not loom just as large in a year's time, as indeed they did in 2006 when Pakistan nonetheless won the right to stage the Champions Trophy. An irreducible degree of risk will attach to any cricket tour of Pakistan, as indeed to daily life itself. For as long as that pertains, Pakistan faces competing in international cricket on an essentially part-time basis, unable, like Sri Lanka in the 1980s, to host inbound tours from non-Asian competitors, at terrible cost to local cricket and its luckless, guiltless fans.

Pakistan, of course, has always been regarded as a bit of a hardship posting—unfairly, as it is a marvellous test of a touring cricketer's mettle. But, just now, cricket values, as well as Western values, are somewhat askew. By making players rich beyond the dreams of mammon, for example, the IPL has naturally increased their scope to discriminate between assignments. Only mouth almighty Andrew Symonds has so far had the nerve to say it, but every cricketer must feel the sensation in some degree: why tour Pakistan, where every bus backfire sounds ominous, when you can drop in on India, where there are also bombs, and some very noisy ones at that, but you can pull down seven figures in six weeks?

This risk business, too, is generating a new clientele. No longer are 'security concerns' the sole prerogative of sovereign boards of control. In the matter of the Champions Trophy, at least as visible have been the CEOs of the players' associations, specifically Paul Marsh of Australia, Heath Mills of New Zealand, Tony Irish of South Africa, and Tim May of that amorphous entity, the Federation of International Cricketers' Associations, who obtained their own security advice on conditions in Pakistan. Marsh was particularly uninhibited in public pronouncements, and well placed to be doing so. Relations between Cricket Australia and the Australian Cricketers' Association will be put to the test in the next year by the negotiation of a new memorandum of understanding; there was no inclination at Jolimont to place them under premature strain.

It is sometimes overlooked that players' associations have been as unsettled by the Twenty20 revolution as cricket boards. Their business is ensuring the best possible deal for their members, yet they can take next to no credit for cricket's new multimillion-dollar milieu: it is the BCCI which has proven the players' great benefactor. But if pay has ceased to be an issue on which associations can mount a case for their existence, then conditions have not. There is little scope in cricket any longer for the bare-knuckled, table-banging shop steward; there remain opportunities for the hard-hat-wearing, clipboard-wielding OH&S man scrutinising the placement of the bollards and saying: 'If you don't fix this, I'm gonna close you down'. 'Security concerns', then, have become an issue by which players' associations can demonstrate their continued relevance, by which it can be proved to cricketers that their dues still buy something.

For Pakistan, meanwhile, the future is bleak. 'The sick man of Europe' was Tsar Nicholas I's appellation for the Ottoman Empire; the Pakistan Cricket Board has become at least the BCCI's frustratingly poorly cousin. There is no more fascinating relationship in the cricket world than the one between these two countries, brought together at the ICC by mutual interests, having been divided by history, culture, disputed territory and nuclear rivalry. The PCB's isolation deepens its acute reliance on BCCI patronage at a time when the BCCI might be pondering the usefulness of such a troublesome satellite, consolidating the BCCI's sphere of influence while also potentially weakening it, for not even the BCCI can afford to shrug off potentially US$90 million of penalty payments to ESPN-Star. And while security has been demonstrated to be a concern of cricketers, it is, even more so, a preoccupation of capital.

Cricinfo, September 2008

SPORT AND RECESSION

Can the Centre Hold?

Throughout 2008, *Forbes*, the American magazine that preens itself as 'The Capitalist Tool', has been publishing a series of special issues on the world's most valuable sports properties, in baseball, ice hockey and footballs (various). The last contained the usual selection of eye-popping figures about NFL: for example, that the average team is valued at US$1 billion, nineteen teams being worth more, compared with just five last year and none five years ago.

Did I say 'is' valued? I meant 'was'. For in years to come, these magazines may not be unlike the Lehman Brothers caps and Fannie Mae fridge magnets now selling on eBay: a reminder of the good old days, when credit was cheap, assets only increased in value and corporate largesse was unending.

An even more pointed reminder of changed circumstances, of course, is the AIG symbol sported, doubtless with some chagrin, by Manchester United, worth £14 million a year to the club when the deal was done thirty months ago, but now as ignominiously conspicuous as mouthing a slogan for Luftschiffbau Zeppelin in May 1937: 'You'll always travel Fuhrer class on the *Hindenburg*!'

Man U will cope. Others may not be so lucky. The Götterdämerung on Wall Street has demonstrated that when asset values rise significantly and over a long period, a misapprehension grows among investors that they will rise indefinitely, that everyone will get rich and that everyone involved is a genius.

How closely, I wonder, does this also apply to the business of sport? Big time sport has enjoyed the sort of revenue growth over the last twenty years that in an athlete would suggest a steroid or illegal hormone: they have also marbled in huge fixed costs, as expenditure has risen to meet then outstrip income, with the assumption that future growth will somehow make it all work.

Sport got a glimpse of what a major financial reckoning might look like in 2002. The collapses within a month of the Kirch Gruppe and ITV Digital brought hard times and austerities to the Bundesliga and the Nationwide League, depriving clubs generally of the broadcasting bounty to which they had grown accustomed.

Present circumstances hit clubs and leagues at a more prosaic and localised level. About a quarter of the US$10 billion in sponsorship monies ploughed into sport comes from the financial services sector. That includes the Premier League's support from Barclays, English cricket's alliance with NatWest, and the London Olympics' fat handout from Lloyds TSB. Who would want to be hustling at the moment? Expect instead injunctions to do more with less. Doves for the opening ceremony? Wouldn't pigeons do the job?

During its gilded age, too, sport has comprehensively thrown in its lot with the high-end consumer now likeliest to change their short-term spending habits. After all, who can enjoy a football match in a £500 seat if one's broker is constantly plaguing one with margins calls, and the bailiff might in-between times have repossessed one's Merc? Particularly worrying is that it is usually the most leveraged and ostentatious fortunes that are most vulnerable: after all, even oligarchs lose money.

Part of the dread pervading securities markets at present is the sheer unfamiliarity of the dilemma. The bull market in stocks is usually deemed to have run since August 1982. You need to be in your late forties to recall a protracted downturn, and in your late fifties to have experienced anything like this kind of confusion and desperation.

That is even more the case in sport, whose management is the province of youthful enthusiasts with sports marketing degrees and iPhones who scatter their conversation with quotes from *Jerry Maguire*. What will they make of a downturn? Which among them will know how to eliminate discretionary costs and to winnow away fixed ones? Above all, how many athletes have had to come to terms with being worth considerably less than they were a year earlier without a serious deterioration in their playing abilities? For it would be a brave man who bet on the next NFL broadcasting rights deal being worth as much as the present US$8 billion. Like I said, enjoy *Forbes*. Things may never be this good again.

~

One sign of the seriousness of the credit crisis has been the surprising dearth of sports metaphors in use among those charged with resolving it: surprising not only because commercial life has become so replete with them, but because they have been the stock-in-trade of the Bush White House. Who can forget CIA chief George Tenet's description of the case for WMDs in Iraq as a 'slam dunk'? Or Bush's promise as president to 'sprint to the line'? That worked out well.

So far there have been no touchdowns or home runs, nor has anybody offered 110 per cent, except perhaps as an interest rate. That's because hardly anyone has stepped up to the plate, what with the general lack of heavy hitters and a playing field far from level, while Congress' attempt at blocking and tackling went badly awry. As for the countercycle, that of business metaphors infiltrating sport, a hard day at the office has taken on a whole new meaning.

~

Dean Rusk once called the United States 'the fat boy in the canoe': when it moves, everyone must adjust. In cricket, that role is filled by India, which makes worth noting the recent launch of what is destined, according to its backers, to become 'the most popular cricket website in the world': www.bcci.tv.

So far it looks rather less like a website devoted to cricket than to the BCCI. Top story yesterday was 'Lalit Modi Wins TV Award', the IPL commissioner having won a coveted CNBC Awaaz Consumer Award—well, *someone* must covet them. Top comment piece was 'In Praise of Sharad Pawar', a 1685-word paean about the outgoing BCCI boss, 'a statesman who is clear of thought, dispassionate and above all a true team leader', by his BCCI colleague Inderjit Bindra. Featured player profile, meanwhile, was 'Yuvraj Singh—Making of a Legend'. Not so much of a legend that he made India's fifteen-man squad for the first two Tests.

This venture bears close watching, for the BCCI is not just offering a Web portal but attempting to exercise a significant degree of control over the coverage of cricket in India, to the exclusion of established rival Cricinfo. They are moving fast: a Google search for 'BCCI' still directs you to the old BCCI website, http://bcci.cricket. deepthi.com/, which looks like it was banged together in an hour by a teenage slacker between puffs on a bong.

So far, though, there is little to allay suspicions that India's hegemonic pretensions in international cricket are less about the game than about the aggrandisement of its political and media elite. And as we are finding elsewhere, no hubris fails to find its nemesis.

The Guardian, October 2008

MUMBAI

Blood in the Streets

'Aussies Dead in Mumbai Massacre.' Thus this morning's poster for *The Australian*. Aussies? Well, yes—a couple, among perhaps hundreds of others. But at times like these, all the gab of globalisation goes by the board, and concentration routinely becomes kith and kin, home and hearth.

Yet there is something shockingly new to the mayhem in Mumbai for distant foreigners, not least of the cricketing kind. Hitherto, terror in South Asia has been seen as a feature of Pakistani and Sri Lankan landscapes, where, especially in the case of the former, it has been regarded as confirming the destination as a frontier of fear.

By contrast, India generally and Mumbai especially have been cricket's candy mountain, offering ever-tastier enticements to the star player—not merely money, but excitement, attention and sense of importance. Non-Indian cricketers love cricket, but in their countries not everyone does; India offers a culture valuing the game as much as, if not more than, the most enthusiastic professional practitioner.

Of course, the distinction was never quite so crisp. India never stopped being a country of extremes, with the possibility of violence. On 11 May 2008, bombs detonated in Jaipur killing or injuring 250 people; three days later, Cameron White, Shane Watson, Graeme Smith and Jacques Kallis played an IPL match there. At the time, though, everything somehow seemed far rosier. Now, confidence is more fragile, and more susceptible to sudden shocks, and India's economic and technological advances work curiously against it.

Almost four decades ago, Australia toured an India racked by civil unrest and economic austerity following the split of the Indian National Congress and bank nationalisation, aggravated by Charu Mazumdar's Naxalite Terror. They were hemmed in by riots in Mumbai and Kolkata, where every window of the Australian team's hotel was broken by demonstrators against the presence of Doug Walters (who was thought erroneously to have served in Vietnam) and the team bus was bombarded with projectiles on the way to Dum Dum Airport.

Yet their countrymen knew next to nothing of this. Mirabile dictu, there was not a single Australian journalist or broadcaster accompanying the team, manager Fred Bennett was indifferent to complaints, and the attitude of Australian players was laconic resignation. According to Ashley Mallett, when the players were under siege in their Eden Gardens dressing room, they simply drank tinnies while waiting for the violence to subside. Bennett burst in at one point and said agitatedly that the crowd were after captain Bill Lawry's blood. 'Hand him over and we'll get on with the drinking', Walters suggested.

Today, Mumbai is a centre of global commerce, tourism and media that reports itself assiduously and comprehensively, for internal and external consumption. When it burns, the radiant heat is felt thousands of miles away. Thus the shock and disorientation of seeing locations familiar to Western tourists in flames and under fire, and the distress of knowing friends and colleagues there.

When the smoke of burning hotels clears, some other phenomena may be seen in clearer aspect. Dazzled by the efflorescence of the IPL six months ago, observers have ignored less exciting but perhaps more meaningful events since. The salient index of stocks on the Mumbai Exchange, which rose sixfold in five years to the end of 2007, has this year shed half its value. Offshore institutions who bought a record US$17.4 billion of stocks last year have sold US$13.5 billion of stocks this year. The Indian middle classes, so fundamental to the IPL's success, have been the chief sufferers.

In October 2008, the rights to broadcast the Champions League were sold for US$900 million to ESPN-Star Sports, making it the highest-valued cricket tournament in history on a per-game basis. Since then, the financial services industry worldwide has had a nervous breakdown, and once-bankable deals have been redefined as wild flights of fancy. When BHP Billiton gave up its pell-mell pursuit of rival miner Rio Tinto this week, the surprise was that it had taken so long.

Sponsors for the Champions League have proven far harder to find than for the IPL, while the tournament has occupied more different dates than the Queen's birthday. In the minds of many fans, in fact, it remains blurred with the similarly benighted Champions Trophy—so many champions, it seems, so little time.

Nor, apart from those domestic cricketers for whom it loomed as the biggest payday of their lives, has it been obvious who exactly benefits from the tournament, or exactly to whom it will appeal. Postponement saves us from pondering, for now at least, who next Saturday was going to watch the West Australian Warriors play the Dolphins at Chinnaswamy Stadium, having not watched the world's top two Test nations duke it out there last month.

The BCCI itself is embroiled in a legal battle with its former chief, Jagmohan Dalmiya, expelled from the board almost two years ago, but now intent on the administrative equivalent of a victory after following on. Just days ago, the High Court in Calcutta ordered criminal proceedings against board president Shashank Manohar, administrative officer Ratnakar Shetty, secretary Narayanaswami Srinivasan and ICC president-to-be Sharad Pawar for swearing false evidence. Pawar's power base may be further eroded if the opposition Bharatiya Janata Party can parlay its tough stand on terrorism into votes at the polls early next year.

In the near term, one jolt may be particularly felt. So far, the BCCI has relied on money to solve everything: to open every door, reconcile every difference, silence every doubter. 'Money doesn't talk, it swears', Bob Dylan sang famously, and for the last year it has carried on like Sarah Silverman. In the face of such horrors as Mumbai has endured, however, money is muffled almost to muteness, and little use to anyone.

The BCCI philosophy, hitherto, has been to tell the rest of the world: 'We are changing everything. Get with the program or be left behind'. In future, however, the board may need to win friends as well as merely to influence people.

Cricinfo, December 2008

INTERNATIONAL CRICKET COUNCIL

No Biggie

The International Cricket Council this year celebrates 100 years as the governing body of the global game. No, strike that. The International Cricket Council this year marks its centenary. Hmmm, not quite right either. OK, let us say that the International Cricket Council's antecedent body, the Imperial Cricket Conference, held its first meeting at Lord's on 15 June 1909. Exactly right ... and so what?

Under the slogan 'Catch the Spirit', the ICC is making quite a big deal of this pseudo-centenary. It has events planned, even if few of these seem directly related to the 100-year landmark. It has a website with a logo which looks like one of those 'commemorative coins' you find in boxes of breakfast cereal. This website solemnly states: 'The ICC Centenary is an opportunity to look back at 100 wonderful years of cricket and is also a time to look forward'. Let's examine these two propositions individually.

First—aye, they were wonderful years, but what exactly was the ICC's contribution to making them so? For most of that time, the ICC had no powers to speak of, and was carefully constrained from developing them by its two 'foundation members', England and Australia: it was an annual beano at Lord's for whomever's turn it was on each member's board.

Even the 1909 date is, arguably, meaninglessly precise. The meeting of 1909 certainly pointed a way to global governance of the game—except that the way was, in the main, a dead end. Sir

Abe Bailey, the South African plutocrat who is the closest thing the ICC has to a father, saw the conference chiefly as an end to his dream of a Triangular Tournament of three-day Tests also involving England and Australia. His country's cricket was then strong—a tri-cornered contest would ratify its progress. Except that because England was ambivalent about the concept and Australia hostile, the tournament didn't occur for three years, by which time South Africa was weak again, and the whole event became a damp squib, never to be repeated.

The ICC reconvened after World War I on a much less ambitious basis. Tours were still concluded bilaterally. Umpires were still appointed locally. Associate membership, which only became available in 1965, meant relatively little, and it's barely twenty years since the ICC obtained a secretariat independent of the Marylebone Cricket Club. What's notable about cricket's international administration is not how much there has been but how little.

If all this seems like a pedant's hankering not to let a story get in the way of a good fact, let's turn to the second proposition and 'look forward'—as the members of the ICC's executive board will do from 31 January. To do so, let us ask a question: how well does the ICC reflect the changing contours of modern cricket?

For all its prominence as an administrative and disciplinary body, the ICC's chief role is to collect 'event revenues' from television and sponsorship rights to its various official events, of which the most significant have traditionally been the World Cups, through its British Virgin Islands–registered subsidiary ICC Development (International) Ltd. In the year of the last World Cup, 'event revenues' amounted to US$285 million, 84 per cent from the Cup itself; US$258 million was then distributed to members, chiefly the ten nations that play (or have played) Test cricket.

Actually, at the risk of further pedantry, to speak of 'nations' is again not quite right. The members of the ICC are actually, as they have always been, the boards of control who have carriage of international and domestic cricket in the relevant countries— indeed, in commercial terms, the ICC might be described as a global cartel of local sports monopolies.

Yet, as we are seeing, not all monopolies are created equal. The monopolies of the Pakistan Cricket Board and Sri Lanka Cricket, in particular, have become licences to shred money. According to new PCB chairman Ijaz Butt, the payroll under his predecessor grew from 300 to 800 in less than two years. What on earth did they all do?

And who knows where the money poured into Zimbabwe Cricket ends up? (Trick question: the ICC do, thanks to KPMG, but they're not telling, thanks to president Ray Mali.)

These monopolies are also changing before our eyes. The BCCI's monopoly is guarded like Fort Knox; the West Indies Cricket Board's is as sturdy as a clapboard outhouse. But in both cases, they are, somewhat uneasily, shared. Subhash Chandra's Indian Cricket League has muscled in on the BCCI's lucrative racket; the WICB has obtained Allen Stanford as a sugar daddy. The ECB, of course, likes the sheen on his bling too.

In fact, the days when the ten individuals on the ICC executive board could claim to represent the ten most important cricket organisations in the world, and collectively to incarnate 'international cricket', are no more. The ICL explicitly works against the grain of that structure already, with its teams in Pakistan, Bangladesh and possibly Sri Lanka, operating a miniature alternative version of international cricket. So, albeit in a subtler way, does the IPL, its participants based not on the state associations constituting the BCCI but city-based commercial franchises—apparently on the (very shrewd) recommendation of broadcast partner Sony.

The emanating strains of these developments are being felt even in pacific and prosperous Australia. In the last week, for instance, both Cricket Victoria and Queensland Cricket have kvetched publicly about not having top players available for the KFC Big Bash play-off that entitles them to entry in India's quasi-domestic Champions League (deferred, after the horrors of Mumbai, to later this year). Cricket Australia gave them short shrift, but their complaints were understandable—the Champions League gives new relevance to state-, province- and county-based bodies, offering revenue they need not share with jealous rivals.

Then there are the players, once stirred only by flags of country, now no less excited by flags of convenience. The England team have just flown to the Caribbean with several key players who have been dickering with their central contracts since September as they wait for Twenty20 opportunities to crystallise. The players are commercial entities to be reckoned with already: Sourav Ganguly has retired wealthier than a few boards of control we could speak of; if he wearies of fishing, Matthew Hayden might be able to engineer a leveraged buyout of Queensland Cricket. The players compete, moreover, in the same market for sponsorship as the boards that have traditionally staged international cricket. After all, why sign your brand up to the West Indian cricket team if the endorsement you really want is Chris Gayle's? Yet how are boards to be recompensed for the possible, nay likely, unavailability of players representing IPL franchises? Answer: not at all.

In some respects, the ICC is now the finished article, representing the culmination of international cricket as the premium form of the game—in a time quite probably past that culmination. As C Northcote Parkinson put it in one of his facetious laws: 'A perfection of planned layout is achieved only by institutions on the point of collapse'. Indeed, a centenary kind of suits it. After all, excepting maybe a telegram from the Queen, too few friends and too many candles, what's a hundredth birthday worth anyway?

Cricinfo, January 2009

INTERNATIONAL CRICKET COUNCIL

The End of Empire

Weak, ineffectual, a sham democracy, a rubber stamp for the powerful: the litany of complaints about the International Cricket Council is a long and damning one. The irony is that this profile essentially entails meeting its design specifications. The ICC's shortcomings have been the preferences of its members.

The inaugural Imperial Cricket Conference was convened on 15 June 1909, the brainchild of Abe Bailey, a South African merchant venturer and cricket fancier who envisioned an 'Imperial Board of Control'. South Africa having just beaten England at home, Bailey was fired by enthusiasm for a Triangular Tournament also involving Australia. Around the table at Lord's, the attitude was more ambivalent, and Bailey's countrymen were a fading force by the time the event took place three years later: the Springboks' weakness, combined with the weather, rendered the event farcical.

'Imperial Board of Control'? No thanks. The ICC survived after World War I as an annual jaunt, administrators from Australia and South Africa putting on their best suits for a day of hospitality from the conference's landlord, the Marylebone Cricket Club: chairman and secretary of the ICC were concurrent offices of the club's president and secretary. The West Indies, New Zealand, India and Pakistan were welcomed, but cautiously. The original trio consolidated their influence at the meeting of 17 June 1958 by becoming 'foundation members', support from two of which would be required for any binding motion.

This was, however, less about preserving power than preventing power concentrating. The founders saw the ICC in Commonwealth terms, as a shop for talk not action, fulfilling what long-serving secretary Jack Bailey called 'the function of Buckingham Palace'. The philosophy was summed up in a meeting fifty years ago of the MCC's Freddie Brown with Australia's Board of Control, discussing the proper forum for arbitrating unlawful bowling actions. 'There is some doubt as to whether the conference has any power', said Australia's Syd Webb warily. 'The conference has no power', confirmed Brown. 'It is the place where opinions can be ventilated.'

Preservation of the members' sovereignty was particularly helpful where South Africa was concerned. Rule 5 of the conference's constitution required that any country leaving the Commonwealth was demoted from the ICC, with the result that Tests against that country became unofficial from the meeting of 20 July 1961. When the conference met again a year later, however, Australia's representative, Harold Bushby, deprecated the technicality, insisting that 'each country should be able to make up its own mind as to whether it wished to play cricket against South Africa'—a position supported by president Sir William Worsley. So South Africa, whose racist institutions were increasingly rendering it an international pariah, remained welcome in cricket's circles, while support of at least one of the continuing 'foundation members' remained a prerequisite in matters of significance.

A fascinating exchange ensued at the ICC four years later. TN Peirce of the West Indies and the Maharajah of Baroda from India expressed reservations about plans for England to host a South African tour; England's Gubby Allen promptly retorted that South Africa's 'present high standard would deteriorate very quickly' in the absence of competition, with 'a disastrous effect on the whole of Africa', while former prime minister and MCC president-designate Alec Douglas-Home opined that 'the game should and must continue whereas politics might change'. When the status of fixtures involving South Africa was raised, New Zealand's ED Blundell added that it would be 'burying one's head in the sand' to exclude unofficial Tests involving South Africa from official records. The maharajah noted drily that 'it appeared South Africa had suffered no loss in cricket prestige through being omitted from membership of the conference'.

Yet even then, the Pax Brittanica was coming under subtle pressure. Pakistan had mooted a 'junior division' of cricket countries, later designated 'associate members'. The first intake on 15 July 1965 included Ceylon, Fiji and the United States, followed a year later by Denmark, Bermuda, East Africa and the Netherlands. On the renamed International Cricket Conference, the foundation members were less able to protect their former ally, and South Africa's twenty-year purdah began. When England, Australia and New Zealand seized on the creation of the ostensibly non-racial South African Cricket Union as proof of progress, for example, it was Pakistan which stood in the way, Ghulam Ahmed stating that 'his Board was definitely opposed to bringing South Africa back unless and until their policy took a completely different shape', and Abdul Kardar threatening that 'if any member country sent a team to South Africa, his board would have to seriously consider the cancellation of any arrangements that may have been agreed upon previously'. In fact, the Pakistani pair had anticipated the shape of the Gleneagles Agreement reached at the Commonwealth Heads of Government Conference in London on 15 June 1977, whose signatories undertook 'vigorously to combat the evil of apartheid ... by taking every practical step to discourage contact or competition by their nationals with sporting organisations, teams or sportsmen from South Africa'. When New Zealand moved and England seconded that 'all members give consideration to readmission of South Africa to membership of ICC' four years later, the associate members ensured the vote would fail.

This hard line withstood the rebel tours, and also restlessness among its old guard. 'The ICC meeting is really only a junket for a trip to the UK', griped the long-serving Australian official Ray Steele after one meeting. 'Most of them never open their mouths and in any event the conference has only very limited functions and powers and where it counts they have no teeth, and I think in future we should be very much on guard to ensure that they do not get teeth.' Increasingly, however, England and Australia were finding themselves on the wrong side of history. The ICC's great brainstorm, the World Cup, began in England, but was won by the West Indies then India. Pushes from the Subcontinent for referees, third-country umpires and the introduction of technology in adjudication could be delayed but not prevented. And although ICC communiqués were still printed in Wisden's least-consulted recesses, the first paragraph on page 1241 of the 1985 edition described events unforeseeably momentous.

To the ICC meeting of 18–19 July 1984, the BCCI, represented by president NKP Salve and treasurer Jagmohan Dalmiya, brought an offer hard to refuse: a proposal for a World Cup on the Subcontinent almost twice as lucrative as the counterproposal from England. England argued that the Indo-Pakistani bid lacked the support of a foundation member; the ICC's chairman, MCC president AHA Dibbs, said it did not matter, and support from the associate members carried the day. 'It was a miracle', said Salve. 'Perhaps for the first time, a battle had been successfully fought in ICC ... India and Pakistan and her friends had shown England and her allies that they were no longer supreme in the matters of cricket administration, their power of veto notwithstanding.'

The meeting also made clear that this 'power of veto' was on borrowed time. When discussion turned to governance, Australia's Fred Bennett and John Warr offered a general defence of the ICC as a 'forum for discussion', whereupon it was 'generally agreed' that 'any changes should be thought out with caution and without undue haste'. Allan Rae, batsman turned barrister and president of the West Indies Cricket Board of Control, then threw in a googly of which his old comrade Sonny Ramadhin would have been proud: the paternalistic 'foundation member' veto had outlived its usefulness, should apply only to matters effecting those countries, and otherwise 'be abolished', 'equal voting rights' prevailing.

One can hear the spluttering. Bennett demanded to know how the veto had been misused, Warr added that he had never even heard of it being applied—even if this invited the question why it was necessary anyway. Rae continued: the ICC should be funded separately of the MCC, a 1 per cent levy on Test match income bankrolling a permanent, free-standing secretariat. Bennett 'intimated that Australia had always believed that the current conduct of ICC affairs by MCC were satisfactory' and that 'there would have to be very strong reasons for change for his country to accept them'. But, while there was no 'undue haste', in a sense the deed was done. The working party designing the newly styled International Cricket Council agreed that the veto 'should not remain in perpetuity', and while agreeing that 'MCC's traditions and impartiality gave the club a strong qualification to administer international cricket', mooted a 'proper ICC office'.

As a result, Lord Cowdrey became the first ICC chairman not also MCC president. He oversaw the end of the veto, and also the end of the MCC's involvement in ICC affairs, except as landlord of its office in the Lord's Clock Tower. The ICC also selected its first International Umpires' Panel and promulgated its first Code of Conduct—although sometimes it seemed that administrators needed as much behavioural supervision as players. Emboldened by the success of the Subcontinent's first World Cup, Dalmiya went implacably about obtaining a second: Cowdrey's legendary serenity was acutely taxed by his last meeting, a thirteen-and-a-half-hour marathon on 2 February 1993, where India again got England's better. The result was a financial triumph, with which, in a sense, cricket is still coming to terms.

With the 1996 World Cup, cricket suddenly loomed as large financially as it had culturally. Yet, now funded by a small levy on the Test nations, the newly independent ICC remained a starveling body. It had as its chairman the respected West Indian Clyde Walcott, as its inaugural chief executive the careful Australian David Richards, and not much else. Members advised of developments in the worsening story of match-fixing, for example, mainly as a means of self-exculpation. As Walcott said, the ICC's powers remained severely circumscribed:

> The ICC has no means of finding evidence, we do not employ
> detectives, and it was not possible for us to act under our rules
> at the time. The introduction of the Code of Conduct meant

the member countries ceded power to us to punish on-field offences. It did not allow us to investigate matters that took place some time before, like an alleged bribery incident.

When Dalmiya succeeded to the new position of ICC president in June 1997, his bid for the chairmanship a year earlier having ended in a deadlock with Australian Malcolm Gray, the council's coffers contained £16 000. The ICC's sales of the television rights to the World Cups and an array of new ICC events including the Champions Trophy radically changed its profile, but left it running fast merely to stand still. When members belatedly empowered the ICC to act on match-fixing, the view of Lord Condon, the former Metropolitan Police chief recruited to run the council's 'Anti-Corruption Unit', was that the ICC did not provide 'an infrastructure to meet the financial and governance requirements of the modern game'.

Richards' successor, the flinty Australian Malcolm Speed, set about rectifying these deficiencies. New committees and subcommittees aided by a bigger bureaucracy improved financial controls and coordinated the development of the game in new locations; the ICC itself hit the road, physically transplanting to the more benign tax environment of Dubai. But as India's proportion of global cricket revenue has grown with each passing year, so have its political ambitions, to the extent that the ICC has begun resembling a subsidiary of the BCCI—exactly the relation, of course, that the ICC once had with the MCC. The climate, however, is less that of the Commonwealth than of the United Nations General Assembly: volatile, grievance-laden, full of unlikely alliances and shameless hypocrisies. Where once India argued the moral case for the excommunication of South Africa, more recently it has cynically protected a similar global outlaw that happens to be an ally—Zimbabwe. Where the ICC once shrank from decisions, now it rushes flaky ones, such as changing the result of the 2006 Oval Test.

The ICC's office-holders and officers used to be determined by rote; now it is by wrangle. The last presidency had to be extended a year while rival successors, India's Sharad Pawar and England's

David Morgan, sorted their differences. The preferred candidate to succeed Speed, South African Imtiaz Patel, developed last-minute reservations; the new chief executive, South African Haroon Lorgat, has the benefit of an Indian 'advisor', IS Bindra. Where the 'I' in ICC once stood for 'Imperial', and now for 'International', there seems no danger it will ever stand for 'Independent'.

Wisden Almanack, 2009

INTERNATIONAL CRICKET COUNCIL

1909 and All That

When, in 1977, England and Australia wished to celebrate the hundredth anniversary of the inaugural Test match at the Melbourne Cricket Ground, they played a Test match on that ground—one of the best in history, decided by a margin identical to the game it commemorated. Simpler days, simpler habits. For its hundredth anniversary, the ICC is doing a bit in general and nothing in particular, the slogan 'Catch the Spirit' for its series of very low-key events having proven as resistible as 'Catch the Swine Flu'.

Fair dos, the ICC has a bit on—the World Twenty20, for one thing. Nor is it as though re-enacting a meeting would cause much excitement, unless perhaps Ravi Shastri was under instruction from Lalit Modi. That pow-wow on 15 June 1909, ironically, was held during a Lord's Test involving England and Australia, one of the Australian representatives, vice-captain Peter McAlister, being unable to attend because he was batting at the time. In 2009, not only is there no game scheduled at what was once called 'headquarters', but Australia has been eliminated, while England is barely hanging on.

Mind you, South Africa, whose Sir Abe Bailey is the closest approximation of a founder the ICC has, is the tournament's red-hot favourite, and one part of Bailey's vision for an 'Imperial Board of Control' has been fulfilled: the Triangular Tournament on English soil he wanted and got was such a fiasco that international cricket on 'neutral' territory did not recur for more than sixty years, but is now commonplace.

There are some other interesting *plus-ca-change* aspects to the genesis of the ICC's antecedent, the Imperial Cricket Conference. Bailey was no Coubertin. In an excellent history, *Empire & Cricket* (2009), edited by Bruce Murray and Goolam Vahed, Murray draws attention to the initial congruence of cricket and commercial interests: not only was Bailey the politically ambitious protégé of the merchant venturer Cecil Rhodes, but England's representative, Lord Harris, was chairman of the London-headquartered Consolidated Goldfield of South Africa. Both had interests in promoting British prestige in South Africa, and vice versa.

Bailey and Harris, however, hastened too slowly to achieve their ends. South Africa's formal proposition, sent to Lord's in November 1907, was for a Triangular eighteen months hence. Thanks mainly to Australia, already scheduled to tour in 1909, and whose newly founded Board of Control was loath to share the profits of the summer, Bailey's brainchild had to gestate until 1912, by which time South African cricket was in decline and Australian cricket in foment: England duly prevailed by forgettable default. Too much dithering and dickering, countries basically suiting themselves—the patterns of the ICC's century, you could argue, were set at birth.

In constituting a body with an explicitly imperial charter, furthermore, Bailey and Harris expressly confined the official game to the pink bits of the world map. As Rowland Bowen observed in *Cricket: A History of Its Growth and Development Throughout the World* (1970), the founders 'excluded Philadelphia, arguably more powerful at the time than the surprising proponents of the idea, South Africa', and also neglected the strength of cricket in Argentina, which hosted a strong Marylebone Cricket Club team in 1911–12, and several teams after the war. The model, then, was that of a club, chiefly about the beneficiation of the existing members, rather than an association, about trying to gather further interested parties. And even when the nature of the body was altered by the admission of New Zealand, India and the West Indies, the power of the foundation members was fortified through special voting rights.

Much of the ICC's history, in fact, has been about the resistance of members to its growing too strong, thereby impinging on their sovereignty and self-perpetuation. Only for the last twenty years has the organisation had a secretariat independent of the MCC; only for the last decade has it been guaranteed even an approximation of the resources necessary to administer the game. A popular genre in punditry in the mid-1990s was the 'Why O Why' column, calling for the ICC to *do something*, usually about match-fixing, illegal actions or glutted schedules, ignoring that it was the organisation's members who kept its structures so weak and loose. Indeed, the instant that chief executive Malcolm Speed looked like taking these imprecations seriously, his lawns and flowerbeds flourished: he spent the last months of his contract on 'gardening leave'. There are noisier churchmice than his successor, Haroon Lorgat.

This week the ICC will be feeling a mite chuffed with itself. The World Twenty20 is ticking over nicely, India and South Africa providing the power, Ireland and the Netherlands the passion. That sensation is unlikely to persist long past Sunday's final. With every success in Twenty20, not only does Test cricket look that tiny bit dowdier, but the ICC's premier property, the 50-over-a-side World Cup, appears a little more archaic. Players ground down by the one-day-international mill must regard Twenty20 as nothing short of deliverance.

Twenty20, too, this global summit notwithstanding, looks likelier to be exploited at national level than international, the BCCI having perfected a club-based model, the IPL, that other countries are striving to emulate. All of a sudden, the talk is of 'windows' in the global calendar—talk that began with players but has lately been echoed by their boards. For the ICC's Future Tours Programme, a decade in the perfecting, the implications are enormous: disliking the view through his particular 'window', for example, IPL commissioner Lalit Modi seems intent on demolishing the decrepit English property he can see next door.

At the moment, however, 'windows' are about all the ICC has to offer, for the IPL, the Champions League and mooted Twenty20 tournaments in England, Australia, South Africa and New Zealand are of the hybrid quasi-domestic variety that their progenitors argue place them beyond the ICC's remit, even though they involve international players, potentially clash with international schedules, have already occurred in international locations and inevitably will again—indeed, Modi has spruiked the possibility of a second IPL each year away from India. In other words, because the players are the same, and because the sponsorship and broadcasting monies available to these ventures come from the same finite pool as that available to the ICC, the international body faces being required to bless national cricket ventures occurring at its expense. At least the ICC had nominal jurisdiction over the spread of fifty-over cricket, even if it had precious little success curtailing its proliferation; it looks like the ICC will have even less say where the diffusion of Twenty20 is concerned.

Invocation of 1977, then, isn't without significance. The back-story to the Centenary Test was that many of the players involved were throwing in their lot with the inchoate professional venture that Kerry Packer would call World Series Cricket: the game's established governors were about to lose their undisputed authority. The ICC's centenary comes at a similar juncture, as control of cricket appears to be slipping from its grasp, the difference being that this control is reverting to members who have never really liked it. As it enters a second century, the ICC's future looms, at least potentially, as running those parts of global cricket with which its members can't otherwise be bothered.

Cricinfo, May 2009

STANFORD SUPER SERIES

The Acid Test?

The fortnight we are amid, at the close of 2008, features an enormously important cricket match. At the risk of sounding oracular, we don't know which one.

It could be the Test that finished last week in Mohali, where not just the wheels but the axles, transmission and beverage-holders fell off Australia. Or it could be the climax on Saturday of the Stanford Super Series, where every misfield will have an impact on the Antiguan balance of payments. It will not, however, be both.

That both these games are broadly defined as 'cricket' attests to how elastic the definition has become. The game in Mohali was more than ten times the length of the Coolidge contest to come. Yet for their triumph, amazing to say, the Indian players received no prize money, while whoever wins across the Atlantic will divvy up US$20 million. This doesn't look as much as it did, what with trillions being bandied about so freely of late. But in an English cricket economy accented to the benefit system, it still represents a lot of celebrity darts tournaments. In the West Indies, meanwhile, it would leave you with change from the purchase of an island or two.

The Mohali Test represented India's rise to mastery of Test cricket, a form of the game 131 years old. The Stanford Super Series reflects India's revelry in Twenty20, a form of the game barely five years young. For without the rise of the IPL, there's no way the England and Wales Cricket Board would be scrabbling for money with the febrile desperation of a junkie couch-diving for coins.

So far, the response from administrators has been a recitation of clichés from long-ago commerce and business degrees. Cricket, they insist, is splendidly positioned, with all these interesting varieties, each appealing to a different demographic. Because, you see, transport companies that prospered a century ago spread their investment evenly between automobiles, landaus and velocipedes, while the airlines that did well fifty years ago maintained an interest in Montgolfier balloons and Bleriot monoplanes as well as jumbo jets. Well, now you put it that way …

In fact, this recitation of half-remembered nostrums about product differentiation from Economics 101 is mainly to soothe everyone's nerves. Cricket is like the subprime mortgage market just over a year ago: everyone knows that something will have to give; they're just hoping it's not too painful. The anxiety shows up in the hollowness with which administrators repeat the sentiment that Test cricket is the pinnacle of the game, the ultimate, the sine qua non, the dog's bollocks … actually, they're seldom so eloquent. Nor do they commonly substantiate the assertion, just possibly because they think it is self-evident, more probably because they haven't the foggiest notion why—it's just something they once heard, and repeating it has always gone down well at all those stuffy dinners and conferences it's their lot to attend.

Were I pressed on this question myself, I would probably put it something like this. Test cricket refreshes the parts other kinds do not because it encompasses the greatest variety of skills, abilities, temperaments and challenges of all ball games. Shane Warne and Glenn McGrath are massively different bowlers and men; Ian Botham and Chris Tavaré were bashing chalk and blocking cheese— put together, they turned Test matches.

Test cricket, furthermore, exhibits these players and their powers over the longest period, in the most varied conditions and scenarios. It is about survival and subjugation, the explosive moment and the marathon effort: it is Andrew Flintoff bayoneting Langer and Ponting in his first over of the second innings at Edgbaston in 2005; it is Flintoff battering Australia's ramparts for eighteen consecutive overs at the Oval a couple of month later. Teams losing

Twenty20 games are merely beaten cricketers; Australia at the end of the Mohali Test looked like beaten men. Twenty20 has exhibited some exciting skills, but they are far more restricted and regimented. Batting isn't just hitting sixes; bowling is not four-over spells. Which is why, if Twenty20 comes to define cricket, in my opinion, the game will have successfully lobotomised itself.

That's only a personal perspective, worth no more than anyone else's. But I am surprised that more people—players, pundits, fans, devotees as well as administrators—have not made so bold. Test cricket will never be able to justify its significance on the basis of money; it needs to be appreciated and advocated for its subtleties and satisfactions. What's curious about my original question is that I am almost certain we already know which was the better game of cricket: the Mohali Test was riveting in its intensity. But that is not, these days, what confers importance.

~

For all its one-sidedness, Mohali staged a superfine match, India prising Australia's fingers off a window ledge with calm deliberation. India have beaten Australia before, of course, but usually on the back of some stirring individual feat, and in 2001 by storming back from the brink. This was cricket of a stern, systematic, almost surgical precision, underlining also how wasteful India was in throwing away the December 2007 Melbourne Test by their indifference to preparation (and omitting both Virender Sehwag and Gautam Gambhir). Greedy programming, in hindsight, might have cost India the best chance it has ever had of beating Australia in Australia—but then, of course, what administrator has ever been held accountable for being too greedy?

~

Speaking of programming, greedy and otherwise, Cricket Australia has finally offered a glimpse of its response to Indian financial hegemony, foreshadowing a city-based, franchise-owned competition in the Southern Hemisphere, including South Africa and New Zealand. 'International stars from overseas' will be welcome—an idea against the grain of traditional antipodean parochialism, but an inevitable emulation of the IPL.

It is the biggest cricket move since the phrase 'safe as a bank' acquired its newly ironic ring, but clearly exploratory, as short so far on detail as money; it mainly bespeaks the pressure on administrators to be seen to be doing something to cash in on Twenty20 mania. CA faces renegotiating its memorandum of understanding with Australia's top cricketers next year, and wishes to be seen as singing from the same song sheet as their restive union, the Australian Cricketers' Association. The Ashes isn't Australian cricket's only challenge, or even the biggest.

~

'Sometimes it is almost liberating when you finally lose.' Ricky Ponting? In fact, the speaker was another modern Indian sporting hero, Viswanathan Anand, in a fascinating interview with *Spiegel* just before beginning the campaign to retain his World Chess Champion's crown in Bonn. While not here referring directly to it, Anand's form going into his clash with Viktor Kramnik was woeful: a last finish in the Master Tournament in Bilbao, where he failed to win a game. Yet he is now within a gambit or two of flattening the fancied Russian, conqueror of Garry Kasparov. If cricket is chess on grass, India is also on the brink of a triumph in the world of grassless cricket.

What did Anand mean by saying that losing was a relief? 'I think to myself, okay, the point is gone, tomorrow you are going to play better.' Happy the man so confident in his abilities that defeat is so easily cast aside. Anand reminds us that greatness is not merely about success; it also concerns losing in such a way that incurs the least psychic damage. Got that, Punter?

STANFORD SUPER SERIES

Gone for All Money

In one of its popular spoof 'news' items, the hosts of *Not the Nine O'clock News* once reported that Sir John Gielgud was anxious to reassure admirers about his appearance in Bob Guccione's wildly expensive shlockfest *Caligula*. Sir John was quoted as claiming that he was as shocked as anyone: none of the scenes of graphic X-rated pornography had appeared in his original paycheque.

Something similar came to mind as England squirmed its way through Sir Allen Stanford's wildly expensive shlockfest in November 2008. Goodness gracious, the players seemed to be saying: here we were expecting a nice, simple US$20 million game of Twenty20. Nobody told us it was all going to be so excessive, so vulgar. In fact, it is hard to think of a team so richly deserving of humiliation as Kevin Pietersen's, who spent all week as moral poseurs troubled by the riches that apparently awaited them then deservedly ended up with squat, who moaned through the year about their inability to cash in on the IPL then found it all a little tawdry when one wrong lap was sat on.

On the other hand, some queasiness was definitely in order. The Stanford Super Series is reportedly set to run five years. Already, though, it feels like an end rather than a beginning. While you'd be pardoned for missing it, given that Durham is still running round blazoned with the logo of Northern Rock and Yorkshire that of Bradford & Bingley, investment markets have reached the end of a cycle of chronic excess, and are gradually meting out judgement on an era of unearned millions: chief executives rich beyond the dreams of avarice who have left the state to clean up their mess; bankers who parcelled up and sold radioactive debt to hit earnings targets and cream bonuses; politicians in thrall to corporations intent on thwarting regulation. Yet the US$20 million for three hours' work in Antigua savours of Wall Street at its wildest—and this in a country where the government's annual revenues are only six times larger.

If cricket is to survive its interpenetration with global commerce, furthermore, then it must be careful to preserve some sort of hierarchy about its own values. When US$20 million is available for an unofficial sub-international Twenty20 game, how do you preserve attachment to the idea that Test cricket is a definitive form of the game? When Shivnarine Chanderpaul and Ramnaresh Sarwan are more than US$1 million wealthier for putting their pads on and waiting to bat for less than an hour, why would you as a Caribbean youth do other than aspire to the mighty green and black? While it's true that it is a player's lifetime of dedication rather than mere happenstance that places them in line for such windfalls, there still needs to be a sense of the rewards being earned, rather than individuals falling arse backwards into a dirty great pile of cash.

Right now it is tempting to see the Stanford Super Series as a saturnalia—a harbinger of more multimillion-dollar moments. Given recent events, some circumspection might be wise. Reassuringly, Sir Allen Stanford is ranked 205th among wealthy Americans in the *Forbes 400*. On the other hand, his privately held fortune is derived from asset management, property and investment banking, with reported funds under management growing 30 per cent in 2007—an interesting financial profile amid present discontents to say the least. Hmmmm. Let's just say that emerging unscathed from the subprime market's upheavals will be a challenge worthy of Sir Allen's mettle. He might even be spending a bit more time with his lap under a desk rather than a WAG.

The sums of money involved in sport are no longer trifling in commercial terms. When Lamar Hunt rolled out World Championship Tennis in 1967, his father warned him: 'If you're not careful, Lamar, you'll go broke in a hundred years'. But corporates now bandy round billions to be part of Olympics and various footballs (association and American), while television rights for the IPL and for cricket's World Cups have wormed their way into ten-figure territory too. 'A billion here and a billion there', as Senator Everett Dirksen aphorised, 'and pretty soon you're talking about real money'.

Nor are those commercial interests there for the feelgood factor: they are expecting, at these prices, to earn commercial returns. For aficionados of the so-bad-it-goes-through-good-and-back-to-bad-again, the DVD of *Caligula* came out a couple of months ago—they are still trying to make it pay. Investors today will not wait nearly so long to extract a worthwhile return.

Wisden Cricketer, November 2008

STANFORD SUPER SERIES

Capacity Crowd

Of all the statements recently released regarding Allen Stanford, perhaps the most grimly amusing was chief executive David Collier's revelation that the England Cricket Board had 'determined to suspend' relations with its former sugar daddy—analogous in some respects to drowning passengers of the *Titanic* determining to suspend relations with the White Star Line.

Contracts are easy to shred; associations linger. And reputation, hard-won, easily lost, is the devil to repair. 'The best of intentions', which is ECB chairman Giles Clarke's self-exculpation for cosying up to Stanford, are immaterial: Wall Street had leaders of impeccable motivations who are no more employable for them today. Essex chairman Nigel Hilliard's claim that due diligence on Stanford was on the basis of 'capacity to pay', meanwhile, suggests that English cricket was fortunate not to see the Medellin Cartel Sunday League.

Managing cricket is about preserving value as well as leveraging price. At a time when the ECB is earnestly seeking a replacement for Vodafone, the continued presences of Clarke and Collier imply that they will whore their cricket team to anyone with 'capacity to pay'—and who would wish to be that sponsor? English cricket has been damaged by association with Stanford; it is now damaged by association with a chairman and chief executive who have such a narrow and technocratic understanding of their duties.

But while the bucks have stopped, the buck hasn't quite. One of the ECB's sternest critics, indeed, might already be felt to have protested too much. English cricket has 'nothing but egg on its face', says Sir Ian Botham, adding that the chairman himself is toast: 'Giles Clarke pushed for this and he has to face the music. He was the one telling everyone Stanford was the way to go—and it has been a huge mess'.

Some, however, might recall the Sir Ian Botham who in June 2008 blessed the Twenty20 for 20 launch at Lord's with his presence, and described Stanford as 'the new Kerry Packer'. Packer 'shook the whole place up', he reminisced. 'I think what Stanford is doing is shaking it up again.' Are these two Sir Ian Bothams by any chance related, to paraphrase *Private Eye*? I think we should be told.

While we're at it, was that not by Botham's side his old mucker Sir Vivian Richards, a juxtaposition bringing back memories of their 1980s entanglement with manager manqué and Rasta rags fancier Tim Hudson—an entanglement which Botham conceded, in hindsight, had made him an 'international joke'?

Sir Viv, in fact, was part of a veritable round table of cricket knights who drew a monthly fee reported to be US$10 000 for sitting in Stanford's 'Legends' group: Sir Garfield Sobers, Sir Everton Weekes, Curtly Ambrose, Joel Garner, Lance Gibbs, Gordon Greenidge, Wes Hall, Desmond Haynes, Richie Richardson, Andy Roberts and Courtney Walsh. Walsh even enjoyed Stanford's endorsement when he narrowly failed to become chairman of the Jamaica Cricket Association in October 2008.

Which is not to say the aforesaid luminaries received anything but the dampest and whiffiest mushroom treatment. But it does mean that, however innocently and inadvertently, they colluded in the perpetration of what the Securities and Exchange Commission is calling a 'fraud of shocking magnitude'. They were the baubles on a Christmas tree that turned out to be a man-eating plant.

Here, then, is an extreme example of the fakery inherent in sports sponsorship. Business craves the company of sport because it looks just a little cleaner, smells a little sweeter, stands just a little taller. And it was ever thus: recall that Gillette explained its support for England's inaugural one-day domestic tournament by saying that cricket was a respectable game 'played by gentlemen'.

It seems a harmless enough coalition of interests, or at least a soothingly familiar one, when a sports star stands there spruiking a car; we nod sleepily at the faint pretence that he actually possesses some superior automotive insight, and ignore the obvious reality that he has been paid for mouthing sentiments he is ill-equipped to verify and has little genuine reason to believe. It is not so harmless when athletes esteemed by generations appear to bless financial disasters that threaten regional economic devastation. The Stanford story is no more over than was the *Titanic* story when the waves closed over its stern.

~

When it comes to distinguishing price and value, Australian cricket administrators have their moments too. The mid-February 2009 Twenty20 match between Australia and New Zealand was decided in the penultimate over by an outfield catch of quicksilver brilliance by Adam Voges. It was the sort of catch you wanted to see again and again, except that a video placed on YouTube was subsequently replaced with the advice: 'This video is no longer available due to a copyright claim by Cricket Australia'.

IP (intellectual property) has been the hot abbreviation in sports management for some years now. In the name of 'monetising' a sport's 'assets', it usually leaves miserable, pettifogging, alienating restrictions in its wake. 'Who owns Adam Voges' catch?' is a question that could tangle lawyers for months, if not years; if you love cricket, the question seems sour and sterile. Fortunately, wiser counsel has now prevailed: the video is back.

To be fair, these dilemmas are becoming more difficult to adjudicate, and grow exponentially more complicated when the website of a major media organisation links to and makes use of a video in the surrounds of advertising. Sooner or later, one suspects, sports organisations will have to decide whether the resources dedicated to chasing IP up hill and down dale justify themselves, or whether the revenues theoretically foregone earn themselves back in exposure and goodwill. Shane Warne's bowling of Mike Gatting at Old

Trafford in 1993 might not have become 'the ball of the century' had it been administered on a pay-per-view basis; as it is, cricket can hardly have been better advertised.

~

Over the last few weeks, the surrounds of Melbourne have been laid waste by bushfires of unexampled fury. Overhead views of areas I know and love lie in unrecognisable ruin. Except that, every so often, the view from above reveals an expanse still faintly green: a sports oval, part of every community, home to the local cricket and football clubs, and now frequently the base for efforts to accommodate the displaced and traumatised. Meanwhile, after the example of the Australian team's visit to the region, every second cricket club seems to be holding some fundraising activity for victims. Sport is usually something Australians celebrate, but at the moment it is showing rarely fathomed capacities as a source of solace.

The Guardian, February 2009

STANFORD SUPER SERIES

Collective Failure

When serial swindler Horatio Bottomley finally and deservedly ended up in Wormwood Scrubs, the prison chaplain reputedly found him in the standard convict labour of repairing a mailbag. 'Sewing, Horatio?' he said. 'No', said a chagrined Bottomley, without looking up. 'Reaping.'

The relationship between sowing and reaping comes to mind strongly at news of the abrupt financial dematerialisation of Allen Stanford, and the humiliation of his uncritical admirers at the cricket boards of England and the West Indies. Still ascertaining the extent of Bernie Madoff's depredations, the Securities and Exchange Commission does not lightly bandy the phrase 'fraud of shocking magnitude'. But there can be no fraud without credulity, and that, in London and Antigua, appears to have abounded.

In truth, something of this kind has been in the stars since Wall Street's great houses began tumbling like dominoes six months ago. Stanford Financial was a privately owned financial services and property group boasting prodigious asset growth and offering exorbitant interest rates even as markets were heading sharply in the opposite direction, while offering next to no detailed earnings or balance sheet information. Sounds like an institution to bet your life savings on, eh? Yet the headline issue of Twenty20 for 20 was who had sat in Stanford's lap. At least the West Indies Cricket Board extracted *some* value from their dabblings with Stanford. The England Cricket Board have made themselves a laughing stock—correction, a *bigger* laughing stock, because everyone's sides are still sore from the revolving door exits of a disoriented Kevin Pietersen and Peter Moores.

The WICB, furthermore, had at least some reason, in their churchmouse-poor region, for accepting Stanford at face value. The ECB is wealthy, secure and apparently populated by *men who understand business*: those ever-so-impressive individuals behind whom sporting organisations have during the last decade or so fallen into obedient lockstep. Chairman Giles Clarke was an investment banker at CS First Boston; chief executive David Collier was a senior vice-president at American Airlines; its board consists, according to the ECB website, of 'ten experienced non-executive directors'. (True enough, in a way: if they weren't experienced before, they're certainly experienced now.)

Little in cricket, of course, is completely without precedent. Sponsors, broadcasters and corporate partners *do* go broke from time to time. Cricket Australia's very first financial backer, Vehicle & General Insurance, which forty years ago bought naming rights to this country's inaugural one-day domestic competition, collapsed after a season. But that dates from days when the game's governance was in the hands of genteel, sinecured amateurs. The ECB boasts income of about £100 million. It claims to have performed due diligence on Stanford Financial. Yet if this wasn't cursory, it must at best have been naive. Something like: 'Rich? Of course! I saw his money: it was there, in the perspex box. He arrived in a helicopter for goodness sake—don't you know anything?' Because if the ECB *did* nurse apprehensions about Stanford's financial status and failed to impart them before Clarke's recent re-election, that raises many more interesting questions. Whatever the case, Clarke's celebration of his new term of office richly deserves to be the shortest in history.

Much more will and should emerge about cricket's entanglement with the enigmatic Stanford, but something is already very obvious about the revolution the game is undergoing. Consider the relationship between cricket and the world economy—consider it, because there is actually not a huge amount to say. Test cricket is 132 years old, yet its success and failure have been relatively little influenced by exogenous economic events. In fact, during both the Great Depression of the 1930s and the stagflation/oil shocks of the 1970s, cricket was strong and vibrant.

In the last thirty years, by contrast, cricket's prosperity has been shaped increasingly by corporate interests: sponsors, broadcasters, licensees and lately the franchisees of the IPL, plus private impresarios like Stanford and Subhash Chandra. Because the investment climate has been relatively benign, cricket and cricketers have benefited handsomely—to the extent of sovereign boards becoming sizeable commercial enterprises and players being paid millions of dollars for a few weeks of Twenty20 in the IPL, not necessarily because they are operating more effectively or playing better but because their assessed market value has risen.

Yet in many respects, the finances of the game remain precarious, even desperate. To choose a news item at random, Cricinfo has just reported that Derbyshire County Cricket Club had declared its third consecutive annual surplus: £14 065. Their chief executive paid tribute to 'the outstanding hard work of the off field team'. Doubtless true, but it is a lot of hard graft for not much.

Perhaps it is time to start wondering exactly how cricket would cope in the event of commercial default precipitating a serious insolvency in its own ranks: the failure of a county, state, province or even a country. The last is more than a reckless fantasy: the boards of Sri Lanka, Pakistan and Zimbabwe operate under perennial financial stresses; the post-Stanford WICB invites a close look too. Would the state bail the failure out? Would the ICC act as a lender of last resort? Would India? Horatio Bottomley always had a plan: when creditors, process servers and discarded mistresses came calling, he availed himself of a secret door in the back wall of his Long Acre office. Where is cricket's emergency exit?

Cricinfo, February 2009

TWENTY20

Technical Correction

Bull markets can be long, bull markets can be short, but they all, at some point, end—and, as of early February 2009, cricket's Twenty20-fuelled boom suddenly looks decidedly shaky.

In short order has come news that the third season of Subhash Chandra's Indian Cricket League has been at least delayed, preparatory to a review of its swollen player stocks, and that Allen Stanford's Twenty20 Challenge has been consigned to oblivion. The ICL might yet endure in modified form, and has already done somewhat better than expected, turning from what began as the expression of a rich man's pique into a spectacle with a certain vernacular charm—like the IPL, without the pretension and grandiosity. Stanford's troubles look less tractable: his opaque financial group faces scrutiny by the Securities and Exchange Commission, Internal Revenue Service and Federal Bureau of Investigation.

The ICL's problems derive in part from the hypocrisies of the BCCI. The IPL exists on one hand to exalt and celebrate the maximum freedom of trade: no national loyalties, no regional loyalties, the highest bidder prevails, turbocapitalist market forces rule. Yet the BCCI runs it as the most anticompetitive of monopolies, leading inter alia to the persecution of players as demonstrably loyal to their countries as Jason Gillespie and Mohammad Yousuf for doing no more than exercising their prerogative as professionals. As reprehensible as the acquiescence to this of the boards of Australia, Pakistan and England have been the supine response of the normally ever-so-outspoken Federation of International Cricketers' Associations, silently allowing its members' free agency to be not just restricted but punished.

Stanford's travails owe more to a business model containing more hope than Barack Obama's election campaign. With colour, movement and general razzamatazz, Stanford helped revive domestic cricket in the Caribbean—something well beyond the endless incapabilities of the West Indies Cricket Board. But the pay-offs were paltry, and the fear must now be that the withdrawal of his resources will leave the region, and the game therein, worse off than when he found it.

In the main, though, the message is that cricket is not impervious to the business cycle, that spectacles of a marginal nature conceived in a time of plenty cannot be guaranteed in a more austere future—call it, if you like, cricket's own subprime crisis. Crises, moreover, are contagious: investors hear and observe that others aren't investing, and the multiplier effect of the healthy economy becomes the divider phenomenon of the weak one. The BCCI already has some experience of this, having failed to sell sponsorship rights for the Champions League—it was spared more public embarrassment by the event's deferral. The enterprises whose futures are still more clouded are the likes of England's twenty-team P20, from which the England Cricket Board is already backing off, and the franchise-based Twenty20 tournament scheduled in Australia, South Africa and New Zealand for 2011.

The BCCI will have surveyed with satisfaction the eclipse of its nemesis Subhash Chandra, and setbacks in the ECB's efforts to establish an alternative sphere of cricket influence using Allen Stanford's moolah—happenings that further consolidate the official Indian game as cricket's exchequer. But even the second IPL, sched-uled to begin on 10 April, begins under somewhat less auspicious circumstances than the first. As English football's premier league demonstrates, the spoils of a league do not distribute evenly: there are winners and losers off the field as surely as on. Last year's com-petition was partly sustained by its novelty, following the famous investment principle that a rising tide lifts all boats. In the next few years, expect more evidence of Warren Buffett's famous corollary: 'When the tide goes out, you learn who's been swimming naked'.

Some set-up expenses incurred in the first year will presumably not recur, and there will be accounting benefits from depreciation and amortisation, but how well the franchises have retained their value will not really be understood until one changes hands, or the franchises mooted for Kanpur and Ahmedabad find buyers—always assuming that these can find sufficient playing strength, when most of the world's choicest cricket talent is already contracted. It might turn out that the time to move on was immediately after the first season, when the euphoria would have guaranteed a sizeable mark-up even for the loss-making franchises. At the time, of course, everyone was chuffed to bits about Lalit Modi's multimedia mardi gras. But another investment maxim teaches that nobody should ever feel bad about taking a profit.

An irony of the moment is that we in Australia have just enjoyed perhaps the most intriguing and involving summer of international cricket in memory. The Tests and one-day matches against South Africa, the one-day matches involving New Zealand and even the Twenty20 internationals have been almost uniformly worth watching—the balance between the various forms of cricket has felt exactly right; the volumes likewise. Andrew Symonds' periodic fatuities apart, there have been no depressing controversies; the cricket, on the contrary, has been played in excellent spirit and with red-blooded conviction. Much of the credit for that should go to the players, especially the fresher faces like JP Duminy and Peter Siddle, but Cricket Australia can feel justly satisfied by a summer not a day long. Were cricket not so confirmed in its capacity to mismanage success and squander goodwill, one might almost feel well satisfied.

It is hard to imagine, in fact, how the summer would have been improved by a Southern Hemisphere Twenty20 franchise tournament, just as it is difficult to make out how the Ashes summer of 2009 would have been enriched by the full-scale P20 originally envisaged. The argument for more commercial 'innovation' in cricket has routinely been the necessity to meet an imagined 'market'; to quote ECB chairman Giles Clarke from July 2008, it is 'about giving the spectator what they want'. Yet this is flim-flam: the *real* market involves selling properties to sponsors, broadcasters, licensees and now wannabe franchisees, which might or might not then catch on with spectators, viewers and consumers. And the question is now: what happens when *that* market materially changes?

Cricinfo, March 2009

PAKISTAN

Lost in Space

It could have been worse—far worse. The rocket missed, the grenades failed to detonate, and the targets did not come to serious harm despite the ramshackle security. To inbound tours of Pakistan, furthermore, the attack on the Sri Lankan team bus on 3 March 2009 probably makes next to no difference: in practical terms, the distinction between near and total isolation is negligible.

Just about everything else to do with the incident, however, is tragic and lamentable. The warm inner glow from England's return to India in December after the horrors of Mumbai has well and truly dissipated. A vague pall of 'terror' has hung over Pakistani cricket for much longer than is commonly imagined: the ambush took place within sight of Gaddafi Stadium, named for the bellicose colonel after some particularly florid anti-Western demagoguery at a 1974 meeting of the Organisation of the Islamic Conference. Maintaining cricket amid the greater game of war-on-terror/whack-a-mole, however, now seems altogether too difficult.

And that is a bigger problem for cricket than anybody has bothered to pretend. So far, the response of the game's other nations to deteriorating conditions in Pakistan has been a reflexive and buck-passing one. That is: we're not going. Indeed, there's already abroad some misplaced self-satisfaction with all those tough-minded 'security analyses', even if it could be argued that timidity about touring Pakistan made cricket a bigger rather than a smaller target. Mere threat having proved so effective at undermining the country's sporting relationships, how tempting must an act of violence seemed?

Whatever the case, the shock of Lahore advertises by worsening a crisis that all cricket has a stake in. Even before the attack, the Pakistan Cricket Board was in disarray, its executive locked in a power struggle with senators aligned to former director Javed Miandad, who recently flounced out, and striving to reduce a staff that mysteriously expanded to 800 during the previous administration.

Now that the last hope of a resumption of inbound tours has been finally snuffed out, the PCB's revenue base is effectively destroyed. The cancellation of Pakistan's series against India cost US$40 million; the departure of Sri Lanka preludes further losses, short and long term. The board's financial problems seem intractable: the rebuilding of Gaddafi Stadium itself halted in January amid claims of 'massive irregularities'. In short, it is as capable of fulfilling its obligations as co-host of the World Cup two years hence as it is of hosting the FA Cup final. Who, then, will salvage cricket in Pakistan? Don't everyone answer at once ...

The obvious answer—or, to be more precise, the answer traditionally bandied about when nothing else springs readily to mind—is the ICC. Except that the ICC today is altogether dominated, in governance and finance, by India—seriously, perhaps even irrevocably, estranged from its neighbour.

There will be forces in India, particularly in an election year when 'security' is a volatile issue, that welcome the calamity in Pakistan, regarding it not only as just retribution for the atrocities in Mumbai, but an opportunity to further humiliate and immiserate the country they hold responsible. The IPL looms as a further opportunity for India to flaunt its global thrall, even as Pakistan is held to ransom by the forces of religious reaction. Six matches in the IPL's second season, which begins in five weeks, are scheduled in Chandigarh, a little over 200 kilometres from Lahore—the plutocrat and the pauper of cricket in South Asia will shortly be living side-by-side.

The other answer to the PCB's travails is the state itself. Some form of national bailout or government guarantee would be less of an ideological stretch than, for example, the Obama administration propping up AIG. But that would entail sacking an administration only six months old, whose chairman, Ijaz Butt, was appointed by president Asif Ali Zardari himself; it might make cricket in Pakistan even more enticing to violent elements, too.

In other words, although it is enervating and dismaying to repeat a worn-out sentiment, there are no easy solutions. Nonetheless, the time when the problem of Pakistan can be reduced to individual security analyses and deferred to an unspecified future is past. The country's blameless cricketers and benighted public need to feel they have allies. Sri Lanka tried to play their part; now others need to fill that breach.

~

One political gesture, small but symbolic, might be helpful: revoking restrictions on Pakistani players in the IPL. Six had contracts suspended and four terminated in the wake of the cancellation of India's tour of Pakistan. The BCCI might regard this as an imposition, but if they did not have elaborate security measures in mind before Lahore, they will be rushing to make them now. The IPL was praised in its inaugural season for smoothing old antagonisms by turning former opponents into comrades: which antagonisms could now be in greater need of smoothing?

A longer-term measure might be some form of ICC equalisation fund to maintain the solvency of its member countries, Pakistan having joined the West Indies and Sri Lanka in dire financial straits. It would be fraught with difficulties, especially when it involved such havens of commercial transparency and management candour as Zimbabwe. But tying grants to specific projects involving player and infrastructure developments might go some way to remedying cricket's incredible income disequilibrium, where three-quarters of the sport's global revenue emanates from India. Eight years ago, Steve Waugh, embarrassed by the disparity in the rewards for Australian and Zimbabwean players, suggested some form of minimum wage underwritten by the ICC. It is worth considering something similar where the finances of national boards are concerned.

The Guardian, March 2009

INDIAN PREMIER LEAGUE 2

Imperialism Redux

You've got to hand it to Lalit Modi. The International Olympics Committee accepts years of free hospitality before it doles Games out; super-Samaranch Modi signs off in two days. So the IPL has a home, even if its degree of Indianess is altered—some would say lessened, although it might also have increased.

The relocation is already replete with ironies. In the 1990s, the BCCI was the great champion of a rather muddled strategy to 'globalise' cricket, personified by the giddying rise of its secretary, Jagmohan Dalmiya, to the presidency of the ICC. Leave out the intervening decade and it might almost seem that his hopes have fructified: the IPL will be organised in one country, staged in another, involve teams represented by players of all nations, and reach a vast global television audience through World Sport Group.

Except that the IPL's progenitor, Dalmiya's sometime nemesis, will not sully his brainchild's name with talk of globalisation. He has stressed that the priority is the entertainment of the Indian fan, game times dictated by the convenience of domestic television timeslots, arrangements to the satisfaction of the lanyard-wearing classes. At his triumphant press conference, Modi's idea of the benefit to South Africa was not such joy and excitement that the IPL might bring, but the sterile measure of the hotel rooms and airline tickets that the IPL will consume.

Watch for subtle changes to this rhetoric: the BCCI might even indulge in some high-sounding rhetoric about building bridges and making new friends. But they'll be faking it: the relocation is a desperate measure that they strove to stave off until it was very nearly too late. The hurry now is an index of the BCCI's obduracy as well as its opportunism. Since Mumbai, it has been impossible merely to wish security concerns away, but it didn't stop the BCCI trying. A few days ago, Modi was still dismissing rumours of a relocation as containing 'absolutely no truth'.

The fact is that the IPL would be occurring in Antarctica if there were direct flights, and it suited World Sport Group. And, in that sense, the Indianess of the tournament is more pronounced because it is imposed: the point is not to bring an attraction to another country, but to create a satellite India on that country's soil. And there is an old-fashioned word for such a form of exploitation: imperialism.

Not a word you hear a lot of in India—except, perhaps, with a contemptuous sneer. But, if by accident and effect rather than strategy and intention, and in the short term rather than the long, this is essentially an imperial exercise. South Africa accepts colonisation, India runs the show for its own benefit, then scarpers home. The Raj took a few hundred years over it; the IPL in South Africa, because its imperialism is of the consumer capitalist rather than the political or religious sort, will do the deed in six weeks. For sure, the IPL will leave some money; it may leave a cultural imprint; it may even leave some goodwill. But that will happen coincidentally: it is not an objective; it is not, really, a priority.

The funny thing is that, if Modi did but know it, cricket has a huge opportunity in April and May. The stars of 2007's World Twenty20 Championship were the South African crowds, who embraced every visiting country with warmth and glee. Games between India and Pakistan haven't been played before more enthusiastic and energised crowds in Lahore or Mumbai. For that reason alone, South Africa is a vastly superior venue to England. The IPL looms as an ideal complement to the recent title fight with Australia: the best Test matches anywhere in four years.

For cricket to make the most of that opportunity, however, the IPL would have to resile somewhat, even if not totally, from the stance that it is purely and simply a 'domestic' tournament—a stance maintained chiefly to remain outside the jurisdiction of the ICC. A genuine cricket visionary would now be playing up the idea of making the IPL a gift and example to the world rather than an Indian self-celebration involving some incidental beneficiation of the South African hotel and airline industries—by reinstating the luckless Pakistanis, for instance, or pledging the franchises to coach locally as the Australians did so successfully on their recent tour. At least at the moment, however, Modi does not seem to be that visionary: he has an eye always on his home market, origin of his power, and, perhaps even more importantly, location of his enemies. And until some gesture towards making the IPL more like an International Premier League, an Imperial Premier League is what it will be. You have to hand it to Lalit Modi all right. One wonders how soon people will get sick of doing that.

Cricinfo, March 2009

INDIAN PREMIER LEAGUE 2

In Praise of Diggler

What's not to love about Dirk Nannes of the Delhi Daredevils? He speaks Japanese. He plays the saxophone. He is an expert skier and runs a snow travel business. His nickname is Diggler, which while not hugely imaginative at least honours a pretty cool Paul Thomas Anderson film, rather than some multiplex shlock with Jim Carrey or Adam Sandler. And he bowls with a wickedly quick left arm that makes good batsmen hurry and the ball go late.

Above all, the well-travelled Nannes, thirty-three years old next week but only three years a first-class player, is demonstrating the good that can come from turning a game upside down, revealing the hitherto concealed: Daredevils captain Virender Sehwag says that his opening bowler is the fastest bowler he has ever faced. But were it not for the worldwide talent search compelled by the IPL, Nannes would still be the answer to an Aussie domestic cricket trivia question rather than the twenty-first-century's answer to CB Fry.

This phenomenon of a household name being created from an outhouse name occurred to a limited degree during the IPL's first season, with the accelerated advance of the likes of Shaun Marsh and Sohail Tanvir, not to mention the sudden profile it made available to Indian domestic players such as Swapnil Asnodkar and Manpreet Gony. It was the first indication of how the IPL could reshape cricket's career structures. The time-honoured progression has been school-club-state-country, with a stop-off on the way in recent years at some high-performance centre or academy. With its enormous audience and relentless coverage, the IPL made everything big and everyone famous that it touched, regardless of pedigree and position.

That is being repeated in IPL 2 with the roly-poly Dolphin Yusuf Abdulla, and more talent from India's first-class circuit like KP Appanna, Shadab Jakati and Shane Warne's rags-to-rupees teen tearaway, Kamran Khan. But Nannes is something else: a soi-disant 'accidental cricketer' overendowed with other talents. The only reason to discount him as the hidden hand behind *Fake IPL Player* is that as a Nipponophile he probably prefers haiku. The IPL, in fact, would seem a pretty good fit for Nannes' lifestyle. Able to earn more cash in six weeks of IPL than in six months as a Sheffield Shield toiler, he can now afford to learn Aramaic or master the harpsichord.

Even in this era of hyperprofessionalism, other sports have allowed scope for the talented dabbler. In American football, there was Robert Smith of the Minnesota Vikings, with his zeal for philanthropy and passion for astronomy. In golf, New Zealand's Greg Turner grew up in a family where brother Glenn was destined to score a hundred hundreds and brother Brian to pen eight collections of poetry: he stretched himself both ways, winning a dozen international tournaments until his retirement in 2000, while also indulging his knack for journalism and interest in politics and the environment.

Cricket loves its renaissance men: Fry, Bob Crisp, Aidan Crawley, the redoubtable Major Poore. But reaching the top today, it is assumed, demands a whole-hearted, hole-headed commitment—the game and nothing but the game. Use the phrase 'well-rounded cricketer' and it is assumed you are alluding to Samit Patel or Jesse Ryder. Some have wondered whether this is all to the good. In complaining that England is surfeited with first-class cricket and cricketers, for example, Mike Atherton has mooted a 'semiprofessional' level, in which players could 'develop interests outside the game, preparing for life beyond cricket'. Dirk Nannes appears to have arrived at a sort of semiprofessionalism from the opposite direction, working his way into cricket from outside the fold.

But perhaps he is also the harbinger of a more interesting kind of cricketer—one whose life is not just cricket, having perhaps started late, and choosing to proceed from one professional assignment to another rather than to set his sights on a Test cap.

Whatever the case, IPL 2 is certainly pointing to another modification of the standard career structure, by demonstrating the possibility of extended twilight. Following the example of Shane Warne last year, Matthew Hayden, Adam Gilchrist, Anil Kumble and Sanath Jayasuriya have been rolling back the years in South Africa after ending careers in the recent past with more a whimper than a bang. What appeared at first a game for youth, élan and elasticity has turned out friendly to the old stager and the deteriorating physique, thanks to Twenty20's limited and specialised skills, and also its brevity. It's arguable, in fact, that Warne and Hayden are still in the best Twenty20 XI in Australia, albeit that they would probably be deemed ineligible for selection because they no longer represent an Australian state.

Next month marks the centenary of the first meeting of what became the ICC—which, somehow, is not marked by a worldwide public holiday. And while Lalit Modi's brainchild is reshaping cricket in more ways that anyone imagined, the ICC slumbers fitfully in Dubai, powerless to influence this ostensibly 'domestic' tournament. Whither a new leader for cricket? The ideal candidate would be someone broad, strategic, eclectic, well travelled, capable of seeing the game in the context of its society, while not regarding it as the most important thing in the world. You know what I'm thinking, don't you? Dirk Nannes for president!

Cricinfo, April 2009

INDIAN PREMIER LEAGUE 2

Commercial Breakage

It's working. Two weeks of the second season of the IPL and it's finally been drummed into me who the damn sponsors are. Thanks. Thanks a lot. Now ... GO AWAY! Actually, had I money to invest, I'd be wondering why DLF, presently being squeezed by slumping property values and a share price a quarter of its peak, and Citigroup, insolvent but for Barack Obama's indulgence, were wasting shareholder's funds on staking sixes and endowing so-called 'success'. As I don't, I'll simply vary that old Bob Hope gag concerning the night he went to a boxing title fight and a game of ice hockey broke out: the IPL is fast degenerating into a series of three-hour advertisements through which are sometimes discernable glimmers of cricket.

Cricket, of course, has much to thank television for. How much richer is our appreciation of a Shane Warne leg break or a Kevin Pietersen cover drive for the luxury of studying it, frozen in time; when we can hover over each detail of the harmonious human mechanism. But either Lalit Modi is pumping nitrous oxide into the commentary box or IPL is bearing out JK Galbraith's observation that television 'allows for persuasion with no minimum standard of literacy or intelligence'.

One expects a certain degree of phoniness from Sunil Gavaskar and Ravi Shastri, who as IPL commissioners are busy getting high on their own supply. But the rest of Modi's fawning courtiers, even super-smooth Mark Nicholas and pawky Jeremy Coney, have been reduced to carnival barkers, whether greeting a full toss slogged for six like the news of VE Day, pretending that the 'tactical time-out' is something other than a sneaky commercial trick, or, above all, hawking the sponsors like Jim Cramer used to ramp shares on *Mad Money*. Could Citigroup be scattering 'moments of success' for its own morale? Can it be that somewhere in the fine print of DLF's sponsorship contract is prescribed a specified number of long-hops and full tosses per hour, a guarantee of a minimum of 'maximums'? The result is that whatever the game looks like, it sounds as forced as the canned laughter in an American sitcom.

Some of the artificiality of season two has simply been made more obvious by the inclement weather, diminishing novelty value, fewer thrills and more spills, which has left the appointed interpreters straining for effect. But that can't explain everything. There was plenty of glitz and hype in the first season of IPL, but the excitement of the fans was stunningly, thrillingly real. Away from India, the IPL lacks that authentication—it is a distant and diluted re-run, with contrivances to redeem its deficiencies. Even when it's right, they somehow get it wrong, as at the end of the most recent Rajasthan Royals v Kolkata Knight Riders, when the best game of the tournament and the best result in cricket was capped by a climax as fake as Sally's when she met Harry. Are the commentators, then, straining to act as proxies for their main audience back in India? If so, it seems a doomed enterprise.

The commentators' clueless desperation now feels as though it is working against the IPL. When something great happens, they have nowhere to go, no upper register left to use. When 20 off 10 balls exhausts your superlatives, how do you describe a hundred off 50 balls? When a young Indian domestic player getting away a couple of beefy blows is so thrilling, what tone do you adopt for Tendulkar? As Gilbert and Sullivan put it in *The Gondoliers*: 'When everyone is somebodee/Then no-one's anybody!' A further complication is Twenty20's inherent unpredictability, its mixing of the sublime and the ridiculous. When commentators hype a batsman up for consecutive boundaries only to watch him perish to an imbecile smear, or praise a bowler to the skies for four dot balls then see him smacked into orbit twice while closing the over out, they subtly erode their own authority—such authority as they had, anyway.

The television commentator has always been sensitively placed. His network has paid good money to broadcast, and thus has an interest in the game being perceived as representing high-quality excitement—even when it is not. Richie Benaud didn't become His Richieness by saying: 'This is a boring game between two medi-ocre teams, and represents an ideal opportunity for you to mow the lawn'.

With Twenty20, however, there is the added imperative of promoting a format in which exorbitant sums and giddying hopes have been invested. The consumer has not just to be sold the game he is watching, but the Twenty20 concept in general; persuaded that he is witness not just to a contest of teams, but a contest of genres, with Lalit Modi responsible for the most exciting breakthrough since the cross-your-heart bra. It forces the commentator even further from the ideal perspective of disinterested critic, bringing to bear a weight of experience and a talent for observation, reducing him to sideshow huckster, flogging the game like a patent medicine from the back of his covered wagon. Nor am I sure it ultimately does the sponsors much good either. There are two sides to brand recognition: one where the sponsor's name conjures up warm and positive associations; another where it stirs irritation and objection, as a result, perhaps, of incessant, cloying, annoying repetition. So, yes, we now know which sponsors to find—and also, if so moved, those to avoid.

Cricinfo, April 2009

Top of the World?

Most cricket clubs have a few older players still good enough for first XI selection who nonetheless prefer to muck around in the second XI, usually on the grounds that it's time to 'give the kids a go', although often as not because they like the easy runs and cheap wickets available when playing slightly beneath one's class. Did the second season of the IPL give a foretaste of a similar phenomenon in the global game?

Eight of the Australian team appearing at the Oval against the West Indies on 6 June 2009 for the ICC World Twenty20 will be there because they are their country's best players. Three will be there because Adam Gilchrist, Matthew Hayden and Shane Warne are not, having demonstrated in South Africa that if they are overripe for Test selection, they still ooze juice in Twenty20. For champions the Deccan Chargers and finalists the Bangalore Royal Challengers respectively, Gilchrist and Hayden hammered a total of 1067 runs at a strike rate of 148.2; Warne took fourteen wickets at 26, gave away just 7.3 an over, and threw himself round in the field, only three fielders taking more than his six catches.

The trio looked, moreover, to have worked the format to their advantage, perhaps because South African conditions asked more questions of cricketers than the benign and controlled environments of the first season—which, all in all, actually made for some quite interesting viewing in the cricket breaks between the advertisements. Hayden was unrecognisable from the stumblebum who shuffled out of Test cricket to the sound of his own feet in January; Gilchrist was entirely recognisable, as international cricket's most electrifying hitter for the last decade. And not since *Rififi* has there been a bigger heist than the Rajasthan Royals' comeback against the Mumbai Indians at Kingsmead on 14 May, with Warne winkling out Ajinkya Rahane, then Jayasuriya and Tendulkar, finally throwing the ball to Munaf Patel for that larcenous final over.

Age and endurance might have been a problem had Hayden, Gilchrist and Warne been pitted in a longer format, but Twenty20 is a basic form of the game, so players with good basics prosper—see also Anil Kumble and Rahul Dravid. So ask yourself. To whom do you think opening bowlers in the World Twenty20 would prefer to bowl? Hayden and Gilchrist or David Warner and Brad Haddin, good cricketers that they are? And against whom would a batsman sooner back himself against? Warne or Nathan Hauritz?

OK, so it won't happen: Australia's selectors are as likely to borrow Hayden, Gilchrist and Warne from the IPL as a Pakistan teammate is to borrow Shoaib Akhtar's protector. The reason is, of course, that the three are officially 'retired' from 'all forms of the game'. But that is actually all. To clarify the situation, I recently inquired with Cricket Australia about whether Australian players had to be chosen from within the ranks of Australian domestic cricketers. The answer took a little while coming back, but it was no. Where 'unretired' players were concerned, it could be a little more complicated: for instance, for the purposes of the calculation of provident fund entitlements (the superannuation scheme for Australian players, which operates on a sliding scale favourable to those with more games), the player would apparently be considered to be starting his career again rather than resuming after a break. But the inference of the reply was intriguing: that, theoretically, nothing prevented David Warner playing only for the Delhi Daredevils and Australia—he need not play for New South Wales. Nor, it implied, was there any impediment to, say, Phillip Hughes devoting himself full-time to banana farming at twenty-five, and only coming to town for Test matches and to represent the Chittagong Challenge Rider Kings or whomever has been added to the IPL by 2014–15.

For Australians, the IPL seems a distant affair, on television at an ungodly hour, involving a kaleidoscope of uniforms and a cacophony of commentary, and competing for attention, none too successfully, with the clamourings of the various football codes. Yet the gravitational pull it is exerting on cricket here is no less significant for its subtlety. Already there has been one instance of an Australian-born player jumping the queue to national selection because of IPL feats, in the form of Shaun Marsh, who aside from back-to-back 70s against the Proteas last summer hasn't quite substantiated his Kings XI Punjab reputation. A potential long-term development might be a gifted Australian under-19 player talent-scouted by an IPL franchise, coming thereby to the attention of an English county or a South African province, and presenting for national selection having bypassed his country's first-class structure altogether.

How much, meanwhile, would Andrew Symonds be looking forward to the prospect of starting next season back in the Sheffield Shield, having partaken of the lotuses of IPL but missing out again on Ashes selection—probably his last chance. The disaffected player once had no choice but to accept the bad with the good. But why mess around with Snakes & Ladders if you can simply play Monopoly?

Among the players of the Test-playing nations, of course, Australians are better off than most. The baggy green is lined with crisp green. If you were a West Indian, how would you be feeling towards the Test cricket that your captain regards as such servitude? Would you perhaps be just a little envious of your pal Dwayne Bravo's Mumbai Indians payday? And look ten years hence. Who will wish to be playing international cricket over the age of thirty if it becomes an inhibition on one's earning capacity, as indeed members of Chris Gayle's team in England already appear to regard it, and if Lalit Modi is as good as his word in mooting a second IPL tournament every year?

These are among the questions that the irresistible rise of IPL continues to pose, and the influence it promises to wield, while remaining, of course, as we're incessantly reminded, simply an

Indian 'domestic' tournament—albeit shaped over the last six weeks in South Africa, even more than last year, chiefly by the talents of players from other countries. This ICC World Twenty20 is one thing; by the next, chances are, cricket will look different again, with the imponderable being not who might be there, but who might not.

Cricinfo, June 2009

CHRIS GAYLE

Follow the Leader

One of the abiding gripes of the hard-bitten hack is the sheer monotony of modern playerspeak. Another day, another press conference consisting of the bleeding obvious, reliant on liberal use of the words 'hopefully' ('hopefully we'll win') and 'obviously' ('obviously, hopefully we'll win'), with maybe a few 'good areas' thrown in. Perhaps the last time a press conference made news was twenty years ago, and not even then for what was said, but rather what was done, David Gower hurrying from his inquisitors at Lord's to attend *Anything Goes*, thus transiting from one mainly pointless farce to another.

On the other hand, maybe it's no wonder that players say so little given the response when they actually do. Witness Chris Gayle, who generally troubles to move his lips as much as his feet but who on the eve of the Test at Riverside wearily confessed in an interview with the *Guardian* that the West Indies' captaincy was 'not something I'm looking to hang on to', and that he 'wouldn't be so sad' if Test cricket faded away, although some English opponents such as Andrew Strauss 'would be sad' because they lacked the panache necessary for Twenty20.

Cue shocked reactions all round, the knightly duo of Sir Vivian Richards and Sir Garry Sobers standing up for Test cricket's epic grandeur, their old mucker Clive Lloyd having already chastised Gayle for arriving hotfoot from representing the Kolkata Knight Riders in the IPL. English fondness for periodic fits of morality was also confirmed, Simon Wilde opining in the *Sunday Times* that Gayle was 'not a leader and never has been', and Steve James in the *Sunday Telegraph* that he certainly shouldn't be a leader any longer: 'Gayle is hardly one of the game's great thinkers. But he is a Test captain of a major nation. And with that comes a certain responsibility. He has abdicated that quite astonishingly'.

Yet the West Indies is not a nation; it is a region, and a troubled one at that, whose cricket has in recent years seemed at constant risk of falling apart, which would have wearied a skipper of sterner stuff than Gayle. And the fact is not everyone wants to be a Test match captain—even Allan Border, who captained Australia in more Tests than anybody else, did not want the job, and took a long time to feel comfortable in it. Had Border been held to Steve James' standards of responsibility, his tenure wouldn't have lasted a year.

The last of Gayle's grumblings, meanwhile, obviously breached that quaint sporting omerta concerning comment about rivals. Last night after watching my Aussie rules team, Geelong, annihilate its opponents, I saw our star midfielder Jimmy Bartel respond to the obvious statement from the television interviewer that it had been a one-sided affair. 'No, they took the game right up to us', he insisted, failing utterly to strike a tone of sincerity, but participating obediently in the charade that every opponent is equally respected and every victory is a brand from the burning.

Frankly, if the alternative is such phoniness, give me Gayle's candour every time. For that matter, give me Strauss' initial candour in chiding Gayle for his belated arrival, which probably coaxed his rival into a little tit-for-tattle. Test cricket looks dour enough at Riverside without honestly held opinion, even annoyance, being held back too.

The chief beef with Gayle, of course, is his breach of that politesse about the 'primacy of Test cricket'. But why the sense of affront? A 2008 Professional Cricketers' Association survey confirmed that more than a third of English first-class players would consider retiring early to take the opportunity to play in the IPL, and a further fifth would court banning by playing in the Indian Cricket League. Responding to a March 2009 survey by the Australian

Cricketers' Association, fewer than half of Australia's elite cricketers believed that representing their country would be the ultimate professional accolade in the next decade.

Personally, I consider Gayle mistaken. I believe Test cricket's welfare matters a great deal, for it is the most thorough and exacting examination of the overall quality of a cricketer. But it also benefits nobody if the 'primacy of Test cricket' is upheld simply by a polite public agreement not to say otherwise, especially if it is simultaneously being undermined by those who run the game.

For a belief in the 'primacy of Test cricket' hardly seems to be shared by Gayle's employer, the West Indies Cricket Board, who cheered on as tens of Allen Stanford's mysteriously gotten millions were lavished on Twenty20 cricket in their region, yet who had to cancel a Test match in March 2009 because Viv Richards Stadium wasn't fit to graze cattle on.

Nor does the idea that cricket concerns more than merely maximising revenue strike much of a chord with Gayle's hosts, the England Cricket Board, who also threw in their lot with Stanford, having studiously sealed Test cricket off from a mass audience by selling broadcast rights to Rupert Murdoch, and putting Dick Turpin and Black Bess in the shade by the highway robbery of their ticket prices.

Heaven knows there aren't many believers in Test cricket at the BCCI, which provides the lion's share of global cricket revenue, while seeing to it that six weeks involvement in the IPL earns most participants more than they stand to make from international cricket for the rest of the year—which cannot but cause any cricketer to reconsider his priorities.

Down here, I'm not entirely sure what administrators believe. I recently made inquiries with Cricket Australia about when they might be selling a DVD of the last Australia–South Africa series— the best of recent years, and the best I can remember here. Naaah, came the answering drawl from the marketing department: Aussies won't buy DVDs of series that their team have lost. I wonder where the empirical verification for that conventional wisdom came from, given that Australia has lost only one other home series in twenty years. But so much for celebrating six of the most absorbing Test matches that Australia has ever played.

In speaking his piece, then, all Chris Gayle has done is leave the hypocrisy to others, and taken global cricket administration at its actions rather than its words. If similar questions began generating similarly honest answers from others, then cricketers might actually be worth listening to again.

Cricinfo, June 2009

CHAMPIONS TROPHY

How to Save One-Day Internationals

Has a cricket cup ever been less loved than the Champions Trophy? Even when one-day tournaments proliferated during the 1990s, outright animus was hard to summon. They came. They went. Who cared? But something about the Champions Trophy—whether its meaningless name, its instant forgetability, its ever-changing structure or its ever-shifting date—actively courts contempt. Somehow it embodies everything that's wrong with international cricket—utterly routine, perfectly perishable, posing as significant, fooling nobody.

To the 2009 instalment in South Africa, wrapped up on 5 October, all the foregoing applied and more. Following directly on from an entirely futile series between Australia and England spanning seven matches but seeming to last seven weeks, the Champions Trophy had a dreadfully anachronistic feel. Some games were good, some were bad, there were some surprises, but no close finishes, and if you can remember the winner in a month's time you'll be doing well. Otherwise, it faithfully reflected the malaise in fifty-over cricket since the World Twenty20 in 2007: a malaise that has prompted Shane Warne, no less, to call simply for its abandonment, and encouraged both England and South Africa to drop the format from their domestic schedules, spruiking forty-over matches instead.

One-day cricket made enemies during its rise; they are paying it back as it declines. Indeed, while Test cricket has bred ardent defenders, the fifty-over game seems to have built no lasting constit-uency. Since the success of cricket in three-hour chunks, games lasting a whole day have smacked of disco in a hip-hop age. And this is a greater conundrum for the ICC than a matter of taste, tradition or aesthetics, because the format is not about to disappear: the global body is committed to television rights sales of fifty-over fixtures for the next six years, out until the 2015 World Cup in Australasia, even as the property it intends selling is one in which confidence, conviction and cachet is steadily diminishing.

Until 2007, fifty-over cricket had a staunch patron in the BCCI, which had waxed fat on its revenues and advocated a variety of artificial remedies, such as Power Plays and Super Subs, to its increasingly formulaic nature. But with India's five-run victory over Pakistan in that epoch-making Twenty20 final at Wanderers, following on from the team's early elimination in the 2007 World Cup, the BCCI's attention shifted, and drastically, the IPL carving its path through the cricketscape. India have played only two one-day series at home since the last World Cup; indeed, their performances in the Champions Trophy were of a team with talent at deviance to concentration span.

Why, then, is one-day cricket in such bad odour? After all, it has made a lot of cricketers famous and a lot of administrations rich: squeezing in yet another rinky-dink tournament has been an effective substitute for strategic thought among boards of control all over the world. The truth is that the fifty-over game has been not only overused in cricket's calendar, but overpromoted. Purporting to be a game about aggression, it concerns as much if not more the dimension of containment, the counteraction of spectacle. Wicket taking is de-emphasised: whether you end the innings two for 320 or eight for 320, of course, is immaterial. The prevention of boundaries is paramount: thus the institution of the off- and leg-side sweepers, than which a captain would no sooner go without than his box. It is not cricket concentrated but cricket diluted. This is compounded by the most enfeebling limitation: the restriction on the number of overs a bowler may bowl, with the implied necessity to extract ten overs from a fifth bowler when most teams choose only four specialists. Which is why the middle overs of a one-day game so often slip by almost below consciousness: unambitious batsmen trying not to get out, part-time bowlers trying not to give up runs, commentators trying not to sound bored.

This, of course, we know. The objections are tried, true and by now, perhaps, also a little hoary, for there is actually rather more to the fifty-over game than critics will allow. For one thing, a day is a naturally occurring length for a game of cricket. Most humble strivers at club level will play a large proportion of their careers in games of a day's duration; in this sense, the fifty-over game is inclusive, presenting top players with dilemmas and challenges everyone can recognise. Bowlers, it is true, are reduced to passive propelling agents, servitors. But if the chief objective of batting is the achievement of centuries, most competent top-order players should be able to obtain a hundred while obtaining a reasonable proportion of the time a one-day innings makes allowable. In 120 to 150 balls, all batsmanship's modes are possible: defence, consolidation, accumulation, attack. Graeme Smith's 141 against England at Centurion, for example, was complete as no Twenty20 innings ever will be.

Indeed, there is more to the condemnation of fifty-over cricket than the merits of the case justify. Among the players, it springs from surfeit, and weariness of the If-this-is-Monday-it-must-be-Mumbai circuit. Among the cognoscenti, if we are to be frank, it derives, at least in part, from snobbery. An expressed preference for Test matches identifies the speaker as a subtle student of cricket; a disdain for the game's shortened form further shores up claims to discrimination and superiority. Were HM Bateman still around, the comic touch he brought to such breaches of good breeding like 'The Man Who Lit His Cigar before the Loyal Toast' and 'The Man Who Crept into the Royal Enclosure in a Bowler' would surely have been applied to modern cricket, with 'The Cricket Purist Who Confessed He Was Quite Partial to Watching One-Dayers'.

Yet, if you are a purist, there seems a great deal in the fifty-over game for which to be thankful, especially in its enhancement of such core skills as ground fielding, catching and running between wickets;

it can hardly be a negative development that modern cricketers are more naturally athletic and elastic than of yore. When pressed, indeed, most purists will allow the last as areas of improvement. If the best fielders are now no better than the best of the past, the general standard is far higher than it was; running between wickets is also more precise, because the penalties for error are greater since the third umpire's advent. And it is this that should interest us in contemplating the format's future.

Consider this: the aspects of fifty-over cricket for which there is more or less unanimous approval are those that are the least restricted, regulated or codified. There is no one-hand-one-bounce rule, no need to run 23 yards for every third run. The game is best, then, where it is most free. This matters because in their slightly panicky response to the cannibalisation of their fifty-over franchise by Twenty20, authorities have taken the very opposite tack: that is, they have striven to make the game shorter, more restricted, more complicated, more artificial, and in the process actually less accessible to the live spectator. The concentration required for keeping up with Power Plays, Super Subs, Duckworth–Lewis calculations, field restriction requirements and other playing conditions in one-day internationals is now quite considerable, and at grounds themselves almost nowhere in evidence. No wonder most people are now there for the beer.

The ICC presumably believes it is adapting fifty-over cricket to a post-Twenty20 world that needs more entertainment, more surprises, more distractions, more concentrated action. They are drawing precisely the wrong conclusions: Twenty20 works not because it is gimmicky, but because it is simple. Fifty-over cricket will not be improved by more restrictions because Twenty20 has restricted cricket sewn up—which is why the smarter course would be to do the very opposite.

The best one-day matches many of us have witnessed were staged a decade ago, during the last World Cup in England. Held early in summer with a white Duke ball, it became a vintage series for fast bowling: Ambrose, Walsh, Akram, Akhtar, Donald, Pollock, McGrath, Srinath, Gough. Bowlers aimed to get batsmen out.

Batsmen had to defend as well as attack. Captains placed attacking fields. Teams collapsed. Teams fought back. There was big hitting, to be sure, from Saeed Anwar to Lance Klusener; more often there was scrapping, scavenging and endless pressure, in games of true Test match texture.

Had I my druthers, this is the model to which I'd hark back. I would redesign one-day cricket so that it reverted to its original nomenclature as involving 'one-day Tests': limited overs, unlimited scope. Captains would be free to use bowlers when and as often as they wished, and place fielders anywhere they pleased, with a limitation only on boundary riders in the last five overs. I would insist on matches being played on a variety of surfaces—greentops and bunsens as well as good batting pitches—and with the longest possible boundaries. And I would encourage attacking bowling, deprecate negative tactics and set a price on wickets by penalising batting teams for every man dismissed—perhaps 20 to 25 runs. Facing an unequal contest? Bowl your opponents out, in the immortal spirit of Foch at the Marne: 'My centre is giving way. My right is retreating. Situation excellent. I am attacking'.

It won't happen, of course, because the idea of making anything look more like Test cricket is simply too counterintuitive for cricket's governing classes: the marketers cordially loathe Test cricket because its variables boggle their neat, orderly, commodifying minds; the administrators think they are doing the game a favour by preserving it as a museum piece, rather than as a viable form of mass entertainment, and otherwise have no wish to think about it. Yet the 'one-day Test' would not be valuable only in its own terms; it would have potential as a means of interpreting Test cricket to the popular audience, the gap between the five-day and Twenty20 forms of the game having grown so vast as to border on the irreconcilable. A tournament like the Champions Trophy, in fact, would be the ideal place to trial such an experiment: it might, at last, give us something by which to remember this gimcrack event.

Seriously Cricket Chronicles, October 2009

CHAMPIONS LEAGUE 2009

Passion Play

Ever wondered how WAG du jour Lee Furlong ended up on television, and thereby on Shane Watson's arm? You might have thought it was something to do with her comely appearance. But no: according to the website of her speaking agency, readily Googleable, it's all about 'passion': 'Lee's passion for the media has already led to a presenting role with Fox Sports News'. 'Passion for the media'? Dear God ...

If ever a word was in the process of being utterly debauched, it is 'passion'. Originally it referred to suffering or agony, as of a martyr. Now it is simply an overheated substitute for enthusiasm of any description. Furlong grew up wanting to be on television; with the yeast of hyperbole, this juvenile yearning germinates into a 'passion for the media'.

With the launch of the Champions League in October 2009 came another passionate outpouring, as Dean Kino, its head of legal and business affairs, explained its raison d'être:

> It increases the passion of grassroots cricketers to be involved for their states and provinces. If you look at the interest in the KFC Twenty20 Big Bash in Australia and the IPL over the last six months, you will see that the result of going to the Champions League has been hugely stimulating. At the domestic level it will drive young cricketers to the game and that will build on domestic cricket and make it stronger.

Some tournament, eh? It's going to 'drive young cricketers to the game'. Looks like Mum will have Saturday mornings off in future.

Kino, who is also Cricket Australia's general counsel, is usually known for his circumspection; he worries if staff visit the water cooler without a QC's opinion. There must be a reason he has so totally quaffed the Kool-Aid now, tarting money up as 'passion'. Because, you see, by Kino's lights, cricketers were not really passionate about representing their states or provinces before. They were just, you know, pretty ho-hum about it. Oh, they'd do it if they had to, but the wife had been at them to pave the patio and they wondered if they could spare the time. But now, they're just so passionate, hugely stimulated, virtually priapic, thanks to the Viagra-like qualities of the IPL and the KFC Big Bash, and now the pornographic punch of the Champions League. Of course, what Kino means is that the Champions League stands to improve the financial incentives for some lucky domestic cricketers. But behind that casual eliding of remuneration with 'passion' lies a universe of self-delusion. And speaking of Lalit Modi …

For when it comes to huge stimulations, Kino has been training with the master. And in his vaunting of the Champions League, the IPL's impresario was almost tumescent with excitement:

> It's a place where we can find young cricketers who then play for their national sides. The IPL is a great example of a domestic club-level tournament, and similarly nations around the world have club tournaments. The objective here is not to make money, it is to build the game, to build club-level cricket, to find and nurture new talent. Money is not the criteria.

Oh, purlease. The Champions League may indeed promote a player who furthers his claims to national selection, but it does not exist in order to unearth talent: it exists because the television rights could be sold to ESPN for the greatest per-game rights fee in cricket history, and no other reason. The IPL, meanwhile, is not a 'great example' of a 'domestic club-level tournament'—it is, so far, the only such tournament, and probably will remain so, the joint venture of Australia, South Africa and New Zealand having failed to get off the ground, the domestic version of T20 in England having remained based on the existing first-class counties. Modi apparently now sees not the world as it is, but the world as he would wish it in five years. Vision? Or hallucination?

As for the objective being 'not to make money' and 'money is not the criteria', where does Modi think all that 'passion' comes from? Not because young cricketers of Otago grew up dreaming of their date with destiny against the Cape Cobras; not because of the thrill of watching the Eagles without needing to know the words to 'Hotel California'. It's because you can get rich quick: New South Wales could lose every match they play in the Champions League and each player would still receive more money than the entire team received for winning the KFC Big Bash.

Which is not to say that the Champions League will be devoid of interest. It will involve some excellent cricketers; it will parade some lesser-known names, which is one of the most appealing and involving aspects of the IPL. From an administrative point of view, it is especially intriguing, offering revenue-raising opportunities to state and provincial administrations hitherto entirely dependent on distributions from the boards of control of which they are members— potentially advantageous for some, potentially destabilising for all. In this sense, it throws a bone to states, counties and provinces which spend vast sums on bringing cricket talent to fruition, only to see that talent suit itself when the IPL hoves into view.

Above all, perhaps, the Champions League hems cricket into a T20-centric framework that little more firmly. The KFC Big Bash, for instance, is now the most lucrative cricket in Australia bar none, international summer included, because it offers access to the Champions League: a bizarre usurpation of the time-honoured hierarchy of competition. The inference, as with all T20, is that future players will not profit according to how their skills work in cricket, but how they work on television.

Yet sometimes one wonders if Modi actually speaks any longer, as distinct from simply letting words tumble from his mouth. In his panegyric to the Champions League, for instance, there was this:

'We must make the competition more broadcast-friendly and show it to countries that have never seen cricket before'. Hang on, isn't the Champions League wholly philanthropic? Such expansionist rhetoric sounds suspiciously like a mantra of business growth. What, too, can he mean by 'more broadcast-friendly'? Advertisements during the advertisements?

Then there was this: 'Like the IPL did, we have to get more women and children hooked onto this game'. Notice the 'hooked': an ugly image, marketing as dope peddling. And notice the 'this': the objective is not the promotion of our game, cricket, but his game, T20. There was more too, with a clear cumulative message: it's Lalit Modi's world, and we just live in it.

As a game, T20 has made some worthwhile strides in the last year, in South Africa and England. Indeed, it would be a perfectly pleasant and amusing diversion were it not for the putrid accompanying dogma. We're overdue some truth in advertising. The Champions League will improve the remuneration for some domestic cricketers, provide access to the Indian market for some local associations, and add a bit more to the coffers of a couple of IPL franchises; it stands also to widen Modi's power base, while weakening some of the game's other institutional structures. It has zip to do with philanthropy, and absolutely damn all to do with 'passion', except the 'passion' one might briefly work up for a dumb blonde with big tits. And no, I'm not talking about Ms Furlong.

Seriously Cricket Chronicles, November 2009

BURNOUT

Everyone's Problem

'Burnout' is back. Until a few years ago, it seemed to be all that players and their union representatives used to talk about, cricket's version of sick building syndrome and yuppie flu. Then, with the rise of the IPL, players suddenly couldn't play enough, and burst with renewed energy that was in some cases remarkable. When Andrew Symonds had a kick of the footy the day after his sale to the Deccan Chargers in February 2008, his Australian teammates pulled his leg: it was amazing that a man could jump so high with so much gold in his pockets.

Now Australian coach Tim Nielsen is worried about 'burnout' ahead of Australia's one-day series against India in the context of those New South Wales players who have just enjoyed a massive Champions League collect. Sounds like the kind of out-burning you could get used to, doesn't it? In a two-week period, Simon Katich's team fielded for 114.2 overs, batted for 111.5 and won US$2.6 million. They might have the aforementioned Andrew Symonds problem, but surely not much else.

Nielsen does have a point, of course, insofar as it is not so much the playing that grinds players down these days as the relentless travelling and the protracted absences from home. He has watched it wear the keen edge from the likes of Michael Hussey and Stuart Clark; he has seen it finally get the better of Adam Gilchrist and Matthew Hayden, relatively young men with good cricket still in them. But hold the violins: these are supremely well-paid professionals, and the modern have-iPhone-and-Blackberry-will-travel professional is mobile, motivated and global in perspective. Twenty20, moreover, can be a high-pressure game, but it is hardly a physically extenuating one. At Oxford University earlier this year, Sourav Ganguly remarked dryly that he sometimes finishes Twenty20 games feeling as though he's hardly played. That was the warm-up, wasn't it? Say, when does the cricket start?

Yet is burnout an affliction troubling only to players? Leni Riefenstahl's camerawork could not have disguised the gaps in the crowds at the venues outside Delhi during the recent Champions League. The organisers were fortunate that the spirit and élan of Trinidad and Tobago gave locals something to cheer for; Indian cricket without its matinee idols, the Tendulkars, Dhonis and Yuvrajs, felt a bit like buskers being given the run of Carnegie Hall.

It's not a year since Australia played six of the most enthralling Tests of the modern era against South Africa; they are just about to begin a best-of-seven, fifty-over, head-to-head tournament in India. Yet between times have been squeezed, inter alia, the IPL, the Wisden Trophy, the World Twenty20, the Ashes, two NatWest Series, the Champions Trophy and the Champions League, most if not all with the capacity to be marquee events, but slotted together instead as tightly as Meccano. Actually, I'm being unkind to Meccano: Meccano is satisfyingly logical and coherent; the cricket year has become like making the Lego Star Wars collection integrate with adobe brick, to slot K'Nex Railroad Pals into Carrara marble.

Crowds, to be sure, are not always a reliable index of interest in cricket. There will have been numberless millions keeping track of the Champions League on their alternate screens at work and fast-forwarding through games recorded overnight. But the sheer disorganisation of cricket's calendar is now itself fatiguing, and cannot but bring cynicism and contempt in its train. One half-expects Lalit Modi to decree an extra month of the year, modestly named Modember, for a Champion of Champions Championship.

Speaking of cynics, the other potential victim of burnout, not that many will be able to summon so much as a glycerine tear, is the media itself. Of course, journalists are terminal malcontents, popular really with neither players nor public. Sit in an air-conditioned press box watching cricket, do you? What a life! Well, yes it is, quite, and one would sometimes wish to do more of it. For it's not so much the journalists feeling the strain of the calendar today as media proprietors. With the decline of newspapers, even big media organisations like News Corporation are becoming picky about tours and tournaments, especially long ones. Online media is not a like-for-like substitute, idly prone to the cheap shortcuts of seating a junior journalist in front of a television in the office, and/or soliciting dashed-off tripe from wannabe pundits and try-hard humorists.

As their own game grows richer than Croesus, the game's governors will not spare too much time worrying about the straits into which daily print media is slipping, with advertising migrating to the Web and circulations continuing their long-term downward-trend line. On the contrary, the recent catfights over intellectual property between boards of control and news agencies have made the former's position abundantly clear: they like the money on their side of the table. The print media, too, can be a little irreverent for some tastes, inclined to making a nuisance of itself by being critical, by being tasteless and tactless, by pointing out problems, by holding administrators and players to account.

Yet, for all its faults, and these are many, the print media has a credibility that a handsome Bollywood star and a popular model walking towards a camera and holding microphones while reading a script just cannot quite attain. And a game so prone to making a horse's arse of itself needs its gadflies. Journalists, for example, did much to reveal cricket's dark match-fixing heart a decade ago; one wonders whether they would now be sufficiently vigilant, curious and numerous to do the same. Players are not alone, then, in suffering from a surfeit of cricket. What they are alone in is also benefiting from it.

Cricinfo, October 2009

CRICKET IN 2009

The Longest Year

For all its obsession with youth, colour and vibrancy, cricket is developing a problem commonest among old men: an ability to remember what happened last year but not last week. Reviewing 2009, events even months ago seem eternities old, having slipped far down the memory hole, perhaps because the hiatuses for reflection and recapitulation have been so few, perhaps because the events themselves have been so brief, matters of an over here or there, rather than an hour, let alone a whole day.

The most significant event of the cricket year, moreover, occurred outside a stadium rather than in it: the attack on the Sri Lankan team bus en route to a Test match at Lahore on 2 March. Yet the show, somehow, had to go on: two weeks after being under machine-gun and grenade fire for twenty-five minutes, Simon Taufel umpired a Test in Hamilton. Lalit Modi promptly packed his caravan and took the IPL to South Africa, where the final was fought out between teams from Bangalore and Hyderabad composed of fourteen Indians, four South Africans, three Australians and a New Zealander—a sentence that even two years ago would have made no earthly sense.

Indeed, for all the talk about cricket's three varieties, 2009 was the year in which Twenty20 hogged the limelight almost completely. In a year of the Ashes and the Wisden Trophy, a year in which South Africa wrested from Australia the status of the world's number-one Test nation and Bangladesh registered their first Test win, Test cricket barely registered. Some of the best Test matches of modern times were played: in half-a-dozen meetings, Australia and South Africa fought one another to a standstill; Sri Lanka stole a match at Galle from under Pakistan's nose by taking eight for 46 on the last day; England saved a match at Cardiff they had no right to, and made Ricky Ponting rue the occasion for the next two months. But India, by playing just three perfunctory Tests in New Zealand and at the time of writing having scheduled no Tests for 2010, conveyed such indifference to what has been considered the game's premium format that it was contagious.

With Allen Stanford bandying billions about, West Indian players had momentarily looked serious about international cricket again. Nobody hit the ball harder or further than their captain, Chris Gayle, against Australia at the Oval, one six disturbing the ecclesiastical serenity of Archbishop Tenison's School. When Stanford proved to be another South Sea Bubble, Gayle's team sulked and pouted through an England tour, then stormed out of commitments against Bangladesh, past master Viv Richards accusing Gayle of a 'total betrayal of the game that raised him'. In the year that Andrew Symonds and Andrew Flintoff also turned their backs on their countries in favour of more casual employment, the West Indies looked for a time like becoming the first cricket team to do the same, making peace with their board just in time to visit Australia, albeit with no promises about the future.

For all that 2009 was meant also to mark the centenary of the ICC, meanwhile, its authority was increasingly compromised by the wealth and vitality of the BCCI. The ICC's years of trying to bring a modicum of order and cohesion to the cricket calendar through the Future Tours Programme were set at nought by the 'quasi-domestic' events that now fall outside the council's purview, despite demanding the services of the same players and venues and offering far greater sums of money.

Although the cancellation of the Indian Cricket League shored up the IPL's claims to premiership, the result was a year in which nobody seemed to know what was next. When was the NatWest Challenge? Was it before or after the World Twenty20? Would the

British Asian Cup coincide with the Wisden Trophy, the NKP Salve Challenger Trophy or the Chappell–Hadlee Trophy? When did the Champions Trophy end and the Champions League begin? At times, 2009 became like a three-ring circus, with lion tamers, then clowns, then trapeze artists, in no apparent order and to no particular end. It wasn't altogether unlike the 1990s, when you could hardly tell an Asia Cup from an Austral-Asia Cup, but for there being Pepsi at one and Coca-Cola at another. Except that now the sums of money were hugely larger, while the cricket was paradoxically briefer. In October, for example, New South Wales took barely three hours to beat Trinidad and Tobago to a purse of US$2.6 million in an evening in Hyderabad—another one of those sentences that would have been entirely unintelligible two years ago. The 50-over-a-side Champions Trophy, meanwhile, was praised not because it proved particularly exciting, Australia taking the trophy in a canter, but because it was short—a back-handed compliment if ever there was one.

Snatches of memorable cricket resisted the trend to instant perishability. It was the year of Dilshan's Dilscoop, JP Duminy's dexterity, dynamic Dirk Nannes, and of the Dutchmen's day out at Lord's—and these were just the Ds. Tellingly, however, it seemed to be players already established who provided the greatest highlights rather than new faces demanding attention: as yet, Twenty20 seems to generate celebrity, brief and efflorescent, rather than fame, grand and lasting. Anil Kumble and Matthew Hayden didn't let retirement hold them back during the IPL; Sachin Tendulkar's defence still looked watertight; Ricky Ponting's pull shot still pulsed with power. Virender Sehwag was Wisden's Leading Cricketer of the Year; Mitchell Johnson, the ICC's choice as International Cricketer of the Year, demonstrated his inexperience by going to pieces during the Ashes.

It was, above all, a year of captains, from Andrew Strauss of England to Daren Ganga of Trinidad and Tobago, Adam Gilchrist of the Deccan Chargers to Shakib al-Hasan of Bangladesh. Captain of the world's top Test team, Graeme Smith of South Africa, led an anti-AIDS campaign in his home country; captain of the world's Twenty20 titleist, Younis Khan, retained his job despite clumsy political interference in his. Mind you, very few cricketers can have so dominated cricket in their country as Daniel Vettori now overshadows the game in New Zealand, as bowler, batsman, captain and now quasi-coach after the sacking of Andy Moles; he'll be cutting the sandwiches next. If it's all starting to come back to you now, that's good. But the problem remains: in the headlong pursuit of sensation, the quest for the memorable appears to be falling by the wayside.

Sports Illustrated India, December 2009

INTERNATIONAL CRICKET COUNCIL

A Modest Proposal

Consistency is an elusive quality in cricket. Not at the ICC. It began the decade in crisis. It has finished the decade in crisis. In-between has been sandwiched one crisis after another, in some of which the ICC has been the unwitting coat-holder for two nations duking it out, to others it has contributed by sheer ineptitude: who can forget the 'database error' that in 2008 led New Zealand judge John Hansen to believe that Harbhajan Singh had a choirboy's disciplinary record?

In some ways, you have to hand it to them: in absorbing punishment to its authority and credibility, the ICC has shown a chin like Jake La Motta's. But surely only the ICC could transform a source of celebration like a World Cup final into a clusterfuck like the one at Kensington Oval in April 2007, then reward the perpetrators with further appointments, so that Rudi Koertzen, for example, could turn his 100th Test, at Lord's in July, into another fiasco.

Nor is the current malaise at the ICC merely a continuation of the same. Ten years ago, when the ICC was bumbling its responses to illegal actions and match-fixing, cricket was at least looking to it for leadership. Now the crisis is one of relevance. The ICC stands for a system of multilateral cricket governance at odds with the economic and cultural forces that have made India, and its board of control, the de facto locus of power in the global game. A problem just as great is that nobody seems to care.

The pity is that the ICC is as well placed as at any time to fulfil its mission: it has resources, professional personnel, a thoughtful chief executive in Haroon Lorgat. It has arrived at this capability, however, as its remit has been curbed. There was a telling exchange in May when Lalit Modi unilaterally announced the granting of 'windows' in the ICC's Future Tours Programme for both the IPL and the Champions League. Lorgat responded that not only were there no such 'windows', there could not be any: the IPL and Champions League, as quasi-domestic tournaments, were not in the council's domain. Modi then denied having asked for the 'windows' in the first place: 'We have never propagated that we should be part of the Future Tours Programme for the IPL or the Champions League because I think there is a natural window for these two events'. 'Natural window'? Sounds a little like renovation by taking a sledgehammer to a wall, doesn't it? Which isn't a bad metaphor for the modi operandi, actually.

Here is where the ICC's abiding public relations problem kicks in. Rather like an International Monetary Fund or World Bank, the ICC is condemned to arrive on every scene last—after misbehaviour has taken place, after a diplomatic stand-off has begun. This being so, it has become naturally associated with frenzies and foul-ups, which it can never resolve to universal satisfaction, and usually ends up resolving to nobody's. As such, it has been an endlessly convenient scapegoat, readily undermined by members, barely tolerated by players, cheerfully ridiculed by media and fans. Even when spreading positive news, the council has demonstrated a talent for ruining the effect, like in November when its five-year-old ICC Awards anointed as International Cricketer of the Year the one and only Mitchell Johnson—the only person to have a lousier Lord's Test than Rudi Koertzen.

Lorgat is continuing the strategy of predecessor Malcolm Speed by building a natural four-year cycle of ICC-controlled events, with a World Twenty20 to be played in even-numbered years and a World Cup alternating with a Champions Trophy in odd-numbered years—and if the ICC's financial statements are anything to go by, this has been effective enough. Irrupting disputes over intellectual property and clashing commercial deals, for example, seem also to be a thing of the past.

For the moment, anyway: because events have placed the ICC in very intense competition—for players, for time, for attention, and above all for broadcast and sponsorship monies—with its largest member, the BCCI. If perhaps not yet fatally, its jurisdiction over cricket's calendar has diminished. The situation is analogous to a local council striving to order and even out its city's central boulevard by permitting building only of determined styles and heights, but being powerless to prevent a particular developer every so often sending up a Burj Dubai or Jin Mao Tower.

This isn't all bad, by the way. After all, who wants a main street of Mies van der Rohe–inspired glass boxes? But if the shadows of the BCCI's supertalls cast the rest of cricket into darkness, and they in due course become the only places its population aspire to work, then the consequences could be considerably worse than the short-term gains.

Another crisis in the making at the ICC is the massive financial inequality of its members, the BCCI being so much wealthier than its near neighbours Sri Lanka Cricket and the Pakistan Cricket Board but providing precious little encouragement to either—quite the contrary in the case of Pakistan. The more successful IPL franchises have probably extracted more money from cricket in the last two years than the PCB in its entire history.

The BCCI's gravitational pull is even felt in the faraway Caribbean: there is no way that Chris Gayle and his fellow refuseniks would have prolonged their feud with the West Indies Cricket Board had the IPL not offered rewards so ample for time so insignificant. Which is not to say, again, that players bargaining from financially firmer positions with their boards of control is an entirely malign development. But competition for the services of international cricketers, as during World Series Cricket and the rebel tours, has caused the game a great deal of pain, at least in the short term. The irony is that, at home, the BCCI is a perfectly brutal monopolist: witness its attitude to the Indian Cricket League. The IPL's effect, however, has been to subtly undermine boards elsewhere in a way the BCCI itself would never tolerate.

How does the ICC remedy that inequality? How does it renew its control over cricket's calendar, to guard against a repeat of this year's absurd and meaningless congestion, and distribute revenues from the game more equitably, so that the game prospers all over the world? There is actually a solution so compellingly simple, logical and obvious that you just know it will never happen: the BCCI cedes control over the IPL and Champions League to the ICC, which makes them into genuinely global tournaments with franchises in every Test-playing country, and in due course perhaps some non-Test-playing ones too.

Presto: the traditional monopoly of the official game is restored, although the players continue to benefit from any market growth, because of the competition for their services from the new franchises, and the fans in other countries are given a stake in the excitement, rather than essentially having to look over Indian fans' shoulders. Other boards can cease so far fruitless and essentially pointless efforts to grow their own Twenty20 attractions; instead, they share the benefits via ICC distributions from a properly constituted and multilaterally governed worldwide competition. Lalit Modi accepts the thanks of a grateful cricket world, and sheers off to star as himself in the inevitable Bollywood biopic.

The obstacles? One is the ICC's reputation, reminiscent of a jest told at the Australian newspaper giant John Fairfax after its ruin in an ill-starred leveraged buyout led by impatient heir Warwick Fairfax: 'How do you create a small business? Give a large business to Warwick Fairfax'. Who would trust the ICC to run a corner store after the shambles of the last World Cup, of which those final nocturnal meanderings were somehow a profoundly fitting culmination?

It's a fair question. By the same token, it's not as though the BCCI is exactly a streamlined model of commercial efficiency either, struggling with such complicated tasks as answering phone calls and delivering mail; were it issued a school report, meanwhile, the teacher would be obliged to make the comment 'does not play well with others'. The greatest strength the BCCI enjoys is India—the fans, the viewers, the market—which it has done no more to deserve than by existing.

No, the chief obstacles to this proposition would be as straightforward as the proposition itself: ego, personal and national. The IPL is about India as much if not more than cricket, about the country's status in its own eyes and those of others; against that, even the welfare of cricket is perhaps a paltry concern.

Yet the influence and significance of India would hardly be diluted at all: the economic epicentre for an International Premier League/International Champions League would still overwhelmingly be where it is now. The only change would be that certain individuals very powerful today would be somewhat less so, even if they would in a sense be yielding their power to a countryman in the ICC's president-elect Sharad Pawar, and that the indigenous pride engendered by the IPL might in the short term be diffused, to perhaps be rekindled in due course by the prospect of Bangalore Royal Challengers v Durban Dik-Diks or Kolkata Knight Riders v Cardiff Kojaks. Whatever the case, cricket's increasingly divided house must be put in order. The ICC's crisis of relevance is, to borrow a line from Barack Obama's chief of staff, Rahm Emanuel, a crisis too good to waste.

Cricinfo, December 2009

CRICKET AND TELEVISION

Crowds and Powerlessness

In November 2009, the generally tranquil links of Kingston Heath were besieged for four days by a noisy occupying army. The reason, of course, was Tiger Woods, who was being paid A$3.5 million to come win another A$270000 in the Australian Masters. The result was traffic jams banked up for miles, a heaving throng over which it was barely possible to see anything, and, to paraphrase Mark Twain, many good walks spoiled. Such was the crowding, you could watch Woods only for a hole every so often, and then usually from a distance. Compelled by the decree of deferential tournament organisers to observe the champion's insistence on sepulchral silence, third-round spectators even had to return to Woods the driver he hurled at them out of annoyance at the temerity of a fan taking a photograph. Mind you, Woods did have to put up with a posse of drunks who between holes insisted on referring to him as 'Eldred': boys, the name is Eldrick.

This, everyone agreed, was a huge success—for the tournament anyway. For the spectators, those misbegotten souls who put up with the jams and jostling for the privilege of the occasional glimpse of the great man through the crook of someone's elbow, who knew? And, well, who cared? The television ratings were good. The sponsors were happy. When it comes down to it, in fact, the punters were only ever props, part of the scenery, there to make it look exciting for the far-more-important virtual audience. Their satisfaction was as incidental as that of a hooker's after sex: the relationship between the Masters and its crowd was wholly transactional.

Makes you glad to be a cricket fan, eh? No traipsing around in quest of an intermittent peek. No need for don't-blink-too-loud quiet. In fact, it's all rather civilised. But for other reasons, cricket has become dangerously indifferent to the lot of its spectators, to the detriment of the game and its culture, and urgently needs a rethink.

If you contemplate the contexts in which crowds are usually invoked in cricket today, you will find that they are almost uniformly negative. Crowds are deplored when they misbehave, whether they are Indians aping Andrew Symonds, Australians being investigated for racist epithets hurled at Indians, Englishmen drowning their sorrows and irrigating their occasional celebrations, or West Indians overexcitedly overrunning their outfields.

But crowds are also deplored, contrarily, when they are not enthusiastic enough, or fail to materialise. Where, for instance, were West Indians during the 2007 World Cup? Thus, too, the ritual of complaint about the paucity of Test match crowds. Where were the Indians last year at Punjab CA Stadium when Tendulkar became Test cricket's highest scorer?

Crowds are deplored when they fail observably to support the home side. Thus the infamous Tebbit Test, articulated by Norman of that ilk in April 1990, when he complained that ethnic minorities in England were failing to assimilate because many were continuing to barrack for their countries of origin.

But crowds can also be deplored when they *do* support their home side. Thus Peter Roebuck's idée fixe with the crowd at the Oval in 2005, who, at the prospect of England regaining the Ashes for the first time in a generation, had the audacity to cheer when bad light favoured the draw their team needed, thereby reducing itself to a 'pitiful state of orchestrated nationalism'.

> A team had been invited to play a series of matches only to be subjected to this abject and crass self-glorification. They had come from a country that has fought side by side with its host

in four wars. Numerous foreigners had also arrived to support their team. Thousands of children were watching ...

Manifestly spectators were more interested in England winning than in watching top-class cricket. They were happy because the interruption meant that their team had a better chance of drawing the match. To that end they were content to spend hours twiddling their thumbs. Anything was better than the possibility of defeat.

Even when cricket was played, the mood of the crowd bordered on the demented. To watch the faces of English supporters in the public stands when an Australian wicket fell was to see a mixture of hatred and hysteria. Not the least shock experienced while sitting amongst spectators was the discovery that the people singing about Andrew Flintoff were not inebriated students but well-heeled 40-year-olds. What the hell are these people doing with their lives? What the hell is happening in this country?

Who knows? Perhaps people were enjoying themselves. Frankly, for what English cricket fans pay to watch Test matches, the security indignities they undergo, the general dilapidation of grounds and the killjoy prohibitions of administrators, they should be allowed to parade in the nude if they so wish. But there's the rub. Crowds, in general, are simply assumed, like sightscreens and drinks breaks, and reported with a similar degree of understanding by journalists high above them in air-conditioned comfort who haven't had to pay to get in. Nobody speaks for them: they have no association, no lobbyists, no agents, no spin doctors, no ghost writers. Who has protested the scurvy treatment of fans in Calcutta and Johannesburg, deprived of international cricket by ludicrous administrative turf wars? Where were the thundering denunciations in England when the ECB cancelled a Twenty20 Cup quarter-final ten minutes before the start because of a dispute about a player's registration, thereby wasting the journeys of 4000 hapless fans? When wronged, fans have no recourse but the withdrawal of their interest—a self-penalisation.

The main reason for this indifference to the spectator's lot, in administrative circles at least, is television. For twenty years and more, cricket has been obsessed with its telegenia—how to improve the experience for viewers, and so to maximise the value of the game as a media property. And as viewers have grown in financial importance, so live spectators have diminished. Twenty years ago, about a third of Cricket Australia's turnover came from 'match revenues'; that is, gate receipts. Now it is less than 10 per cent. When CA consented in 2004 to the broadcast of international cricket in Australia live against the gate in the host city, it was an act not of caprice but of accumulated indifference. In key economic respects, in fact, the home viewer is greatly preferable to the ticket purchaser: no need for authorities to build expensive infrastructure, to deal with grasping booking agencies, to lay on particular comforts or additional attractions.

The subordination of the game to television's priorities has had many perverse outcomes, but one of the strangest is this: where the accent of television coverage of the game used to be about making the viewer feel like he or she was 'there', today the opposite is true. Televised cricket, shot from every angle and at every speed, screened in a uniformly pleasing light and reported in a uniformly upbeat voice, bears no resemblance to sitting in the crowd. Yet it, rather than actually being physically present, has come to be regarded as the definitive experience: the emphasis at grounds is now on striving to replicate what the game would be like were you watching at home. There are big screens for replays of every boundary and wicket, and advertisements at every break; there are entertainments in each intermission so you need never feel unamused or, heaven forbid, reflective; there are radios for sale so you can listen to the television commentary, and frankly, you sometimes need them, the playing conditions having been made so absurdly complicated in one-day internationals that games can border on the incomprehensible—just ask John Dyson. Are we in the first Power Play or the second? How many players are allowed outside the circle? Why is there a VB ad on the scoreboard when I want to know how many overs Mitchell Johnson has left? And why does CA object so strenuously to the Barmy Army's bugler when it is intent on turning our stadia into discos for the middle-aged with non-stop prog rock from the 1980s?

To be fair, by comparison with most boards of control, CA appears to give half a damn about its country's live fans. It has kept tickets affordable and available; it has gathered data on their expectations via market research; it has striven to maintain consistency of fixturing so that people know basically that there will always be, for instance, a Test on Boxing Day in Melbourne, and a Test around New Year in Sydney. Would that other boards gave even a tinker's cuss.

The protracted shambles of the last World Cup was a case in point. The organising committees of the West Indies Cricket Board prolonged the tournament's proceedings to the point of pain, and pitched admission prices as high as US$120 in the first round and US$390 for the final; attendances, mysteriously, were only two-thirds of the claimed ticket sales. The environment was so torpid that, as Adam Gilchrist admits in his autobiography, it communicated itself to the players:

> The tournament itself didn't seem to be going very well, with high ticket prices blamed for low crowds and a lack of atmosphere. There were perceived to be too many games with too-long breaks between them. It was during one of those long breaks that I dropped to another low, missing Mel [his wife] and the kids so badly I pretty much wanted to go home.

It was worse for the fans, as Tony Cozier reported pithily in *Wisden*:

> Strict regulations everywhere ... conspired to spoil the usual Caribbean revelry, before public and media pressure prompted officials to relent. No alcoholic drinks could be taken through the gates (a ban defied by Trinidadians who sneaked in their rum in plastic suncream bottles); musical instruments had to be prevetted; conch shells—an identifiable sound of West Indian cricket—were disallowed, as they were deemed a potential weapon; and initially no pass-out tickets were issued.

Security was understandably tight, given the safety fears that have haunted all such sporting occasions since the 2001 terrorist attacks on New York, not to mention the sponsors' demands for utmost vigilance against ambush marketing. It was also often excessive, even after the furious public reaction when World Cup stewards were pictured frisking police officers at a warm-up match in Barbados.

Indeed, it is in cricket's showcase series that the contempt for fans seems to be at its greatest. In 2008 in India, for instance, the BCCI held a Test series involving Australia that they seemed not to care if it was attended at all. Tickets were absurdly difficult to obtain, often requiring a visit to a specific bank branch; at Mohali, the crowds consisted of a few intrepid Australians and some uniformed schoolchildren bussed in to take up space; at Nagpur, it was necessary to buy a ticket for all five days, for a game at a new venue 19 kilometres from the centre of town. Perhaps the most egregious recent example of a casual disregard for the paying public, however, was seen at the last Ashes, when the ECB was cajoled by cash into scheduling the First Test at Sophia Gardens, capacity 16 000, so that even fewer people could attend than usual. Not a kilometre away stood the silent reproach of Cardiff's plush 75 000-seat Millennium Stadium.

In this unspoken shared belief among administrators that somehow it is immaterial if crowds no longer gather, and that only the vast, diffuse, invisible audience of viewers counts, lies the seeds of a grave crisis for cricket. In the most straightforward sense, crowds matter aesthetically, in a way that ratings never can. They ratify by their presence an occasion's importance; they dramatise by their passion a game's excitement; they negate by their absence an event's significance. Sachin Tendulkar's 12 000th Test run should have been one of the great moments of Indian cricket; it will be remembered instead, as even ICC chief executive Haroon Lorgat noted, with dismay and disillusionment.

Those who trouble to attend cricket are also its core constituency; to set aside a day for a Test or a one-day international involves a huge investment of time and money, which deserves proportional return. Yet the members of this core are being treated as political parties sometimes treat their most loyal voters, and listed corporations treat their most steadfast small shareholders, marginalising and alienating them as they take them for granted—and no party or company has done this long and prospered. On the contrary, commercial organisations dependent on public patronage lavish extraordinary efforts on keeping their most loyal customers, encouraging them to return by loyalty cards, bonus programs and other incentive systems. Why does cricket, so purportedly savvy in the ways of commerce, care so little? Australian golf might have looked a little ludicrous at the Masters last month with its serpentine queues, star-struck melees and strivings for church-like quiet—but at least it was trying.

Seriously Cricket Chronicles, December 2009

TEST CRICKET

Good Bad Publicity

Test cricket is in trouble. I know. I read it in the papers, saw it on television and heard it on radio. It's all over the internet too. That modern Zeitgeist-o-meter, the Google search, reveals a panoply of greats past and present opining about the eclipse of the five-day format: Sachin Tendulkar, Kumar Sangakkara, Greg Chappell, Shane Warne, Ricky Ponting, Rahul Dravid, Matthew Hayden, Richard Hadlee, Gary Kirsten, Michael Vaughan. Not to mention Chris Gayle, for whom, of course, it's no biggie: he is more concerned about his next haircut.

Oh, and there's a survey too, on which *The Age* and the *Sydney Morning Herald* went to town in November 2009. Commissioned by the Marylebone Cricket Club, which not so long ago would have solicited public opinion by offering whisky sours all round at White's or the Athenaeum, it sought the views of fans in India, New Zealand and South Africa on their preferred forms of the game. There were horror-struck responses to its statistics. 'The results do not make for pretty reading', said Peter Roebuck, beneath the sober and restrained headline: 'The truest form of the game is on the brink of extinction'. 'Only 7 per cent of Indians, 19 per cent of Kiwis and 12 per cent of South Africans put Test cricket above its peers. Most Indians favour Twenty20, while Kiwis like ODIs.'

Well, yes, kind of: 58 per cent of Indian respondents did indeed nominate Twenty20 internationals as their preferred form of the game. But this was downright weird: since the first in December

2006, India have played just nineteen such games. Meanwhile, only 4 per cent of Indians professed consuming adoration for the IPL, which we're constantly being told is all about the fans, has changed the game irrevocably, and is to Test cricket as Godzilla is to Tokyo. It would have been just as factually correct to present the headline: 'Test cricket still more popular than IPL'.

In the case of India, furthermore, the poll was conducted in a year without a home Test until the end of November—a lack which invites the question: if Test cricket has become a minority interest in India, how much does that have to do with visibility and access? At a time in which so much cricket of such variety is being played, views are susceptible to all manner of short-term influences. How different would the results have been had the poll been held after: a) the 2007 World Twenty20; b) the first IPL; c) the India–Sri Lanka Tests just completed, after which India ranked number one on the ICC World Test Championship?

Let's be blunt: this survey was dodgier than a genuine Armarnee suit from Arthur Daley's lockup. The conclusion was based on the views of 500 fans in each country, which in India amounts to 0.000417 per cent of the population. According to the MCC's Tony Lewis, cricket 'would be foolish if we didn't think it was universal', but really the opposite was true. Here was a classic case of evidence from which the preconceived was extracted (dwindling support for Test cricket), the unexpected ignored (the insignificant interest in IPL) and grounds for doubt overlooked (the statistical insignificance of the sample). Cricket is meant to be a game full of stattos, but where were they when we needed them?

Worse, the interpretation indulged a widening streak of masochism among cricket's elites—its top players, senior administrators and commentariat—about Test cricket. For after the West Indian capitulation at the Gabba, the Murdoch press took up the theme of the imminent death of the five-day format with necrophilial gusto, star columnist Shane Warne leading the way. Beneath another cool and dispassionate headline, 'Don't let Test cricket die', Warne offered the helpful advice: 'Test cricket needs an injection of something to capture the fans across the world'. An 'injection of something'? At least he's moved on from diuretics, you might say, but he hasn't become much more discriminating. And there was much more besides, with hectares of print devoted to tiered championships, night Tests, field restriction circles and the like, accompanied by exhortations to 'Have your say: Vote in our online poll on what can be done'. Welcome to *Cricket Idol*.

Sure, this is a debate worth having, for it is true: five days to decide anything these days seems an extraordinary, maybe even anachronistic, luxury. But *plus ca change*. It was in a famous interview with the Murdoch press in January 1982 that Kerry Packer's factotum, Lynton Taylor, then charged with promoting cricket in Australia, said he'd basically given up on the long-form game: 'The game of Test cricket as it's presently constituted is archaic ... I don't know that Test cricket can be saved'. And truth be told, Test cricket is as prone to spasms of hand-wringing as the English public, in Macaulay's droll judgement, to periodic fits of morality. Ask any journalist round for more than five minutes how many times he's written the 'death of Test cricket' piece. It's the modern equivalent of the Bradman obituary—something to keep at the ready, just in case.

Amazingly, too, the torrents of dross evaporated the moment the West Indies fought back at Adelaide Oval, which shows how phoney was the concern for Test cricket, and how pants were most of the mooted innovations, in the first place. Or actually, not so amazingly, for herein may lie some of Test cricket's malaise that has nothing to do with Twenty20, the IPL, the global hegemony of the BCCI, or the gradual marginalisation of the ICC: the general insufficiency of 'news'.

Think about it. Ten years ago, to choose a season at random, the Australian summer was reverberating not just to the heroics of Adam Gilchrist and Justin Langer at Bellerive and Shane Warne's pursuit of Dennis Lillee's wicket-taking record, but Shoaib Akhtar's sudden rehabilitation, Joe the Cameraman's abrupt unmasking, and Darrell Hair's latest showdown with recalcitrant touring teams. Hansie Cronje was about to be unmasked as a cheat, joining Mohammed Azharuddin and Salim Malik in purdah. Perhaps it is age, perhaps it is a journalist's fondness for scandal-mongering, but a few such stories today would be a relief from the modern monotony of non-stop touring and contextless competition.

In a typically shrewd piece for the 1973 edition of *Wisden*, Richie Benaud summed up the Ashes series of 1970–71 and 1972, with their combination of skilful cricket and space-grabbing controversy, from England's walk-off in Sydney to Australia's piss-off at Headingley. At the time, Benaud had an unusual dual perspective, being both commentator for the matronly BBC and columnist for nubile *News of the World*; he wrote accordingly.

> Everyone will have their own ideas on this question of whether or not controversy harms cricket but, over the past two series between Australia and England, I think the game has come out of it very well. The type of controversy which I believe harms the game is where the cricketers are providing poor fare for the spectators, whether that be at the ground or on the television screens ... That sort of controversy I feel does harm in the game because it will be written up or talked about by the media and agreed with—as it should be by the cricket follower ...
>
> Personally I think the last two series between these two countries have provided the best cricket of any dual series since the war ... I believe a great deal of this is due to the fact that in both series the cricket has been very good and the teams roughly equal in strength and intent on providing good entertainment. In addition they have provided their share of controversy—or had it provided for them—and I regard that as a contributing factor to the success of the last eleven Test matches between England and Australia.
>
> Gods or flannelled fools? Voiceless robots or men of character, willing and able to express their feelings? Well, you can take your pick, but I am inclined, having been both in the centre and in the press and television boxes, to prefer the latter any day.

Benaud was writing before cricket controversies involved revelations of corruption, and became proxies for racial tensions and religious squabbles. But his argument is not redundant. Test cricket still commands phenomenal hours of air time and hectarages of space; it is faltering not just because of exogenous factors like Twenty20, but because it is not providing the dramas, the dilemmas, the raw meat of scandal for a ravening media and a public craving thrills and spills, sin and redemption. Had the MCC held its precious survey two years ago in the wake of Bhajigate, when Indians were incinerating Steve Bucknor in effigy and fuming about Harbhajan Singh's martyrdom, would only 7 per cent of them have given a monkey's about Test cricket?

Is Test cricket, then, with its corset-tight Code of Conduct, its pre-modern puritanism about 'the spirit of the game', its post-modern obsession with technology, its abiding ambivalence about aggression, its very contemporary paranoia about 'damaging the brand', caught in a trap of its making, as well as a potential victim of market forces? Because for as long as it fails to provide grist for the media's mill, it will be at risk of becoming that grist itself.

Seriously Cricket Chronicles, January 2010

ICC WORLD TEST CHAMPIONSHIP

Who Rules the World?

The afternoon of 2 August 2009 at the Oval was cold and wintry, not the best for cricket; for Australian cricket, in fact, it could hardly have been worse. Ricky Ponting's team, hanging in gamely after losing a crucial toss, were abruptly up-ended in the 21 deliveries it took Stuart Broad to nip out four for 8. After Graeme Swann chimed in with four for 18 from 43 deliveries, England ended the day with a 230-run lead and seven second-innings wickets in hand, a deficit Australia could not make up for three further days' trying. So it was that the Ashes changed hands.

But it was worse than that, if such a sentiment can be believed from an Australian. Had Australia won that Fifth Test, and thus the series, they would have maintained their status atop the ICC World Test Championship. As it is, they slipped to fourth, an ignominy not experienced in a generation. To all intents and purposes, Australia had led the cricket world since 3 May 1995: the date it recaptured the Frank Worrell Trophy, ending the West Indies' twenty-two years in the Caribbean without defeat. So their fourteen-year dynasty crumbled in an afternoon. It should have been the proverbial 'shot heard around the world'—but it wasn't.

Why? For one thing, the ICC World Test Championship table is almost as obscure to the general public in its workings as the Duckworth–Lewis method. For another thing, Australia's was only a partial eclipse: they remain atop the ICC One-Day International Table, an ascendancy ratified in India, and are not about to slump as dismally as the West Indies after their prolonged premiership.

Yet the main reason is that there was no obvious inheritor of the champion's mantle. It wasn't the handing over of a blue riband, yellow jersey or green jacket, or even a Richie Benaud–style blazer: South Africa rose to the top like a bureaucrat being promoted because of the incompetence of his predecessor. Now there is also Twenty20, cricket's richest and most glamorous format, to consider. Pakistan beat Sri Lanka in its global summit this year, where South Africa fell short again in a global tournament, and Australia was a listless muddle.

So it's all become a bit of a mess. Indeed, you could liken global cricket supremacy to umpiring: certainty disappeared the minute science and technology were introduced to make definitive judgements. But the overriding difficulty is simple: the game has been allowed to grow so diverse as to make consensus impossible about what cricket 'is'.

Think about trying to answer the simple question that anyone new to cricket would ask: who is the world champion? Where football or rugby was concerned, the answer would be succinct: you would name the last winner of the World Cup. But cricket's World Cup is decided in a fifty-over format, and the trophy's last instalment was so dire that you'd be pardoned for wanting to forget it. In general, Chris Gayle always excepted, cricketers think of Test matches as the fullest and most searching examination of a team's skills. But fans are increasingly drawn to the lickety-split spectacle of cricket in twenty-over chunks.

So what would you say? 'In the five-day format known as Test cricket, South Africa are the best, although they lost their last series at home to Australia, who are now rated fourth, and India are third even though they've only played three matches so far this year and at the moment aren't scheduled to play any next year. In the one-day format …' Too late: your interlocutor is glazing over; he's forgotten his next question about the Kolkata Knight Riders' wacky helmets, and is staring into space. Sheeesh, how are you going to explain the Champions League?

Administrators keep insisting that the three forms of cricket are cosily complementary. Actually, Test cricket, one-day cricket and Twenty20 hang together like an Italian political coalition, because of slight momentary convenience rather than innately long-term coherence; in the free market of entertainment, they are more naturally destined to compete, even to cannibalise one another, searching out the same broadcasters, the same sponsors and many of the same fans. Already, it seems, countries are more precisely calibrating their ambitions. India, certainly, is contemptibly marginalising Test cricket, hosting its first five-day match of 2009 in November, and leaving Eden Gardens without a Test match for two years. None of which bodes well for the future of international cricket in the face of the rivalry from the soi-disant 'domestic' IPL and Champions League. As the good book tells us, a house divided against itself cannot stand.

To be on top, to be the best, to have conquered all comers and to be garlanded for doing so: this, for players and for fans, is the summit of all ambition. On how that is constituted in cricket, alas, agreement has been made almost impossibly elusive. In hindsight then, that spell of Stuart Broad's was even more seminal, and undersung: it ended not just a dynasty but the last such dynasty, and perhaps the whole idea of dynasties itself.

Cricinfo, November 2009

ICC CODE OF CONDUCT

Hail the New Puritan

Of all the statues that now ring the Melbourne Cricket Ground, the most readily identifiable features Dennis Lillee. More than twenty years after he last bowled in big cricket, his predatory leap and mephistophelian mien remain somehow unmistakeable. What a bowler. What a character. But, of course, he wouldn't take half the wickets today he did in his own era. Why? Not because he would be any less the nemesis of batsmen, but because he would spend most of his time suspended under the ICC's Code of Conduct.

In the Boxing Day Test against Pakistan thirty-three years ago, Lillee rained bouncers on the unhelmeted openers. Scolded by the umpire, he mimed an under-arm delivery. When an official warning for intimidatory bowling was then issued, he picked up a balloon blowing across the arena and shaped to bowl it. Told soon after to bowl his overs more expeditiously, he defiantly did the opposite. Members booed him when he was slow changing position in the field; the outer cheered him to the echo in response. And the cheers steadily drowned the boos as, from the deadest of pitches, he uprooted ten wickets for 135.

Today, such behaviour would have broken at least half-a-dozen ICC statutes—there's probably one concerning balloon abuse. In this most recent Test, for example, teenage tearaway Mohammad Aamer was chided by an umpire for blowing a kiss at Australia's Shane Watson, alluding to the latter's alleged 'softness'. Just as well he didn't send flowers.

Cricket, of course, has always agonised over what constitutes acceptable aggression, having been freighted with moral expectations during the Victorian age, then exported to the far-flung colonies as a civilising influence. Nor is it a bad thing that cricket should retain vestiges of that politesse. A game of defence as well as attack, it should involve restraint as well as aggression. But when Test cricket is held to be of waning relevance to this hurry-scurry, harum-scarum age, questions are worth asking. How many games are actually less demonstrative and more censorious than thirty-three years ago? And are we judging red-blooded young men playing a demanding, often frustrating and endlessly scrutinised game too puritanically?

Nor are these merely questions of authority. Consider the December 2009 'incident' in Perth, where three committed and competitive cricketers—Sulieman Benn, Brad Haddin and Mitchell Johnson—became entangled. Some mild inadvertent contact was made, followed by some milder advertent contact—the kind of push back one might indulge in if clumsily nudged on a crowded bus. The result was effectively two days in parallel: a day at the ground in which 500 deliveries were bowled, and a day on Channel Nine in which one delivery was replayed about 500 times—although, to be fair, the commentators, most of whom owe their eminence to having been similarly red-blooded cricketers, refrained from pronouncing too judgementally.

The print media were not so circumspect. Journalists, many of whom had just finished damning the West Indians for their casualness and penning obituaries for predictable and monotonous Test cricket, dwelled minutely and sententiously on five seconds of a five-day contest evincing the opposite. Here, we were told, was a 'physical clash' involving 'pushing and shoving' from a 'cantankerous' West Indian with a 'history'—the degenerate fiend had been penalised for insubordination on a youth tour almost eight years earlier. The game itself—excitingly skilful, intriguingly poised—was almost completely overshadowed by the 'news'.

For by now, 'big, bad Benn' had copped a two-match suspension from ICC referee Chris Broad—in his time, ironically, a pretty truculent cricketer, whose son Stuart appears to be taking after him.

Quaintest of all, in fact, were Broad's explanatory comments on Benn ('It just all looked bad on TV') and Haddin ('I think he realises it didn't look good on television'). Yes, the incident looked *so* terrible on TV that Nine replayed it incessantly. In an age of reality television, YouTube and other phenomena of mass exhibitionism, cricket must be the only pursuit in the world where participants are under orders to *tone it down* when cameras are around.

In any event, this attitude is emblematic not of consideration for the audience but of contempt, containing as it does an assumption that the average cricket watcher is incapable of independent judgement and slavishly imitates everything seen on television. The children! Think of the children! Give me a break. Did viewers conclude that Shane Watson's operatic send-off of Chris Gayle in Perth was recommended behaviour? Or did they more sensibly decide that Watson, frankly, is just a bit of a tit?

Mind you, sympathies here should lie with the players, who must by now be seriously confused. Competing strains of cricket rhetoric have emerged: the first insists that the players must be entertainers, putting on a show to excite and engage their audience; the second holds that the players must be moral paragons, exhibiting no evidence of such everyday emotions as disappointment, anger, shock or indignation lest they somehow damage the televisual product. These are nearly impossible to reconcile, unless one holds a vision of cricket/entertainment involving automata executing perfect cover drives between advertisements all day.

Here, then, is a case of lost perspective—not cricket's only one. Because there lurks a belief that the heavens will fall if a single batsman is given out mistakenly, for example, millions of dollars are being spent on a referral system that might improve the accuracy of decision-making by a few per cent if it doesn't render the game farcical first. Behaviour is, however, an area where more robust and grown-up attitudes might go a long way. I was at the MCG thirty-three years ago when Dennis Lillee behaved so petulantly then bowled so brilliantly, and it left a trace neither on me, nor my cricket—if only.

THE BCCI

Talking to the Taxman about Cricket

The name Kerry Packer is often invoked in the context of modern Indian cricket, the revolution being led by the BCCI being paralleled to the made-for-television spectacular conceived thirty-three years ago by the Australian plutocrat. It turns out that the parallels run deeper: like Packer, the BCCI doesn't like paying tax.

Packer spent much of his life fighting a running battle with the Australian Taxation Office, on the premise that anyone who didn't minimise their tax 'wanted their head read'. Now the BCCI is being challenged over tax exemptions claimed on the basis that its promotion of cricket is a 'charitable' activity—a proposition as sustainable as the idea that the United Nations is about democracy, or that India is about curry.

Chances are, of course, the issue will fade away: someone will talk to someone, and some luckless official will have his arse kicked. The BCCI, insouciant as always, is simply saying nothing, leaving the *Times Of India* to surmise that they 'don't seem too worried'. But to go with their challenge, India's Income Tax Department has issued a fascinating and scathing assessment of the BCCI that raises a host of questions cricket has been studiously avoiding.

'The Board of Control for Cricket in India (BCCI) has become totally commercial and all its activities are being carried on commercial lines', argues additional director of exemption Rita Kumari Dokania. 'Cricket is only incidental to its scheme of things. It is more into prize money for every run or wicket, which is nothing short of a gimmick.'

The BCCI has apparently twice altered its constitution to broaden its permissible activities—as Dokania adds, to an utterly unsurprising end:

> The conduct of certain activities and receipt of income from these activities clearly show that these activities are totally commercial and there is no element of charity in the conduct of BCCI. The characteristics of volume, frequency, continuity and regularity of the activities accompanied by profit motive on the part of the assessee have been held to indicate an intention to continue the activity as business.

To the actual promotion of Indian cricket, the tax authorities estimate, the BCCI allocates just 8 per cent of its stupendous revenues.

On the detail of the assessment, it is impossible to comment, because the BCCI's financial statements circulate only among its members—which, again, hardly savours of an open, inclusive and public-spirited institution. But the taxation position of the BCCI resonates with the philosophical dilemma of all modern cricket administrations, which can be condensed to a single question: does cricket make money in order to exist, or does it exist in order to make money?

Cricket in its history has done both, sometimes simultaneously, although generally one or the other predominates. When English cricketers first came to Australia 150 years ago, it was primarily to make money; when Australian cricketers began reciprocating those visits, it was chiefly to satisfy a colonial longing to express both rivalry and fealty. Generally speaking, however, the boards of control that came to administer international cricket in the first half of the twentieth century ran rather like the cricket clubs that provided their governance models, treating money as a means to an end rather than an end in itself. They did not build up reserves; they did not acquire assets; they did not even seek to maximise returns. On the last of these, in fact, did the diffusion of cricket depend. Had return on funds employed been a paramount concern to Australia and England, they would simply have played each other every year. There was a general acceptance that spreading the game was A Good

Thing—even if it was not always done with grace and judgement, or without a whiff of condescension. Nor was this creed honoured without a certain hypocritical piety, for honorary administrators believing themselves best placed to judge what constituted cricket's benefit looked severely on players agitating for better-than-subsistence incomes. If there was an end, however, it was chiefly that of national honour: on-field success, particularly in Test cricket. And the surprising aspect of this model is that, although some boards knew financial exigencies and some players led hardscrabble existences, there was always enough money to go round.

Everyone can suggest a date when this model bumped into modernity: 1963, with the abolition of amateurism; 1977, with the incursion of Packer; 1987, with the coming of the World Cup to the Subcontinent; 1995, when the Indian supreme court freed the BCCI from the archaic *Telegraph Act* to sell broadcasting rights to the highest bidders. But a very deep Rubicon was clearly crossed when the BCCI invited corporates to participate directly in the commercial exploitation of Indian cricket by owning IPL franchises, essentially issuing them licences to participate in a massively lucrative oligopoly. Reliance, Indian Cements, Kingfisher, Deccan Chronicle and other owners are not solely motivated by profit: ego, vanity, competitiveness, a gluttony for glamour and even a spirit of adventure play a part. But a philanthropic concern with the long-term welfare of cricket? Would these companies have invested in franchises whose value they expected to dwindle? And even if you did not regard IPL as about the enrichment of a privileged commercial and media elite rather than cricket per se, the idea of the BCCI operating with charitable intent is so preposterous that only ... well ... a well-heeled tax lawyer could argue it.

Yet these questions should not only be piled at the BCCI's door. There isn't a cricket board in the world reluctant to prostitute itself to Twenty20, with the most aggressive being those who need the money least: the England Cricket Board, happy to snuggle up to any spiv with a big billfold and a new helicopter, and Cricket Australia, eager to squeeze the Sheffield Shield for the sake of an even Bigger Bash. The BCCI at least had a rival, the Indian Cricket

League, to counteract; the ECB and CA have no such rationale, except for some glib management-speak about 'growing the game', building 'new markets' and tapping 'cricket consumers', whereupon expenditure will presumably rise to meet income. To the question of how much money cricket needs in England and Australia, the answer seems to be: always more. This is the logic of late capitalism mouthed unthinkingly; mixed with vestiges of muddle-headed paternalism and sentimentality, it persuades administrators that they are somehow acting in 'cricket's best interests'.

Running cricket in the era of KPIs and TRPs is a great deal more complicated than in the days when what mattered was winning the next match, the next series, the next tour. The temptation to set great store by perceived financial acumen is a great one—it provides a straight answer to the straight question of 'how are we doing'? In fact, in key business disciplines such as disclosure, corporate governance, financial controls, strategic planning and contractual fidelity, the administration of cricket worldwide is generally abysmal. Until a week ago, the most recent set of ICC accounts on its website was for the year of 2007; there are now three cursory pages for 2008. But when the Pakistan Cricket Board and the West Indies Cricket Board are among your rivals, it's not that difficult to look good by comparison.

All the same, the game's administration is becoming so absorbed in what it is doing that the reasons it is doing it seem to be slipping from consideration. It takes a reality check from a disinterested observer, in this case India's tax authorities, to convey the essence of change, as distinct from the fact of it. And for all that he perceived a 'little bit of the whore in all of us', Packer himself grasped that not everything of value could be priced. What, an interviewer once tackled him, would he have given to represent Australia at sport? A million dollars? A billion dollars? 'Anything', he said. Nobody had to ask him whether that was before tax or after tax.

CLUB V COUNTRY

T20 Nation

In 1921, the American journalist Lincoln Steffens returned home from a visit to the Soviet Union with a spring in his step and a famous line on his lips: 'I have seen the future and it works'. Cricket's equivalent nowadays is a study of the IPL. The headline of a foretelling of cricket's future by Mike Atherton, published in *Wisden Cricketer* in January 2010, is unequivocal: 'Club v Country? No contest'.

Atherton is, to my mind, the game's premier analyst, speaking with the authority of 100 Tests, not to mention ten O-Levels, three A-levels and a BA (Cantab). When he concludes that 'international cricket will eventually be superseded by club cricket', we are bound to listen. His argument, typically considered, is that while countries are constrained by the talent within their borders, 'clubs can sign whomever they wish, from wherever, finances and availability allowing'. Thus: 'Over time competitiveness, which is at the heart of good sport, is much easier to maintain'.

Atherton is not the first to so prophesy. Some, especially those who have deplored what they see as sport's tendency to nationalist excesses, have already celebrated the rise of the franchise-owned club as the game's chief organising unit in the twenty-first century. No less than the former under-secretary-general of the United Nations, Shashi Tharoor, looks on the IPL as cricket's proverbial melting pot, blurring former allegiances and dissolving old antagonisms: 'Thanks to the mixture of nationalities in each of the IPL teams, partisanship has suddenly lost its chauvinist flavour. In the IPL, the past poses no impediment to the future'.

Peter Roebuck has foreseen and welcomed the substitution of the values of the corporation for those of the country: 'The ICC will be more important after the franchises have taken over domestic cricket because it will be empowered not by self-centred countries but by businessmen with high expectations. Free from impossible responsibilities and the petty politicking that mars this most ungovernable of games, it will focus on matters of discipline and co-operation'.

Interesting—and such wise judges are right to note the tectonic shift the IPL represents. Yet there's something familiar about such sentiments, maybe even ironic, given the liberal dispositions of the commentators involved. The inefficiency of the state; the purifying efficacy of competition; the fundamental rationality of free enterprise: is there not here a nostalgic waft of 1980s economic dogma—Reaganomics, Thatcherism, call it what you will? The 1980s also saw all manner of prophecies about the necessity of dismantling public institutions, empowering private capital, and the general global globalness of globalism. How odd, meanwhile, to hear such pronouncements regarding cricket at a time when they are so deeply out of fashion in economic policy circles, when the American government owns the bulk of the country's auto industry, the British government runs a sizeable chunk of the country's banking industry, and France's Nicolas Sarkozy has declared that the global financial crisis presages 'the return of the state, the end of the ideology of public powerlessness'.

Nor is the IPL, involving the socialist principle of a salary cap and the protectionist mechanism of quotas, perhaps the best example of a market left flourishingly to its own devices and dynamics. As for those 'businessmen with high expectations' focused on 'discipline and cooperation', this does not reconcile easily with stories of corporate babble in the boardrooms, Rolexes scattered in the dressing rooms, US$600000 paid for Mashrafe Mortaza, and Australian cricket's man of the moment, Cameron White, not representing his franchise at all during the IPL's second season.

Leaving aside for a moment the principle of private ownership, which involves another set of issues altogether, the club model has a great deal to recommend it. Indeed, one can hardly argue the contrary. The club is, after all, the basis of cricket everywhere, long predating the nation, and even the county, state and province, as a unit of cricket competition. With a bit of imagination you can draw a line of descent from the Bat and Ball Inn's corporate sponsorship of Hambledon to Kingfisher's ownership of the Bangalore Royal Challengers, even if the soi-disant 'King of Good Times', Vijay Mallya, has yet to emulate Richard Nyren by mixing punch to 'make a cat speak'. So does the reinvention of 'the club' via the medium of the multimillion-dollar franchise prelude in cricket the eclipse of the nation?

For the most convincing counterargument, it is useful to recall the world three years ago, when the BCCI was still resisting Twenty20 for fear of endangering the golden calf that was one-day international cricket. One impetus for the IPL is generally well understood: the irruption of Subhash Chandra's Indian Cricket League, which looked like bringing Twenty20 to India anyway, and potentially cornering the market. The other impetus tends to be forgotten: India's defeats, by Bangladesh and Sri Lanka, in the 2007 World Cup, which sent the team reeling from the tournament before the Super Eights stage. Bad as this was for Rahul Dravid's team, and also Greg Chappell's coaching career, it was a calamity for those broadcasters, sponsors and advertisers on the Subcontinent who had priced their investments in the tournament on the assumption of prolonged Indian involvement.

Lalit Modi was a man whose time had come, having conceived of a tournament in which India was guaranteed participation right the way through. When MS Dhoni's ensemble prevailed in the World Twenty20 in South Africa, the argument could also be made that the IPL was somehow the best of the best—even if that contention has since been belied by India's poor showing in last year's World Twenty20 and the abject failure of IPL teams, despite home ground advantage and friendly schedules, in the subsequent Champions League.

With this understanding, the formulation of 'club v country' can be seen as simplistic. Far from 'partisanship having lost its chauvinist flavour', as Tharoor argues, the IPL is nationalism's ultimate triumph: a global tournament in which the same nation always wins. Indeed, the IPL is in India a national champion like the computer services giants Infosys, Wipro and TCS, bringing pangs of patriotic pride as it outdoes the world's best. 'I am extremely proud that whatever we have seen over the last 44 days is a product of India', said Sharad Pawar at the first final. 'It [IPL] is a global representation of India, and what the modern day India stands for and its successes', added Modi. When the tournament was relocated to South Africa in its second season, in fact, its Indianess was somehow emphasised, by lying so lightly on the landscape while simultaneously effacing the location beneath.

At the player auction for the third IPL, the nation won again, with the franchises unanimously shunning players from Pakistan, many of whom had been invaluable in the first IPL before their exclusion from the sequel after the horrors of the Mumbai attacks. This was not economically rational behaviour in a borderless world: at US$200 000, for example, Shahid Afridi was a snip. But the franchise owners were unwilling to wager their popularity on the market and/or political acceptability of Pakistani players. Where the BCCI, to their considerable credit, could see a greater good served by the resumption of cricket relations with the Pakistan Cricket Board in 2004, the IPL's self-serving cartel had no such wider or deeper focus: no sense of symbolism, no notion of the good of the game, and no goal greater than pleasing the financiers by not running the risk of displeasing the fans. In doing so, the perceptive Ashok Malik argued in *The Pioneer*, they have paradoxically served the ends of India's Ministry of External Affairs, demonstrating 'cricket's potential for coercive diplomacy'.

> The IPL franchises have placed the equivalent of an economic embargo on Pakistan. India has very little leverage—political or socio-economic—within Pakistan and its ability to 'impose costs' in the face of provocation is limited. The IPL boycott

of Pakistan, the income loss to individual cricketers and the open snubbing of that country's cricket community, represents just such an 'imposition of costs'. This has been done by civil society. Yet, it would be foolish to expect Indian diplomacy not to use it to its advantage.

The contention that the IPL somehow leads us to the sunny uplands of a post-nationalist cricket utopia, then, lacks force. Indeed, one is left to wonder exactly what the IPL's admirers in this context find so objectionable about nationalism as cricket expresses it. To be sure, George Orwell famously described international sport as 'war minus the shooting'. But for all Orwell's greatness as a thinker, this was one of his least felicitous lines, analogous to murder minus the death or life minus the breathing. Yes, follies and frictions can occur when countries clash head to head in sport, but international cricket's impacts have been, by most standards, almost overwhelmingly benign: we still talk about Bodyline and the Stop the 70 Tour campaign because they are exceptional, not character-istic. One could even argue that cricket in this postcolonial age is worryingly lacking a nationalist edge. West Indies v New Zealand? Sri Lanka v South Africa? Afghanistan v Ireland? Compared with such rivalries, it's no wonder that the IPL, with its hyperbolic promotions and hypertrophic team names, seems to represent a veritable clash of civilisations.

'Club v country'? For sure, the club may well be the face of the future, but behind it will always lurk the country—which is not going anywhere. And if the IPL does represent a recrudescence of nationalism beneath a corporate veneer, it is perfectly possible that the future we have seen will not work at all as we imagine.

Seriously Cricket Chronicles, February 2010

INDIAN PREMIER LEAGUE 3

All a Twitter

Shane Warne has given his view on the best innings he has ever seen. Having bowled to Tendulkar and Lara in their pomp, to Laxman and Dravid in Calcutta, having watched Steve Waugh in Antigua and Adam Gilchrist in Johannesburg, he has nonetheless opted for ... Yusuf Pathan's hundred for the Rajasthan Royals against the Mumbai Indians in the IPL at Brabourne Stadium in March 2010.

From the greatest bowler of his generation, such pronouncements are bound to be noticed, especially as Warne is already on record—or, at least, on Twitter—as confirming that the zenith of his career was the Royals' victory in the inaugural IPL. This was during an exchange of mutual endearments with the IPL's equally tweet-happy impresario, Lalit Modi.

Actually, it's one of Warne's most admirable characteristics that he is so liberal with his praise. With age can come the attitude that all was better in one's own day; Warne might be on the far side of forty and only plays six weeks a year, but the day, he feels, is still his. One with ample reason to dwell in the past is uncompromisingly a man of the present.

These days, however, Warne is a veritable praise machine, spreading the gospel of IPL to parts far and near. In the recent snafu over security concerns in India, it was Warne, alongside Matthew Hayden and Adam Gilchrist, who argued against his former captain Ricky Ponting, his erstwhile spin twin Tim May and their old joint interest the Australian Cricketers' Association. When the Royals unveiled their Royals 2020 venture with Hampshire, the Cape Cobras and Trinidad and Tobago in London in February, Warne was the senior spruiker: 'I am delighted to be part of this new innovation, and I am excited by what we can achieve, given what we have already achieved. Yet again, the Royals are leading the way'.

So what to make of Warne's encomium for Pathan? Firstly, it makes little sense. Pathan batted for 37 balls. The bowlers of which he took greatest toll, on a storied but small ground seating only 20 000, were Ryan McLaren, Rajagopal Satish, Ali Murtaza and Sanath Jayasuriya. His team lost. When Warne said of taking on Tendulkar that 'it was a pleasure to bowl to him', it was a meaningful and heartfelt tribute. Exalting Pathan was simply succumbing to the tumescence of the moment—a sensation, of course, to which Warne is not exactly a stranger.

Yet there is more to it than that, for Warne's views mesh perfectly with the general IPL communications strategy, conveyed alike in its advertising and its commentary, sometimes indistinguishable in their hucksterism: that *this is it*, and the rest of cricket simply does not exist; or that cricket began two years ago, when Modi whipped it into shape from the drawn-out and economically inefficient activity it had been for a century and more.

That is certainly Modi's self-perception. 'Either we innovate and bring in new fans,' he told *The Times* last week, 'or we don't innovate and we let the sport die'. There is something more than a little messianic about this, with its inference that cricket was devoid of innovation and in danger of dying before the IPL—one half-expects Modi to start paraphrasing Lt William Calley, and urging that it will be necessary to destroy cricket in order to save it.

It's arguable that, for all the entrepreneurship unleashed in India, cricket globally was actually in better shape two years ago; there were certainly some boards of control, like Pakistan's and the West Indies', in ruder financial health than they are now. And for all its reputation for conservatism, cricket in its history has demonstrated a remarkable capacity for innovation. What game has survived subjection to such extraordinary manipulations, having been prolonged to ten days (in Durban seventy years ago), truncated to as few at 60 balls (in Hong Kong every year), and remained recognisable in each instance?

One keeps looking out for innovation in the IPL, but of late it hasn't been all that obvious. Lionel Richie as an opening act? Johnny Mathis must have been busy. Matthew Hayden's Mongoose? Looks a bit like Bob Willis' bat with the 'flow-through holes'; Saint Peter batting mitts are surely overdue a revival. The only genuinely intriguing step this year, bringing the IPL to YouTube, was forced on Modi by the collapse of Setanta; otherwise, what Modi presents as 'innovation' is merely expansion by another name, in the number of franchises and the number of games.

There's certainly fun to be had in the IPL. The players are doing their best, and with so many high-class cricketers there is always the chance of seeing a sublime stroke—a Dravid cover drive or a Gilchrist pick-up, and you could hardly not enjoy watching Yusuf Pathan hit the ball to infinity. But calling it 'great' or the 'best ever' made as much sense as saying the same of a pop video. The risk is, as ever, that the cricket in the IPL will simply become a pretext for celebrity circle jerking; perhaps the members of the IPL's cheer squad should stop listening to each other and start listening to themselves.

Cricinfo, April 2010

THE FALL OF LALIT MODI

Transparent Lies

In the aftermath of the first final of the IPL in 2008, its impresario, Lalit Modi, had no doubt what the event embodied. 'It [IPL] is a global representation of India,' he argued, 'and what the modern day India stands for and its successes'.

Modi was right then, and he is still pretty right now, except that how it represents India is assuredly rather different. In the heady days of that first tournament, it stood for India's vitality, imagination and economic heft; if even a fraction of the allegations recently aired are true, it shows the country at its corrupt and dysfunctional worst.

'What must you think of us in Australia?' emailed an Indian friend last week—an unanticipated role reversal given the recent state of Indian–Australian relations. The good news, I assured him, is that we do little thinking here, at least in the sports pages. During the biggest cricket story in a decade, football-obsessed newspapers in my home town have been delving in depth into such big issues as 'Is Jonathan Brown as Good as Wayne Carey?' and 'The Return of the Power Forward'.

A strapline in *The Age* last week shrieked of 'Sport's Greatest Scandal', but it referred, *horribile dictu*, to a salary cap breach by the local rugby league team. 'Sport's Greatest Scandal'? Dear God, it wasn't even sport's greatest scandal *of the day*. The IPL? Oh, there was some coverage when a bomb went off in Bangalore with all the force of a car backfiring and an Australian cricketer in the same postcode might have had his hair mussed or spilt his margarita, because that fitted with the cliché of violent, unpredictable, scary Asia; but when Indian turbocapitalism meets Indian Realpolitik, it's all a little esoteric for the average Australian sports editor—and they are *so very* average.

Yet here was a story that everyone should have seen coming. On the eve of the first tournament, I prophesised on the ABC's *Offsiders* that the IPL would be rocked within five years by a corruption scandal that would 'knock Hansie Cronje into a cocked helmet'. But that's not to claim great foresight. It simply stood to reason. Opaque finances, negligible regulation, a host of related party transactions, asset valuations plucked from thin air, an overmighty chief executive, supine non-executive directors, politicians already with their hooks in—here were all the preconditions of Enron, if one did but recognise them. To fail to grasp that, you needed to be either ignorant or implicated—alas, rather too many kiss-arse commentators and columnists were both.

Now, of course, they're all feigning outrage, like Captain Renault in *Casablanca*: 'I am shocked, *shocked*, to find gambling going on this establishment'. 'Get Off the Front Page', read the headline on Harsha Bhogle's say-nothing column for Cricinfo. But why? The front page is an excellent discipline. Jamie Dimon, boss of JP Morgan Chase, the only American bank to come away from the global financial crisis with reputation enhanced, tells his staff that they should undertake no financial transaction they wouldn't be happy to see described on the front page of the *New York Times*. And the front page is *exactly* where the IPL belongs.

The magic word is now *transparency*—transparency will apparently set us free. But transparency where? The owners are only one constituency. Will the commentators be forced to declare their interests? Will the journalists have to reveal their connections? Will the various state governments be compelled to divulge the extent of their subsidies to the IPL in the form of grounds, facilities and taxation relief? Will the state associations that compose the BCCI be required to lay open their finances to public scrutiny? Will the BCCI make its elections genuinely democratic?

The truth is that genuine transparency in the IPL has been impossible from the inception because of its adoption of a private ownership model. You know why they call it 'private ownership'? Because *it's private*.

In fact, as Shashank Manohar reminded Modi when he tweeted the night away about the equity holders in the new Kochi franchise, conditions of confidentiality are integral to commercial transactions. You might not like this, but it is the way of business. And if business has imposed its values on the IPL, that's only because it was invited, even entreated, to do so, in order that the maximum sums be extracted from the sale of franchises. Face it: the moneychangers aren't *in the temple*; they were sold the keys *to the temple*, and since then they've changed the locks.

Coverage of the story in India has dwelt in exhaustive detail on the money sluiced through numerous entities in Mauritius. Yet almost half of the foreign direct investment in India comes through Mauritius, because it has a tax treaty with India and insignificant corporate tax rates, and members of the Indian elite also use it freely, clearly subscribing to the view of New York property diva Leona Helmsley that 'only little people pay tax'. As a prophetic article in *Africa-Asia Confidential* explains:

> Round-tripping via Mauritius involves the use of the *1983 Double Tax Avoidance Agreement* (DTAA), a tax holiday advantage provided by Mauritius and other tax havens, to re-route money transferred illegally out of India. The illicit funds are then transferred back to India as legitimate foreign investment in the Mumbai stock market via participatory notes. These 'P-Notes' are used by overseas investors not registered with Indian regulators, allowing them to acquire shares anonymously, which triggers allegations of widespread money laundering. Much of the money invested through P-Notes is legal and comes from sources like hedge funds, which seek to benefit from the non-taxation of capital gains on Indian stocks bought in Mauritius, but Indian officials worry because they cannot separate the good money from the bad.

So even if more exacting disclosure requirements were introduced, they would be facile to avoid: throw enough investment bankers, corporate lawyers and tax accountants at a corporate structure and any trace of beneficial ownership can be effaced. In pursuing its franchise dream, then, Indian cricket laid itself open to becoming a vehicle for tax minimisation and money laundering. This just took longer to dawn on some people than others.

Why? This, perhaps, is the most intriguing question of all. The IPL exercised strict controls over its coverage, suborning some, excluding others, demanding an atmosphere of constant celebration, deriding doubters as rheumy-eyed romantics. Modi moved fast—faster, sometimes, than the eye could see. He was the chairman of the IPL's fourteen-member governing council, but came to be called the 'IPL commissioner', in imitation of that role in American professional sport. The distinction was more than semantic. A chairman implies consultation; 'commissioner' implies ... well ... committing, which Modi clearly did, to a fault. Courtiers as considerable as Ravi Shastri and Sunil Gavaskar competed to praise him. Possible party poopers, like the ICC Anti-Corruption Unit, were held at arms-length. No wonder Modi operated in an atmosphere of impunity. And no wonder rumour and innuendo accumulated around the IPL when it showed so little interest in giving a proper account of itself.

Modi's modus operandi was to keep doubling the bets on his own charisma, and, indeed, the story of his triumph enjoyed widespread appeal. Here was the personification of India Shining, bringing moolah and market forces to a game that, so the story went, had previously languished in the dead hands of Anglo-Australian overlords. In fact, India has been the most significant force in global cricket for a decade, but until then the IPL may have kept that fact from itself; the league became an annual celebration of that development for Modi's countrymen and a few well-paid guests. About its second- and third-order effects on cricket, the impact on other countries ... well, who cared? *They* were having fun. And how could all those DLF Maximums and Citi Moments of Success be wrong?

My friend Sambit Bal of Cricinfo may be right that this is a scandal the IPL needed. It certainly brings fans face-to-face with the tangled reality of their amusement, based as it is on a self-seeking, self-perpetuating commercial oligopoly issued licenses to exploit cricket as they please. Whether the fans care is another matter: one of the reasons Indians have embraced economic liberalisation so fervently is a shoulder-shrugging resignation about the efficiency and integrity of their institutions. Given the choice between Lalit Modi, with his snappy suits and his soi-disant 'Indian People's League', and the BCCI, stuffed with grandstanding politicians and crony capitalists, where would your loyalties lie?

And if Modi *is* toast, it will in one sense be a tremendous pity. In his way, he represents a third generation in cricket's governance. For a hundred years and more, cricket was run by administrators, who essentially maintained the game without going out of their way to develop it. More recently it has been run by managers, with just an ounce or two of strategic thought. Modi was neither; he was instead a genuine entrepreneur. He has as much feeling for cricket as Madonna has for madrigals but, perhaps because he came from outside cricket's traditional bureaucratic circles, brought a vision and a common touch unexampled since Kerry Packer. It's arguable, in fact, that the more culpable in this affair are the likes of Sharad Pawar and Inderjit Bindra, allegedly wise heads who pandered to Modi's ego and ambition because it suited their particular purposes. The clock is now ticking for the fourth IPL. It may look quite different to the third—indeed, it had better.

Seriously Cricket Chronicles, May 2010

THE FALL OF LALIT MODI

Brand from the Burning

When Lalit Modi came to the podium after the final of the third IPL with minutes ticking away on his reign, he had what few administrators at presentation ceremonies can claim to have enjoyed: a captive audience. What would it be? You won't have Modi to kick around anymore, à la Richard Nixon? Old BCCI vice-presidents never die, they just fade away, à la Douglas MacArthur?

Not quite, although Modi, for him, flirted with rhetoric: 'Indian People's League … I have lived a dream … Humble servant of the game'. Then there was the quote from the *Bhagavad Gita*, which some oblivious viewers may have mistaken for another sponsor (coming soon: the Mahabharata Moment of Success). Finally, there came a defiant roar: 'We should not allow this brand to be diluted *and we will not*'.

What Modi meant, of course, was that nothing should be permitted to harm the IPL's reputation, although that he dropped so easily into the jargon of Marketing 101 shows how thoroughly this patois now pervades sport. Manchester United. New York Yankees. Chicago Bulls. If you still think of them merely as sporting clubs, you are *so* five minutes ago: they're brands, ripe for extending, leveraging, repositioning and spinning off from. As for diluting said brand … well, it's equivalent as a commercial taboo to stepping on Elvis' Blue Suede Shoes. Knock me down, step in my face, slander my name all over the place … just don't dilute my brand.

Since inception, the IPL has worn its brand value like a corroboration of inner virtue. On the eve of this tournament, under the headline 'Brand IPL touches the sky', the league's website reverberated with the announcement that Brand Finance, a branding consultancy, had valued the brand value of the IPL brand at US$4.13 billion worth of brand—which is a lot of brand, brandwise.

Indian breasts swelled with pride. Here, at last, a country which had traditionally imported sporting brands had built one of its very own.

How Brand Finance arrived at that figure was unexplained, of course, because such exercises, involving as they do mainly guesswork, marketing mumbo jumbo and a few spreadsheets for appearance's sake, rejoice in their sense of magic, the illusion of money conjured from nothing by gee-whiz branding gurus. In the case of the IPL, of course, Modi started with rather more than nothing. There was already a deep and abiding Indian passion for the game built over generations which, with the backing of an entrenched monopoly for its promotion, he set to exploiting— although to mention that runs the risk of spoiling the illusion.

Since Modi's Mumbai sign-off, much of the commentary has been focused on the brand dilution potential inherent in its scandals. MS Dhoni doesn't think we should worry: 'IPL as a brand can survive on its own'. Shilpa Shetty, 'brand ambassador' of the Rajasthan Royals, tweets that we should: 'Custodians of Cricket must not hamper d Brandvalue of this viable sport'. Hampering d Brandvalue, insists new IPL boss Chirayu Amin, is the furthest thing from his mind: 'IPL's brand image is strong and nobody can touch that'. Harsha Bhogle, however, frets for the nation: 'Within the cricket world, Brand India will take a hit'.

Not much more than a week after Modi's first tell-all tweets, the media was anxiously consulting Brand Finance's managing director, Unni Krishnan. Had there been any brand dilution yet? It was, said the soothsayer gravely, 'too early to say'. He could, however, confirm the following: 'The wealth that can be created by the brand is going to be substantially significant for many stakeholders. A conducive ecosystem has to be created to move the brand to the next level ... We have to build the requisite bandwidth to monetise these opportunities'. Errrr, yeah ... what he said. Anyway, placing a value on the IPL brand has clearly been quite beneficial to Brand Finance's brand—it's obviously an ill wind that blows no brand any good.

What's missing from these bromides of the brandscape is any sense that there is a game involved, that cricket might be at risk of sustaining collateral damage. Ten years ago, the spectre of match-fixing caused fans to despair of the damage to their beloved game; some of us still can't look at cricket in quite the same way. The assumption now is that the interests of the brand and of the game overlap to the degree that cricket need hardly be mentioned.

But do they overlap so exactly? A game is a cultural activity, operating at myriad levels, all of which need to be maintained, nurtured, protected. In the world of the brand, all that really matters is the face shown the public, the spectacle, the image. A game depends on fair dealing, robust processes and good people prepared to place their individual interests second. A brand requires nothing of the kind. Both a game and a brand are at reputational risk, but in the case of a brand only the appearance of respectability and integrity is essential, and that can be achieved, or so it is usually felt, by sound media management, and at worst post-hoc damage control. Nike runners produced in Asian sweatshops? Not a problem ... unless it affects sales. Tiger Woods a compulsive, multiple adulterer? Better try keeping it quiet ... lest 'Brand Tiger' be imperilled.

So this is not a problem confined to the IPL or India. It applies wherever sport meets big corporate interests and, these days, that means everywhere. Australia, moreover, has little to teach anyone on this subject. Consider this country's scandal of the moment, involving the National Rugby League and its premier team, the Melbourne Storm. The Storm, vanguard of the code's push into the south, has been stripped of honours after the revelation it has been systematically and fraudulently breaching the NRL's salary cap limitations.

Salary cap rorts are a common Australian phenomenon; the attitude to them recalls the philosophy popularly applied to gays in the US military: 'Don't ask, don't tell'. The Melbourne Storm CEO implicated in this particular debacle argues that 'everyone does it'; 92 per cent of respondents to an online poll last week agreed. But the NRL declines to widen or deepen its investigations because, frankly, the stakes are too high; better to scapegoat one club *pour encourager les autres*. The situation is exacerbated by the NRL being half-owned by Rupert Murdoch's News Corporation, which has no interest in the scandal worsening because of the risk of further dilution of its hard-won brand.

Has something similar happened in the IPL? One of the more candid critiques of events has been provided by MAK Pataudi, member of the governing council that either knew everything and did nothing (by Modi's account), or knew nothing and will henceforward do everything (by its own). According to Pataudi, he and his fellow council members simply assumed 'things were okay'; indeed, they were 'carried away with how well everything was going'. Then this: 'I saw the crowds, the IPL was very popular … the dirt that has been attached to it is sad … but as long as the product was good, I was happy'. When one of Indian cricket's greats attends a game and simply sees a 'product', then the brand truly has become a graven idol. But, then, it's perhaps not so surprising. So transfixed has the BCCI been by its own commercial prowess over the last three years that agencies with the potential to impede have been held at a haughty arms-length. Move along, ICC Anti-Corruption Unit. There's nothing to see here, World Anti-Doping Agency. Don't bother us now—we're busy brand-building.

The brand mentality is now at odds with the thorough investigation that cricket surely needs. The BCCI will be anxious to contain the damage, to look nowhere it does not absolutely have to, and to place as much blue water between itself and Modi as possible. Because to a brand, as distinct from a game, administrative corruption is no biggie, providing it remains out of sight. Crooked players? That would be a party-pooping diluter. But do IPL fans care about conflict of interest and nepotism, about free-floating facilitation fees and freely given sweat equity? Well, certainly not if they don't hear about it. A slightly seedy reputation? That can be lived with. Some have already conjectured that an aura of sleaze will invest the IPL with further tawdry glamour. 'What drama and sleaze', said 'social scientist' Shiv Visvanathan, quoted recently in the *Times of India*. 'People don't go to watch Modi. They go to watch Dhoni and Tendulkar ... It's a delight to see someone like Modi next to a clean Tendulkar.' Dawood Ibrahim—your D Company franchise is ready.

Where's cricket in all this? Good question. Because if that US$4 billion of brand is scraped away, somewhere beneath lies a worldwide game whose value cannot be priced, even by the mavens of Brand Finance. The BCCI, then, has a grave responsibility—a responsibility that's actually greater than simply protecting an oh-so-valuable brand from the unspeakable horrors of dilution.

Cricinfo, May 2010

AN ENGLISH IPL?

Anyone for Cricketainment?

To extract the maximum hilarity from the email of Yorkshire chief executive Stewart Regan to his fellow county bosses, imagine it read with the accent of one of PG Wodehouse's upper-class nincompoops. 'The IPL model relies heavily on "star players" and this is why they have been so successful', pants Regan. 'Matches include fashion shows, after-match parties and entertainment. They have launched the word "CRICKETAINMENT" which I think is really innovative.'

I say, that Lalit Modi, a jolly clever fellow, eh? He's launched a whole new word, dontcha know? In India, they have 'star players' and what-not. You can't miss what Wodehouse called the 'certain what-is-it' in Regan's voice. Here's someone who seems to have just found out that cricket concerns more than the forward defensive stroke. Perhaps this is news in Yorkshire, where they proverbially don't play for fun, tha knows. But is it any wonder that Modi looks like a genius when he keeps this sort of company?

Let's just refresh our memories. Because Twenty20 cricket actually started in England in 2003 and attracted no interest in India for the next four years. Indeed, the BCCI regarded the game's new variant with distinct unease. They had a nice fat fifty-over racket running: why endanger it with anything 'really innovative'? If anyone can be credited with the idea of 'cricketainment', it's the England Cricket Board's marketing director, Stuart Robertson, who enticed the ambivalent with all manner of entertainment epiphenomena—as enumerated by Hugh Chevallier in *Wisden*:

Jacuzzis, fairground rides, bouncy castles, face painting, barbecue zones, boy bands, girl bands—you name it, it was there as a sideshow. Rather more in your face were the banks of loudspeakers blaring out frequent musical snatches—'I don't like cricket, I love it!' from 10CC (remixed for our times by the United Colours of Sound) greeted boundaries, while Queen's 'Another One Bites the Dust' taunted dismissed batsmen as they sprinted for the dug-out.

And credit where credit is due—bank credit, mainly, in his case—but nobody outcricketained Allen Stanford at Coolidge, with his carnivals, mobile discos, and hot and cold running WAGs. 'The purists lose sight of that', lectured Stanford. 'It's entertainment, that's it ... Dancing, music, Twenty20, this is the way we play it, for entertainment.' So it's a strange oversight for someone like Regan, suddenly so smitten with 'fashion shows, after-match parties and entertainment', for he is actually detecting innovation exactly where it is not. The IPL does not succeed because of Modi's much-vaunted 'cricketainment'. It prospers because India has an economy finally growing fast enough to improve standards of living for its 1.2 billion people, and because cricket is one of the few passions those people share, thus providing corporations with access to the country's growing consumer markets. You could scrap the fashion parades and celebrity self-celebration tomorrow—indeed, the BCCI has foreshadowed just that—and the IPL would be just as big, possibly bigger.

Where Modi was genuinely innovative was in the matter of private ownership: that is, he basically bypassed the state associations composing the BCCI and sold franchises to big businesses and venture capitalists. But before English counties sign up for a system from which they extract a fifth of gross revenues, essentially running their game on the crumbs from the rich man's table, perhaps they should compare notes with the Indian state associations currently complaining about the two-thirds of three-eighths of not very much they're deriving from the IPL. 'They are absolutely convinced we are sitting on a goldmine!' chortles the excitable Regan in his email; it might just as easily be a shaft.

There's all manner of strains in the structure of English first-class cricket. It's hard to blame counties, however previously hidebound, for seeking solutions wherever they might emerge. But they have picked a peculiar moment to get religion. It is difficult to believe, too, that they truckled so cringingly to Modi during a meeting in which, if the minutes are to be believed, he advocated that IPL franchises simply desert official cricket 'if governing bodies try to block the development of IPL20', and talked freely of usurping the ICC's role by staging 'IPL Tests and ODIs', relying chiefly on the greed of players to achieve his ends. Oh, who cares if it helps us save county cricket, eh?

What's particularly striking about Regan's communiqué, however, is not its cloying naivety, but its utter defeatism. It is swept up in the IPL fiction that cricket is really a bit of a naff old relic, and thank goodness Lalit Modi arrived in the nick of time with 'cricketainment' to save it from itself. Does anyone talk about 'footballtainment' or 'golftainment'? No, because football and golf are confident enough of their own intrinsic excellence not to need 'fashion shows, after-match parties and entertainment', or at least not to treat such juvenilia as evidence of Mensa-esque cleverness. Only cricket suffers from administrators who feel so frustrated by the game with which they have been entrusted that they must constantly be manhandling and mangling it in order to wring out an extra dollar.

Modi has at least the redeeming feature of a vision with a certain epic grandeur—*folie de grandeur*, anyway. It betrays the decadence of English cricket administration that its proudest county is now run by a desperate coat-tail rider like Regan. Time was when cricket administration was the preserve of rattletrap reactionaries so besotted with the game they would rather it rot than reform. Now it seems dominated by a caste who essentially wish they were doing something else, something with a bit more glamour, celebrity and money, and hanker to change cricket into a product more congenial to them, airily invoking 'the fans', but largely in their own interests.

To be fair, one can sympathise with the counties' position, even if the malaise is largely of their own making. Nor is there anything wrong in cricket with a feeling for social change, a spirit of adaptation and even a touch of disgruntlement. But one would wish its governors started from an attitude to their game, again to borrow from Wodehouse, rather more gruntled.

Cricinfo, May 2010

THE GOVERNANCE OF CRICKET

Officers' Mess

The title under which Cricinfo began aggregating its coverage of l'affaire Modi in April 2010 was a spontaneous decision, but would now be hard to improve: 'The IPL Mess'. The affair carries the hallmarks of scandal, it has threatened to become a meltdown, but of its characteristics as a mess there can be no dispute.

One of the more delicious stories to emerge, in a recent edition of the *Times of India*, was that the BCCI was forbidding employees from taking work home, not out of a noble commitment to work–life balance, but because they were afraid of still more documentation going astray. Profound significance was attached to Lalit Modi disgorging 15 000 pages of IPL material to the BCCI, but what was significant surely was that it had to be disgorged in the first place: Modi was seeking credit for surrendering to the BCCI its own documentation. Huh?

Of course, we now also know that the IPL governing councillors didn't believe it was their job to handle this information. Ravi Shastri has complained that his role was to 'ask cricket questions', which makes it sound like he thought he was quizmaster at a trivia night. The BCCI's chief executive, Shashank Manohar, was only half-right when he complained: 'An institution functions on trust'. Better is the philosophy that Ronald Reagan applied to the Soviet Union, which also fits an institutional framework snugly: 'Trust but verify'. The BCCI approach of 'trust then panic and blame' would disgrace a corner store, let alone an enterprise like the IPL which, as we're often reminded, is a brand worth not US\$4.12 billion or US\$4.14 billion but US\$4.13 billion—a branding consultancy said so.

If Modi and the BCCI *do* part ways, it is unlikely to be chiefly because of a dubious facilitation fee or a rigged franchise auction, but fundamentally because they can no longer work together, assuming they ever really did: the 'behavioural pattern' part of the charge sheet. Such a parting would actually be perfectly defensible. 'I just don't like you', explained Henry Ford II on sacking Lee Iacocca, the most celebrated auto executive of his generation, soon after Ford Motor Company had posted a US\$2 billion profit in 1978. There was no question of the competence or integrity of Graham Halbish when he was booted out as chief executive of Cricket Australia in 1997; he simply could not coexist with his chairman, Denis Rogers.

Modi has complained of being 'public enemy number one' at the BCCI for some time; indeed, he might well have been ousted from his position last December, remaining only on the understanding he cooperate more closely with Manohar. That this was allowed to continue beggars belief. Chief executives serve at the pleasure of their boards; when they lose the confidence of a majority, or even a significant minority, they become a debilitating liability, because they cease to be completely effective. Modi's eagerness to stay on is understandable. He had money, motivation, a chorus of sycophants, and his most acerbic detractor, Narayanaswami Srinivasan, was more conflicted than Kashmir: BCCI secretary, IPL governing council member, president of the Tamil Nadu Cricket Association, and proprietor of the Chennai Super Kings, which employed India's captain as its captain and India's chairman of selectors as 'brand ambassador'. In such a *tu quoque*-rich environment, the temptation to brazen it out would have been overpowering. But what was the BCCI doing allowing such a situation to fester?

As it is, if Modi and the BCCI now do not part ways, the perception will be that it is because they have a mutual interest in the containment of the controversy, in which case Ratnakar Shetty's so-called 'investigation' will look a little like the long-forgotten Chandrachud inquiry into match-fixing in 1997, absolving everyone and everything, and derogating allegations of corruption as nothing but media mischief. All that talk now of government interventions, probes by taxation and foreign investment authorities, Rahul Mehra's unflagging campaign for the reform of all national sporting bodies to make them less like personal fiefdoms ... well, who knows where *they* might lead, eh? Here, then, is one of those scenarios where whomever prevails will be undeserving, and the system, such as it is, will have utterly failed. The time is ripe, in fact, to look beyond the 'mess' and to that system itself—how, and not just in India, cricket is governing, and failing to govern, itself.

Corporate governance is not as much fun to discuss as the doosra or the Dilscoop. Not even corporate governors find it all that interesting, routinely treating it as a box-ticking exercise, in which the priority is technical compliance rather than genuine effectiveness: Satyam Computer Services won the Golden Peacock Award for Corporate Governance under Risk Management and Compliance Issues five months before the depredations of chairman Ramalinga Raju were revealed. But in a game turning over billions of dollars, there must be questions asked about the coping capacity of cricket's historic institutional structures.

The basis of cricket's government everywhere is geography. Every national board of control is constituted on the basis of representation selected by the states, provinces, counties or islands composing it; these states, provinces, counties or islands are themselves usually a gathering of smaller geographic units. The ICC is this concept writ large, a coming together of emissaries from those national organisations.

This has been an immensely robust and stable model, with the benefit of being easy to understand, and at least superficially democratic and equitable. It has, however, always had a number of disadvantages. The boards are unable to influence who sits on them: they must accept whomever a constituent body elects, often in circumstances where the electoral process is far from clear. Unless well supervised and suitably motivated, the representatives themselves will tend to create not a genuine forum for policymaking but an arena of competing sectional interests, prioritising the extraction of short-term benefits for those who have chosen them over the long-term welfare of the body on which they sit, and standing solidly in defence of the status quo, because reform will involve some people sacrificing hard-won eminence. Thus Malcolm Speed's droll line in reference to Cricket Australia: 'You'll never get the turkeys to vote for Christmas'.

In India, this situation has further entrenched itself in the twenty-first century because so many politicians or their proxies now run state associations, coveting membership of the BCCI not out of an abiding commitment to cricket's betterment, but as a political credential: step forward some prize butterball turkeys in Sharad Pawar, Arun Jaitley, Farooq Abdullah, Narendra Modi and Lalu Prasad Yadav, to name but the plumpest. Not that there isn't something to be said for having a can-do politician in one's corner, but it's also an admission of a lack of faith in the fairness and efficiency of bureaucratic processes. And is this what India would wish to be known for?

Modi illustrates many things, meanwhile, but one is surely that cricket benefits from ideas that come from outside its own gene pool. Yet in order to make his way at the BCCI, he had to win the aegis of the cricket associations of Himachal Pradesh, Rajasthan and Punjab, and cosy up along the way to the right patrons. Not surprisingly, the IPL was in its way a response to the malaise of the BCCI, of a governance structure geared chiefly to the division of spoils provided by a huge market, and of actual administration reduced to a clerical function, with all the strategic vision of your average goldfish. Creating the IPL as a free-standing entity and providing it with IMG manpower suited both Modi and the BCCI: Modi because it gave him mastery of his own domain; the BCCI because it obviated any requirement to cultivate itself the nimble, responsive and disinterested leadership necessary for such a venture.

The solution, of course, brought with it a host of problems. In a bizarre vestige of the traditions of honorary officialdom, Lalit Modi was paid no salary by the BCCI, thereby exuding an aura of independent wealth, even of philanthropy. But when the IPL introduced the innovation of private ownership, to whom was Modi ultimately accountable? Was it to the BCCI? Was it to the IPL as embodied in its governing council? Was it to the IPL as constituted by the franchises? Was it to himself, whether (symbolically) to his vision, or (practically) to the Modi Entertainment Network?

The result is not simply the murk around several of the IPL's key contracts, but changes that already stand to affect the game around the world while being chiefly in the interests not of cricket, nor even of the BCCI, but of the franchises: in particular, the stealthy but relentless expansion of the IPL in number of teams and games. We have it on MAK Pataudi's authority that the IPL governing council was divided on the matter of this growth, which is turning a window in cricket's calendar into floor-to-ceiling glass. Yet a faceless unelected majority prevailed, regardless of the consequences for other stakeholders, like those international players whose presence is being insisted on even as their workload is being hugely expanded, like those national boards without a say in the further depletion of their expensively generated human resources, like those cricket fans outside India who will see less international cricket in their own countries as a result.

To repeat, we arrive at this pass because the BCCI was so wedded to a structure of politicians and bureaucrats helping themselves, that it preferred to avoid the question altogether and permit the IPL near complete autonomy. Yet the strains on the BCCI's broad-based geographic model, which has resulted in the country hosting international cricket at no fewer than forty-five arenas, are being felt nonetheless. As Ramachandra Guha recently pointed out in Calcutta's *Telegraph*, populous Uttar Pradesh, Madhya Pradesh and Bihar, in which dwell one in three Indians, remain unrepresented in the IPL; Kerala, Tamil Nadu, Karnataka and Andhra Pradesh, accounting between them for less than a quarter of India's population, will from next year each host a franchise. 'This maldistribution of IPL franchises undermines its claim to be "Indian", and is in defiance of sporting history and achievement as well', noted Guha. 'The truth is that citizenship and cricket have been comprehensively trumped by the claims of commerce.'

The other problem with purely geographic models of governance, conceived as they were in response to methods of transportation and communication arrangements long obsolete, is that cricket has been left unrepresentative in basically all other respects. For example, it is almost a decade since Lord Condon in his report to the ICC on match-fixing commented that part of the crisis arose from the fact that players were 'not sufficiently involved in the administration of the game and ownership of the problems'; he retires with the situation entirely unchanged, except that in the meantime players have drifted in some countries into collective bargaining arrangements.

Again, this seems a lost opportunity. Although they are, of course, being amply rewarded for it, of no group in cricket today is more being expected than players. Cricket administration, meanwhile, is desperately short of firsthand cricket knowledge. While CA has raised a flutter in the dovecotes by promoting John Howard for the ICC vice-presidency, Janette Howard knows more about cricket than the incoming ICC president. Sharad Pawar's chief qualification for the job is a mastery of power politics in Maharashtra. The idea that he can be an effective operator in time off from being India's minister of food makes a mockery of both jobs.

The IPL, for all its claims to innovation, is in this respect an old-fashioned autocracy. Where players are concerned, Modi follows Alfred Hitchcock's advice about dealing with actors: 'Pay them heaps and treat them like cattle'. Modi makes goo-goo eyes at Shane Warne occasionally, like Hitchcock with Tippi Hedren, but otherwise plays the role of distant sugar-daddy, occasionally morphing into the role of plantation overseer. Players *will* be available; shirkers, such as Australians wishing to play Sheffield Shield, *will not* be tolerated.

Lest this critique be dismissed as singling out India for its inadequacies, it is worth pointing out where Australia is falling short, particularly in an era obsessing over broader horizons and finding new audiences. Examine the identikit parade of directors in CA's annual report and you will find men who look like they could have been running the game in the 1950s, selected in state-by-state ratios barely changed in 105 years. Harry Harinath excepted, where are the non-Anglo faces? Where are the women? Where are the younger people? Perhaps this accounts for the 1980s disco atmosphere that now pervades Australian cricket grounds: it's old people's condescending idea of what young people like. Whatever the case, and whatever the capabilities of the individuals, it still resembles an assembly chosen on the basis of Buggins' Turn.

Nor is this same document remotely as informative as it should be. Ten years ago, there were seven pages of financial accounts in CA's annual report; last year, despite the prodigious growth in the quantum and complexity of cricket's finances, there were four, with the accent on meeting statutory requirements rather than providing genuinely instructive evidence of cricket's financial strength.

To be fair, comparisons are odorous in studying financial activity within cricket, because no two years are alike. And one would talk about the disclosure standards of the BCCI if these actually existed. But CA has fallen into bad habits, by comparison, for instance, with the England Cricket Board and Cricket South Africa, which produce impressive and voluminous documents on time every year. CA's chief executive officer, James Sutherland, is an accountant by background: the organisation should be doing better than what is analogous to a cricket scorecard featuring only fall of wicket, leg byes and who won the toss.

Such criticism can be more generally couched. Never has more money sluiced through cricket, yet the game's attitude to disclosure remains a mixture of the grudging and the apathetic. A corporation with the disclosure regime of the ICC would be a market pariah. KPMG were sent to pore over the books of Zimbabwe Cricket; perhaps they need to pay a visit to Dubai Sports City, too. As for Pakistan and Sri Lanka, contemplating their finances simply gives one a headache.

The dearth is not simply of up-to-date information but of meaningful analysis, and not merely of how money is being raised but how it is being allocated. Indian observers are transfixed by the aforementioned US$4.13 billion valuation ascribed to the IPL by Brand Finance, a figure almost entirely meaningless: because the IPL is not for sale, the value is unrealisable. They remain perversely incurious about how the BCCI spends its vast resources. During their dispute with the Indian board in January, India's taxation authorities came up with a figure of mysterious provenance but extraordinary implications: on the actual promotion of Indian cricket, the BCCI spends just 8 per cent of revenues. Never mind Lalit Modi—why is this not a scandal?

Anyway, to simplify, here are half-a-dozen modest proposals for the improvement of cricket administration at national and international levels:

- Reconsider the geographic basis of representation on boards of control. Encourage all responsible bodies to appoint at least a sizeable minority of competent non-executive directors, with specific areas of expertise: law, accounting, marketing, finance, broadcasting, sports medicine. Their explicit mandate should be to make decisions in the interests of the country as a whole, rather than any particular region. To quote a shrewd Australian businessman, Garry Pemberton: 'The easiest way to obtain good corporate governance is to obtain good corporate governors'.

- Establish the clearest possible reporting lines, and remove all ambiguities of responsibility, such as arose with Modi's role at the IPL. Hold individuals to the most demanding standards where potential conflicts of interest arise.

- Where private ownership is concerned, remember your mother's admonition: it's all fun and games until someone loses an eye. Cricket in India has had two hearty paydays as franchises have been auctioned; those franchises now will act in nobody's interests but their own, and every cricketer and every fan in all the world will have to live with the consequences.

- Given the convulsive change cricket has undergone in the last three years, a board of fifty-something suits is an anachronism. A global game requires a diversity of backgrounds. Work on making cricket's government representative in all respects, with a range of ages, sexes and interests. Promote more players with recent experience, rather than famous names who gave the game up twenty years ago and more; tell them they will be expected to do more than 'ask cricket questions'.

- 'Sunlight is the best disinfectant', said the American jurist William O Douglas. Improve disclosure standards at all levels, with an emphasis on information that is timely, meaningful and intelligible, rather than required by statute. Boards of control around the world receive huge financial distributions from the ICC: it's arguable that as a prerequisite of membership, they should be able to give a coherent account of how that money is allocated. Consider regular publication of decisions reached at meetings—after all, it's not as though national boards have any competitors in their own countries. Maybe hold some meetings in public. It is, after all, the people's game.

- Don't treat cricket's governance as too established to reform or too esoteric to matter: it should be a concern of everyone involved in the game. If it is not, cricket's future will be strewn with many more messes than the most recent.

Cricinfo, June 2010

JOHN HOWARD AT THE ICC

The Augean Stable

Shortly after leaving the White House, Calvin Coolidge had to complete an application form for the National Press Club. Under the heading 'occupation', he scribbled: 'Retired'. Faced with the heading 'remarks', he paused, reflected, and finally wrote: 'Glad of it'.

Not every politician is so sanguine. Limelight deprivation syndrome is common. Which is not to say that the emergence of John Howard as a candidate for presidency of the ICC is so motivated. An alert observer might have detected a continuation of the parallels between Howard and his political inspiration, Sir Robert Menzies, one of whose retirement roles was also in cricket administration, as president of the Kent County Cricket Club—a position he assumed while Lord Warden of the Cinque Ports, and which probably engaged him rather more.

But the assertion was open to be made, and hastily was. 'For many years the W. G. Grace of Australian politics, a man never willing to declare, Howard is perfectly suited to life after politics as a cricket administrator', said one of Howard's former political antagonists, Mark Latham, in a newspaper column as sparkling and insightful as this concluding line. For what Latham is suited, meanwhile, is a question not only unanswered, but of negligible interest. He is the Jason Krejza of Australian politics: a brief glorious flourish, a protracted subsidence into oblivion.

Actually, cricket's governance deserves better—which is Cricket Australia's objective in promoting Howard. Since the ICC was overhauled thirteen years ago and the office of president created, it has been filled by a collection of characters as dubious as the police line-up in *The Usual Suspects*. The incoming president, whom Howard would succeed, is a senior Indian politician with a chequered past. Previously, the president was an abusive drunk from South Africa who luckily died halfway through his term. A leading candidate for the top job until recently was a Sri Lankan bookmaker and political king-maker once prosecuted for issuing a forged passport to a crime boss who was then conveniently shot.

The ICC's reputation for management of the game, meanwhile, is not so much in the toilet as right around the bend. Self-marginalised by relocation to Dubai for tax reasons in August 2005, it specialises in ineffectual announcements and muddled compromises—which rather suits the boards of control constituting it, jealous of their sovereignty as they are.

Howard has to get there first, too. The system—like almost everything to do with the ICC—is convoluted. Best man for the job? Too easy. The ICC presidency is filled every two years by a new representative from the ten Test-playing nations, which are for this purpose divided into five regions, one of which Australia shares with New Zealand; nominees serve first as vice-president, then as president.

When New Zealand Cricket wrote to CA in September 2009 about their candidate, it assumed that no objection would be taken to a New Zealander, Australia having taken precedence at the countries' last turn. NZC was further fortified in its view by its promotion of Sir John Anderson, a career banker who now chairs the board of TVNZ—as respected a name as exists in the game's traditional governance circles.

Anderson's cricket credentials are almost as extensive as his commercial qualifications. A quality first-grade all-rounder in Wellington, he had his first experience of administration there when he bailed his Karori Cricket Club out of a deep financial hole in the mid-1970s. He later oversaw reforms at the Wellington Cricket Association, presided over the liquidation of New Zealand's old board of control and its replacement with a full-fledged board of directors fifteen years ago, then engineered a new constitution for the ICC when the old one had led to a deadlock over leadership between India and Australia in 1996. Of a superior curriculum vitae for the job at issue, it is hard to conceive.

CA's argument is to agree that Anderson's credentials suit the job perfectly—but the job *as it is now*, rather than as it *needs to be*. As across every contemporary cricket issue falls the shadow of the BCCI, both the ICC's biggest member and its greatest rival. The BCCI accounts for about three-quarters of global cricket revenues, but its supranational Twenty20 competitions, the IPL and Champions League, are outside the ICC's jurisdiction, being ostensibly 'domestic' tournaments. India's board thereby exerts de facto control over what looms as cricket's most lucrative future format.

The BCCI is a sporting administration, but it is also, increasingly, a political organisation. Many of its constituent state associations are led by local chief ministers or their proxies. The BCCI's Sharad Pawar, who will become president of the ICC in July, is a classic example of a politician harnessing cricket for his powerbroking ends. After splitting from the Congress Party ten years ago in protest at the ascendancy of Sonia Gandhi, the 'King of Maharashtra' strengthened the support base of his new minority party by ousting former Indian captain Ajit Wadekar as chairman of the Mumbai Cricket Association in 2001, then levering out businessman Jagmohan Dalmiya as boss of the BCCI. It's paid off: despite a scandal-strewn past, he remains agriculture minister in Manmohan Singh's cabinet.

Because little happens at the ICC without the BCCI's explicit say-so, international cricket has become hostage to a range of Indian political and commercial fortunes. In this context, CA, whose board includes former Howard minister Ian McLachlan and former Labor premier John Bannon, regard Howard's political acumen and experience as potentially of value. A selection committee has been constituted: current NZC chairman Alan Isaac, former chief of New Zealand rugby Chris Moller, and CA directors Geoff Tamblyn and Wally Edwards, with the respective chief executives Justin Vaughan and James Sutherland present as non-voting observers.

Several layers of risk remain. To New Zealanders, CA's stance smacks of 'typical Australian bullying', as a former senior administrator puts it. There is also considerable distrust of the selection committee's chairman, Rod Eddington. Infrastructure Australia's ubiquitous chief is remembered across the Tasman as erstwhile chairman of Ansett, whose subsequent collapse prostrated Air New Zealand. The committee's representatives did not budge after interviews of Anderson and Howard in New Zealand on 28 January, and if no resolution is reached can leave the ICC to split the candidates, but this would hardly be a dignified solution.

In the meantime, unwanted attention on Howard's candidacy also has the potential to affect CA's relations with Canberra. It's a fair question whether the right time to be cosying up to a successful conservative prime minister is while also negotiating with a surly Labor communications minister for removal of one's sport from the anti-siphoning list. Yet it's Howard who seems to be courting the gravest risk. Even if his name did go forward, he would not assume his mantle until July 2012, by which time, on present trends, presidency of the ICC will be less influential than presidency of the Kent County Cricket Club. Life as a retired politician might then look, as it did to Coolidge, pretty damn attractive.

The Spectator, March 2010

JOHN HOWARD AT THE ICC

A Confederacy of Dunces

All those in favour of John Howard, say 'aye' ...

Come on, I know you're out there. I can hear you breathing. And for any politician, so it goes. It is a paradox of democracy that politicians, desperate to court popularity, and living or dying by it, are doomed to widespread unpopularity. Politicians are almost invariably elected by bare majorities, meaning they start with the disapproval of at least a sizeable minority; these ranks gradually swell with disillusioned former supporters, and the previously indifferent. There being no policy that does not disadvantage someone, this number grows inexorably, until ... one day ... you're looking at your post-political options. As is John Howard at the moment.

One option in particular, vice-presidency leading to presidency of the ICC, is not exactly a plumb job. The pay is non-existent. The company is pretty dubious. The powers are heavily circumscribed. The largest and most important member holds the body in contempt, and undermines it at every opportunity. The cricket public everywhere think the organisation is a joke. That Howard is willing to accept such a frankly thankless task reveals a hitherto-unsuspected streak of masochism. Except that Howard raises the hackles of certain of the ICC's members, with no objection in particular but every objection in general.

As the debate has made partisans of everyone, a preliminary note is necessary. I write here as someone to whom Howard the politician did not appeal, and who cast his every available vote against him, even to the point of voting for some I knew to be total plonkers. I even have reservations about whether he is entirely the right person to assume the presidency of the ICC. On the other hand, in reviewing the objections expressed to him, I'm not persuaded he's the wrong person. Let us examine them, as coolly as we can …

HOWARD IS A POLITICIAN: This is the easiest objection to dispose of, because Howard is not a politician. He is a former politician. Same difference? Former politicians the world over would beg to differ. After Winston Churchill lost the British election of 1945, he 'wished every day for death'. John Winston Howard's perspective, I imagine, would not be nearly so extreme, but I suspect he can give you chapter and verse on the distinction between the two states of being. A politician out of office is like a batsman without a bat: just a man, of greater or lesser ability. Howard, in fact, is twice-removed from power: he is retired, and the party he once led is undergoing a spell in opposition that, at least until very recently, looked like being long and protracted.

There is an argument that even former politicians by the murk of their prior doings bring the risk of controversy to their role. But if an extensive, ongoing and chequered political career hasn't stood in the way of Sharad Pawar's rise to eminence, then what conceivable objection can be made to Howard? Say what you like of him in other respects, he remained in his career almost boringly free of the taint of financial corruption. Want to stop John Howard? You'll have to do better than this.

HOWARD IS NOT A CRICKET PERSON: This is the objection of Sri Lanka Cricket, whose interim committee chairman, Somachandra de Silva, believes that 'on principle it is the wrong thing to do to bring someone from outside for the vice-presidency'. But from outside what? From outside cricket's governing circles? Does the game's existing administrative elite so abound in talent that it would not benefit from the expertise and disinterested perspectives of a well-credentialled outsider. Sorry Mr Mandela, if only you'd served the afternoon teas at the cricket games on Robben Island, we might have been able to get you in on a technicality. Sri Lankan sports minister Chandrasiri Ratnayake recently deemed his cricket board the country's 'third most corrupt organisation'; not exactly a ringing endorsement of those on the inside of the virtuous administrative circle at Sri Lanka Cricket.

The evidence, in fact, is all the other way, that the traditional means by which cricket has promoted from within are failing hopelessly, generating a succession of shonks and non-entities, many of them from the self-same countries now trying to impede Howard's progress. From South Africa comes Percy Sonn. From Sri Lanka comes Thilan Sumathipala. From Pakistan comes Ijaz Butt. Not that Australia is exemplary in this respect either. Jack Clarke is a likeable fellow, but is he really the individual best qualified to chair its cricket board?

In any event, and with all due respect to de Silva, who at stages in the 1970s may have been the best leg spinner in the world, the eligibility for office at the ICC of those without a direct involvement in cricket administration is not his to deem. The ICC's constitution does not disallow it; on the contrary, Pakistan nominated Ehsan Mani as ICC president seven years ago when he did not even live in his home country, and nobody batted an eyelid.

Howard's non-cricket personhood might also be argued to derive from his knowledge of the game. It's an old line in Australia, usually made by someone asserting their own superior knowledge: 'That bloody Howard—*I* know more about cricket than he does'. Short of entering Howard in *Cricket Mastermind*, with perhaps Sharad Pawar, Lalit Modi and Giles Clarke as fellow contestants, I'm not sure how this is to be established, nor whether it actually matters. The skills important to a presidency or chairmanship are not the ability to bowl a doosra or quote the hit-wicket law from memory, but those of being able to take wise counsel, ask intelligent questions and run effective meetings. Eleven years of balancing interests and corralling a cabinet as a country's prime minister seem ample evidence of these skills in Howard.

There remains in Sri Lanka, of course, residual ill-feeling about Howard's remarks six years ago concerning Muttiah Muralitharan. Fair enough, too. The comments were ill-informed and tactless; they also caused grave disappointment at Cricket Australia, which had been keen for Murali to tour. In straining for a populist sound bite, Howard forgot the considered views both of his political hero, Sir Robert Menzies, that world sporting competition when used for 'stirring up sensation, for looking for trouble, and if necessary creating it' could do 'almost as much to create international bitterness as any political factor', and his cricket hero, Sir Donald Bradman, that the problem of illegal actions is 'the most complex I have known in cricket, because it is not a matter of fact but of opinion'. On the other hand, all he expressed was *that*: an opinion. Less dogmatism and more understanding would have served him better, but the straightforward expression of an honestly held view is not to be deplored merely because one happens to disagree with it.

HOWARD IS A RACIST: For many Australians, Howard was a disappointing leader, ever the politician, seldom the statesman. He grappled uneasily with the politics of race, as every Australian prime minister has and probably always will. He pursued policies towards refugees that were iniquitous and inhumane in application, even if mandatory detention was an innovation of the administration before his. He made little headway on improving the lot of Australia's benighted Aboriginal population, and his behaviour at the Reconciliation Convention in May 1997 was ignominious at best, although there was also an argument that symbolic gestures towards reconciliation in advance of an amelioration of Indigenous living standards were premature, if not empty.

The common cliché used to describe Howard as 'divisive', however, was often rather casually applied. Politics in a democracy is inherently divisive, insofar as it involves the implementation of one from a range of policy options, thereby antagonising the advocates of others. Those fondest of the word 'divisive' in a political context are usually those on the wrong side of the divide.

To Howard's perceived political sins, moreover, patterns could be difficult to detect. He was too conservative for some, too radical for others; he was disparaged both as too much the ideologue and too much the pragmatist. In this sense, he was the classically supple modern political operative, in perennial and opportunistic pursuit of electoral advantage, as succinctly expressed by his biographers,

Wayne Errington and Peter van Onselen: 'At various points in his administration, Howard has promoted regulation and deregulation, freedom and authority, self-interest and community feeling ... Because of such inconsistencies between action and rhetoric, supporters and critics cannot recognise the John Howard described by their respective foes'. A condensation of his politics simply as 'racist', then, will signify more about the speaker than Howard.

This whole debate, in fact, has revealed much more about its participants than the object of their ire. It has been difficult to keep up with some of the misinformation in circulation. To choose one example, in Pakistan's *Dawn*, Sohaib Alvi revealed exclusively that 'in 2002 Howard snubbed President Pervez Musharraf's assurance of VVIP level security and disallowed Australia's cricket team to tour Pakistan'. This, said Alvi, conferred on the Pakistan Cricket Board's embattled Ijaz Butt 'the opportunity to become an instant hero among all his detractors by casting a vote against' the Australian.

Pakistan must be sadly short of heroes at present if this is how they are reduced to minting them. Alvi also happens to be 180 degrees wrong. Howard was strongly in favour of Australia touring Pakistan that year, precisely because this country, like the United States, regarded Musharraf as a bulwark against Islamic extremism. He urged CA to accept the PCB's invitation; it was CA who for security reasons insisted on the fixtures being relocated offshore. Few plights are sorrier in world cricket than the isolation in which Pakistan cricket fans languish through no fault of their own, and Australia in not touring for twelve years has nothing to be proud of. But Howard, who visited Pakistan less than five years ago and bowled perhaps the most replayed long-hop in history, isn't to blame.

The sentiment Alvi expressed in his piece, furthermore, was actually worse than misinformed; it was malevolent. There is a lot of this about. In cricket's global governance, sad to say, the chief priority seldom seems to be that of promoting the game's interests or preserving its cohesion; it appears far more important to exact mindless retribution for past wrongs, real or imagined. The culture is no longer of give-and-take, or even civilised disagreement, but of a kind of smouldering umbrage, permanently on the verge of exploding. In this case, one might as well name and shame. The casus belli of the dispute over Howard's nomination is that he argued against, and finally insisted on the cancellation of, an Australian tour of Zimbabwe.

This insistence represented a shift of philosophy for Howard. Over the Liberal Party he joined in the 1960s was the long shadow cast by Menzies, who publicly supported the continuation of cricket links with South Africa in the midst of a growing sporting boycott. Menzies' view was conditioned by his belief that nations had absolute sovereignty over their domestic affairs, however much they be disapproved of by other countries; he also had a sentimental attachment to South African cricket as it was then constituted.

Howard inherited and adhered to these attitudes to the extent of anachronism. But he has changed rather more positions than might be expected from one with his reputation for intransigence. The efficacy in South Africa's case of sporting sanctions as an expression of disapproval persuaded Howard that they were appropriate in the case of Zimbabwe, whose rancid, democidal president is patron of the nation's cricket governing body.

That Zimbabwe's Peter Chingoka should be making the most noise about Howard's nomination is not surprising; that he should be regarded as doing so in good faith is entirely remarkable. Chingoka's international pariahhood is the reason the ICC board has to convene not in any of its traditional homes but in Singapore; that he has a seat at cricket's table, let alone influence, brings dishonour to the game. His transparent purpose here is to expedite Zimbabwe's rehabilitation as a Test nation, and to shore up his political support at home. All sorts of benefits in money and prestige will flow his way once Zimbabwe is re-established as a client state of India's. For what it's worth, I hope for Zimbabwe's return too: a touch of their amateur zeal would be a tonic in this grimly professional day and age. But it should be a decision based on the best interests of world cricket, not on the best interests of Peter Chingoka.

In any case, what sort of bastardised governance is this that takes its cues in moral arbitration from associates of one of the cruelest and most corrupt political criminals of modern times? Whom else would Zimbabwe and its suggestible South African allies have us be rid of in international cricket? How about Andy Flower, who wore a black armband in the 2003 World Cup, mourning the death of democracy in his home country? How about Richie Benaud and Ian Chappell, because one managed and the other played in a Wanderers XI in South Africa after that country's exile from Test cricket? Let's be thorough: why not withhold accreditation for ICC events to any journalist who has criticised Robert Mugabe? This would at least be entirely consistent with Zimbabwe's attitudes to freedom of the press.

The countries arguing against Howard's nomination for the ICC vice-presidency disgrace themselves. They purport to be on an idealistic crusade for the purity of cricket government, but their real purpose is to preserve its sleazy deal-doing dysfunctionality, while enjoying the sensation of rubbing Australia's nose in it along the way. They travesty a great and noble cause, the fight against racism, by using it as a decoy from their motivations, to the extent that the cry of 'racist' in cricket now has barely any moral utility left. In doing so, irony of ironies, they also present the strongest possible argument for the recruitment of someone from outside this rotten system, be that John Howard or another figure of stature owing no fealty to anyone, to reform it.

Cricinfo, June 2010

JOHN HOWARD AT THE ICC

I Do Not Like Thee, Mr Howard

Say what you like about the members of the ICC, they are utterly consistent. No matter how far you lower your expectations, they always find a way to underperform.

The ICC presidency has existed for thirteen years. It has rotated among the ten Test nations six times. Not once has the nomination caused a murmur: it has been accepted as the nominating nations' prerogative.

Australia and New Zealand, after a rigorous and orderly process, offered Australia's second longest-serving prime minister as the next holder of that office. John Howard was content to serve a waiting period of two years as vice-president, without a vote, without remuneration: quite a gesture of humility for one who has been a country's leader. Now he has been knocked back—and knocked back without even an opportunity to address the rejectionists.

Why? Nobody will say, because nobody so far has had the nerve to stand behind such a calculated insult, both to the individual, and to the country that elected him, for better and worse, four times. The best the ICC can do is a press release stating that his nomination 'did not have sufficient support'—making it sound like a chiropractic problem rather than a political one.

There were all sorts of reasons to develop a distaste for Howard the prime minister. I've expressed a few of them myself. But were any of them relevant to his ability to hold the presidency of the ICC? It involves chairing the board of a sporting body, a job for which he was content to serve a two-year apprenticeship, not holding bringing peace to the Middle East or resolving the Schleswig-Holstein Question. Rather like Tom Brown's objections to Dr Fell, the main objection seems to be that ... errr ... people object to him.

What little we do know is that the first hint of opposition came a couple of months ago from Zimbabwe, which had their own bone to pick with Howard for his disapproval of their indefensible government. Like Alexander Pope's critics, however, Zimbabwe were 'willing to wound, afraid to strike'. This role was left to Cricket South Africa's chairman, Mtutuzeli Nyoka, who appears to have set himself up as a kind of arbiter of racial okayness. Howard, it's rumoured, was once disrespectful of Nelson Mandela, even if nobody seems to know when or how, and this must have been a while ago, because Howard was also responsible in November 1999 for making Mandela an honorary companion in the Order of Australia. Perhaps Nyoka is sincere in his objections, perhaps not. He has so far exhibited no courage in his convictions, and from the organisation that inflicted Percy Sonn on cricket, objection to a former Australian prime minister is pretty hard to take seriously.

Ultimately, however, responsibility lies with the chaotic, fratricidal, law-unto-itself BCCI, for had it chosen to back Howard, the decision would have gone through on the nod. The BCCI likes to think of itself as cricket's leader—as, indeed, it is, by any economic measure. But where was it when actual leadership was required? Sunk in its own Machiavellian intrigues, busy trying to claw back a facilitation fee from World Sport Group, and poring over Lalit Modi's hotel and limousine expenses. Suggestions in the Indian media are that the rejection stems from internal upheavals at the BCCI, where ICC president Sharad Pawar, who supported Howard's nomination, is on the nose with his former colleagues for being too close to Modi. Who knows? And who, ultimately, cares?

This mixture of hopeless shillyshallying and posturing has brought cricket's global governance to a grave new low. The decision is neither constructive nor forward-looking; it reeks of enmity and envy. How ironic that the nomination of Howard should have been deemed so 'divisive', and 'divisiveness' such an unforgivable sin—what could be more divisive than rejecting a nomination of Howard's eminence without explanation?

OK, so now expect one of those high-quality cricket debates involving the generalised, free-floating, received-wisdom idea that Howard must be a racist, because of something someone once heard from somebody who remembers reading something on the internet about stuff. He said that thing about Murali, didn't he? And what about those Indian students, eh?

But there are no highfalutin principles involved here. Six member boards of the ICC have decided, jointly and severally, that it will play well in front of their home constituencies to rub Australia's noses in it. In this context, some remarks recently vouchsafed by Ozias Bvute, the unloved chief executive of Zimbabwe Cricket, are worth examining.

Bvute began by insisting that reports of Zimbabwe's opposition to Howard were all a beat-up: 'A section of the international media has erroneously created the impression that we have been at the forefront of a motion to block Mr Howard's nomination'. Hard to see where the international media got that impression from: the presence of Howard in Harare with Cricket Australia chairman Jack Clarke must have been a complete coincidence.

Bvute continued: 'This is not only maliciously incorrect but also ignores the fact that our structures dictate that such a decision can only be taken by the ZC Board which is in fact still to meet and state a position on the matter'. Please enjoy: instruction in democratic processes from Zimbabwe, whose president has made such a fine art of the principle of 'vote early, vote often'.

Bvute concluded: 'Our concern has and always will be the welfare of the game. Our final decision and vote will be guided by what is in the best interest of cricket in this country'. Except that Mr Bvute manages to contradict himself in a single bound, because 'the welfare of the game' and 'the best interests of cricket in this country' are not the same, even if they may on occasion be parallel. It would be in the best interests of Zimbabwean cricket to play India every week, but this wouldn't be much good to the welfare of the game in general.

Let's give Bvute some credit. While others cower, he is prepared to stand by his cock-eyed thinking. But if his remarks can be taken as indicative of attitudes at the ICC, then its members have given up trying to be a FIFA, a body acting in the international interests of its sport, and are content to be a tenth-rate United Nations: all piss, wind and parish-pump politics.

Cricinfo, July 2010

THE ICC

A Crisis of Legitimacy

'I'm not worried because it's a democratic organization', said Sharad Pawar, the ICC's new president, after the June 2010 executive board meeting in Singapore. The mystery is about which organisation he was talking. Amnesty International? The Boy Scout Movement? It certainly can't have been the ICC.

On the other hand, there seem to be others claiming in the aftermath of John Howard's thwarting to have glimpsed democracy in action, six out of ten constituting a majority. They prove only that they can count; otherwise, they demonstrate a decidedly loose grasp of how democracy operates.

People in a room having a vote is not democracy. It depends on who they are, how they got there, and how faithfully they follow the rules of their organisation. Not even lots of people voting freely does a democracy make. Lots of people voted freely in South Africa in the days of apartheid; many more did not. Lots of people voted in Zimbabwe in 2008; guns spoke louder.

To be legitimate, democracy depends on several preconditions. One is an open and transparent election process. Can the ICC executive board boast of this? So far there has been neither a vote, nor even a discussion, merely a letter, giving no reason for the opposition to Howard, or the last-minute changes of heart of several countries.

To be legitimate, too, those making decisions require legitimacy themselves. And here, I think, it becomes quite interesting. By disputing John Howard's credentials to be ICC vice-president, the nay-sayers turn attention on their own credentials—and, to be fair, on those of the pro-sayers too.

The executive board of the ICC is not elected. Individuals are appointed by the boards of control that are its members. How are they appointed? It varies. There are chairmen. There are presidents. There are chief executives. Some have been selected by constituent associations, some by governments; the default route into the BCCI, for instance, seems to be to become the chief minister of the state of the local cricket body. Easy really. All you have to do is join a political party, suck up to the right people and knife the rest for twenty years or so—presto, you're a cricket administrator.

How, meanwhile, did Ijaz Butt get the job of being chairman of the Pakistan Cricket Board? Myself, I think he was appointed to make him feel better about being Ijaz Butt. But it might also have a little to do with his brother-in-law, Ahmad Mukhtar, being the defence minister of Pakistan, chairman of Pakistan International Airlines, and a key ally of president Asif Ali Zardari. Mukhtar probably told Zardari that Butt was a 'safe pair of hands'. Yep, just as smooth and steady as Kamran Akmal's.

Anyway, you're getting the idea. Here are a couple of questions. By what measure are cricket administrators actually representative of their countries, as distinct from the self-perpetuating administrative autocracies that bear those countries' names? What empowers them to pass political judgement on anything or anyone? Because if you're going to start brandishing the D word, you really should be able to invoke some sort of mandate yourself.

And, while we're at it, is the ICC executive board genuinely motivated by the interests of world cricket, or those of its members increasingly pressing short-term needs, like the desperation of Pakistan to renew cricket competition with India, or of Zimbabwe to sneak back in via the side door? Because if it's simply the latter, then there is no point to it: a system of bilateral relations, with India at their centre, would serve just as well, and actually be more honest.

Legitimacy is something cricket's administrative bodies have tended to overlook, mainly because they regard themselves as outside politics, and from mutual politeness: we won't mention your tin-pot dictatorship if you don't mention ours. But it's starting to matter. India's overwhelming economic heft means that every position a member board takes on an ICC policy must have at least half an eye on its effect on relations with the BCCI. There are also new and powerful influences on the game's governance. Vijay Mallya and Mukesh Ambani, for instance, are already more important men than Ijaz Butt ever was. And whatever you may think of the IPL, its franchise owners have made good on promises to fans and to players—they have set out to earn legitimacy, as well as to buy it. In this respect, the IPL amply deserves its popularity: as the BCCI never has, franchises have given fans a fair deal, and players probably more than a fair deal. To what degree can this be said of any of the boards of control currently so proud of themselves for signing a one-paragraph letter and opting out of further discussion?

But why pick on India and Pakistan, apart from the fun of seeing the Cricinfo comments section phosphoresce with fury? Australia's system is a 105-year-old antique. It has a certain vernacular charm: basically you join the committee of a first-grade cricket club, gather together enough mates to boost you to a state association, then wait for sufficient numbers to float you on to Cricket Australia. A degree of sucking up and knifing may be expedient here too; you will certainly have to buy many rounds of drinks.

Now, the board of CA are a pleasant bunch of coves. But they're not exactly dynamic, nor would one say they were over-qualified; on occasion they can be pretty damn parochial. How big is the talent pool from which they are drawn? Decidedly small. How representative are they of all cricket's constituencies—men, women, children, players, fans? Not very. CA is not the worst cricket government going round, by any means. But phew … is that bar set low or what?

A criticism of CA's nomination of Howard runs this way: was there nobody else in the circles of Australian cricket administration with the nous, gravitas and willingness to fill the ICC presidency? I'm bound to say it's a very good question, and after an embarrassing pause the honest answer has to be not really. Regrettably, if Australia took the job of ICC presidency seriously at all, an appointment from outside traditional cricket administration was unavoidable—perhaps also because anyone with a background in the ICC's history and its characters would run a mile.

There's a good argument, too, that this applies more generally. Cricket has changed more in the last three years than the previous thirty. If ever past knowledge was trading at a discount and new thinking was at a premium, it is now. Yet cricket administration still languishes in the era of Ijaz Buttheads. Chief executives today flit between industries as a matter of course: it is nothing to see oil men running banks, and management consultants running IT companies. Yet some running cricket still see their realm as so unique that they will accept nobody who hasn't put out a slips cradle or erected a set of nets. Who are they kidding? Apart from themselves, I mean.

OK, so who in these circumstances were CA and New Zealand Cricket to choose? The criteria ... well, there weren't any. And this, one can only imagine, was a planned absence. Remember: this presidential rotation system is only as old as the wrangle about which of David Morgan and Sharad Pawar went first as ICC president. It was conceived of because, perhaps wisely, nobody thought the council capable of handling a process that involved other than a rubber stamp.

So there were no prerequisites of involvement in cricket administration; no requirement to be other than a sentient biped. All the nomination had to be was the duly-chosen representative of CA and NZC, and, apparently, have no criminal record. It could have been Kylie. It could have been Russ. God knows, it could have been Hoges. Loves cricket. Some administrative experience, from involvement in the set-up of World Series Cricket. Popular overseas—more than in Australia, actually. Similar attitude to tax as the ICC. No criminal record—well, not yet anyway, unless you count *Almost an Angel*. Mick Dundee's knife might have added a frisson to executive board meetings too.

It must have been assumed that Hoges had his hands full with the Australian Taxation Office, because the nomination went to John Howard. I won't rehash the arguments for and against him: they are worn out, and, in the absence of further and better particulars about the ICC executive board's objections, speculative. Howard was a controversial politician with a populist knack that sometimes expressed itself in policies that were punitive, draconian and base—although, irony of ironies, Australia was actually a more culturally and ethnically diverse country at the end of his prime ministership than before it.

I don't doubt the sincerity of several of his critics now; if there was an Australian whom Howard did not at one time infuriate and antagonise, I have yet to meet them. By the same token, some self-appointed experts on Howard in India at the moment seem to have a fairly casual acquaintance with Australian domestic politics: one tabloid TV jock who interviewed me recently kept calling him 'the prime minister of Australia and New Zealand'.

Consider this, too: Howard's candidature was disclosed at the beginning of January. His selection by CA/NZC was announced two months later. The response at the time, or so it appeared, was shrugs all round. Sharad Pawar rang Howard to express pleasure at the prospect of working with him; Haroon Lorgat rang to introduce himself and his organisation. Sri Lanka were imagined to hold reservations, but their board secretary, Nishantha Ranatunga, stated:

> We know that Howard as prime minister ruffled a few feathers calling Muttiah Muralitharan a chucker, but that is now a thing of the past. We don't want to harp on it any more. We have to look to the future and try to work cordially with whoever is elected to the ICC post. We have no control over people elected to that position.

About that 'no control' bit—you could argue that this was stupid, and you wouldn't have a bad case. Theoretically, if not practically, the ICC presidency is cricket's number one job: it is a travesty that it should basically be an empty slot to be filled for two years by whomever's go it is. Other sports administrators create dynasties: Joao Havelange, Avery Brundage, Kenesaw Mountain Landis. ICC presidents take turns: the guy from India, him from England, that bloke whatsisname from Pakistan.

It is, however, a travesty of the ICC's own, and very recent, making. And it *was* the process. But then, apparently, the process changed. We still don't know when. We still don't know why. It may be as simple as the process dragging out, giving the opportunity for second, third and fourth thoughts. The ICC executive board were meant to vote in April, but the attendance was disrupted by Eyjafjallajökull. It came to pass that the executive board did not make a view known until six months after Howard was known to be in the running for the job: if his existence was so obviously a mortal offence to all right-thinking persons, why did his antagonists wait so long, so that the ICC now has no vice-president, and a high-profile and very fully employed president who'll be able to give his job at least half an hour a fortnight … every other month … with a bit of luck … if he's not too busy?

There is now a perverse pleasure in circles in Asia and Africa that Howard was scotched—*sic semper tyrannis*, and all that. But what transpired was a pathetic, even a cowardly squib. Howard tried to meet Mtutuzeli Nyoka in Johannesburg. Nyoka decided to go to the football instead. Howard went on to Harare to meet Zimbabwe's Peter Chingoka. Chingoka, apparently, was charm personified—the term, I believe, recently popularised by Hank Paulson, is 'grinfuck'.

So what transpired in Singapore last week was the deployment of a teeny-weeny fig leaf of democracy to cover a dirty great embarrassment of decrepit and disintegrating oligarchy, for it reflects not the ICC executive board's profound commitment to good governance, but its growing crisis of legitimacy. The boards involved are watching their sovereignty being eroded on all sides—by India, by the IPL, by the players' increasing commercial mobility, by fans' desertion of their marquee Test match product, by the encroachments of their governments, by the priorities of corporations. All they have left are cynical, populist gestures like saying boo to John Howard. And, as they say, never stand between a politician and a cynical, populist gesture—you will be trampled in the rush. Politicians do have their uses, of course, even at the ICC. What's wrong is that this bunch are mediocre, self-protecting, sinecured politicians posing as cricket administrators who speak not for their countries but for their board's predominant clique, and whose supervening policy is to remain on India's right side. Say what you will of John Howard, and also of Sharad Pawar, but at least they know what an actual democratic mandate feels like.

Seriously Cricket Chronicles, July 2010

WORLD CUP/IPL 2011

A Land Fit for Heroes?

Cricket loves its heros. Tendulkar, Dhoni, Sehwag. Warne, Kallis, Steyn. For the next few months, the game's hero should be the Indian fan. Here come the world's two biggest cricket attractions, right on top of each other. The tenth World Cup is underway, somehow strung out to forty-nine games. Then on 8 April, less than a week after its final, begins the first of the seventy-four games of the fourth Indian Premier League.

In any other country, this would be too much of a good thing. In India, too much is barely enough. The games fixtured in Sri Lanka and Bangladesh notwithstanding, it will be Indian television audiences that somehow make Canada v Kenya and Ireland v the Netherlands work as the tournament effectively spends five weeks deciding whether West Indies or Bangladesh go through to the quarter-finals. Then they'll swap their horizontal tricolours for the IPL replica gear of their favourite franchise and follow that all the way too.

It's a source of wonder. Forty years ago, India had issued fewer than a quarter of a million television licences. Now there are sets in more than half the nation's households, and they never shine more incessantly than for the number one game. India is not just obsessed with cricket; it is, as Santosh Desai puts it in *Mother Pious Lady* (2010), 'obsessed with being obsessed.'

For cricket elsewhere, that poses a growing dilemma. The World Cup is a misnomer. Cricket is not a global game (that is, followed in a majority of countries in ways not based chiefly on national identity), but a multinational one (dependent, like rugby, on an essentially fixed minority of countries) depending, as perhaps as no other sport, on the latterday financial heft of a single country.

The size and vitality of India's economy has divided an ancient and widely-loved sport into two streams – the fixtures involving India, as competitor and consumer, and those not. The former are so staggering more lucrative that the latter have a diminishing relative existence. Every new cricket initiative worldwide involves trying to monetise Indian passion, whether it's Australia's mooted Big Bash League or New Zealand's Cricket Holdings America LLC. Young cricketers everywhere hanker for the easy money of IPL: Australian domestic cricket stopped almost to a walk during the IPL auction as players hung on every tweet and text message. Where once the objective might have been to become the next Ricky Ponting, now it is to become the next Dan Christian, made a millionaire overnight last month by the lightning strike of an offer from the Deccan Chargers.

You'd be forgiven for regarding Indian domination of the cricket world as a tired theme. Although it was simply temporarily obscured by Australia's on-field strength and *amour propre,* the domination probably dates back more than fifteen years old, to the 1996 World Cup and the Supreme Court's liberalisation of India's airwaves.

But what needs to be understood is that the intrinsic qualities of cricket are coming to have less to do with this than Indian gross domestic product and gross political ambition. Ashis Nandy's contention that cricket is an 'Indian game accidentally discovered by the English' has been vindicated not by culture but by capitalism, and also the ballot box.

It's as simple as this. First imagine that you are a broadcaster or a manufacturer of consumer goods surveying the extraordinary cultural, ethnic, religious and linguistic diversity that is India. Especially if you are a Samsung surveying the scene from Seoul or an LG Group from Yeouido-dong, how baffling it must seem. So many Gods. So many markets. How to span them all? Bollywood? Soap opera? Cricket outdoes them all, partly because it effortlessly enfolds elements of the other two – narrative, character and *tamasha*. No wonder cricket attracts eighty-five per cent of the advertising monies lavished on sport in India.

Now imagine that you are politician. It's easy really – just abandon all your moral scruples. Think about the appeal to your constituents of a cricket-friendly face and a cricket-minded administration, what an IPL franchise, a new cricket stadium or even just hosting a one-day international might be worth. What a way to evince your common touch, your affinity for vernacular culture.

When the World Cup was last in India, the dominant administrative figures, like Jagmohan Dalmiya and Inderjit Singh Bindra, had deep roots in the game. The administration of cricket in India in the last fifteen years has been transformed by the presences of such political heavyweights as Arun Jaitley of Karnataka, Rajeev Shukla of Uttar Pradesh, Narendra Modi of Gujarat, Anurag Thakur of Himachal Pradesh, Ranjib Biswal of Orissa, Dayanand Narvekar of Goa, Jyotiraditya Scindia of Madhya, Ranbhir Singh Mahendra of Harayana, Lalu Prasad Yadav of Bihar and/or, just lately, Shashi Tharoor and Kuruppasserry Varkey Thomas in Kerala – although, perhaps above all, by Sharad Pawar, the 'King of Maharastra', now poo-bah of the International Cricket Council.

So cricket in India is not big only because of its fans' unique passion, its players' great skills, the game's incomparable appeal – and it is certainly not big because of the talent of its administration. It outstrips the game in rival nations because India contains lots more people who want to buy mobile phones and televisions while aspiring to whitegoods and other consumer durables, and also because of the exuberant self-admiration of India's political and media elites.

What does this mean for cricket? In the near-term, it has meant great rewards for players, who have no objection to being told where to go and what to do providing a king's ransom is involved, and also improved access and better deals for fans, because they are now also consumers whose disposable rupee is suddenly worth hustling for.

A pre-industrial game, however, does not make a natural fit with a late capitalist economy. At risk is its hold on any independent existence, as a game, as a cultural form, as an institution. Cricket, it is true, has never been truly outside economics and politics – in India, as has been eloquent argued by Ramachandra Guha in *A Corner of a Foreign Field* (2002), it has been an heir to the fissures and tensions of race, cast, religion and nation.

But within it has been preserved something spontaneous, romantic, transcendant, inspirational – something beyond the market forces to which it is today increasingly in thrall. In this latest incarnation, cricket is mainly an effective means of conveying goods to market; in and of itself it is arguably of dwindling significance.

This happens, by the way, everywhere. At times this summer in Australia, watching the Ashes felt like visiting a shopping mall – and there was something deliciously subversive about watching the team that had come to play cricket win, and the team wheeled out to interrupt the advertisements get rock'n'rolled.

But India's playing is like the effect of any other two nations squared. Which is actually a diminution of cricket worldwide. One of the qualities of Indian cricket fans has always been their global awareness. They were international followers of the game, long before it was straightforward to be so. They would follow events in, say, Australia or the West Indies almost as closely as they followed their own favourites.

An irony of Indian cricket's resistless rise is that the game is becoming less global, relatively speaking. While football and the Olympics have maintained their relentless onward march, Test cricket remains a small club; one-day international cricket is little larger. As Amit Gupta notes in *Cricket and Globalisation* (2010): 'There are no cricketers who have become global icons and advertising brand names in non-cricket-playing countries – as David Beckham, Tiger Woods and Michael Jordan have done for their sports in countries like China.'

China developing a taste for cricket might change the landscape – cricket's string-pullers would like that, because there are lots more consumer markets to conquer there. But, really, who cares? They're creaming it at the moment without having to look anywhere else. Let the ICC parachute in some plastic bats. In the short- to medium-term, the name of the game is exploiting a core market that is still growing.

Elsewhere, in fact, cricket is becoming subtly less local. When India visits Australia later this year, it will be transported in an Indian commercial bubble, with its home television audiences in mind: even the hoardings in the grounds will be allocated to Indian brand names. Series that don't involve India, meanwhile, drift into the twilight of obscure pay-TV channels.

The quasi-domestic Champions League is perhaps the most bizarre artefact of Indian hegemony, a tournament that even when it is not in India is all about that country. Last year's instalment in South Africa remains in the memory only because of its eeriness: bad cricket being played by ordinary cricketers in front of handfuls of spectators, gyrating cheerleaders and overexcited commentators simply because ESPN, frustrated at having failed to bid for the IPL, had forked out $US1 billion. Here too can be seen most clearly the distinction between what the fans want and what the cricket-industrial complex want them to want. That's no way to treat heroes.

India Today March 2011

WORLD CUP 2015

Swinging Irish

In their famous spoof version of British history, W. C. Sellar and R. J. Yeatman describe Gladstone as having spent his twilight years trying to resolve 'the Irish Question'. Alas it is to no avail: 'Unfortunately whenever he was getting warm, the Irish secretly changed the Question.'

Something similar applies to cricket's Irish Question, which could be about any number of things. Is it about the size of the Cup? Is it about the length of the Cup? Is it about the venue of Cup? After all, India and Sri Lanka had no problem with a fourteen-team tournament. Why do Australia and New Zealand seem so keen on winnowing the participants away to ten? Perhaps there's an argument for World Cups only being held on the sub-continent: it is, after all, where the crowds, the cash and the television audiences are.

Is it, on the other hand, about Zimbabwe, that ghost in flesh at the ICC executive board which somehow retains full voting rights and financial entitlements despite not playing Test cricket, and despite being considerably the inferior of Ireland at one-day cricket, and probably the Netherlands too? At the moment, the president of Zimbabwe Cricket cannot even visit the next host nation, such is his global reputation.

Or is it about T20, given that the ICC is offering associate members participation in a bigger World T20 as a sop for their exclusion from the World Cup? A positive of the dispute is that the associates have proven smarter than the full members gave them credit for: understanding that T20 is most congenial to the mediocre, they have refused to be infantilized. The irony is that part of T20's appeal is its capacity for creating upsets, which might be felt to have offered associates a shorter cut to success. Kudos to the Irish and the Dutch for seeing past that, and seeking the right to master a form of cricket that isn't just about keeping advertisements apart.

You might by now have worked out that my sympathies lie with the associates; actually, I find it difficult to believe that a cricket lover could feel any other way, given that it is other cricket lovers who sustain the game in its outstations, and that they deserve as much nurturing and encouragement as it is in the ICC's gift to give. All power to the popular outcry against Ireland's treatment. Credit even to ICC president Sharad Pawar for putting the matter back on the agenda – temporary credit anyway.

I fancy, too, that the World Cup needs associate members rather more than the ICC executive board has hitherto been prepared to acknowledge. Sri Lanka defeating India in 1979; Zimbabwe overcoming Australia in 1983 then England in 1992; Bangladesh routing Pakistan in 1999; Kenya rolling West Indies in 1996 and squeezing into the final six in 2003; Ireland stitching up Pakistan in 2007 and England in 2011: you will forget many World Cup deeds before you forget these. And as exciting as it is to see a six peal from the bat of Virender Sehwag, there is something even a little more thrilling about a similar blow from Hiral Patel.

To be fair, there is merit in the contention that a ten-team round-robin is the most efficient and fair preliminary stage for the World Cup, even if the total number of games will barely differ. The management of the ICC originally brought forth a plan for 2015 under which the top eight countries would qualify automatically, and the next six countries (two full members and four associates) would play off for the last two places: it was the executive board that insisted on automatic qualification of full members.

Four years out from the tournament, it also requires some precognition to evaluate the future strength of the associate members: their talent pools are small, and susceptible to one-off setbacks and key retirements. Ireland and the Netherlands have handy teams now; by 2015, they might have gone the way of Kenya.

They are, however, surely likelier to develop more competitive national XIs if they have World Cup participation to aim for. And as an incentive for associate members of ICC, whether in the matter of players, media or sponsors, nothing trumps a shot, however optimistic, at the international one-day crown. The Cup structure surely exists to serve cricket, rather than the other way round.

The play-off, too, might have less to recommend it than seems. Because the difference between entitlement and non-entitlement to a World Cup distribution amounts to tens of millions of dollars, participants in such a competition would be competing for the equivalent of Allen Stanford moolah, introducing budget uncertainty to already precarious finances. When all is said and done, the most equitable solution still appears a twelve-team cup. Perhaps fourteen competitors was too many; ten, however, feels like too few.

The Irish Question is an interesting one to have to consider at all, because it seems to imply a new stage in the diffusion of cricket round the world. Consider how cricket internationalized in the first, second and third places.

For almost the first half century after the commencement of the cricket rivalry between England and Australia, the only addition to full-scale competition was South Africa, and then on rather fluctuating terms: Australia toured there desultorily twice; teams sent from England were barely representative.

In May then September 1926, nonetheless, the Marylebone Cricket Club hosted Imperial Cricket Conferences at Lord's at which not only Australia and South Africa were represented but India, New Zealand and West Indies, these last three all indicating a desire to bring teams to England.

New Zealand had had a board of control for about three decades, but the West Indies' board had barely formed, and India's would not be established until the end of 1928. Despite this, agreements were reached for the interchange of visits and, at the second meeting, a definition of Test matches arrived at: 'Matches played between sides selected by recognised governing bodies of cricket representing countries within the Empire'. England duly played their first Tests against West Indies (1928), New Zealand (1931) and India (1932), while West Indies paid their first visit to Australia and New Zealand (1930–1).

This was a most remarkable climacteric; in hindsight, it was from these conferences that international cricket really sprang, doubling the number of participants, rather than from those in 1909 whose centenary the ICC marked two years ago. For an organization as formal and ceremonial as Marylebone, it now seems deliciously ad hoc, reminiscent of the historian Sir John Seeley's remark that the British acquired their empire 'in a fit of absent-mindedness'.

The idea of a junior tier of involvement then dates from July 1965, when the Imperial Cricket Conference changed its name to the International Cricket Conference, and its rules so as to accommodate members from outside the Commonwealth. Ceylon, Fiji and the United States became the first 'associate members', their ranks swelled further the following year by Bermuda, Denmark, East Africa and the Netherlands.

In 1971, augmented by Argentina, Bermuda, Canada, Gibraltar, Hong Kong, Israel, Malaysia, Papua New Guinea and Singapore, associate members received voting rights. Four years later, for no screamingly obvious reason, Sri Lanka (formerly Ceylon) and East Africa were invited to put the 'world' in World Cup when the first event was staged in England; only the 1992 World Cup, also an ANZAC enterprise, has gone without associate member involvement since.

The third phase of globalization commenced as an Indian initiative, with the presidency of Jagmohan Dalmiya at the ICC. Casting envious eyes on the 'world game' that soccer had become, he exhibited a missionary zeal for expanding the game's horizons. If his modus operandi sometimes looked as if he was throwing darts at the map of the world, he provided cricket with its first specific development bankroll: the inaugural ICC Knockout in 1998 was staged expressly to endow the council's development programme. And with the revolution in cricket's finances over which Dalmiya presided, the ICC could finally afford to make associate membership mean something financially, and affiliate membership too. Numbers of affiliate members grew from six then to sixty today.

On elite cricket, however, this process left negligible trace. It remains true that while no former British colony has won soccer's World Cup, only former British colonies have won cricket's. Boards of control consented to development not because they saw it is a priority but because it seemed like A Good Idea, and perhaps also because they sounded so weighty when they said things like: 'Of course, we're looking at China.' In particular, they exhibited negligible interest in scheduling fixtures with associates, their attitude being that by signing off on ICC development budgets they had, as it were, 'given at the office'.

The ICC's development strategy has changed in the last few years, from a horizontal model, spreading cricket to as many countries as it could conveniently colour in on the globe, to a vertical one, investing most heavily where results are most promising. Fearless, feisty Ireland is a success story – or, at least, it was.

What's also changed in the last five years, ironically, is India itself. A decade ago, globalization was explained as a long-term strategy to enhance cricket's cultural and eventually its commercial potential. Today, long-term thinking is *so* twentieth century: it's far more satisfying and filling to gorge on the low-hanging fruit in the Indian orchard.

This, one suspects, had a subtly negative impact on cricket's interest in new frontiers. It's a corporate logic: the core product is ticking over nicely; why bother with research and development? It's also an organizational outcome: each member of the ICC executive board represents a national board of control; what do any of them gain from spreading cricket's reach as opposed to increasing their own share of the growing spoils? Especially when, India's aside, boards worldwide are strapped for cash *right now*: if you're following *WICB Exposé*, the Jamaica Cricket Association seems barely able to keep pace with president Paul Campbell's Burger King cravings.

Cricket's Irish Question, then, is inseparable from this hinge point in the game's development, and is a test of its administration's good faith. That being so, it is hard to feel confident. A shrewd Australian prime minister – not *that* one, but the one before him – once said: 'Always back self-interest. At least you know it's trying.' Here, however, that will turn this Irish Question into an Irish Joke.

Cricinfo, April 2011

Part III
Australia Felix
and Infelix

ALLAN BORDER

Leader of the Resistance

When he came to write his epic narrative account of Australian politics in the 1980s, Paul Kelly chose the title *The End of Certainty*, encapsulating the period's reforms, realignments and reverberations. To a history of Australian cricket in the 1980s, the same title could be fixed. After a hundred years in which Australians had come to expect a top two position in global cricket as a right, they found themselves rooting for a middling team: callow, fragile, susceptible even on home soil, ranks thinned further by rebel tour recruiters.

Throughout these austerity years, one presence was constant. When Allan Border took his first faltering steps in first-class cricket, Australian cricket was in rude health. Within a year, plundered by Kerry Packer's private enterprise, its vulnerabilities had been exposed. And although Packer's incursion had the effect of expediting Border's progress to international level, the after-effects lingered. For the next decade, the scar left by World Series Cricket was apt to itch and ache and weep when the patient was under stress.

To Border more than any other player would be left the task of repairing what, especially against the West Indies, was sometimes irreparable. His career record attests the tenor of the times: he was on the winning side fifty times in 156 Tests, on the losing side in forty-six. He played, moreover, in sixty draws. An old Australian joke runs that draw(er)s are for swimming in; in Border's time, they often seemed the best that could be hoped for.

It was tough. It could be gruelling. On forty-eight occasions, Border batted with Australia either responding to a first-innings of 400, trailing by 150 on first innings or following on. But the times also probably rather suited Border, leeching from him reserves of deep concentration, organisation and obstinacy. At the end of his career, he might have wished to start again: Australia's painstaking investment in youth was about to fructify, and a period of dominance impended. But nobody plays against their predispositions for fifteen years. Interestingly, he was significantly more effective away, when Australia needed him more often, than at home, when his team tended to slightly be more comfortable. He averaged 45.94 in his own country, 56.57 in others; he never made a Test hundred at the SCG, but he compiled a couple in Madras. For the role of stern, stoic resister, Border was sent by Central Casting.

To a generation of Australians accustomed to the overdog role, it is hard to flesh Border out. A stocky 177 centimetres, he approached the crease with a businesslike bustle. There were no showy rituals or preparatory mimes, just a two-handed shake of the bat with a flex of the forearms when he was about halfway out, as unconscious as a boxer touching gloves. His technique was genuinely ageless. 'His straight backlift is controlled', wrote that closest of observers, Ray Robinson, in 1979. 'His level-eyed stance, once side-on, now shows his left toe-cap. His low-grip makes less use of handle leverage than Kim Hughes, but forearm power makes him one of the most effective drivers and back either side of the stumps.' As an identikit portrait of Border at the end of his career, it could hardly be improved on.

Above all, he was versatile. Against fast bowling, Peter Roebuck once likened him convincingly to a boulder; against slow bowling, he moved nimbly, with eagle eyes and twinkling feet. In a boom-or-bust batting line-up, he was as reliable as a bank cheque. His average as player was 50; his average as captain 51. His average up to the age of thirty was 50.35; his average thereafter was 50.74. He was one of the top three scorers in 129 of the 265 Test innings in which he batted. Conditions, climes and other considerations seemed immaterial: his sixty-eight first-class hundreds were achieved on thirty-three different grounds. If you recall the era in Australia, you'll remember how news of the cricket then passed around. The first question would be: do you know the score? The second would be: is Border still in? If the answer to the second was yes, then even the grimmest answer to the first was somewhat mitigated.

To a world that identifies Australia with jagged aggression, it is also hard to explain Border's demeanour. When Australia toured England unsuccessfully under his captaincy in 1985, captious judges found fault with his friendliness towards the likes of Ian Botham and David Gower. Border was nettled. 'Victory has nothing to do with being ultra-aggressive towards opponents', he claimed. 'I've been through both experiences, seen both attitudes ... If you're being outplayed, you're being outplayed. Hard luck but fact.' Yet even an Englishman, Chris Broad, in his golden summer of 1986–87, found the Australians' reticence strange: 'The problem for the Aussies was that the captain Allan Border and his deputy David Boon were both quiet blokes and said hardly anything on the field'.

More than any other player, Border then turned such remarks into quaint curios of a bygone age. On the Ashes tour of 1989, Australia's on-field dominance had an acrid verbal edge. 'I've been through all sorts of downs with my team, but this time I thought we had a bloody good chance to win', Border confessed to Gower afterwards. 'I was prepared to be as ruthless as it took to stuff you.' This became the prime directive of Australian teams thereafter; likewise was friendliness identified with failure. Twenty years after Border was chided for his pacifism in 1985, Ricky Ponting copped similar criticisms as his team turned the Ashes over.

In Border's defence, it could be said that he was no tougher on opponents than on his own team. From a shy and retiring sort who looked after his own game, he became as captain a martinet, demanding absolute commitment. That could be traced to a night in a bar in Sharjah in April 1985, just months after his unruly succession of Kim Hughes, where he'd solemnly laid out objectives for his captaincy, without realising that several of the nodding heads had already done similar nodding over contracts to tour South Africa. Border remained bitter even with the four who withdrew from the tour—Murray Bennett, Wayne Phillips, Dirk Wellham and Graeme Wood—and had to be persuaded to accept them as members of his team in England. They underwent a pre-tour interrogation as unsparing as anything Gower had to cope with: Wellham, who emerged from his 'white as a ghost', thought it an 'outrage', and said he would 'not forgive Border his stupidity'. Nine months later, Border spontaneously laid his captaincy on the line during a one-day series in New Zealand, pouring forth his frustrations at an impromptu press conference by the practise area at Lancaster Park. 'They're going to have to show me whether they really want to play for Australia', he groused. 'And whether they really want to play for me.' Seldom has Australian cricket been so hostage to one man's humours.

Yet through a rocky period that followed Greg Chappell's picking and choosing of tours and Hughes' unhappy role as his locum, Border was also sustaining the idea of the game as a passion rather than a profession. Grittily, grumpily, he restored in his country a sense of the honour inherent in national representation, eroded by decades of animosity between players and the Australian Cricket Board. He was available and chosen for all thirty of the tours in his fifteen-year career. He learned he had become a father while wearing his pads, awaiting his innings during an Australian collapse at the SCG—which was curiously fitting, as he had a tendency to watch cricket as anxiously as an expectant father, compulsively fondling his 'worry ball'. His thoughts made easy reading on the field too, hands seemingly always trending towards his hips to form that famous 'teapot' pose. His moves were studied intently by all the next generation's Australian luminaries: Shane Warne, Steve Waugh, Mark Taylor and Ian Healy.

The turning point in his captaincy was in India, where Australia was a decidedly unfancied participant in the 1987 World Cup. The transformation in his leadership turned an old cliché on its head. Previously, he had led from the front, valiantly but unavailingly, because there was nothing much to follow him; here he led from behind, with the aid of a sharp and sagacious coach, Bob Simpson. The only survivor of Australia's previous World Cup campaign, where a talented but disunited team had disintegrated under pressure, he had absorbed all its lessons; henceforward, he would go on learning.

What he and Simpson were not destined to accomplish was victory over the West Indies, although they went closer than any other country, coming within 2 runs of the Worrell Trophy on Australia Day 1992. Border, as has recently come to light, had also already achieved one unacknowledged victory over the West Indies at the inception of his captaincy, in an episode where the respective ends of certainty, Australia's and Australian cricket's, intersected.

When Cricket Australia made its archives available for research a couple of years ago, its records revealed the efforts of prime minister Bob Hawke in the summer of 1984–85 to install Clive Lloyd as Australian cricket's guru, a position the government was prepared to fund. Hawke's infatuation was publicly evinced when Lloyd was honoured with the Order of Australia 'for service to the sport of cricket, particularly in relation to his outstanding and positive influence on the game in Australia'—a rather masochistic honour, given that Lloyd's West Indians were even then beating Border's Australians black and blue. Privately, the board nursed more misgivings, and waited for Hawke's ardour to cool, which it did; Australian cricket moved on, investing long term in competence rather than short term in charisma.

In an era so smitten with charisma, in fact, Border's complete lack of it was among his most appealing attributes. He did what came naturally. There were no ostentations or gimmicks; there was no testimonial or farewell tour. Instead, Border dropped back to Sheffield Shield for a couple of years after quitting international cricket, although not for fun; he was as grim and combustible with Queensland as he was with Australia, leaving a forceful impression on the young Matthew Hayden.

Australian cricket, meanwhile, went from strength to strength. In Border's last year of international cricket, a popular Australian troubadour, Doug Parkinson, recorded a sentimental ballad, 'Where Would We Be without AB?' The answer was: top of the world. This, perhaps, was Border's signal achievement. Great players often leave great holes behind them; it is a very rare great player who effectively renders himself redundant. Certainty might have become a thing of the past in Australian politics and society; to Australian cricket, Border had helped restore it.

Cricinfo, March 2010

STEVE WAUGH

Buried Treasure

Steve Waugh is an Australian Living Treasure. That is not the airing of an opinion, but the statement of a fact: he is one of a list of about a hundred nominated and elected by this country's National Trust. It's an eccentric and obviously subjective list. Erstwhile prime minister's wife Hazel Hawke is there; the erstwhile husband who left her for a younger woman, Bob Hawke, is not. Hugely popular, widely admired and softly spoken Indigenous athlete Cathy Freeman is there; hugely popular, widely admired and extremely noisy Indigenous athlete Anthony Mundine is not. In other words, this is no place for controversialists. It is a pantheon in which Steve Waugh fits snugly.

Nobody has played more Tests than Steve Waugh. No Australian has played more one-day internationals. It's a record as uncompromising as the man himself, and the team he led to success upon success. It was built, moreover, in a relentless forward march. 'What about the next game, Steve?' asked a journalist after one night game in January 2000. 'Who are we playing?' Waugh responded, adding amid chuckles: 'We just get on a plane and go somewhere and find out who we're playing'.

At the time, he was one of three to-die-for wickets in international cricket, while having nothing in common with the other two: the classically correct Sachin Tendulkar, and the altogether irreverent Brian Lara. Waugh was neither a straightforwardly orthodox, nor even a particularly gainly batsman—crouching, jumping, cutting all sorts of capers as he refrained from hooking. All the while, however, he would be accumulating, like compound interest, occasionally essaying a signature slog-sweep to ratify his ownership of the crease. He was a batsman of his era: at home in all conditions, never daunted, always ready, ever hungry.

Yet for a figure whose cricket was so embedded in the modern, the terms in which Waugh is usually understood are deeply traditional. No sooner had he appeared on the scene in the mid-1980s than Bill O'Reilly was describing him as Stan McCabe reincarnate; he became known for his friendships with past masters Hunter Hendry and Bill Brown. When he made his first real impact as a Test batsman twenty years ago in England, the praise was for his model technique, of a purity no local batsman could emulate. When he came to the Test captaincy a decade ago, he was lauded for his regular appeals to the past, and an almost demagogic espousal of the cult of the baggy green. Even in articulating the doctrine of 'mental disintegration', Waugh was seen as following time-honoured Australian mores: he was the old-fashioned, indefatigable Aussie who did not give up a chip of a bail, while expecting what happened on the field to stay there.

His career knew torrid times. There was the claimed catch of Brian Lara in April 1995, for which, as he put it, he was 'carved up' by the likes of Michael Holding and Viv Richards. There was the manipulation of the points system in the World Cup a decade ago, in an attempt to progress the West Indies at New Zealand's expense, after which Waugh famously explained: 'We're not here to win friends, mate'. Nor did he shore up relations with the media when he muttered, less famously but more pithily, that his press conference inquisitors were a 'bunch of cockheads'.

Yet this was a rare dropping of the guard: for a cricketer who played so ruthlessly, and whose team was wont to push the line of acceptable aggression, his career had few personal black marks. He never transgressed the ICC Code of Conduct himself, and was once even its beneficiary, Ian Healy's suspension in South Africa in March 1997 smoothing his path to the vice-captaincy. A stroll through the index of his magnum opus, *Out of My Comfort Zone*

(2005), underlines how seldom he became part of public disputes. One lights hopefully on 'moped incident, Bermuda', only to find it refers to minor hijinks at the end of the 1991 Caribbean tour rather than being Australian cricket's secret Pedalogate.

Off the field, Waugh maintained an almost sunken profile. In person a shy and self-effacing man, he was instrumental in welcoming wives into the Australian team's fold as a kind of civilising influence, receiving the phone call that offered him the Australian captaincy while watching *Sesame Street* with his daughter. When Shane Warne publicly dissed Adam Gilchrist's leadership aspirations by philosophising that a captain should be more like The Fonz than Richie Cunningham, it was possible to fit Steve Waugh into the scenario as a kind of Howard Cunningham, all rumpled integrity, paternal wisdom and comfortable domesticity.

Speaking of Howards, the period of Waugh's ascendancy in Australia was encompassed by the prime ministership of John of that ilk, the self-styled 'cricket tragic' who cheerfully acknowledged himself the most conservative leader his conservative party had ever had. Waugh was not an exact fit with this period. He welcomed the compulsive innovator John Buchanan into his team's inner circle; he sought, with a touch of the New Age guru, to 'get to know the guys as human beings and not just cricketers'. As his fame grew, and he was compelled to become a public figure, he became as famous for exchanging pleasantries with Mother Teresa and Nelson Mandela as he did for exchanging unpleasantries with Curtly Ambrose, putting his reputation to use in a variety of philanthropic works on the Subcontinent.

Nonetheless, in an age of compulsive extraversion, Waugh cut a taciturn, even an inhibited figure on the field, lean, dour and unsmiling, to complaints about which he retorted: 'If you're in your office trying to work, do you smile all the time?' Instead of flamboyance, the keynote of Waugh's captaincy was continuity. He existed, even in an age of abundance, as a reminder of leaner times in Australian cricket, the last of his generation to have an Ashes defeat on his conscience. He pressed also to create 'new' traditions, having a special cap minted for the first Test of the 2000s modelled on the cap worn in the first test of the 1900s, involving himself in the manufactured memorabilia industry as a shareholder in the firm Blazed in Glory.

Nor was it just the surname that lent his leadership a martial air. His Tests were frontal assaults, carefully plotted, relentlessly executed. No captain to lead their country in more than ten Tests has a higher proportion of wins or a lower proportion of draws. He believed in rank, in esprit de corps, even in the power of a uniform, embodied in his storied cap, so distinctive in an era of helmets and sunhats. His nationalism was of the same unselfconscious, celebratory if sometimes defensive character that flourished during the eleven years of Howard's premiership. 'I'd like to see Australian people own more of Australia and not sell it all off to overseas companies and corporations', he told an interviewer fifteen years ago. 'It seems to me that the Japanese own half of Queensland—that's one thing I'd like to see changed.' But if all the John Williamson songs and odes to the Southern Cross sometimes seemed contrived, nor were they easily imitable. Waugh initiated the numbering of players' headgear and attire, inviting eminent past players to hand new caps over to Test debutants, beginning with Bill Brown's welcome to Adam Gilchrist ten years ago. England have tried something similar, but watching Nasser Hussain hand Jonathan Trott his new lid at the Oval in 2009 was, quite clearly, qualitatively different. Taking his teammates to Gallipoli sat more naturally with Waugh than with any other leader; when England dropped in on Flanders before the last Ashes series, it looked phoney even before Andrew Flintoff elected to drink for his country.

Quite why Waugh reinforced his captaincy with so many props and symbols is an intriguing psychological question. Some saw it as self-promotion; even now, Waugh has a quiet caucus of detractors in Australian cricket, who see him as out primarily for number one. Waugh himself has answered to the charge: 'Life as a full-time professional teaches you to be selfish in many ways'. A personal suspicion is that Waugh coveted the captaincy before quite grasping what it entailed, and as a self-contained man found it at first an uneasy fit. The activities and artefacts with which he surrounded his leadership were a means of distributing the burden; he could thereby make himself less an individual, more the representative of a lineage.

Waugh was famous for his diaries and his photographs. Both can act as means of ordering and controlling experiences, putting a comforting distance between the act and the observer. Sport, of course, is replete with ego, and Waugh could not have competed without a sizeable one. But his wife Lynette, who writes as perceptively of her husband as anyone, has noted: 'Stephen has never—even as a baby, I'm told—liked a lot of attention'. And it's telling, I think, how swiftly and completely Waugh has receded in public consciousness since that final, rather fevered farewell season five years ago; not for him the love of and comfort in the limelight of his most eminent contemporary, Shane Warne. 'Treasure', of course, is something proverbial tucked away, not necessarily recognised as such, even when in plain sight. In this sense, the National Trust truly knew its man.

Cricinfo, August 2010

272

SHANE WARNE

Fame Is the Spur

Shane Warne will probably never play at the Melbourne Cricket
Ground again, but a corner has been marked out for him. In
October 2009, in the bowels of the ground, the National Sports
Museum activated 'Shane Warne: Cricket Found Me', in which a
three-dimensional image of Warne speaks for more than ten minutes, seemingly ex tempore, while appearing to walk around a
dressing room.

The technology is remarkable; Warne's adaptation to it is more
remarkable still. He was required to speak about his career to a
camera, without prop or prompts, in one uninterrupted take. As
you will observe, he did so effortlessly, without ever breaking eye
contact—or, perhaps more accurately, lens content. Elsewhere in
the museum, a simulacrum of the Australian Rules footballer James
Hird, an intelligent and well-spoken young man, goes through the
same routine in a similar display: his attention falters, his eyes dart
away, his body language is tentative. You watch Warne again. You
hate to admit it but it's true: he seems to be taking *to you*. Now *that*
is charisma.

Warne was an extraordinary bowler. It can't really be said often
enough. He will personify leg-break bowling for as long as the skill
exists. If and when an outstanding new purveyor achieves note, the
question will be: how does he compare with Warne? As fascinating
to watch as were Anil Kumble and Mushtaq Ahmed, Warne's
was the style to study and emulate—so simple, so unadorned, so

apparently artless. So epic were his feats, too, that it is hard to recall leg-break bowling before him. In the 1980s, of course, there were the mysteries and intrigues of Abdul Qadir. But Qadir's wickets down under cost 61 runs each. Had Cormac McCarthy written a novel of Australian cricket at the time, it would surely have been called *No Country for Young Leg-Spinners*. That was certainly the attitude, when Warne first played Sheffield Shield, of his captain Simon O'Donnell and coach Les Stillman. Seldom has received wisdom been more promptly and utterly routed.

Warne cut a swathe through batsmen in the early 1990s who had seen nothing remotely similar for generations—which was amazing. Then he cut another swathe, and another—which was miraculous. After his Test debut in England, with its fabled 'Gatting ball', Warne's bowling average was 28. It diminished to 22.55, grew to 26.7 and finally settled at 25.4. Until then, leg spin had been cricket's blue sky investment; Warne made it into bowling bricks and mortar. Everything told you it should be otherwise. Batsmen would get used to him. Coaches would work him out. Curators would prepare flat pitches. All these were before the physical dangers Warne posed to himself, for leg spin involves colossal efforts at pivotal points in the human anatomy. And, to an extent, all the aforementioned possibilities eventuated. In each case, Warne rose to the challenge of counteracting them. He kept getting batsmen bowled. He kept getting them LBW. He kept getting them WTF. He had almost no right to, but he did.

Even so, this doesn't quite do him justice, for Warne was no more to be considered simply a bowler than Marilyn Monroe was to be deemed merely an actress. He was a presence, on the field, in the game, in the media, in the mind. To each delivery, there was a whole preamble, sometimes theatrical, sometimes languorous, always captivating. As he dawdled before his trademark saunter, he would curl the ball from hand to hand, an action both predatory and dainty, feeling his own powers of torque communicated through the ball, keeping the batsman in his crouch that little longer than perhaps was comfortable—time for thought, time for doubt. That pause: it was almost imperceptible, yet time would seem to stand still. It called to mind Paul Keating's parliamentary retort when quizzed by his rival John Hewson as to why he did not call an early election: 'The answer is, mate, I wanna do you slowly'.

In the last few years of his career, these performances of Warne's bordered on burlesque. The Ashes of 2005 and 2006–07 were series divided: there was the cricket featuring Warne, then the rest. There was brilliance, there was bluff; he was the beamish boy one moment, the blowhard the next. He was seldom outbowled, hardly outfoxed, never outtalked. His manner with dissenting officials was straight from the WG Grace playbook: 'They've come to watch me bowl, not you umpire'. Nor was it always a pageant of success. A day that sticks in the mind is the fourth at Perth in December 2006. Warne toiled for almost two sessions from the Prindiville Stand End, on a perfect batting wicket, in temperatures well over 40 degrees, taking one for 100. Yet every ball was full of willingness and willpower. Every time he paused at the top of his run, you felt like the batsman was simply there for his delectation. Every time he whirled into his action, you expected a triumphant appeal to follow. At the time, it transpired, he was contemplating the retirement he announced before the next Test. You'd never have guessed: he seemed to be setting himself to bowl forever. Late that day, McGrath, spared work for the afternoon, struck crucially with the second new ball, and afterwards commented that the wickets were as much Warne's as his: how often, by the pressure he exerted, by the yakka he soaked up, that was true.

On fame in cricket, meanwhile, Warne rewrote the book. In this, to be sure, he had some help. On television in India, Sachin Tendulkar has exerted perhaps the single greatest influence; on tabloid culture in England, Ian Botham left indelible inky fingerprints. Yet Warne blazed a trail of fame everywhere cricket took him, and everywhere he took cricket. He oozed action. He radiated star quality. An expectation surrounded him, including his own of himself, as it has done few other players, and as it was once summarised by another Australian cricketer: 'Every time Warne bowls he expects to take wickets. Every time he bats he expects to make runs. Every time he sees a woman he expects to get laid'.

His weakness, particularly in the last of these, was an incapacity for saying 'no'—to others, to himself. But you could sort of understand this apparently infinite suggestibility: after all, most of the time 'yes' worked so damn well. And, in the end, Warne pulled it off, so to speak: even after all his tribulations, Warne has ended up being a good advertisement for fame. Certainly, he always seemed to enjoy it—sometimes to a fault. 'He loves to be loved', said his captain, Steve Waugh, and the media has never outgrown its infatuation with him. For all his sometimes tetchy relations with them, too, Warne has returned the media's embrace. No past master has fitted as seamlessly into commentary as Warne—insightful, irreverent, irrepressible, even in his recent permatanned petrifaction.

Warne also remained, above all, absolutely true to his gift. Fame had opposite effects on Tendulkar and Botham. Tendulkar preserved his excellence by sequestering himself from a clamouring public; Botham swallowed celebrity whole, and spat out self-parody. Warne swaggered down the middle of the road, living large, but always bowling bigger, revelling in the attention while never losing the love of his craft. Even now, at forty, in the IPL, he looks completely engaged in every game. There are those who say he obtains wickets because he is Shane Warne; to this, Warne would undoubtedly reply: 'Thanks for the compliment'.

Warne has inspired books, busts, bottles of wine, hagiographies, hatchet jobs, mountains of memorabilia, even a musical. But in some respects, the MCG's new installation of him is his most faithful reflection. Many, many more people saw Warne as image than reality; he is a man of comparatively few close friends and millions upon millions of acquaintances. Yet somehow, despite all the layers of mediation, all the received opinion, all the manufactured outrage, the naturalness came through, and we felt we knew him.

Cricinfo, July 2010

SHANE WARNE: THE MUSICAL

Fanfare for the Common Man

Consider these three vignettes from the storied life of Shane Warne, involving something that happened, then something that didn't, then something that is.

On 10 June 2000, London's *Daily Mirror* publishes front page allegations that Shane Warne had harassed a nurse, whom he had met in a nightclub in Leicester, by bombarding her with explicit voicemail messages. Australians respond by bombarding the offices of Cricket Australia with telephoned complaints. Although Warne is at the time representing his English county, Hampshire, rather than on national duty, he has been Australia's vice-captain for a successful eighteen months. CA's chief executive flies to England, testily confronts him, then oversees a meeting of directors stripping Warne of his office, thereby thwarting his captaincy ambitions.

Five years later, almost to the day, London's *Sunday Mirror* publishes a still spicier story, about a buxom budding glamour model whom Warne had purportedly pestered for sex that then proved embarrassingly perfunctory. Warne is actually representing Australia, and the story is in some respects more damaging than the episode in 2000—in particular, it undermines a reconciliation Warne had been trying to affect with his long-suffering wife, Simone. CA switchboard operators brace for the torrents of complaint— and receive not a single call. In fact, receiving no demand, the organisation makes no public comment, and Warne bowls as well in the next five Test matches as he ever has—that is, perhaps as well as any man has bowled in cricket's history.

Finally, at Melbourne's Athenaeum Theatre, on 10 December 2008, a four-piece band strikes up an introductory medley beginning with Emerson, Lake and Palmer's 'Fanfare for the Common Man'—and, at once, he is among us. Warne moves shyly but visibly to centre front in the dress circle, to watch a musical based on his life, encompassing all the above and more. The audience exult—a mood that doesn't alter for the entire evening. When creator Eddie Perfect struts to centre stage as his bumptious, been-there-done-that subject, the atmosphere is almost that of an evangelical revival. The audience laugh and cheer and applaud their way through almost three hours of his infelicities, infidelities and infantilities—and so does Warne. Paul Keating lent his imprimatur to Casey Bennetto's hugely successful musical, although only after waiting about six weeks for signs of visible success. Warne knows no such inhibition: he materialises on stage at the end to make public his endorsement, walking off hand-in-hand with his parodist.

At the end of this third vignette, everyone knows they have seen something special, but perhaps how special is elucidated only by considering the first two also: Warne, it would seem, has cajoled the public out of its tendency to moralising to one of relaxed celebration of personal folly, through a midpoint of indifference. When Perfect/Warne sings that he's 'just another chopped tall poppy/That's what they do when you're an Aussie', he's actually overlooking his show's evolving contribution to the legend: apparently, a chopped poppy can grow back twice as large, providing it remains true to its nature. The subject is one of the greatest of cricketers; it is also of the growth of one of Australia's greatest, cheeriest, most companionable and inclusive of jokes—a joke all the funnier for the fact that once we took it so seriously.

You could fault *Shane Warne: The Musical* for perhaps not quite having the courage of its satire, for throwing a stone or two and running away: Warne's media scolds and cynical handlers get off lightly. You could quibble with its portrayal of Warne as the most demotic of cricketers and also the supreme individualist—a tension it doesn't quite reconcile. There'll be some Australian teammates who get a giggle from Warne delivering an entire song, 'We're Going There', extolling the camaraderie of the beer drinking school. There's a delicious glimpse of Warne in Jason Gillespie's autobiography, *Dizzy* (2007), holding court during a Gabba Test when a group of Brisbane Lions players dropped in:

> He decided to grab a beer out of the fridge, sit in his corner, put an ice pack on his knee and have the fags nearby. Maybe he wanted to portray a bit of an 'old school' image to the Brisbane lads. The rest of us all looked at each other and thought to ourselves, What's going on here? Warnie with a beer? We were all having a bit of a giggle, and in came the Lions lads to say 'Hi'.
>
> Nothing was really said until Glenn McGrath walked in. He sat down, noticed Warnie with a frostie and asked, 'What the hell are you doing with a beer?' Warnie replied, 'Bowling day, mate—just finishing the day with a beer.' Glenn responded, 'I've never, ever seen you with a beer.' Warnie came back with, 'Oh, hang on, mate: I always have a beer at the end of a bowling day.' We all pissed ourselves laughing, because none of us had ever seen him have a beer after a bowling day.
>
> For the rest of the summer, Darren Lehmann, Gilly [Adam Gilchrist] and I took it upon ourselves to make sure that at the end of each bowling day, Shane had a beer in his spot in the rooms. We chortled away, thinking we were the funniest blokes in the world. After about six months, he said to me: 'Dizzy, enough is enough, you've made your point—well done.'

But faulting the factual fidelity of *Shane Warne: The Musical* is pointless: one might as well bring an elephant to a production of *Oklahoma!* to see if the corn reaches eye-high. Because Perfect has gotten something brilliantly, uncannily right: he has made his musical a love story. On the face of it, Warne is a man of sex rather than of love; but he is also an incurable romantic. Perfect has written some wonderfully, waspishly funny songs, but the numbers that nail the story down are the most poignant. At the end of Act One, Warne sweeps his young bride, Simone, off her feet, promising that one day she will be 'Dancing with the Stars'—as came to pass, when she was recruited for that television show as Warne's ex-wife. At the end of Act Two, Warne having delivered the gloriously self-justifying anthem 'Shine Like Shane', Simone retorts with 'What about That?'—all broken metre and frail rhyme.

> Think of all the times I got on a plane to meet you and the boys
> at the end of another tour
>
> They would smile and hug me knowing full well what you'd
> been up to
>
> I thought they were our friends
>
> But they were just yours
>
> Do you know how that feels, Shane?
>
> Knowing your friends are not real, Shane?
>
> What about that, Shane?

Having listened, head bowed, Warne/Perfect confides laconically in the audience: 'As you can see, not everything went entirely to plan'. It might be his accounting for a spell of none for 100. There's a stoic chagrin as he heads into the climactic 'The Ashes': 'The landscape looks black/But the Ashes are a sign it's time to grow back'. Twinned with its life toll, Warne's career triumph is seen in starker relief.

Warne is also a sponge for adulation. As perhaps no other cricketer, public affirmation rejuvenates him—it is one of the reasons for his whole-hearted embrace of the IPL, when he doesn't need the money and hardly needs the fame. His manager, James Erskine, apparently read the script for *Shane Warne: The Musical* in advance, but it would have taken the experience of watching it in an excited and joyful audience to finally convert him. If he is a stranger to musical theatre, he knows all there is to know about crowds.

Shane Warne: The Musical has been almost three years in the making. You can see the work—and also not see it. One song is a notable omission since the previews at last year's Comedy Festival:

in 'So Take the Pill', Brigitte Warne was played as a *Sylvania Waters* virago, forcing the fabled diuretic pill on her dopey, suggestible son. It was a good song in the wrong musical—cruel, gratuitous, and rightly deemed unnecessary. The dream sequence that follows is now a little long and shapeless—it is the only period where the musical loses momentum. But there's an expansive generosity about the two and three-quarter hours that is quite Warnesque; songs are tossed up as gamely as leg breaks, then as cunningly as flippers and zooters. It is Warne's past, and all our pasts. The year 2000, once the very definition of the future, now savours of nostalgia: before 9/11, economic pessimism and climate catastrophism, when sportsmen's peccadillos still had the power to shock. These days, that's entertainment—as Warnie always sort of said it was.

Shane Warne: The Musical also has that unusual quality of seeming like an incredibly obvious idea the minute that you hear it, although cricket and the stage in Australia are nodding acquaintances rather than bosom pals. There was a *Botham: The Musical*, which toured Australia in the early 1980s, although it took the Cambridge Footlights Society to mount it. Nonetheless, Perfect's production has one interesting antecedent. When WG Grace first toured Australia 135 years ago, Melbourne's most popular Christmas pantomime was Garnet Walch's *Australia Felix; or Harlequin Laughing Jackass and the Magic Bat*. The allegorical plot concerned a magic cricket bat gifted by the 'ethereal genius' Mirth to a country lass, and used by her betrothed, Felix, in a game at the Melbourne Cricket Ground.

Australia Felix was partly a reply to Anthony Trollope's acid views of the antipodes in his *Australia and New Zealand* (1872). Walch offered cricket as a civilising counterinfluence to the corrupting powers of Mischief, representative of horse racing. Mirth describes the bat as 'the symbol of the manliest game/To which I've ever lent my royal name/Type of true British sport, without alloy/Where you, friend Mischief, are *de trop*, old boy'. Australia, in fact, was in the process of building a better Britain than the original; Britain's pompous dimwit ruling classes were embodied in Kantankeros, the 'demon of Dullness'.

When Warne/Perfect arrives in England on his maiden Ashes tour in *Shane Warne: The Musical,* two hoity-toity toffs mince past, commenting severely on 'that frightfully blonde man from the colonies'. The Australians, dontcha know, are 'nothing but a bunch of criminals and chronic masturbators': the familiar caricature of Englishmen as effete snobs goes down a storm, as we know they'll shortly be getting theirs. It is reiterated at regular intervals thereafter that, for all the global game's cups and kudos, no cricket matters quite so much as the ritual humiliation of the hated Pom. During the finale, lights on the illuminating backdrop form the outline of the Ashes urn. Perfect's triumph, then, is not only to demonstrate how much can change in eight years, but how much can stay the same in 135.

The Monthly, February 2009

SHANE WARNE IN THE IPL

Yeah Yeah

One of the truisms with which Australians have traditionally grown up involves the captaincy of their cricket team. Prudish Poms, it has been said, pick their ten best players, and only then pick a captain, whereas we no-nonsense Aussies always choose our best eleven, then appoint the best of that best to lead it.

The contradistinction is now probably a bit old hat, but not only because England seem to have abandoned hang-ups about an 'officer class'. For with each passing year it grows a little more curious: Shane Warne, the best cricketer of his generation, perhaps the best of all Australians bar the eternal exception of Bradman, did not occupy the office to which his abilities clearly entitled him.

The sense grows almost every time Warne leads the Rajasthan Royals into the field in the IPL, when he reminds you of John Ford's famous remark about John Wayne. Ford could take or leave Wayne the actor, but one quality he could not deny: 'The sonofabitch walked like a man'. Some captains hold the job without ever really becoming leaders; Warne would be a leader even were he not captain—as indeed he was for Australia.

Alan Crompton, a former chairman of Cricket Australia who managed several of Warne's early tours, once described his impact in terms of the dressing room. Wherever Australia went in those days, it was around Warne's corner of the dressing room that activity seemed to concentrate: teammates hovered; visitors descended; noise and laughter emanated. Crompton said that no other Australian player in his long experience had quite the same effect, except perhaps Rod Marsh, another cricketer's cricketer who coincidentally also missed out on captaining Australia despite having all the credentials for doing so.

On the field, too, Warne was never happy unless fully engaged. David Lloyd, then England's coach, recalls the final afternoon of 1997's Old Trafford Test. Warne, Lloyd could see, was a little non-plussed by the atmosphere, or lack of it, on the field, so he started clapping his hands at slip, and noisily exhorting each of his teammates in turn, addressing them by their nicknames. 'C'mon Australia!' he bellowed finally, loud enough that all the crowd could hear it. 'This is what it's all about!' And so, to Warne, it is: communal input, collective effort.

Leading in ascendancy, of course, isn't altogether a challenge. But even under the cosh, Warne was not the kind to retreat into himself. In India in 2001, Warne faced some of the most gruelling cricket of his career: out of form, out of condition, against a home team suddenly galvanised, part of a visiting side steadily losing focus, and facing criticism even from his own coach, John Buchanan, for his palpable lack of fitness.

Warne and Buchanan were never again quite on the same page; hardly unlikely, really, when they were like leaves from different books. When I quizzed Buchanan about this series a couple of years ago, however, the coach paid Warne generous tribute. After a long absence recovering from a broken finger, Warne was clearly far from his best, and struggling desperately in the heat. But around the dressing room at each interval, he was the loudest and longest in urging comrades on, and by a long way the last man beaten.

That Warne never captained his country parallels the fate of Keith Miller, Australia's don't-give-a-damn all-rounder of the 1950s, thought by conservative cricket authorities to be too hot to handle. That Warne had the most public private life of perhaps any cricketer before or since discomforted administrators more instinctively at home with Steve Waugh's old-fashioned family values. Nor was this exactly a state secret. 'Shane's a good boy', his mother is said to have told an officer of CA. 'He just can't keep his dick in his pants.'

Another factor told against him. Warne had two spells as captain of Victoria, neither long, but both seemingly indicative, winning just two and losing six of eleven games, and paying 52 runs for each of his twenty-seven wickets. Long absences on international duty were a handicap, but there seemed something about being first among equals that did not suit him; in a team of strong characters including Dean Jones, Darren Berry, Matthew Elliott and Brad Hodge, he failed to achieve the distance and disinterest by which good captains set themselves slightly apart in order to express their authority. Nor did four-day cricket on slow, flat wickets suit a personality that needed the reinforcement of individual performance.

On the other hand, had Warne made a success of leadership in the Sheffield Shield, and had he rather than Steve Waugh succeeded Mark Taylor as Australian captain in February 1999, there might not now be this fascinating coda to his career in Jaipur. As it was, even after 1000 international wickets, Warne retired from Australian cricket with worlds to conquer. He had enjoyed the experience of coming from the outside and building a young team at Hampshire in 2004 and 2006, yanking them from the second division of the county championship to within a whiff of the title; the money was resistible when the Royals job was offered, for Warne could earn more from the media punditry for which he has revealed unexpected gifts, but the opportunity was not.

The disincentives, meanwhile, actually made the job more beguiling rather than less. Warne had everything to lose and by no means much to gain from becoming then the league's only foreign captain. He had achieved so much. What did it profit him again putting his reputation on the line? He had never prospered in India, paying 43 for each Test wicket there. Nor had he had much impact in Twenty20, Hampshire winning one game in eight during his last season at the club. Yet what could be more exciting than routing the doubters, who became just that little more audible after Rajasthan were monstered by the Delhi Daredevils in their first match?

Two factors have worked in his favour. First, he designed his own job: a role that suited him of captain, coach, guru and go-to guy. It looked to the outside world like a derisive middle finger to

Buchanan, whose contribution to Australian supremacy, Warne often argued, was always glimpsed after the fact; it certainly resonated with the views of Warne's old mucker Ian Chappell, who loudly proclaims the obsolescence of coaches at every opportunity. But the position certainly fitted Warne, always prepared to accept that the buck stops with him providing he also starts it. Unlike other franchises, there has never been any confusion at the Royals about the man in charge: coaching director Darren Berry (from Victoria) and chief executive Sean Morris (from Hampshire) know enough of Warne to give him his head.

The young squad has also been made to measure. Warne is a charismatic man: gregarious, personable, good company, capable of the up-and-at-'em motivational address but also of the arm-around-the-shoulder believe-in-yourself one-to-one, and, above all, a contagious enthusiast for cricket, who enjoys the game as he enjoys himself. Nor does the world have anything to teach Warne about media management: he plays journalists and broadcasters like guitars. At Hampshire he was renowned for using press conferences and newspaper columns to promote the county's coming men, like Nic Pothas, Dimitri Mascarenhas, Michael Carberry and, most famously, Kevin Pietersen; whether it has been Sohail Tanvir, Swapnil Asnodkar, Kamran Khan, Yusuf Pathan or, lately, Paras Dogra, Warne at the Royals always seems to be bigging up someone.

The second factor in Warne's success at the Royals has been the slightly surprising one that Twenty20 suits him. Spinners weren't expected to influence the IPL overmuch; the boundaries were too short and the bats too powerful. But the restricted format gets the best from him. One of the reasons Warne never quite adapted to Indian conditions, for instance, was his inclination to spin the ball massively. The distance of the break was often exciting, but opened up width and angles for batsmen to exploit. Twenty20's zero tolerance policy towards wides compels Warne to bowl as perhaps he always should have on the Subcontinent: straighter, within tighter lines, and with the trademark big leggie as a variation.

In his forty-first year, and without regular first-class exposure, Warne would now find Test cricket a serious challenge. But the three-hour game could have been devised with him in mind, not simply because it is not so physically strenuous, but because it magnifies the potential significance of the brilliant individual delivery that is still well and truly within Warne's capabilities. It also makes more useful his potentially damaging hitting. No match has been as significant in Warne's tenure than the Royals' clash with the Deccan Chargers in Hyderabad, when with fourteen needed from the final four balls, Warne clouted Andrew Symonds for a boundary then for consecutive straight sixes.

The result brought to the fore Warne's talismanic qualities. Nothing conduces to doing the unexpected like the experience of doing it before, and Warne was already the hero of a thousand fights. He was the man who had turned whole Test matches, and seen them turned by others; the fluctuations of Twenty20, wilder but simpler, were meat and drink to him. That win in Hyderabad was the first of a dozen wins in fourteen games: Royals haven't made a bigger comeback since the Bourbon Restoration. Rajasthan have failed to quite repeat that title-winning form, but have never been less than dangerous, and in this most recent season have loomed large again.

Warne appears in his element in the IPL, whether exchanging admiring glances with Bollywood's brightest or swapping mutual endearments with Lalit Modi via Twitter. And make no mistake, Warne likes money. Not that he is particularly greedy, or motivated by mammon; on the contrary, through his foundation in Australia, he has been a generous donor to children's charities. But he is comfortable in money's company. Some squirm at the IPL's wealth and ostentation. Warne is not one of them. Raised amid the cheerful and unabashed materialism of Australian suburbia, he likes beautiful, expensive things—big houses, flash cars, eye-catching bling.

Warne's incalculable gift to the IPL, all the same, is his sheer undisguised pleasure in the contest. Not that he's there for the carnival; his enjoyment comes chiefly through winning. But he plays because he wishes to, not because he needs to, persuading you to forget, at least momentarily, the billions at stake, the commercial agendas, the political machinations. Perhaps, in hindsight, the

Australian captaincy was too solemn an office for a man of such unquenchable energies; whatever the case, he makes a snug fit with the biggest, boldest, ripest, richest game in town.

Sports Illustrated India, May 2010

RICKY PONTING

Big Ask

Preparing for his delivery of the Bradman Oration at the August 2008 celebrations of the Don's centenary, Ricky Ponting carefully set out a speech that at normal pace would comfortably fill half an hour. The hushed auditorium and harsh lighting of the evening got the better of him: he galloped through his words in less than eighteen minutes. It happens, to be fair, to the best public speakers. Yet the story is also, as it were, Punteresque: when in doubt, or under pressure, Australia's captain goes hard, even headlong, about his business.

Doubt and pressure now accompany Ponting to India. Of course, not even the most imposing Test records are without their soft spots. Tendulkar and Dravid don't average 40 in South Africa; Hayden averages less than 35 in England; Shane Warne paid more than 43 runs for each of his Test wickets in India. But Ponting's five-day performances in cricket's modern centre aren't just middlingly poor. An average of 12.28 from fourteen innings implies that about the only thing he has been getting right is turning up on the required days.

Theories, inevitably, have been advanced. Ian Chappell says Ponting is inclined to bat as he speaks—there is too much hurry too soon. It is arguable the conditions restrict him. The lower Indian bounce deprives Ponting of opportunities to essay his pet pull shot; nor has he ever been a confident player of the sweep. Whatever the case, he still has much to prove. It was Steve Waugh who christened

India the Australian team's 'final frontier'; injury having deprived Ponting of a share in Australia setting that to rights four years ago, he arrives looking for a vital validation. How will he respond?

The likely answer is: by sticking to what he knows. Ponting has the classically Australian characteristic of not being a fiddler or a faffer with the basics of his technique or approach. He ascribes his failure in India seven years ago to tampering with the tried and true after a failure or two. Under his captaincy, too, Australia has played a brand of percentage cricket, convinced that quality will out as long as the game plan is observed. The scheme hasn't met with uniform success: Australia's predictability cost them in the Ashes of 2005. But with Warne, McGrath, Gilchrist and Ponting himself, quality has proven a wise investment. The team has continued setting standards worldwide.

Even without that mighty trio, Ponting will be priming Australia to assert themselves, to radiate the prickly, up-and-at-'em aura that he doesn't trouble to euphemise as 'mental disintegration'. Although it is a commonplace that Australia is the world's most aggressive team, it is actually more accurate to describe them as the world's most *consistently* and *uniformly* aggressive team; that is, where a number of teams exhibit aggression in spasms and phases, and certain individuals from other countries are inclined to throw regular weight around, Australians are better at maintaining a lounging, low-level hostility at all times. Indeed, one of the bones Ponting has picked with India is that their players appear to vary in their willingness to contest. He complained, for instance, when the hosts, chock-full of cheek in the first two games of last year's one-day series, suddenly took umbrage in the third: 'If the Indians can play the sort of cricket they did play for the first couple of games and then completely turn around and go the other way in the other games, it showed us how fake, if you like, the first part of the series was as far as they're concerned'. One of the reasons Bhajigate festered on in January, I suspect, was a residual annoyance about what Australians see as an Indian tendency to periodically redefine the acceptable level of on-field belligerence. Thus Ponting's hankering to obtain an ICC determination of what was beyond the pale—not a wise move, really, when the ICC needs a committee to determine the day of the week.

How closely Ponting can hew to his old ways, however, will not be entirely of his own volition. The cricket world is waiting to see whether Australia can remain its reserve currency, as it were, without the watermark of former greats. The absence of Symonds, furthermore, removes a huge, brooding stumbling block, sometimes sullen but always intimidating, in both Australia's middle order and its fielding formations: his physical presence may be missed in India almost as much as his skills.

Just returned from surgery on his right wrist, Ponting himself is a cricketer increasingly conscious of the limits of his own body; thirty-four in December and newly a father, he can glimpse life beyond the game. He has never really had Waugh's presence as a captain: where Waugh exuded a lurking, predatory toughness, Ponting tends merely to look surly. But while never as demonstratively patriotic as his predecessor, Ponting has let slip more often in recent times an elder statesman's anxiety about international cricket. In his Bradman Oration, he dwelt on the old-fashioned continuities of his upbringing—how his junior years were as concerned with community as cricket.

> For me they are the things like the smell of Aeroguard which is something that sticks in my mind about junior cricket. The smell of cut grass is something even to this day, I can still remember ... I remember jumping on my BMX at the age of seven or eight years old and riding all over Launceston to find where my local A-grade side were playing. I was always the first one there and inevitably the last one to leave. I would sit ... in the corner of the change rooms, listening to whatever the club legends of the time had to say about the game and to this moment today I still feel that's where I learned most about the game of cricket.

There was more—much more—in this vein. And although reporting of the Oration emphasised Ponting's (fairly anodyne) opinions about Twenty20, the context of those views seemed much more significant. For all his rapid-fire delivery, Ponting was, unbidden, taking the side of tradition in the pending debates about the game's future. Not even Waugh at his most sentimental dwelt so long on cricket as a local activity, and even as a rite of adult passage. Ponting recalled his youthful chagrin, for example, when the local park of his childhood insisted that cricket games be played with tennis balls: 'For me that wasn't what cricket was all about; cricket was about a cricket ball, pads and gloves, playing in the park, playing against kids who were a lot bigger, a lot stronger and for me that's when my journey really started'. Not a view much heard in these days of plastic balls, plastic stumps and inclusive modified games.

In coming to India, then, Ponting is not simply on a mission to improve his own record; he will be hoping, by a memorable Border–Gavaskar Trophy, to shape the game's future in the country destined to determine it. 'I personally look forward to emulating Sir Donald and leaving the game in better shape for having been a part of it', he concluded his speech. And granted that the circumstances probably called for high-sounding sentiments, and that pressure then made them fast-sounding, Ponting deserves in this instance to be taken at his word.

Cricinfo, September 2008

RICKY PONTING

Nag Poor

When Australia beat England narrowly in the dead Sydney Test of January 1987, having already lost the Ashes, a journalist at the press conference put a proposition to the visiting captain, Mike Gatting. Wasn't it really rather good that the hosts had won a consolation victory? Didn't he, deep down, feel a little sorry for the Aussies? Gatting wasn't a man for baleful glares or even Simon Katich–style brush-offs, but he imparted some advice to remember. Beating Australia was always great, he insisted. And nobody, but nobody, should ever feel sorry for a cricketer in green and gold.

Under present circumstances, however, it's hard not to extend some sympathy to Ricky Ponting, who stands accused of surrendering the Border–Gavaskar Trophy in November 2008 with a single stroke of captaincy: a decision that seems to have set at nought all his previous achievements. Even the newspaper for whom Ponting writes, *The Australian*, has joined the accusers, having spun for him like Alastair Campbell all the way through Bhajigate.

Indeed, Ponting might well have lost Australia the Test, but on the first day, when he lost the toss; ditto Mohali. It's no fluke that Australia's best performance during the series followed the only occasion of it winning the privilege of first innings. The way the Australian bowlers that Ponting didn't use have been described, meanwhile, you'd think he had Ray Lindwall, Dennis Lillee and Glenn McGrath at his disposal. In fact, the pace attack at Ponting's disposal had taken five wickets for the match, and on tour had paid 45 runs per wicket.

Where Ponting does deserve criticism is not in bowling whom he did when, but in so marooning himself behind the over rate that such a choice became necessary, although that bespeaks a lapse in concentration rather than a failure of judgement. Having watched Dhoni's captaincy on the Saturday, he may have been suckered into slowing the pace of the game without realising the pressure it might put him under later. Australians are not hugely adept at defensive cricket, and weren't even at their peak. In the context of the 2003 Antigua Test where the West Indies successfully chased 418, Adam Gilchrist comments in his autobiography: 'We were great frontrunners and liked to accelerate the tempo of a Test match; but when the momentum moved away from us we didn't seem able to arrest it. Once we were slipping, we couldn't slow things down. Our liking for a fast attacking tempo turned against us'. If not then, it has now.

So in the cool light of day, Ponting might wish he had made different choices, chivvied his bowlers earlier, thought ahead about his narrowing options. But the cool light of day is hard to find at Nagpur in November at the end of a gruelling tour, especially without the senior helpmates on whose wisdom he has been able to call for so long. On Saturday, the ABC Radio commentary team threw every toy out of the cot—pacifier, diaper and all—and they were only contending with a lost satellite link to Australia. Ponting made other captaincy calls that earned him no praise, but at which a lesser leader might have baulked, like first choosing then persevering with Jason Krejza.

With all the praise and blame flying around, I suspect we are missing something. To my mind, Ponting has done the game a favour, by showing how neurotic we have become about Test cricket in these Twenty20-centric times. On Saturday, critics were lamenting the day's poverty of entertainment, the teams' insensitivity to the legitimate expectations of the paying public. On Sunday, they turned to lamenting an attempt by a captain to meet one of the arbitrary indicators that those legitimate expectations are being met: the requirement of ninety overs in a day.

By a mixture of ICC regulations and critical consensus, we seem to have arrived at a quantification of what constitutes a good day of Test cricket: a minimum 350 runs from a minimum ninety overs (bowled, in the latest insistence, by specialists). The fine print in various broadcasting contracts probably dictates 375 advertisements and eighty-seven pop songs too.

Yet how many great days of Test cricket have ever been exactly like that? Three of the most dramatic days of the Ashes of 2005 involved 407 runs for ten wickets, 282 for seventeen wickets and 104 runs for two wickets—each of them supersaturated with tension, and yielding memories to last a lifetime. Glorious uncertainty sometimes entails profound disappointment; but without disappointment, excellence becomes prosaic, banal. Why is it that we are so anxious to guarantee Test cricket as an entertainment package? After all, this is a game, not a pop concert. It can only be because we live in an age where a game crossed with a pop concert—Twenty20 cricket—is imposing its standards on everything else.

This has been a good series: tight, tough, intriguing, rich in variety of skill, full of stuff to write about—for which every journalist can be grateful. In fact, the wrangling of the moment is a kind of tribute to the game's long form. What Twenty20 game could rattle so many bones of contention? For this reason, Punter, while Gatt reckons I can't feel sorry for you, I'd like to offer my thanks.

Cricinfo, November 2008

THE FUTURE OF TEST CRICKET

Match Drawn?

In Brisbane fifty years ago, Englishman Trevor Bailey put his name to a Test match innings destined to go down in infamy: a score of 68 spanning 458 inglorious minutes in a doomed attempt to turn a rout into an orderly retreat. During one particularly soporific period, a journalist asked what time Bailey had scored his last run. '3.30 p.m.', the scorer responded. After a pause, another voice called out: 'Today or yesterday?'

Whatever transpires at the Gabba in the [November 2008] Test against New Zealand, it will seem almost riotous by comparison. But it will also not nearly be exciting enough for a new generation of Test cricket critics.

For outsiders finding cricket unintelligible, there have always been a host of consoling anecdotes. 'It sure is swell', Groucho Marx is reputed to have said after watching a couple of hours of cricket at Lord's. 'But say—when's the game itself going to begin?'

Now the chorus is more from insiders, wondering aloud if Test cricket's formula is not anachronistic. In a world hooked on the values of 'entertainment', what place have distant whiteclad figures on a green sward? In fact, this is an old problem. Cricket is an English pastoral game, devised chiefly for participants, and only then attracting watchers. The playing of it long predated the paying for it. Although the first game at which admission was charged was in 1744 at London's Artillery Ground, not until the 1890s were total gate receipts thought important enough to be regularly published in Australia.

And now as then, cricket's action concentrates on a 22-yard strip of earth a long way from spectators—or, as we call them today, consumers. The most companionable of cricket acts is the big hit, with the ball deposited in the crowd. But that does not happen often; indeed, eleven of the thirteen participants actively involved in the game at any particular time are bent on it not happening at all. From an entertainment point of view, this makes no sense. It would be the equivalent of having a group of people at an Amy Winehouse concert dedicated to turning the sound down—admittedly an idea with potential, but hardly in vogue. Increasingly, too, it is the values of broadcasting and marketing that must prevail. The subtle, intimate drama of the contest between batsman and bowler is desperately difficult to convey. Cricket is a product, and products, it is felt, must deliver measurable outcomes.

In an effort to meet commercial expectations over the last decade, cricket has absorbed the dogma that the entertainment value of a day's play is to be ascertained by the runs scored, and the boundaries struck and cleared. As Australia's captain, Steve Waugh was hailed for professing that 350 runs a day would be his team's standard operating procedure.

This has now spun back like a wrong 'un into Ricky Ponting's goolies. His batsmen in India, without the snap and dash of Adam Gilchrist or Andrew Symonds, and chasing big first-innings totals in three of the four Tests, struggled to assert themselves. And because there is now a competing variant of the game, Twenty20, in which 350 runs in three hours constitutes a veritable coma, even quite sage observers are walking around like Private Frazer in *Dad's Army*: 'We're all doomed. Doomed!'

That lack of confidence is instructive. In December 1977, Kerry Packer staged the first of his Supertests at VFL Park in Waverley, which coincided with a Test match at the Gabba. After it, Packer's public mouthpiece, Christopher Forsyth, issued a controversial press release to the effect that the eye-catching, high-concept Supertest was hugely superior to the tense, low-scoring traditional match because its final day's play in Melbourne had featured three times as many boundaries as in Brisbane. Said Forsyth: 'This alone is enough to stamp WSC's first Supertest as memorable and far superior to what went on in Brisbane—superior for cricketers, superior for crowds, superior for television'.

The result, says Eric Beecher in *The Cricket Revolution*, was 'instant embarrassment'. 'In these few words is revealed how little many of Mr Packer's men know of what cricket is all about', wrote the *Times*' venerable correspondent John Woodcock. The press release turned even the archetypal Aussie hard nut Jack Fingleton into a blimpish colonel from Surrey. Forsyth was 'talking rot', Fingo protested in *The Age*: 'Chris, old chap, fours have not a single thing to do with it'. Times have changed: what thirty-one years ago was philistinism has today become accepted wisdom.

Yet there is still something missing from this model. The exhibition of skills is one thing; the tang of competition and the exhilaration of the unexpected are also integral to sport. After all, which modern Test series stirred more excitement, and following which was there a greater surge in participation levels here than in any other season? That's right: the Ashes of 2005, which Australia, after fifteen years in the ascendant, unexpectedly lost. It turned out that while we savour victory here, we revel even more in a red-blooded contest.

Those five Tests, if you recall, featured two draws. And who remembers how many runs per over were scored or overs per hour were bowled? So while it might seem perverse and/or unpatriotic after an era in which we have been so spoiled by excellence, who knows how much more interesting Test cricket might become were Australia to start losing more regularly.

Sunday Age, November 2008

THE 2009 ASHES

A Thing of Rags and Patches

There is always something special about an Ashes summer. The summer of 2009 was so special as to be disturbing. The Ashes introduced to cricket the concept of the five-Test series; it has become the final fastness against its phasing out. England have not played a country over five Tests apart from Australia since 2004–05; Australia have not played a country over five Tests apart from England since 2000–01. Thus were two teams stretched in ways quite unfamiliar to them, like teenagers being expected to graduate from SMS to iambic pentameters—and it showed.

The wins were conquests. The losses were capitulations. The bating collapses were ruinous and utter. The bowling collapses—see Johnson at Lord's, Panesar at Cardiff—were complete. Have teams played more contrasting consecutive Tests than Headingley and the Oval? Have teams struggled as much with putting consecutive deliveries in the same place?

One phenomenon that received a long-overdue debunking was the ever-popular concept of 'momentum': the notion that success inevitably begets further success. Australia had all the momentum coming into the Second and Fifth Tests, and it availed them nought. England mowed Australia down in the Third Test, then were mown down in two and a half days in the Fourth. Momentum is classically defined as the product of mass times velocity; in 2009, it was revealed in cricket to be the sum of the past plus cliché.

Stretched over two and a half months, the effect was of the slow unfolding of very abrupt events, like an Ingmar Bergman film remade in the style of *The West Wing*. It was often fascinating; it was also, sometimes, not very good, or of a particularly high standard. It revealed, too, just how much cricket has lost in the gradual eclipse of the five-Test format. You genuinely *did* see teams and individuals in every circumstance, lifted by luck, taxed by trials, and feel as though you came to know them better—that, indeed, they also came to know themselves more completely.

For the Australians, even though they held the trophy, the series presented perhaps the greater demands, not merely in adapting to England's unfamiliar conditions, but also to the Ashes' unique duration. They arrived off the back of one-day series in South Africa and in Abu Dhabi; they played some bad Twenty20 cricket, then had two weeks in the nets in Leicester. How often do cricketers have no games for a fortnight? How often do they spend that fortnight in the home of Showaddywaddy and Gaye Bykers on Acid? How many interviews and press conferences can they give explaining that they are 'looking forward to the challenge'? The Australians were forced to find out.

'We were really happy with the way the people in Leicester looked after us', says Ricky Ponting in his *Captain's Diary 2009*, and ... errr ... that's it for the Australians' longest stay in any city during the year. Not that one was expecting an account of a visit to the Abbey Pumping Station or a salute to the excellence of Walker's crisps, but it is a kind of comment: the modern cricketer is fully alive only when playing. And the longer the tour, the more broadly spaced the games, the greater the need for self-regulation, for self-direction, for the individual to find a balance between discipline and relaxation, exertion and rest.

The Australians did not make the same mistake as in 2005, in programming games outside the Tests of a derisory two days—no more than glorified net sessions. Again, though, there was a sense of time killed rather than used to advantage between the big events. The old-fashioned tour involving proper first-class matches against states, counties and provinces is a thing of the past, we are told, for economic reasons. Yet the ideal structure to succeed it, ensuring competition for places among players, providing an opportunity to retrieve form and confidence and to rehearse match conditions, has never really been found. On this longest of tours, the effect was even more pronounced than usual: the gaps between Tests were first and foremost about rest for those not playing, and then and only then for giving Andrew McDonald something to write about on his postcards home.

Like an army campaigning far from home, its supply lines stretched, Australia also had multiple centres of authority. There was a captain and a vice-captain. There was a coach and his staff. There was a duty selector, liaising with colleagues back in Australia. Only the last had a vote in choosing the teams. This is a recent arrangement and so far, as sportsmen these days are wont to mangle the expression, the proof is in the pudding. It is not at all clear how individuals 17 000 kilometres away and at least thirteen years out of international cricket are better equipped to choose teams than those on the spot.

Not that Australian players can complain overmuch; it was they who traded involvement in selection on tour away, thanks to the residue of Steve Waugh's decisions to exclude Shane Warne from the St John's Test of 1999 and Michael Slater from the Oval Test of 2001. Waugh and Warne in particular were never on quite the same terms thereafter. To borrow William Safire's description of Richard Nixon and George Meany, they were 'diametrically allied': 'That is, they respected and admired each other and did not like or trust each other'.

Quite how the decisions of the selectors from their far remove to exclude Phillip Hughes at Edgbaston and Nathan Hauritz at the Oval inflected the series can only be conjectural. But Ponting's matter-of-fact comment in mid-November that he should be a selector, and that he had told Cricket Australia just that, suggested misgivings about the process that had grown rather than diminished since the Ashes.

When Australia plunged into the series at Cardiff, there seemed no holding them. The spirit they had bottled recently in South Africa was obvious. It was startling, however, with memories of the constant pressure and events of 2005 still fresh, to watch international cricket of such low intensity as on the fourth day, as Australia coasted towards a declaration against bowlers and fielders so devoid of energy and ambition. All teams look shabby under the cosh, of course, but some look shabbier than others: England here looked a great deal poorer than Australia in similar circumstances, awaiting a declaration, as at Lord's. Marcus North was there capable of a brilliant direct hit run out, to dismiss Matt Prior, almost from the backward point boundary; England awaited Ponting's move at Sophia Gardens like fidgety boys sent to the headmaster's office hearing the swish of a cane.

Then, on the last afternoon, Australia faltered, as both sides would throughout the series, releasing the pressure so assiduously built. Ponting had come to the series excited by his team's feat in overcoming South Africa on their home pitches; he owed loyalty, he felt, to the players who had delivered for him there. He relied on two in the game's closing stages: Johnson and North. Neither broke through, nor looked like doing so. Hilfenhaus, despite five top order wickets, was granted just thirteen of the last day's ninety-eight overs.

If this was a glimpse of Australia's limitations, the first session at Lord's revealed them in stark relief. In his book, Ponting paints a dainty but disturbing picture of his young players' preparation: 'I could hear the excitement in their voices and see an almost glazed look in their eyes when they first looked out over the ground they've dreamt about playing a Test on since they first thought about playing for Australia'. Australian eyes at Lord's are meant to be gimlet not glazed; on the other hand, perhaps the only way to watch was between one's fingers, as Andrew Strauss and Alastair Cook hit twenty-two boundaries before lunch.

When a team has played so badly, there is always the nagging sense, among themselves and their opponents, that a repeat is possible, maybe even probable, especially over cricket's maximum course. It was Australia's batsmen rather than their bowlers that plumbed the depths from then on, but in hindsight it was the first two hours of the Second Test that was a touchstone for England over the long, ensuing summer.

The institution of the five-Test series is due its next revival at the end of 2010 when England trip to Australia, and it is hard to know what to expect after the English prodigies of 2005, the Australian pageant of 2006–07 and the alternating predicaments of 2009. Which is, of course, exactly as one would wish it.

Wisden Almanack, 2010

AUSTRALIA IN 2009–10

The Fork in the Road

Not so long ago, it would have looked liked business as usual: Australia has won five of its last six Tests, and lost only four of its last two dozen one-day internationals. Nobody who watched Australia turn the Ashes over last year, however, will regard the progress as other than preliminary steps towards restoration. At the peak of its powers, Australia simply went out and won; this summer of 2009–10, it has depended a good deal, perhaps even a little overmuch, on its opponents losing.

The West Indies, ambushed in Brisbane, belied their eighth place in the ICC Test rankings by taking Tests right up to their hosts in Adelaide and Perth. Australia then disposed of a poorly led Pakistan team rivalling Shane MacGowan in its propensity for self-destruction, although only after trailing by 206 runs on first innings in Sydney.

Almost every member of Ricky Ponting's team has suffered unwonted media pressure about their performances at some stage, even the captain himself. When he top-edged his first ball to long leg at Hobart, he was facing his worst Australian summer in a decade. But when Mohammad Aamer filled his trousers, Ponting filled his boots, batting almost twelve therapeutic hours in the match. As cricket it's been pleasingly involving, as reflected in the television ratings. But just because names like Shane Warne, Adam Gilchrist and Michael Slater remain in free circulation doesn't mean that times haven't changed: they're commentators now, whose feats set a high benchmark for those they are commenting on.

The Ashes? If not too close to call, it's certainly too far. Australia would frankly expect to win, based on Leonard Hutton's rule of antipodean ground advantage that the team expecting to beat Australia down under must be at least 25 per cent their superior. Man for man, they have also progressed further than England since the Oval Test. Most meritorious has been the further advance of Shane Watson, who this season has bulked like a right-handed Matthew Hayden at the top of the order. His pretensions to the status of all-rounder, too, were enhanced when his batting average finally exceeded his bowling average during the Boxing Day Test.

With the slow fade of Brett Lee and Stuart Clark, Australia has also welcomed the happy-go-lucky left-armer Doug Bollinger, as adept with the new ball as Mitchell Johnson is apparently averse to it, and already an after-dinner speaker's delight. New South Wales teammates, for example, describe his efforts one day in the dressing room to extract toast from a recalcitrant toaster with a knife. Concerned comrades intervened, explaining patiently that it was best not to plunge knives into live electric appliances. Bollinger nodded, pondered, then tackled the toaster again ... this time with a fork.

Where the Ashes are concerned, nonetheless, days are early yet. And if Bollinger appears to be filling a Merv-shaped hole in Australian cricket, much else about this summer has seemed altogether less nostalgic.

Chief among the successes of 2009–10 has been the KFC Big Bash, a domestic Twenty20 competition as subtle as its name, enhanced this summer for the first time by overseas players, such as West Indians Dwayne Bravo, Kemar Roach, Chris Gayle and Dwayne Smith, Pakistanis Shahid Afridi and Naved-ul-Hasan, and New Zealanders Ross Taylor and Daniel Vettori. For Big Bash, read Big Cash: a place in the final translates to a place in the supranational Champions League later this year, and a share in its stupendous revenues. Not surprisingly, state associations hitherto dependent on distributions from Cricket Australia are agitating to embiggen the Bash at the expense of the Sheffield Shield.

Australia's venerable first-class competition is also being squeezed from the other end, its last round this season coinciding with the IPL, an overlap which the league's ubiquitous commissioner, Lalit Modi, warned rather forbiddingly 'could mean penalties on such players, including termination of contracts, jeopardising future participation'.

Ponting, among others, has expressed misgivings about the impingements of cricket's new order:

> I'd hate to see the day where we start playing more Twenty20 cricket at the expense of Sheffield Shield. One thing I think we have had over other nations over the last 50 years is great strength in our domestic cricket. You don't want to tinker with things that are working so well. We have always been very protective of our domestic cricket because we think it has developed and brought on a number of very good players throughout the course of the last 100 years.

So far, the pretence is that nothing need give, and that Australian cricket can somehow follow Yogi Berra's famous advice: 'When you come to a fork in the road, take it'. But internal tensions are building, among players, administrators, agents and media.

Ponting, retired from international Twenty20 and whose IPL contract has just been bought out by the Kolkata Knight Riders, reflects one tendency, keen to stretch his Test days out for as long as form and fitness permit—a sense of priorities he has imparted to his baggy green brethren, only one of whom will appear in India's forthcoming extravaganza. The opposite tendency was simultaneously on show at the Gabba, as Andrew Symonds succumbed for 1, spooning a caught-and-bowled while representing Queensland in the Big Bash preliminary final against Victoria.

Three years ago, Symonds made a match-winning hundred in an Ashes Test at the MCG. This summer, Australia's pioneer of freelance cricket has scraped together 88 runs and bowled eight overs in half-a-dozen Big Bashings, preparatory to rejoining his six-weeks-of-the-year teammates at the Deccan Chargers. It was a sad sight, and a salutary one, for England, it implied, is no longer Ponting's only looming rival.

The Times, January 2010

MICHAEL CLARKE AND LARA BINGLE

A Woman's Place?

'Women are very often keen followers of the game, but their excitement over a match and their sympathetic interest in the players are offset by the uneasiness and disquietude of mind they create in the team's family circle.' Thus Australia's cricket captain 100 years ago, Monty Noble, who did not marry until he was forty, and long retired. How far we have come—and yet not.

Australia's captain, Ricky Ponting, is an exemplary husband and father. Ditto his role models in the job, Mark Taylor and Steve Waugh. But the flight of Ponting's presumed heir, Michael Clarke, to the side of his embattled fiancée, Lara Bingle, has revealed curious assumptions about sport, sex and celebrity held by some who should know better.

Bingle has in the past fortnight suffered a cruel public humiliation, with the publication of a photograph of her showering that slunk mysteriously into the public domain via *Woman's Day*, whose supremely disingenuous argument was that 'it was going to come out at any point anyway'. The photograph may date from Bingle's ignominious fling with footballer and cretin Brendan Fevola three years ago. Sordid stuff—feel free to turn away. But you will have to do the turning, for the media has gone on staring with prurient, voyeuristic abandon, relying on essentially two justifications.

Firstly, Bingle has what, by the media's improvised and mutable moral standards, is a chequered past. She is a bit flash. She is a bit saucy. She once slept with a married man, Fevola. 'Villain or Victim' reads the cover of this week's *New Idea*, announcing another in-depth investigation. There is no question mark. The sentiment hangs there, as if suspended by its own stupidity, an echo of the rapist's excuse that 'she dressed up all sexy so she had it coming'.

Secondly, on the advice of her outré agent, Max Markson, Bingle sold an interview expressing her distress to the same magazine that had caused her woes. It was an almost masochistic reaction, like a beaten wife returning to an abusive husband; it also had the effect of inciting further coverage.

By the same token, Bingle has since her teenage years been part of a celebrity milieu whose inhabitants feel compelled to confide in hundreds of thousands of readers if they burn their toast. 'My Toast Pain.' 'Why I'm Standing by Toast.' 'Brangelina's Toast Feud.' When one is conditioned to a public life, public response must seem almost a reflex.

Why, even yer interleckchals can't help themselves: witness, in Friday's *The Australian*, Mandy Sayer's whimper for partner Louis Nowra, currently being kicked around for his bilious attack on Germaine Greer. And he *did* have it coming.

In the meantime, Michael Clarke was returning to Sydney from a one-day series in New Zealand, his manager explaining that it was 'to support Lara through this tough time'. Now it was the cricket media's turn to scoff. 'Support'? Surely, Clarke should be demonstrating that he was the stuff of a future captain by ditching his fiancée immediately in favour of resuming that terribly important one-day series whose results will be forgotten next week.

Ex-players such as Ian Chappell and Michael Slater argued that being Australian vice-captain came prior to any relationship, both speaking with the experience of first marriages that did not survive their cricket careers. The case was made most explicitly by Peter Roebuck, who saw the issue as being that Bingle is beautiful, and that 'beauty and danger have always been a potent combination'.

From his Fairfax bully pulpit, Roebuck is Australia's most influential and admired cricket columnist. He was also, some years ago, treated with deep malice by the tabloid media. What he published this week, however, bordered on the tawdry gossipmongery of which he was once the victim. 'Restaurateurs complain about her manners and the poor company she keeps', he wrote in respect of the hapless Bingle. 'Fashionistas talk of her headstrong ways and dubious customs.'

Roebuck then cited the damage this was doing to poor, vulnerable Australian cricket, which must at all costs be protected from the ... errr, well ... apparently the disapproval of restaurateurs and fashionistas.

Yet, amazing to say, Australian cricket seems to have survived the corrosive influence of Clingle—to belatedly give the couple the moniker, à la Brangelina, they surely deserve. Australia has lost two matches this summer; Clarke was joint winner of last year's Allan Border Medal, and second-placed in this year's. Were Bingle to parade nude down Macquarie Street, Australia would presumably be unassailable. Over to you, Max.

Roebuck contrived finally to sound like Monty Noble a hundred years ago, endorsing as the model of a cricket wife a kind of doting but distant pastoral carer who refrained from making 'any extra demands'. Like Elin Nordegren, perhaps. Except that she *has* made a few extra demands lately, such as fidelity, which may mean that she is no longer an appropriate model.

Now, according to 'management', Clingle has demerged. We don't know a fraction of the story and, I dare say, never will. But we have had a lesson or two.

At times like this, Australian cricket becomes terribly huffy and concerned with its good name, and recycles that bollocks about the Australian captaincy being the land's highest office, more important than the prime ministership etc. Which is fine: where would sport be without a little mythology? But when that mythology comes attached to such dubious and dated moralising, it isn't Lara Bingle who is dragging cricket into disrepute.

Sunday Age, March 2010

AUSTRALIA IN 2010–11

Fiasco

Cricket boards are like wicketkeepers, most effective when least conspicuous. By this measure, Cricket Australia is having a summer every bit as bad as its cricket team. It's one thing to fail during the Ashes, another to fail so abjectly that the whole surrounding structure is called into question. But such has been the riot of arse-covering and buck-passing since the end of the Sydney Test that it almost seems that the cricketers themselves will get off the hook.

It started with a disastrous press conference in the immediate aftermath of the Fifth Test in which chairman of selectors Andrew Hilditch announced himself satisfied that he and his three colleagues had 'done a very good job as a selection panel'. Worse, his response when criticized for unwarranted self-satisfaction took him to new heights of unintelligibility: 'To the extent that someone thinks that we're not disappointed with the result, I'm disappointed those comments were taken that way. The reality is nobody could be more disappointed than the national selection panel. We picked what we thought was a squad capable of winning the Ashes and it wasn't capable of winning the Ashes, so that is disappointing.' Hilditch is a lawyer. You have to wonder what his advices read like.

That same day, Australian coach Tim Nielsen gave a press conference little less odd. Asked whether any members of his team had improved over the last year, he responded: 'It depends on how you measure improvement.' Well, Tim, it's not rocket surgery: wickets and runs might be a start. 'If we sit back and look at the series results,' he added, 'it would be easy to say none of us have.' But it's far from obvious that the view would vary according to the posture from which it was made. Were Nielsen a coach in any other sport, he would only have avoided the sack by resigning. In fact, thanks to a fortuitous extension of his contract last August, he will be around for the next Ashes.

Chief executive James Sutherland has promised a thoroughgoing review of the season. So far, however, the only parties he has criticized have been Phil Hughes and Michael Clarke for the heinous crime of briefly attending a charity breakfast of the Shane Warne Foundation on Boxing Day. 'That was a supreme error of judgement on their part,' Sutherland said last week. 'The players decided that of their own will. I would be surprised if we see that happening again.'

Players attending a breakfast is a 'supreme error of judgement'? Come again? It's not like they launched a line of lingerie or read the weather on *Sunrise* wearing a tutu. Was Sutherland seriously contending that the performances of either Clarke or Hughes were compromised by attending a function raising money for charity? If so, if their games are so sensitive that they can be derailed by having their vegemite in the wrong place, then arguably neither player should be in the side. Sutherland is normally supremely circumspect in his public utterances: three weeks ago, for example, he shrank from criticizing Ricky Ponting's obnoxious harangue of Aleem Dar. One would have thought that Clarke's and Hughes's hardly compared as a breach of protocol.

If we're going to start talking judgements, in fact, it's best not to look too closely at Cricket Australia's. Test match watchers this summer would have been forgiven for drawing the impression that CA is now a marketing organization that dabbles in cricket on the side. The barrage of idiotic distractions, the desperate attempts to look hip and youthful, the overexposure of the fading Doug Bollinger, the involvement of players in customer-friendly rigmarole, hitting balls into the crowd, shaking babies, kissing hands, etc. – all of them have added up to a sense of a cart so far ahead of the horse that no-one has noticed the horse turning into a three-legged, one-eyed camel. Players can just get away with being advertising billboards when they are winning. When they are losing, so are the products. To paraphrase Bjorge Lillelien: 'Commonwealth Bank! Vodafone! Betfair! Colonel Sanders! Can you hear me, Colonel Sanders? Your boys took one hell of a beating!'

It's CA's marketing services department and its general manager Mike McKenna who have been responsible for the summer's bamboozling cycle of stunts, from projecting Ricky Ponting's face onto Big Ben to the seventeen-man squad shemozzle at Sydney Harbour Bridge. It's McKenna, too, who whenever he spruiks the Twenty20 Big Bash League suggests that he has spent most of his five years in cricket caressing his Blackberry rather than absorbing anything about the game.

McKenna recently suggested that the objective of the Big Bash League was to 'enable us to make a hero out of Shaun Tait or David Warner, two great cricketers currently not playing for Australia [in Test cricket]'. If a 'supreme error of judgement' has been perpetrated in Australian circles lately, it's been the promotion of such permanently stunted mediocrities as Shaun Tait and David Warner as 'great cricketers'.

In fact, CA has chosen an unfortunate time to become infatuated with T20, the game's bitch goddess. It will be striving to regenerate its team in the most complex, challenging and longest form of the game, an effort requiring a sense of common purpose and shared mission, even as it carves domestic cricket into a city-based competition involving cricket's shortest and crudest variant. Not the time to be dividing one's energies, one might have thought; not the time to be pandering to parochialism, populism and short-term greed either.

McKenna justifies this by appeal to other sports: 'Every other sport makes its money from their league format, whether they are rugby or football, from a club-versus-club competition. That's where the passion is.' Hmmmm. So cricket has had it wrong all these years. That passion we felt for our country, our state, or even just for the game ... well, it felt like passion, but it must have been something else – indigestion, perhaps. Where cricket's administrative circles were once a bastion of the idea of their game's difference, specialness, uniqueness, now the obsession is with making cricket look the same as every other sport. Why is it that when Australian cricket administrators talk these days, they sound like they have no confidence in their game's enduring fascination or charm, and as though they really wish they were selling something else?

So crummy a summer has CA had that some are even questioning its future. Two of the most influential voices in the Australian cricket media, Peter Roebuck in *The Age* and Malcolm Conn in *The Australian*, have argued for a total governance makeover, replacing the existing system of a board composed of representatives from the six state associations sitting in long-fixed ratios with something more like the commission that runs the Australian Football League.

The chief executive of Australian Cricketers' Association, Paul Marsh, added his voice to that clamour at the weekend, by calling the current model 'fundamentally flawed' and demanding a group composed of 'captains of industry and other highly qualified people': 'You've got a situation where directors of the Cricket Australia board also have to be directors of their respective state boards. This produces an unavoidable conflict of interest, where directors have responsibilities to CA and their state associations.'

It's pretty hard to disagree with the proposition that a system basically devised in 1905 is ripe for renewal; that South Australia's votes, for instance, are hopelessly out of proportion with its net contribution to Australian cricket when set against Queensland's two and Tasmania's one; that the Buggins' turn principle of the chairmanship is a recipe for mediocrity; that a distribution system in which Cricket Australia simply disgorges its profits to the state associations militates against long-term planning; that an organization with no say over who sits on its board is a weird archaism; that an organization claiming to reach out to non-Anglo communities and women but without non-Anglo or female members among its directors is a nonsense.

On the other hand, it's not so long since Australians flattered themselves that they had the best cricket governance in the world. CA's board may not be a dream team of commercial and cultural nobs and nabobs, as fantasized of by Conn, Roebuck and Marsh, but the direct connection between it and Australia's underperformance in the Ashes is pretty hard to establish. It's not like Shane Watson can't run between wickets because South Australia has three votes on the CA board, or that Shaun Tait is an overhyped nonentity because he's confused by CA's financial distribution model.

Australian cricket has a federal structure because Australia has a federal structure, and because nation and game arrived at their modes of governance at roughly the same time. It is arguable that a key virtue often claimed for it, that it is representative of and in touch with cricket at its lowest levels, has weakened, that market research, onto which CA holds like a drunk to a lamp post, has been substituted for actual direct bottom-up input into the formation of national will. But any substitute for the existing model, even if the personnel were more talented, would almost certainly be less representative. At least with football, members can go to their clubs, vote for whomever and feel as though their view counts. Where is that mechanism in cricket?

The best-represented constituency in Australian cricket at the moment are the players, as evinced by the loud voice in all matters of Paul Marsh. Mind you, based on current performance, it's far from clear that the players deserve such eminence; it's even arguable that the ACA is part of the problem. Twelve years since the first memorandum of understanding between CA and the ACA which placed first-class cricket on a full-time professional footing, players have never been wealthier, more cosseted, more protected. Yet over that same period, partly because you can earn a tidy living these days being not very good, standards in the domestic scene are widely regarded as having fallen. Thanks to the IPL, meanwhile, perversely discrepant pay and incentives are turning the Australian playing community into an every-man-for-himself society of haves and have-nots, with neither rhyme nor reason: one hopes, for instance, that the next time Daniel Christian and Steve O'Keefe run into one another during the Aussie summer, $900,000 Christian at least shouts $20,000 O'Keefe a drink. What sort of trade union is it that condones rewards bestowed so unevenly?

As for the rest of us in Australian cricket, a contagious and debilitating cynicism is spreading: there is a feeling that something is amiss, that something is being lost, that the players are overpaid numpties and/or B-list celebrity haircuts, that the administrators are beige bureaucrats and/or shonky spivs, and that those who care about cricket, who have it in their blood, who think it a fine thing and worth fighting for, are being marginalized and excluded, because they are at odds with the fast-buck mentality, because they object to being slotted into demographics of 'cricket consumers'.

Such impressions are visceral rather than fair or reasoned – at all levels of the game in this country can be found able, well-motivated people who care a great deal about what they do. But they are impressions too widely felt to be ignored. Relations between Cricket Australia and its players might be tense at the moment, but they face parallel challenges, both having a lot of work to do to restore their respective credibilities.

Cricinfo, February 2011

Part IV
Giants of Asia

IMRAN KHAN

Yes, We Khan

When the West Indies toured Pakistan in the late 1980s, the story is told, one of the visiting batsmen noticed Imran Khan assiduously picking the seam. Better put an end to that, he thought, and counselled the umpire, whom he then saw bend Imran's ear. A few balls later, what should the batsman see but Imran again giving the seam a thorough work-out. 'I thought you'd told Imran to stop', the batsman complained to the umpire. 'I did', the umpire replied. 'But he said that he didn't want to.'

It could be accurate; it sounds apocryphal; it is almost certainly 'true', in the sense of conveying a truth, that, as nobody before or since, Imran Khan was the cricket master of his proud and unruly nation. In these troublous times for Pakistan, Imran himself having become one its more erratic demagogues, both country and cricket team are sometimes regarded as ungovernable. Yet as batsman, bowler, captain and advocate, Imran ruled as majesterially, even imperially, as any cricket leader of the twentieth century.

Fixed as is this hindsight image, furthermore, it is forgotten just how unexpected was his success. His board appointed Imran out of desperation: neither Javed Miandad nor Zaheer Abbas would play under the other. The appointment came shortly after the brief, ruinous reign of Ian Botham—some argued that Imran's lot as a match-winning all-rounder was difficult enough without the additional burden of captaincy. For burden it was, as Imran recently confessed: 'When I became the cricket captain, I couldn't speak to the team directly I was so shy. I had to tell the manager, I said: "Listen, can you talk to them? This is what I want to convey to the team"'.

If there was to be little talk, there would be much action. His first Test as captain, at Edgbaston, brought him face-to-face with Botham, rejuvenated by his return to the ranks, and coming off Test cricket's fastest double-century against India. Botham came to bat wearing a sunhat, swinging his arms in great arcs. As Imran approached, the Englishman took his familiar back-and-across step, bat upraised; it wasn't even halfway down as off-stump demateri-alised like a dynamited chimney. Imran's seven for 52 that day—to that stage, the best Test figures by a Pakistani—were a proclama-tion: he would not be following Botham's example.

Imran might not have fancied his rhetorical skills, but he found ample motivation in his own career example. Nobody in the Pakistan team he first joined had any interest in coaching the callow youth who slung hooping inswingers. He pulled himself up by his own cricket bootstraps to become an outstanding new ball bowler: a lithe, bounding run culminating in a sideways leap that brought the ball back into the right-hander in the air but also obtained movement away off the pitch; the strength to hit top speed immediately; the stamina to bowl spells of epic length.

In some the experience might have instilled a belief that others could simply do as he had done. In Imran it inculcated a conviction that nobody should have to. The most generous of mentors, he built pace reserves in Pakistan second in depth only to the West Indies: not just Wasim Akram and Waqar Younis but Aaqib Javed, Salim Jaffer and Mohsin Kamal. In his autobiography, Akram describes how Imran at mid-off would orchestrate his overs for him: 'Inswinger, outswinger, good-length ball, bouncer if he doesn't fancy it. Keep your head still and line up where you want to pitch the ball. If you want an inswinger, aim at first slip, and the ball will end up around middle and off-stump'. He recounts, too, the humanity and humility of Imran in his public comments, how it inspired him when his captain professed: 'Look at Wasim. He's far more talented than me'.

All that kept Imran from becoming a batsman of the first order, meanwhile, was his bowling: he could otherwise have held down number four with ease. With the straightest of backlifts, he hit further down the ground than almost any batsman in the world. Here again he led by example, to the extent of declaring with himself on 93 at Sialkot in December 1991 so Pakistan could take a Sri Lankan wicket before the close. His all-round statistics as leader, 2408 runs at 52.3 and 187 wickets at 20.3, can scarcely have been bettered.

Yet it's the captaincy, and the general control Imran enjoyed over cricket in his country, that make him remarkable, because nobody since Pakistan's original captain, Abdul Hafeez Kardar, had enjoyed such stature before, and nobody has since, nor perhaps ever will. It was made possible, perhaps, by political stability, or at least continuity, in the form of a military strongman, General Zia ul-Haq, who most notably dissuaded Imran from retirement after the 1987 World Cup, regarding him as the only captain able to 'heal our national wounds'.

For much of his time, too, Imran had the advantage of a cousin, Javed Burki, as chairman of selectors. Not that Imran's rule was nepotistic: he ended the gilded career of another cousin, Majid Khan, shortly after taking over, leading to a decade's estrangement. But in being able to shape the teams he led, Imran enjoyed an advantage over almost every captain of his era. He could protect Abdul Qadir, for instance, from the Karachi lobby who favoured their Iqbal Qasim; the likes of Tauseef Ahmed and Mansoor Akhtar played more international cricket in Imran's era than they would have in others, Asif Mujtaba and Qasim Umar perhaps rather less.

Imran had bigger ideas still, especially in his advocacy of an elite umpiring panel with video support, set out in his eponymous 1983 autobiography: 'It would be a move towards professionalism, and if gadgets could help make the umpires' job easier, why not try them?' Imran was instrumental in bringing PD Reporter and VK Ramaswamy from India to umpire the Lahore and Karachi Tests against the West Indies in November 1986, after Pakistan had unexpectedly beaten the world champions in Faisalabad; his absence a year later when England visited was almost as significant in events as Shakoor Rana's presence. Bringing the Englishmen John Holder and John Hampshire to umpire Pakistan's potentially combustible home Tests against India in 1989–90 was an initiative of profound diplomatic finesse, demonstrating an acute understanding of Pakistani pride, Indian sensibilities and English amour-propre—it would prove instrumental in disarming objections in England to third-country umpires, leaving Australia the last hold-out.

Imran's ease in England and with the English was a crucial factor in his captaincy—perhaps rather more crucial than he would now wish to remember. He was recruited to join Worcestershire by its improbably named club secretary, William Shakespeare. His controversial move to Sussex was blessed by no less than Justice Oliver Popplewell, chairman of the Cricket Council. Like cousin Majid, and Pakistani politicians in the making, including Farooq Leghari, Wasim Sajjad and the Bhuttos father and daughter, he read PPE at Oxford; Asians at Oxford, noted Benazir Bhutto, were treated as 'rather exotic individuals who did not fit into any particular class of category'. The *Times* and the *Guardian* reported Imran's doings with more sympathy and accuracy than *Dawn* or the *Star*, and the King's Road flat and social whirl of London suited him. 'Imran did not so much embrace society in the 1980s', observed his first biographer, Ivo Tennant, 'as allow society to embrace him'. He certainly found it far easier to couple in England than in his own country.

It is no bad thing for a cricket leader to be set slightly apart from his men, and Imran's effortless cosmopolitanism certainly had such an effect. The rugged grandeur of his features and the constant swooning of his female retinue can't have hurt either. In his 1988 autobiography, on the cover of which he smoulders like a Mills & Boon fantasy, Imran confides improbably that he grew up with a complex about his looks, so adamantly did his older sister insist that he was ugly. 'It came as a pleasant surprise when I first began to be thought of as good-looking', Imran says. 'I suspect that this coincided with my cricket success.' There is an obvious link, albeit one that cricket purists have been strangely loath to make, preferring to dwell on the aesthetics of outswingers and cover drives: show me a heterosexual male who does not feel more confident for acknowledged attractiveness to women and I will show you a liar.

It is this confidence that has been missing in the erratic trajectory of Imran's politics, which has veered towards Pakistan's most paranoid and puritanical political elements. He is identified today with a conservatism and isolationism that is, at bottom, strangely diffident, profoundly pessimistic. Christopher Sandford may be right to argue in his life of Imran that politics is not a departure from Khan's sporting career but a 'straightforward, logical progression'. Yet sport and politics engender pride in different ways; Imran seems to lack the patience for the latter.

What's certainly true is that Pakistani cricket since Imran has become a reflection of the country rather than an example to it. Indeed, it is testament to his influence just how quickly Pakistani cricket collapsed into individualism, intrigue, parochialism and corruption after Imran climaxed his career with victory in the 1992 World Cup; without him, the sense of collective will dissolved. With the bans imposed on Younis Khan and Mohammad Yousuf, Pakistan will shortly be auditioning its fourteenth Test captain since Imran. The days he did pretty much as he pleased are long ago; in more recent times, it has been his country's administrators acting on impulses and initiatives a great deal less pure.

Seriously Cricket Chronicles, April 2010

JAVED MIANDAD

Agent Provocateur

Javed Miandad objected to what became the cliché routinely recycled in descriptions of him. 'Street-fighter'? What did that mean? Sure, he grew up playing street cricket in the lanes that crisscross Karachi's Ranchore Lines. But so did everyone he knew. It made no more sense than calling Allan Border an 'Oval-fighter'. Such was Javed's lot. However many runs he made, or victories he led Pakistan to, something about him remained irreducibly different, foreign, Pakistani—not that he'd have had it another way.

Most cricket autobiographies include some boilerplate about the national pride inherent in Test selection. Javed's *Cutting Edge* (2003) is fiercely, almost floridly patriotic. 'As far as I was concerned,' he states unambiguously, 'cricket was war and I was at war whenever I played'. In fact, he says it more than once, and describes in some detail the 'terrible embarrassment and shame' he suffered in defeat, while crowd support 'brought tears to my eyes and a chill down my spine'.

There's none of the patrician grace or cosmopolitan veneer of his great contemporary, Imran Khan; such politeness is for 'Oxbridge Pakistanis', whom he always affected to cordially despise. The air is uncompromisingly martial, and the intensity all-consuming. Indeed, as Mushtaq Ahmed relates in his *Twenty20 Vision* (2006), it could be hard to bear:

> He always wanted to consider the conversations about cricket
> throughout the evening after a hard day in the field when we

were tired and wanted to relax. I was frightened to be on his table at dinner because I knew he would bombard me with questions about what I had done wrong on the pitch during the day.

What's curious is that at the crease this manifested as the opposite. No batsman looked more relaxed, more self-amused than Javed. Even Viv Richards—there was a high-strung energy to his swagger. Javed sauntered to the centre like he was already 180 not out; he'd chat; he'd sing; he'd jest and joke. Of his 271 at Eden Park in February 1989, John Wright described him as batting as though 'sitting on a sofa in his front room'. Ian Smith recalled him turning at one point to chirp: 'Nice day today. Would be a lot nicer for you boys at the beach'.

Richards merely made it look as though you weren't good enough to bowl to him; Javed said it to your face. He'd pick on the Indian Dilip Doshi, for instance, charging down the wicket then dead-batting him, hissing contemptuously: 'I should have hit that for six!' He persecuted the slow-moving Doshi in the field, too, calling as he hit to him: 'Come on, there's two! It's only Doshi!' In a workplace, this would now be called bullying, victimisation, psychological cruelty. On the cricket field, it was 100 per cent pure Javed.

The piss-taking air took you in. There was nothing light-hearted about it: in fact, the worst response was to reply in kind, for Javed relished provocation. And while his two-shouldered stance was a picture of relaxation, the release of the ball acted like a hair trigger, combining all his faculties: quick feet to position him, quick hands to adjust to late moment, quick reflexes to make something out of apparently nothing. He placed singles with a pickpocket's opportunism, squeezing no fewer than forty-five into an unbeaten 59 in the first match of a World Series Cup in December 1992. Loose balls were never the same again. There is one particularly flavoursome photograph of Javed turning the ball off his pads. In the stock shot of the flick off the toes, batsmen usually look limber and elegant. In this particular Patrick Eagar image, a bare-headed Javed has absolutely monstered the ball. The feet are blurred, the body is tilted forward at more than 45 degrees, like the forward surge of the hood ornament on a Jaguar. He's not tickled this to fine leg for 1; he's smashed it through square leg, already sensing 3, keen to make it an all-run 4 if he can.

Javed wanted the most of everything, off the field as well as on. Runs alone were insufficient. He pursued records and milestones avidly. Six pages of *Cutting Edge* are dedicated to kvetching about the day in Hyderabad that Imran declared when Javed was 280 not out. He had a very modern taste for bling, setting himself to win the player-of-the-series award during the Perth Challenge because he fancied the Longines watch on offer. He thought that 'the single most important achievement of my professional career' was the Austral-Asia Cup final in April 1986, when the match-winning six that climaxed his 116 not out from 114 balls poured forth coin like a fruit machine: from a US$80 000 diamond-encrusted bracelet to a Mercedes, not to mention a promotion at Habib Bank. Mushtaq Ahmed describes how Javed created a 'Celeb System' for the distribution of prize money after Pakistan's successful 1992 tour of England. When junior players complained about the sliding scale favouring those with more caps, and Javed with the greatest number of caps most of all, he browbeat them: 'Why are you always thinking about money instead of playing cricket? You have only just started playing for Pakistan and you are becoming greedy'.

Javed, nonetheless, was a player always to have at one's side, if only because playing against him could be so unpleasant. And here he joins a very select group in the game's history, whose unbridled and unconcealed competitiveness has been integral to their cricket, as much a gift as a quality cover drive or outswinger. The lineage can be traced back to WG Grace; it takes in more Australians than seems polite to name. Javed was the player who brought that cocky strut to South Asia, the likes of Arjuna Ranatunga and Harbhajan Singh being unthinkable without him. Indeed, it's no coincidence that the pricks all three have kicked against have been chiefly Australian. Australians have been sledging's main exponents and apologists; to sledge an Australian back involves an insurrection of the first order.

One of Javed's early patrons, in fact, was that pioneer Aussie-baiter Tony Greig, who brought the teenage prodigy to Sussex, and then to Sydney for the second season of Kerry Packer's World Series. Asif Iqbal recalled Greig posting Javed at silly point to Derek Underwood when Ian Chappell was batting: 'Javed kept up a barrage of talk in Urdu with the name Ian Chappell figuring prominently. And although none of it was abusive, Ian, unable to understand any of it, probably thought it was. He gradually reached the end of his tether and ended up holing out to deep mid-wicket'. Then, of course, there was the tangle with Dennis Lillee in Perth, too infamous to need further description, although worth more elaboration than it usually receives.

These were red-blooded, bare-knuckled days. Test cricket before the ICC Code of Conduct was a little like Hollywood before the Hays Code, constantly pressing against the bounds of acceptable behaviour, and risking disapproval. Lillee in his Perth hometown was a law unto himself. The WACA had been the scene of his first great triumph, against Rest of the World ten years earlier, and his most protracted pout, over the aluminium ComBat eight years later. With a worshipful local crowd and the famously bouncy local pitch, he felt unassailable. In Australia's first innings against Pakistan, he sat down between deliveries to make plain his disapproval of the visitor's over rate, and also his annoyance at Javed's chiacking from short leg. By the time their passions boiled over, Pakistan were two for 78 chasing 543. In other words, Javed's was a challenge on par with spitting at the firing squad about to shoot you. But symbolic acts make for enduring myths, and Javed intuitively understood that this was one:

> I don't think Dennis or any other Australians had expected to see a Pakistani player like me who simply refused to back down ... We were after all only from Pakistan and he felt he could take liberties with us. Had I been captain of England, I wonder if the idea of retaliating with a kick on the pads would even have entered Dennis' mind.

Here, in fact, Javed grasped something as few previous cricket leaders: the motivational power of grievance. It could be ugly. It could be obnoxious. It could even, sometimes, be sneaky, and Javed had a Machiavellian flair for off-field intrigue too. But it was every bit as effective as Imran's captaincy-by-charisma. Both men won fourteen Tests as leader, but Imran lost eight and Javed six; Imran, furthermore, usually had Javed's services, but Javed not always Imran's. It also left a deeper mark, and a model to follow. No wonder Javed disliked being defined; he was, in every sense, himself a definer.

Cricinfo, June 2009

KAPIL DEV

India Rising

In 1982, Scyld Berry, the very excellent cricket correspondent of *The Observer* who has lately become the editor of *Wisden*, published a fine book on an England tour of the Subcontinent, entitled *Cricket Wallah*. No English writer to that point had studied India with such clarity, sympathy or, indeed, rosy prophecy, for he far-sightedly concluded that the country would become 'the capital of cricket': demography, he believed, was destiny.

In one judgement alone was *Cricket Wallah* amiss. On the basis of the tour's two one-day internationals, Berry thought that limited-overs cricket held 'no great attraction' in India. Batsmen were still technically correct, and spin bowling endured, 'integral, not an adjunct' to the game, for it 'suited the rhythms of Indian life'. In fact, he had just watched the cricketer who, more than any other, would challenge both those appealing preconceptions.

Two hundred and seventeen of Kapil Dev's 432 Test wickets were taken in the heat and dust of India by uncompromising toil; he brought a gaiety to batting in a team that sometimes seemed unaware that Tests were no longer timeless. Above all, by leading India to the World Cup of 1983, he turned his country's cricket priorities on their head—and all this from most inauspicious beginnings.

'There are no fast bowlers in India', fifteen-year-old Kapil Dev was told when he complained about the short rations at lunch at a training camp at Brabourne Stadium in 1974. The judgement was hurtful, but not unfounded. In the First Test of India's last home series, for example, the new ball had been taken by Eknath Solkar (two overs) and Sunil Gavaskar (one over), then surrendered to the slow bowling wiles of Bedi, Chandra and Prasanna. It had not, however, been ever thus. Peer back to pre-war, pre-partition India, and the country's opening attack was probably superior to Australia's. The likes of Tim Wall and Ernie McCormick had nothing to teach Mohammad Nissar and Amar Singh, except that Nissar's best years were swallowed by World War II, while Singh succumbed to pneumonia aged thirty.

A 'feeling of loss' pervaded Indian cricket in their wake, according to its historian, Mihir Bose, which intensified over the next forty years whenever the country's batsmen crossed paths with bowling of real pace. Ray Lindwall and Keith Miller made them suffer in Australia, Fred Trueman lorded it over them in England, and Charlie Griffiths nearly killed Nari Contractor in Barbados. Most ignominiously, Clive Lloyd's pacemen set about Bedi's batsmen like sadistic thugs in a dark alley at Sabina Park in April 1976.

By that stage, Kapil had been a first-class cricketer for one season, without much encouragement. In his second game for Haryana, versus Delhi, he played against Bedi, who was selling one of his Gray-Nicolls bats, and had set a reserve on it of Rs500. With help from his friend Ashok Malhotra, Kapil scraped together Rs475, but there were no discounts, and no gimmies either: his first tour, to Pakistan, was played on pitches apparently prepared for the diplomatic parity of drawn Tests.

From the first, nonetheless, Kapil Dev upset cricket's prior balances of power. In *Spin and Other Turns*, Ram Guha describes the first morning of Kapil Dev's Test career, how in his second over the teenager sent a bouncer past the pentangle on Sadiq Mohammad's cap, 'very likely the fastest delivery from an Indian bowler since independence'. Sadiq's summons of a helmet was so unforeseen that it took some overs to arrive; as Guha notes: 'It is a wonder there was one at the ground at all'. When the West Indies toured India soon after, they dished it out, as was their wont, but Kapil Dev was no less hostile. Normally above the fray, *Wisden* described the Chepauk Test as 'a bumper war' in which India 'for once gave as good as they got'. Bose believes it a hinge point in Indian cricket history.

Kapil Dev altered also the Indian team's internal dynamics. The dominant presence in the country's cricket to that time had been Gavaskar, batting's classical sculptor: patient, implacable, self-sufficient, self-involved, a peppery temper beneath a surface urbanity. Kapil Dev provided a rival to national affection, and a new source of national self-definition. Gavaskar, great as he was, could never emulate the bravura styling of a Viv Richards. Kapil Dev, in an era of the international game uncommonly blessed with fast bowling all-rounders, more than held his own against them.

Remember? Botham, Imran, Hadlee: all fierce rivals. You could imagine them in a Western saloon. Botham would be the one chesting open the swing doors and shouting the bar, Imran the one comfortably encircled by comely belles in crinoline, Hadlee the one staring fixedly at his ice water. But that Injun, Kapil Dev—he held aloof. He had the liveliest and least imitable action of all, a skipping, bounding run of gathering energy, and a delivery stride perfectly side-on but exploding at all angles, wrists uncoiling, arms elasticising, eyes afire. Which was part of his significance. No fast bowlers in India? Kapil Dev could have hailed from no other country.

All that stood in the way of Kapil Dev's bowling was his batting, full of generous arcs and fearful cleaves, signed with an exuberant pull shot that featured a chorus-line kick from his crossed front leg. At first, teammates took Kapil Dev's run-making more seriously than he did himself: he reached the first of eight Test hundreds at Delhi thirty years ago only because Syed Kirmani sacrificed himself, a cacophony of calls sending them to the same end. He retained a sense of play and adventure into which even opponents sometimes entered. At the Gabba in December 1980, he launched Jeremy Coney over the roof of the Clem Jones Stand and into Stanley Street during an innings of 75 off 51 balls; the puckish New Zealander waved his white handkerchief like a flag of surrender.

Selectors were sterner, benching Kapil Dev after the Madras Test of December 1984 when he hit his second ball for six and his third down long-off's throat as India stumbled to defeat against England. But Kapil Dev, for all that he accomplished, never really repented. He won the Lord's Test of May 1986 with three fours and a six from Phil Edmonds; he saved the follow-on there four years later with four consecutive sixes from Eddie Hemmings. It was the year of the building of the Compton-Edrich Stand, and I happened to be amid a throng of ecstatic Indian supporters in temporary seating in front of it. I can still hear the glorious 'thunk' of those straight drives, each faster and flatter than the last, into the building site behind us: they lent new meaning to the expression 'hard hat area'.

Lord's was the venue, too, of that fabled match twenty-six years ago, after which Kapil Dev could have retreated to an ashram but remained one of the most significant players who ever lived—all because of one catch. It came from the top edge of the bat of Viv Richards, then on course to be matchwinner for the third consecutive World Cup final, and it looked suspiciously like providence.

Kapil Dev had deposed Gavaskar as captain, in one of those Indian intrigues that outsiders find unintelligible, and led his country with expected spirit and unexpected smarts. Gavaskar, never a one-day natural, had had a wretched tournament, and been first to fall that day in India's ramshackle 183. The West Indies in reply had charged to one for 50.

Now Madan Lal bowled a bouncer—a bouncer *to Richards*. What's Hindi for chutzpah? The crowd on the mid-wicket boundary began shrinking back; even Father Time ducked. In the event, Richards miscued, but the ball would have fallen safe had any other fielder been stationed near the drop zone. As it was, Kapil Dev turned, ran back with the flight of the ball, loose stride eating up the distance, cast a split-second glance over his shoulder, and collected the descending ball in his finger tips—making even this look deliberate. Has a more difficult catch been made to seem easier at a more critical moment in the annals of the game?

India had won one game in two previous World Cups, against East Africa; now they won what remained their only global trophy until the Twenty20 World Championship in 2007. Both wins similarly tilted the cricket world off its axis. One-day cricket went forth and multiplied on the Subcontinent, to the extent that the next Cup was held there four years later, just as Twenty20 did twenty-four years later, making India its social, cultural and financial fastness.

Kapil Dev was part of that shift, too, shoulder-to-shoulder with Subhash Chandra's Indian Cricket League, while Gavaskar was firmly in the camp of the official IPL. Much else had transpired between times, but it was almost as though their unspoken rivalry had never quite ended. The ICL has floundered and the IPL prospered, so Gavaskar might consider his the last word; yet today's stylish, aggressive Indian stars, like Dhoni, Sehwag, Sharma and Zaheer Khan, are more obviously Kapil Dev's spiritual heirs.

Cricinfo, September 2009

334

MUTTIAH MURALITHARAN

Sharp Elbows

In the cricket match between the villagers of Champaner and the local British garrison that climaxes the sprawling Bollywood epic *Lagaan*, the filmmakers pay an implicit tribute to Muttiah Muralitharan. The villagers' captain, Bhuvan, played by a bare-chested Aamir Khan, calls to the bowling crease his friend Goli, whose self-taught method is to bowl from a standing start after a dozen anticlockwise rotations of his arm. At once, there is consternation. 'He should not be able to bowl like that', the beastly British cad Captain Russell complains to the umpires. 'It is improper.'

The umpires look like acquiescing until the cad's comely sister Elizabeth intervenes. The memsahib, inevitably in love with Aamir Khan and better-versed in cricket than some ICC referees, avers that the Laws are not so prescriptive where bowling actions are concerned; the umpires nod sagely, and the game proceeds, although the cad and his fellow bounders continue griping. 'Damn ridiculous', complains one defeated batsman. 'Dangerous too.'

In its majestic, longer-than-a-Twenty20-game sweep, *Lagaan* has a lot of fun with cricket past and present: the English, for instance, perpetrate the first 'Mankad', while an Indian pioneers the Dilscoop. But the Goli sequence is perhaps the most obvious take on a contemporary theme, and repays some consideration as Test cricket's greatest wicket-taker nears the end of his extraordinary career, having hardly bowled a legal delivery—at least as far as many Australians are concerned.

No English rose was ever going to smooth over Murali's action with honeyed words. Allan Border faced his first few deliveries in Test cricket, interpreted the tangle of arms and bulging eyes as portending leg breaks, and watched in bemusement as they turned massively in the opposite direction. Even before the matter of his legality, he stretched the game's lexicon to breaking point, being an off-break bowler whose rotations were more a function of a rubbery wrist than dirty great Gibbs-esque digits. Off-spin is cricket's rubbish skill—something easy to do in a mediocre fashion, and the eternal preserve of the untalented. John Howard bowled off-spin—as, indeed, do I, and utter filth it is too.

That said, off-spin is supremely difficult to do excellently. The game's annals contain perhaps fewer great bowlers of off-breaks than leg breaks. After Trumble, Laker, Tayfield and Prasanna, who? Murali, then, shone a bland skill through the prism of his wrist to reveal a rainbow of possibilities. He made it turn, he made it bounce; he made it unintelligible, scrambling the seam, so that the ball approached, as it were, in a cloud of white noise. Most renownedly, he and Saqlain Mushtaq fostered the doosra, the googly's evil twin, the finger-spinner's revenge.

As a result of a congenital deformity, of course, Muralitharan also bowled with an arm that was not straight—and bowling is traditionally a straight-arm exercise. Oddly enough, nobody knows why. The best Rowland Bowen can do in his finest of cricket histories is to advise: 'At some unknown stage, the idea took root that "cricket" bowling involved a straight arm'. We can point at least a little more precisely to when, in the sense that it probably wasn't until the 1890s that the Law was strictly enforced, the Marylebone Cricket Club and its chief agent, the Australian umpire Jim Phillips, imposing a fatwa on 'chuckers' in English county cricket.

Murali could still be within the Law providing he did not straighten his arm, and whether he did or didn't became one of the most intractable controversies in cricket history. The answer was pursued with fantastic zeal, by combinations of naked eye and lay opinion on one side, and medical and technological analysis on the other. And the answer was: it depends. Yes, Murali's arm bent, but no more, and in some instances less, than the arms of every bowler. This was not an answer anyone had really expected. Science was meant to provide answers, not to furnish further questions. But it left lawmakers with a choice, between a zero-tolerance approach based on assertion, or a scheme with a 15-degree shade of ambiguity derived from biomechanics. They went the latter route—and the five years since seem to have proven them right.

It is worth saying that while the vast majority of complainants about the tolerance limits have been Australian, the limits seem to follow Sir Donald Bradman's oft-quoted view of throwing as being 'so involved that two men of equal sincerity and goodwill could take opposite views'. The limits haven't dispelled doubts around the doosra, so physically difficult to bowl that it must inevitably skirt the borders of legality. But they have calmed tempers in a debate that inevitably generated more heat than light, and they also invited disputants to contemplate the essence of Murali's alleged transgression.

The assumption underlying critiques of Murali's action is that he obtains from it an undeserved advantage. Yet cricket is hardly a stranger to advantages that aren't quite deserved. How does a batsman *deserve* a flat, lifeless wicket? How does a seamer *deserve* a greentop? For that matter, how does a captain *deserve* to win the toss and take advantage of either? If you were a conspiracy theorist and a bowler, you might be trying to make out figures on the grassy knoll right now. For the last decade, bats have become so powerful as almost to demand licensing as assault weapons; boundaries have been reined in to rinky-dink proportions. Cricket is currently involved in mandating a potentially huge advantage to batsmen—two-faced bats, effectively a doubling of the batsman's effective hitting area—amid no discussion whatsoever. What are degrees of extension in a bowler's arm by comparison? What is the ability to spin the ball more against the capacity to hit it further, more productively and more flexibly?

For this is, in essence, the edge that allegedly accrues to Murali: he spins the ball more than it is felt he ought be able to. A fast bowler who chucks poses a potentially enhanced physical danger; no such consideration attaches to a comparable slow bowler. And, to be sure, powers of rotation do matter where slow bowling is concerned. But if they were an advantage as decided as some critics seem to believe, then David Sincock should have been the greatest spinner of all time. Murali's greatness rests only partly on his capacity to set the ball in motion: there is his accuracy, his keen grasp of batting weakness, his encyclopedic knowledge of opponents, his unflagging love for a game that has on occasion treated him pretty unkindly. In his affable autobiography, *Bully For You, Oscar* (2000), Ian Austin provides a lovely vignette of Murali's assimilation at Lancashire:

> I've never known anyone who knew so much about cricket—or anyone who could talk about the game for so long. There's a hell of a lot of international cricket being played all year round these days, but Murali knew all about it … He knew more about Lancashire's record than Lancashire players themselves. We'd be sitting in the dressing room or in the bar in the evening at an away game and he'd suddenly start talking about one of our games from years back. He'd know all the facts and figures and couldn't believe that the rest of us didn't remember every last dot and comma of the game he was talking about.

It is hard to reconcile such a paragraph with the conviction that Murali's has been an altogether malign and Pandora-like presence. But this belief has always been non-specific about where the exact harm has been inflicted. A common assertion through Murali's career has been that his example would condone and encourage other dubious actions, and there seemed some grounds when Sri Lanka fielded Jayananda Warnaweera. But the only international bowler to attract attention since the 15-degree latitude was recommended in October 2004, Johan Botha, seems to have been dealt with efficiently by the system.

The doosra was subject to suspicion and condemnation when it came into the game—as, indeed, was the googly, whose double-dealing nature was in some quarters regarded as unethical. Yet the doosra proved as harmful as helpful to co-inventor Saqlain, unable to bowl anything else by the time his international career was through, while Daniel Vettori ended his doosra dabblings when he found that the habit of stretching his front leg and opening up his action was interfering with his accustomed rhythm: there were easier and simpler variations almost as effective.

An abiding annoyance about Murali, particularly in Australia, arises from the conviction that the ICC was acting ultra vires in legitimating his methods. 'In Murali's case, the Laws were changed to bring him inside the scope of legality', complains Adam Gilchrist in *True Colours* (2008). 'That's a poor precedent to set.' But the precedent was ancient: it's how cricket progressed from under-arm through round-arm to over-arm bowling, the Law adapting in each case to the efforts of innovators. Nor is it unknown for games to alter rules in response to the prowess of individuals: in Australia, witness Walter Lindrum and the revision of the baulk-line rule in billiards.

Gilchrist's book is actually worth reading for what else he writes about Murali, especially in relation to Australia's tour of Sri Lanka in March 2004. This often-forgotten visit is one of the signal achievements of Ricky Ponting and his team, and a neglected classic of the modern era: Warne (twenty-six wickets) v Murali (twenty-eight wickets), with Australia prevailing in three tight encounters.

> The more I batted, the more I loved the challenge of facing Murali. I couldn't pick him out of the hand, but gradually I taught myself to become familiar with his body shape and the flight he put on the ball, and to select shots where it didn't hurt me if I misread the spin. He varied his position of delivery on the crease, and I grew to predict the spin from that. I started trying to read his plans and counter them with plans of my own.

What Gilchrist describes is worth celebrating: a great batsman's response to the challenge of extraordinary bowling. There was, in fact, much excellent Australian batting in that series, including two hundreds from Damien Martyn, who gambled on playing back to almost everything, and two hundreds from Darren Lehmann, who kept altering his guard, outside leg one ball, standing on off the next, going right back, then scampering down the track. Gilchrist concludes his account proudly: 'It has to be said that this was one of our most "intelligent" series all round'.

Marcus Trescothick and Alastair Cook provide similarly informative expositions about combating Murali in their respective books. Cook recalls Trescothick's shrewd advice not to be distracted by the whirligig of arms: 'The ball does not lie'. Trescothick notes drolly: 'As time passed, I grew to appreciate that views in the dressing room over whether he chucked the ball tended to depend on whether he had just got you out and for how many'. Murali cajoled even unheralded batsmen into new approaches. Jason Gillespie enjoyed some success simply by reference to the line: the wide ball, he deduced, was probably the off-break; the ball on the line of the stumps was probably going straight on.

Even in the anticipation, Murali has been a force to be reckoned with. New Zealanders readying for him have trained on rough ground like used, dry and foot-holed pitches, in order to replicate his unpredictability. The result? Vettori makes the canny observation in his *Turning Point* (2008) that opponents he met during his career who had just come from playing against either Sri Lanka or Australia always seemed more adept and composed against spin than others. In other words, Murali and Warne helped batsmen, and therefore cricket, improve: what could be a greater compliment to them?

To anticipate any player's legacy is fraught with difficulty. Warne has left a wonderful trove of memories, but also an enormous gap: there has been no renaissance in Australian wrist spin to speak of. Because it is hardly less difficult to imagine a copyist of his methods, the same may prove true of Murali. Yet he has also, in an era of unprecedentedly intense coaching and 24/7 television coverage, with their homogenising influences, struck blow after blow for heterodoxy, for tackling cricket according to one's own lights. It can hardly be a coincidence that Murali's teammates now include the world's three most innovative young players: Tillakaratne Dilshan, Lasith Malinga and Ajantha Mendis.

Again life imitates *Lagaan*. In the movie, Goli's effectiveness proves temporary—the English work out that he grunts just before he lets go of the ball, allowing them to pick him off. It is the Mendisian mystery spin of the untouchable Kachra that proves decisive. Ultimately, however, art is outdone by reality, because Aamir Khan is nothing on Kumar Sangakkara.

Best Australian Essays, 2009

TENDULKAR IN PERTH

The Little Master

At the time, there was nothing much about the Australian summer of 1991–92 to arrest its easy slide into cricket past, the home team winning Test and one-day series easily, India and the West Indies slipping out of the country to the sound of their own feet. Only in hindsight has more been detected to it—so very much more.

For Australian fans in particular, it was a summer of four fascinating premonitions. They enjoyed their first glimpses of Shane Warne, of Brian Lara, of Sourav Ganguly and of Sachin Tendulkar—of the last, a baby-faced nineteen year old who blasted more than 1000 international runs in those few months, the impression was nigh unforgettable. In a triumph, it would have been special; in a badly beaten side, it bordered on uncanny. By summer's end, Allan Miller was writing in *Allan's Annual*: 'Bow, bowlers, to the great and mighty Tendulkar!'

Think back to international cricket circa 1991–92. It's not twenty years ago, but it seems an eternity. There were seven full Test nations. There were only two umpires per Test, and the standing officials of that Australian season were all locals—thus the sense of martyred grievance when eight lbws befell India in Adelaide, and only two were upheld against Australians.

India had not visited Australia for six years, had played one Test in the preceding fifteen months, and it showed. In match after match, batsmen shambled across their stumps, fended at balls they should have left, ducked balls they should have played. A much-vaunted line-up steadily ran out of vaunts: Sanjay Manjrekar seemed incapable of an attacking stroke, Kris Srikkanth of a defensive stroke, Dilip Vengsarkar of any stroke at all.

Vaunts of Tendulkar, meanwhile, steadily became a chorus, especially after he became the youngest player to score a Test century in Australia, taking particular toll of the callow Warne. In the crowd at a one-day match in Sydney soon after was seen a banner: 'Oh, what a feeling ... Tendulkar!' The invocation alluded to a popular television advertisement for Toyota: the tyro was being added to the common culture.

The innings that really quickened the pulse, however, was played on the other side of the continent, in conditions quite opposite, and also quiet alien to those in which Tendulkar had been trained. Perth's WACA ground in those days was a little like a lonely, windswept pass in the Wild West, where ambuscades awaited unwary travellers. The bounce was almost vertical, the carry far and fizzing. Not even Australian teams liked it much: the arena was known for sparse, parochial crowds mainly interested in watching fellow Westralians.

On their first visit to the WACA that summer, in November 1991, India had been bundled out by Western Australia for 64, a prelude of their future problems with the rising delivery. In pursuit of Australia's 346 in the Fifth Test three months later, they looked shaky at once. Srikkanth was hit a glancing blow on the helmet by Craig McDermott, and turned to watch it bang into the sightscreen after a few bounces, rolling his eyes expressively. By stumps on the second day, the tourists were a punch-drunk five for 135, and lost their nightwatchman without addition the next morning.

By this stage, Tendulkar was poised to counterattack, and did so thrillingly. New cap Paul Reiffel thought the Indians looked 'jaded' during the Test, as well they might have trailing 0-3. For Tendulkar, though, there was the familiar challenge of Australia but also the new assignment of number four: he welcomed it, his tiny figure crossing the crease to square cut at the top of the bounce, easing into line to drive down the ground, swaying from harm at the inevitable short stuff.

The people of Perth had, as was their wont in those days, stayed away in droves: there were fewer than 5000 spectators, and the Channel Nine cameras could not avoid panning across empty terraces. When Tendulkar stood on his toes to slash McDermott, Reiffel, Merv Hughes and Mike Whitney, the crack from his bat seemed to echo round the stands like the report of a Lee-Enfield. Tendulkar cut, in fact, more often than seemed wise, and at balls closer to his body than a purist probably would have liked; it was the cricket of a batsman trusting his nerve, following instinct rather than instruction. Every ball looked likely to get him out until it came near him, when it was subdued, controlled, countered.

In truth, it was a race against time, with the innings expiring at the other end, a race into which Tendulkar hurled himself with 81 between commencement and lunch, racing from 50 to 100 in 55 deliveries, and putting on 81 in ninety-one minutes with Kiran More: an Indian ninth-wicket record against Australia. Nor had the cares of cricket quite taken their toll on Tendulkar. When he drove McDermott through mid-on for four to reach his hundred, he removed his helmet to show a brief, boyish smile, unselfconsciously reminding onlookers that he was only just old enough to vote, and barely looked old enough to shave.

When Tendulkar skewered Whitney to backward point to finish on 114 from 161 balls with sixteen fours soon after, the Perth crowd did their best to honour him: 5000 had a reasonable stab at sounding like 50 000. More, inspired, prolonged the innings another 32 runs and thirty-three minutes, limiting India's arrears to 74 if only slightly narrowing its eventual defeat margin of 300 runs: it would be some time before India abroad were a fraction as formidable as the team they were at home.

Nonetheless, against the evidence of the results, there was something to Sunil Gavaskar's remarks after the series: 'India got a lot from this tour'. What might have been a rout at Perth was really only a defeat: Australia would lose the corresponding Test of the following summer in just over two days, by which time India would be utterly annihilating England. A year after that, Tendulkar, who had arrived in Australia with a Test average less than 40, had a Test average greater than 50, and there was no looking back—until, perhaps, now.

SACHIN TENDULKAR

Twenty Years of Mastery

Many twentieth anniversary tributes to Sachin Tendulkar will begin with a recollection of one of his epic innings. I wish to cite one of the shortest. It was in Melbourne, my home town, on Boxing Day 2003. It was a day rich in entertainment, containing a Virender Sehwag century full of eye-popping strokes. Seldom, however, have I sat in a crowd so obviously awaiting one player, and when Tendulkar appeared they radiated happiness and contentment, bursting into heartfelt applause. Tendulkar at the MCG? Delayed Christmas presents come no better.

Except that it was all wrapping and no gift. Tendulkar feathered his first ball down the leg side and was caught at the wicket—a miserable way to fall for any batsman, in addition to being a lousy anticlimax. The crowd had hardly ceased cheering than it was compelled to resume, cheering Tendulkar off, and the feeling afterwards was almost of devastation. You could hear the sibilance of conversations, as connoisseurs ruminated that cricket sure was a funny game, and fathers tried explaining to sons that even the greats had bad days. About three overs later, three spectators at the end of my row got up and left. It was mid-afternoon, Sehwag was still mid-spectacular, and *they left*. This was not what they had come for, and they would accept no substitute. I had to stay—it was my job—but I could easily have followed them. The hollow feeling persisted all day.

When it comes to communicating Tendulkar's place in cricket history to future generations, I suspect, this is what will be most significant, and also the hardest to convey. In the twenty years of his career, international cricket has been changed beyond recognition: elaborate and ceremonial Test cricket has been usurped, economically at least, by the slick, shiny, celebrity vehicle of Twenty20. Yet even now, Tendulkar makes time stand still: every time he comes to the wicket, no matter the game, no matter the place, there is a sense of occasion. It needs no pop music, no cheerleaders, no word from his many sponsors. He is announced by his accumulated excellence, the effect somehow magnified by his tininess: little man, big bat, great moment. His entry could not seem more dramatic was he borne to the crease on a bejewelled palanquin by dusky maidens amid a flourish of imperial trumpets.

This, moreover, has been the case almost for longer than one can remember. I first saw Tendulkar bat live in England in 1990. He looked so young, so small, like a novelty item on a key chain. Any sense of frailty, however, was quickly dispelled; instead, there was a sureness of touch not just impressive but altogether ominous. You told yourself to remember him this way; you wanted to be able to say you were there; he was going to be good, so good. By the time he first toured Australia eighteen months later, he simply oozed command. All that held him back, and it would be a theme of his career, especially abroad, was his sorely outclassed team.

Sometimes, this looked almost eerie. Ten years ago in Melbourne, there was another Test involving India and Tendulkar. To distinguish between the two was only fair. India were terrible, a shambles. Kumble dropped the simplest catch imaginable from the game's second ball and took two for 150; Dravid batted more than three and a half hours in the match for 23 runs; Laxman and Ganguly failed twice, the latter playing on to Greg Blewett of all people.

Tendulkar batted as if on a different pitch, to different bowlers in a different match. Shane Warne came on with Australia in the ascendancy in front of his home crowd. Tendulkar promptly hit him into that crowd beyond mid-off. Brett Lee, in his debut Test, bowled like the wind. Tendulkar treated him as a pleasant, cooling breeze. The follow-on loomed, apparently unavoidable. Tendulkar guided India past it, toying with Steve Waugh's formations, making the fielders look as immobile and ineffectual as croquet hoops.

Had it not been for his ten teammates, Tendulkar could have batted until the crack of doom. As it is, he had to rest content with 116 out of an otherwise bedraggled 238. And this wasn't just an innings; it was, at the time, a synecdoche of Indian cricket. No matter where he went, Tendulkar was the main event, preceded by acute anticipation, followed by grateful wonder, seasoned with sympathy, that such a flyweight figure had to bear such burdens.

There is no discussing Tendulkar, even in cricket terms, as batsman alone. He is also, of course, Indian cricket's original supercelebrity; as Pope wrote of Cromwell, 'damn'd to everlasting fame'. In this sense, he has been preternaturally modern, at the forefront of developments in the culture of stardom in his country, with his telephone-number television entanglements and sponsorship deals, and his reclusive private life. Without Tendulkar's prior demonstration of cricket's commercial leverage, Lalit Modi and all his works would have been unthinkable.

What's truly amazing, nonetheless, is that the simulacrum of Tendulkar has never overwhelmed the substance. He has gone on doing what he does best, and has done better than anybody else in his generation, which is bat and bat and bat. Like Warne, albeit for different reasons, cricket grounds have been a haven for him: in the middle, he always knows what to do, and feels confident he can do it. Life is full of complications and ambiguities; cricket, by comparison, even shouldering the expectations of a billion people, is sublimely simple.

Tendulkar's fame, then, is of an unusual kind. He is a symbol of change, but also of continuity. What's astonishing about his batting is not how much it has changed but how little. He set himself a standard of excellence, of consistency, of dominance, and challenged the rest of Indian cricket to meet him up there. Gradually, in the twenty-first century, albeit not without setbacks, stumbles, financial excesses and political wranglings, it has. His presence now is an ennobling one. First it was his excellence that rubbed off; now it is his integrity. Cricket today specialises in the manufacture of instant stars, temporary celebrities, glorious nobodies. Tendulkar acts as a kind of fixed price or gold standard. To choose a well-loved and well-worn advertising catchline, he is 'the real thing'.

In his sheer constancy, in fact, Tendulkar unwittingly obscures just how completely cricket has been transformed, to the extent that it is almost impossible to imagine his fame being replicated. Who in future will play international cricket for twenty years, losing neither motivation nor mastery? Who in future will master all three forms of the game, capable of spontaneous spectacle and massive entrenchment alike? Who in future will excite us simply by walking onto the field, just a man and a bat, and disappoint so seldom? Recalling how shocked, even grief-stricken, was that crowd in Melbourne six years ago as Tendulkar's back was swallowed by the shadows of the pavilion, I find myself brooding anxiously on the thought of what it will be like when he disappears for the last time.

Times of India, November 2009

SACHIN TENDULKAR

Pure Genius

The Tendulkar blood book: it is surely the cricket freak story of the year. The impresarios behind Tendulkar's forthcoming autobiography, *Tendulkar Opus*, have commissioned an extra-limited limited edition of ten into which drops of the great man's blood will be mixed on the signature page. The other pages of the 37kg tome will be trimmed in gold leaf too, but it's the corpuscles and platelets that will be the selling point of the volumes priced at $US75,000 each and … oh, hang on, sorry, they've already been sold, sight unseen.

'Only in America,' people used to groan at one of those news stories about some Bible Belt ecstatic who'd seen the face of Christ in a tortilla, or some millionaire eccentric who'd had the head of their favourite dog cryogenically frozen. 'Only in India,' is the modern-day cricket equivalent, the country being a byword for an ecstatic cricket rapture that makes the enthusiasm of other countries look mild – all effigy burnings, crazy television, eye-bugging bling, and Bollywood glamour.

Yet how often it is, even in the era of 'Captain Cool' Dhoni and/or 'See Ball, Hit Ball' Sehwag, that the Tendulkar stories trump them all, like the teenager who committed suicide a few years back when Tendulkar's back injury threatened to end his career, or the plot to kidnap him hatched by Pakistani terrorists? 'The key thing here is that Sachin Tendulkar to millions of people is a religious icon,' said the mastermind of the Tendulkar blood book. 'And we thought how, in a publishing form, can you get as close to your god as possible?' Dhoni, Sehwag, Ganguly, Kumble – superstars all, but earthbound. Of only Tendulkar can you speak in terms of God and religion, and even then you might still be guilty of understatement. Perhaps the reason that the BCCI has been so reluctant to sign up to the WADA code is the probability of a black market in vials of Tendulkar's other secretions.

The most intriguing aspect of the *Tendulkar Opus* is not the ten copies that almost nobody will ever see but the thousands they will. At 852 pages, it will bulk larger even than Steve Waugh's personal apologia: another big record for the Little Master. What will it reveal? Easier to imagine what it will not. Lovechild? Lifelong battle with depression? Daily telephone banter with Shobhan Mehta? There'd be bloodshed then, and it wouldn't be the profitable kind. Actually, it's hard to conceive of what the book can disclose without causing the kind of controversy which to Tendulkar is anathema. Let's be frank: expect lots of respectful hat-tipping to famous rivals, reverent and touching glimpses of family, maybe the odd behind-the-scenes story of Team India, but with an overall impression as enigmatic as the Mona Lisa's smile.

Nobody will feel genuinely let down either, for Tendulkar has so conditioned us. 'I have taken stands before, but often whatever I say gets misinterpreted and meanings are attached to it,' he has complained. 'If you know that whatever you say will become a controversy, why get into it unnecessarily?' The best cricketer of his generation, in fact, has been among the least scandalous, keeping his head while all about him have not just been losing theirs but throwing them high in the air. Not for him the talk-show couch, or the newspaper pulpit; while he is no longer the stilted youth of his first few television advertisements, cameras still seem to embarrass him slightly, and one would no sooner expect a cheesy product placement from him than a casual doosra.

India has been transformed in his cricket lifetime, from a supplicant at the IMF to its modern tiger economy. So has the country's media, once staid and dowdy, now served by 125 24-hour television news services and more than 1100 TV channels, ravening for content and contention. Tendulkar's phlegmatism is sometimes contrasted to the flamboyance of his contemporary and boyhood companion Vinod Kambli, a batsman extravagantly gifted whose head was turned by adulation and celebrity. Kambli, it is averred, had talent to burn, and did; Tendulkar kept his nose not only clean, but to the grindstone. The comparison is flawed: Kambli was never *that* good; Tendulkar never *that* reticent. But they aren't the worst antitypes. When it has counted, Tendulkar has been preternaturally focused, a cricketer of Gandhian self-denial and Anandian self-containment.

Not that he has been altogether Sphinx-like. Look back in the annals and you will find that Tendulkar grants interviews quite regularly, or as regularly as one could reasonably expect in the absence of any great economic incentive for his doing so. In some of these interviews, he even goes into detail, at least about his batting, exhibiting a flair for succinct expression. Take this for example: 'The mind always wants to be in the past or the future; it rarely wants to be in the present. My best batting comes when my mind is in the present, but it doesn't happen naturally. You have to take yourself there.' Or this: 'The older I get the more I realise how important your breathing is to good batting. By that I mean, if you focus on breathing and relaxing, you can force yourself into a comfortable place to bat.' Not hugely original, but mature and reflective. Tendulkar on batting: it's not quite as good as Tendulkar batting, but there's substance to it, and an intelligence behind it.

As far as his fans are concerned, too, Tendulkar has been consistently generous. He is a quiet supporter of charitable and philanthropic causes, including Apnalaya, a Mumbai-based NGO assisting underprivileged children associated with his mother-in-law, Annabel Mehta. This year he even harnessed the internet as a means of scattering his blessings and benedictions, acquiring 88,000 followers within a day of his joining Twitter; that number now exceeds half a million. It is difficult to imagine that he personally sits there all day attending individually to his well-wishers – 'Thanx. Good luck to u n ur family. I wish u all the best in life'; 'Wish u good luck in life. Keep smiling'; 'Thanx a lot. I m humbled.

Wish u n ur family all the good health n happiness in life', etc. –
but easy to imagine how such apparently personal confirmations
are individually received. The Tendulkar tweet is to India as the
Bradman autograph is to Australia: they abound, but somehow
each one is special.

Of Tendulkar's views on other subjects, however, we know
little or nothing – which may not, of course, be any great loss. A
story is told, probably apocryphal, about an interview in the 1980s
in which pop idol Kylie Minogue was asked her opinion of South
Africa, possibly with the intent of extracting an undertaking she
would not play Sun City. 'I think they should stop shooting the
rhinos,' La Minogue is reputed to have replied, on the basis of
some half-remembered wildlife documentary. From fame cannot be
inferred a natural flair for entering into public debate; indeed, the
contrary may be true, that fame entails such concentration on the
self as to preclude profound interest in most other matters.

But Tendulkar has never 'spoken out' as he might have in
cricket contexts, in the issues-rich environments of the nineties
and noughties, when the game has been menaced by match-
fixing, sledging, ball-tampering, illegal actions, administrative
incompetence, greed, connivance and corruption. Did he not share
with fans the pangs of hurt, of disappointment, of disgruntlement
at cricket's travails? Did he not feel incited to a calming, diplomatic
word, or even an expression of some sort of moral code?

One reason he perhaps did not is the fastidiousness with which
he has quarantined his cricket life from that time he devotes to wife
Anjali, and children Sara and Anjun. 'When I cross the boundary
line, it's not cricket, it's family,' he has explained. 'And when I
think about cricket, it's only cricket.' Given Tendulkar's single-
mindedness at the crease, one can imagine the cordon sanitaire
around his sport. He famously does not consume news media about
his own performances; it would be a departure from type were he to
consume news media concerning other issues.

Chances are, too, that he may not be particularly interested.
The cricketer of Tendulkar's time has needed to cultivate a high
tolerance for boredom: nets, hotels, departure lounges, airliners.

Another hundred throwdowns? Suppose I'd better. Another hundred catches? Might help. It's not an environment conducive to broad perspectives or piercing visions, but to highly selective and heavily concentrated effort. If Tendulkar has kept his eye on his own particular ball, it may be because those other balls do not directly aid him in his superordinate goals of making runs and winning matches.

The predominant reason, however, is that hinted earlier: because it has simply never been worth it. Here is a man who cannot go shopping or dine in restaurants because of the inevitability of public interruption. Here is a man who experiences freedom most while driving around Mumbai at 25mph in the wee hours of the morning. Here is a man who in public must adopt disguises and false beards lest the discovery of his presence cause a riot – one a few years ago, which involved 10,000 people in Bangalore, required 200 police to control it. When such unswerving intensity of attention is a fact of life, who would not wish to avert it at every opportunity? Balzac once ruminated of his fame that he wished it permitted him 'to break wind in society, and society would think it a most natural thing'. Tendulkar breaking wind in society today would hit India like a monsoon.

Every hero says something about their times, and perhaps this is one of the silent commentaries Tendulkar passes on his era, that the media and public are so conditioned to a climate of constant controversy, exaggeration and misrepresentation that participation is hardly worth the candle. Your view can be thoughtful, nuanced, lightly held, tentatively expressed, but after simplification and amplification by the various modern apparatus it will sound like a combination of abuse, insult and battlecry. If it is not in Tendulkar's nature to initiate such a process, then perhaps he is saner than the rest of us.

Perhaps, in fact, it is partly the ridiculousness of his world that has kept Tendulkar going so long: the pleasure, relief and solace with which cricket provides him in his splendid isolation. For here is the paradox of his extraordinariness – his making light of challenges on the cricket field that would daunt even very good international cricketers, while shrinking from the everyday experiences that seem simplest. Murali on a turning wicket, Steyn on bouncy one? Bring them on. One hundred to win in the last 10 overs of an ODI? He can feel his sap rise.

Cricket? He has done it before, and never seems to tire of the idea of repeating himself. But driving round the block? Walking down the street? Taking his children to the park or the beach? No way; not now; maybe never. And given the value imputed to his bodily fluids by *Opus*, Tendulkar cutting himself shaving should almost be covered in the business pages. Hang on again ... I shouldn't make jokes like that, because it's perfectly possible that one day it will.

Genius Unplugged (2011)

SACHIN TENDULKAR V SIR DONALD BRADMAN

Who's the Boss?

Bradman. Tendulkar. Even on their own as words, they have an incantatory power. Put them together in a sentence and they combine like a magic spell. 'Bradman Tendulkar': guaranteed to make bowlers disappear. Stick a little 'v' between them, too, and you're inciting one of the most fervid of sporting debates, even if it is one that usually generates more heat than light.

I mean, Bradman v Tendulkar? Why not Shakespeare v Dickens? Or Tagore v Naipaul or Narayan? Or apples v oranges? Because, on reflection, there isn't a lot of the common coinage that makes for straightforward comparison. Bradman arose seventy years ago in a country of six million people; Tendulkar is the hero of a thousand fights in a land of 1.3 billion. Bradman played cricket in two Test countries, Tendulkar in ten; worldwide war left its ugly slash across Bradman's career, while Tendulkar has lived mostly amid peace and plenty.

The careers of both span roughly two decades, but are as different as their statistical breakdown: Bradman's encompassed 52 Tests and 182 other first-class matches, Tendulkar's has featured 176 Tests, 442 one-day internationals, 103 further first-class games and then some ... so far. In Bradman's time, bowlers were roughly equal partners in the cricket enterprise; in Tendulkar's, thanks to a cricket calendar that seems to squeeze fifteen months activity into every twelve months, they have been reduced to serfs in a feudal batting society. Bradman's challenges came chiefly from his opposition;

Tendulkar's challenges flow, increasingly, from himself, finding new ambitions, new directions, staving off satiety.

Don't underestimate the difference in equipment too. Pick up a bat of Bradman's and prepare to be amazed that he spread such terror and dismay: it is as light and slim as a switch. Impregnated with oil, it would have been a little heavier to use, but not much. Wield a bat of Tendulkar's and ... actually, it gives you the shivers. It looks almost as thick as Bradman's was wide, yet picks up like something half its actual weight. You'll also grasp why, while Bradman hit only six sixes in his international career, Tendulkar has hit 247. Add to this the advent of the helmet and of feather-light protective gear, and not only can Tendulkar's blessings be seen to have abounded, but the difficulty of comparison can be gauged.

If their crickets are perhaps remote from one another, however, their fames may make more fruitful comparison. Bradman was and Tendulkar has been their country's best-known local and international figures for much of their lives. It is one thing to become famous; it is another to remain famous. Fame requires great deeds; its continuation involves an avoidance of the pitfalls that follow. Their feats have been not only to succeed but also not to fail: no two cricketers in history have disappointed their countrymen so seldom.

They made batting, that most complex, various and precarious of arts, appear as secure an occupation as going to work in an office. Cricket is proverbially a funny game, full of chance, luck, coincidence and fluke; they made it seem controllable, replicable, even predictable. On being wished 'good luck' by a comrade as he went out to bat, Geoff Boycott is meant to have retorted: 'It's not luck. It's skill.' Bradman and Tendulkar come as close as any cricketers to rendering that an absolute truth.

They had an appeal, too, that struck countrymen in the heart. Both have been progressive rather than traditional figures. They symbolised new possibilities – that their respective countries could be better than all the world, that they could rise above national ignominy. Bradman achieved fame during the Great Depression, Tendulkar in the aftermath of the India's 1991 economic crisis. They became captives of their fame – wary, reclusive, even a little aloof – but their popularities have made them wealthy. They have sought out commercial opportunities without incurring public displeasure. On the contrary, their peoples have cheered them on.

In the early years of Bradman's career, he seriously entertained abandoning Test cricket because the rewards available in the Lancashire Leagues were so lucrative; he shifted states in search of greater financial security when it was virtually unheard-of. In the early years of Tendulkar's career, he put himself in the hands of the savvy Mark Mascerenhas, who turned him into his country's biggest billboard; his net worth now exceeds $US1 billion. Nobody begrudged either of them the fortunes they accumulated. What Ray Robinson wrote of Bradman is true of Tendulkar too: he did not make money so much as overhaul it.

In doing so, they became the fullest expressions possible of the professional cricketer in their eras, exploring the limits to the potential for the monetisation of cricket talent. These possibilities had until Bradman's era remained untapped outside England, which for much of the twentieth century had the world's only full-time professional cricket circuit; Tendulkar brought them to the greatest cricket bazaar of all. Bradman began the displacement of England as cricket's citadel; Tendulkar has completed it. Bradman made contemporaries see that a man with a bat could change the world; Tendulkar wakened us to by just how much. If Bradman could be expressed as a question, the answer would be Tendulkar.

Outlook December 2010

SACHIN TENDULKAR V RICKY PONTING

Parallel Lives

It's one of those challenges whose resolution will be both satisfying and sad. For nigh on a decade, the statistics of Ricky Ponting and Sachin Tendulkar have stood like pillars, suspending aloft a great arch of batsmanship. When their day is done, one or the other will have achieved the monumental proportions of *the* record for Test run-scoring: a record that, given the dwindling incidence of Test matches, may last for all time.

The respective records are already extraordinary. Tendulkar has 13 447 runs at 55.56 from 166 Tests, plus 17 598 runs at 45.12 from 442 one-day internationals, including a total of ninety-three hundreds. It's an eloquent attestation of the industrialisation of the global game. Tendulkar has played twenty years, as long as Bradman, and scored four times as many runs, despite several injury-related absences. Could even Bradman have maintained such intensity of productivity? Given the different values of his period, would he even have wanted to?

Ponting, meanwhile, has 11 859 runs at 55.67 from 142 Tests, plus 12 731 runs at 43.30 from 340 one-day internationals, having given Tendulkar a six-year head start, and being eighteen months his junior: Australia's captain turned thirty-five in December 2009; India's champion turns thirty-seven in April 2010. Ponting's 209 against Pakistan at Bellerive in January represented his thirty-ninth three-figure score in Tests, while his 106 against the West Indies at the Gabba a month later was his twenty-ninth three-figure score in limited-overs internationals. It bespeaks an appetite for runs, and for cricket, almost unappeasable.

There is an epic sweep to the achievements of both men, not least because they have chosen to ennoble the game's oldest international form. In a country that bequeathed pyjama cricket to the world, Ponting has persevered with the cricket equivalent of dressing for dinner. In a country gone crazy for the dirty limerick of Twenty20, Tendulkar has steadily written the Mahabharata of batting. In a world of braggarts, both are resolutely humble. In an era when bigger is always assumed better, both are small men punching way above their relative weights and heights. And in a game bent now at every opportunity on selling itself to the highest bidder, both Ponting and Tendulkar have put national responsibilities beyond price. They feel the honour of representing their countries; you, the fan, feel the honour of being represented by them.

Scrutinising their respective records is a little like listening for bum notes in Mozart. Tendulkar's batting may have been slightly inhibited by captaincy: he averaged 51 as leader, 56 otherwise. Ponting averages 55 as leader, having averaged 55 in the ranks.

Tendulkar, on the other hand, averages 55 at home and away. Wherever he is playing somehow becomes Sachinland, a secure principality of batting excellence. The borders of Rickyworld are a little more porous. He averages 60 at home, 50 away, and, strangely, only 44 in England—an oversight that may account for his eagerness to return there for the Ashes of 2013.

Both men have reached that stage where their opponent is time, as much as any particular country or bowler. For which of Tendulkar and Ponting ends with batting's blue riband depends somewhat, as did the duel for the wicket-taking record between Shane Warne and Muttiah Muralitharan, on which is the last man standing. Time has taken a toll on the physiques of both, like the elements leaving their mark on a statue. No elbow in history has been as discussed as Tendulkar's; Ponting's back and right wrist are feeling his age.

In recognition of the march of time, both are shunning distractions, as they have sometimes abjured particular strokes. Like silent-film stars loath to embrace talkies, they have had little impact on the game's newest and most lucrative form. Ponting has quit the IPL and retired from international Twenty20. Tendulkar has been a low-key presence in the IPL so far, and played precisely one Twenty20 international, against South Africa in December 2006. Tendulkar approaches Test innings now with such system as to seemingly negate all variables. 'Watching Sachin Tendulkar bat these days is almost like watching a re-run of one's favourite TV show', wrote Cricinfo's Sriram Veera after studying Tendulkar at work in Chittagong in January, somehow capturing not just Tendulkar's surety of touch, but also the contribution of television to the spread of his legend in this vast, sprawling, populace nation.

Over their futures, however, the chief influence is probably that of their respective national administrations. Cricket Australia, which has argued at the ICC for a world Test championship, still takes five-day cricket seriously. The BCCI, the largest obstacle to a world Test championship, eyes five-day fixtures as mistrustfully as a property developer discovering a church occupying a city block: yes, it's pretty and all that, but wouldn't an office building or a car park make more sense? Were the BCCI to acquire the Taj Mahal, it would not be long before a television mast had been thrust through the dome.

CA will ensure that Ponting has a steady supply of Test matches, and thus a solid chance of overhauling whatever benchmark Tendulkar sets. He will finish this year involved in another five-Test series; Tendulkar has played only three such in his entire career, none at home, and his Test engagements are becoming so few that he can hardly afford to fail.

Say it soft, in fact, but Tendulkar the batsman is verging on anachronism. To the most historically and commercially significant game of his era, the final of the World Twenty20 in Johannesburg, which ignited India's passion for the game's newest and richest form, he was an onlooker. To one of the crowning triumphs of his career, his fording of the 12 000 Test-run barrier in Mohali in September 2008, there were virtually no onlookers at all.

So for all the splendour of this batting rivalry, cricket is in the process of debasing it. As observed at the outset, the likelihood is that even if Test cricket survives, nobody will play enough in future to parallel the feats of either man. It is like two mountaineers racing one another to the summit of Everest only to find that there is more kudos in climbing ladders—yet further evidence, if it were needed, of how the fast buck has travestied cricket.

Sports Illustrated India, March 2010

Part V
My Trade

FAKE IPL PLAYER

True Lies

'Let the games begin.' So ended the first post, dated 18 April 2009, of a blog beguilingly styled *Fake IPL Player*. It was, indeed, the eve of the second Indian Premier League. The 'games' of the next two months, however, revolved mainly around the identity of the writer, who appeared uncannily well informed of events within Shah Rukh Khan's troubled Kolkata Knight Riders.

FIP, as he shortened himself, quickly gathered an online audience, intrigued by his insights and amused by his nicknames, puckish (Saala Slimeball for Lalit Modi), punning (Junta Tormenter for Ajantha Mendis) and penile (Vinnie Dildo for Khan himself). When, after a few days, the blog was linked to by Cricinfo, a *succès d'estime* became a *succès de scandale*. At its peak, FIP's blog was receiving 150 000 visitors a day—equal almost to the traffic on Aamir Khan's site.

Journalists followed FIP compulsively. KKR's management reportedly went on a hunt for the blogger in their own ranks, and rumours surrounded the departure from their camp of Aakash Chopra and Sanjay Bangar. FIP subsequently flirted with revealing his identity, before changing his mind and posting a YouTube video of his shadow. The change of mind is now explained: FIP, still anonymous, has now novelised his prank in *The Gamechangers*.

Assuming, of course, it's the same *Fake IPL Player*. It could be an impostor. One wonders how a Fake *Fake IPL Player* could be discredited. On the contrary, given that the original flaunted phoniness in his name, *Fake IPL Players* could multiply endlessly, like Agent Smiths in *The Matrix*, or the eponymous lookalikes of *Being John Malkovich*.

The novelist—let us call him that for convenience's sake—seems to grasp this. Transplanting events from South Africa to England, introducing various subplots and changing the IPL to the IBL (Indian Bollywood League), KKR to the Calcutta Cavalry, Shah Rukh Khan to Sigwald Raees Kahn and Lalit Modi to Lalu Parekh, he has produced a work of fiction about a blog of fiction concerning a club of fiction that nonetheless resonates with reality, because it is a book concerned with a writer declining to divulge his identity written by a writer declining to divulge his identity.

The Gamechangers is a sharp, slick and funny read, with a droll take on its characters' delusions of grandeur. 'To succeed in politics one needs to rise above one's principles', it is observed of the IBL's founder at one point. 'Being a man of low principles, Lalu Parekh had an unfair advantage in this matter.' Sigwald Raees Kahn is persuaded by a lackey that his club should simply be called Cavalry: 'People support Calcutta Cavalry because you own the team, not because it's named after Calcutta … We shall quietly remove the word Calcutta from our logo. No one will even notice it'. Young Indian players used to be so inarticulate, it is mused. No longer:

> These days, young Indian cricketers entered the arena with a much wider vocabulary, thanks primarily to exposure to Australian cricket. Now they knew at least a dozen variations of the word 'fuck' and their appropriate usage in different contexts during a game. The India under-19 captain player once famously used the word as a noun, adjective and verb in the same sentence. The smarter of the lot had learnt to pepper on-field conversations with pleasantries like 'asshole' and 'son of a bitch', and end every interview with 'cheers', irrespective of what preceded it. And when posed with a question they couldn't understand, they had programmed themselves to automatically say, 'I play my natural game'.

The focus of *The Gamechangers*, however, is subtly different to that of the original blog: the novelist is as exercised by the question of *Fake IPL Player*'s spontaneous popularity as by the IPL. His ruminations on authenticity emerge in the asides of the blogger's fictional pursuers, detective Parminder Mahipal Singh and sidekick geek Ashok Ramaswamy, who finally conclude that 'in this circus that's going on, he's probably the only thing that's not fake', and who as the book ends feel so complicit in the deception as to contemplate colluding in it.

In an interview posted on his site, the novelist invokes as inspiration Barry Levinson's movie *Wag the Dog* (1997), in which a White House strategist hires a Hollywood producer to stage a foreign war requiring American involvement in order to distract from a presidential sex scandal. The parallel is useful but inexact; Levinson's plot stretched credulity too far. A better comparison would be *Primary Colours* (1996), the roman à clef of Bill Clinton's 1992 American presidential campaign published anonymously by *Newsweek*'s Joe Klein.

Klein's novel about the charismatic but priapic senator Jack Stanton was an immediate sensation on its release, becoming to the Beltway what OJ would become to the rest of the United States. First there was the guessing game about the characters' real-life counterparts: whether the narrator, Henry Burton, for instance, was really Clinton's campaign manager, George Stephanopoulos. Second was the guessing game about the writer: Stephanopoulos was again a suspect.

Primary Colours succeeded for a variety of reasons, not least because it was a very good novel as well as an entertaining parlour game, but also because of something it was not: it was not authorised. It radiated a deep cynicism not only about politics but about the way politics was reported by what the novel called 'the scorps'—short for the press corps, but also suggestive of their malign nature. It provided a fictional counterpart to DA Pennebaker's audacious fly-on-the-wall documentary *The War Room*, in which Stephanopoulos and his colourful confederate, James Carville, were seen harnessing the suggestibility of American voters in a campaign of attractive nothingness.

Although it turned out to have been written by an outsider, *Primary Colours* felt real, felt 'true'—truer at least than the reporting of the compromised, captive media. It was brave; it was provocative; it contained sufficient corroborative detail to, as Pooh-Bah puts it in *The Mikado*, 'give artistic verisimilitude to an otherwise bald and unconvincing narrative'. It came to occupy the space in the political narrative that had previously been filled by investigative journalism, as during the later scandals of the Clinton presidency did the seemingly disreputable but increasingly unmissable online news website, *Drudge Report*.

FIP was a third, hybrid creation: a *Primary Colours* posing as a *Drudge Report*. Or, to be more precise, it was a *Primary Colours* that its readers wanted to believe was a *Drudge Report*: a well-constructed fiction, composed to cohere with well-established stereotypes but sprinkled with close observation, whose public grew inclined to treat it as the good oil, the inside dope. Because, of course, a sizeable proportion of its readers were journalists, as Parminder Singh exposits towards the end of *The Gamechangers*:

> He knew that they [the media] wanted sensational stories and he put it out for them. Just think about it—an anonymous fringe player in a high-profile team, feels hard done by the system and is using this opportunity to unmask people and destroy reputations. Wow! What a story. Could there be anything more dramatic? He knew that the media would lap it up. And once they did, all he had to do was keep them hooked with his scandalous revelations. Every time the media went cold on FIP, he would come out with the next Big Bang ... This was all news, to be printed, broadcast and consumed.

This is the most interesting dimension of the FIP phenomenon: what it says about the public's ambivalent relationship with established news sources. Two factors seem to be mingled in its success: firstly, its apparent subversion of the sports–industrial complex, reflecting a belief that the media is simply in thrall to power; secondly, a sort of indifference as to whether news is actually true—as long, at least, as it is entertaining and tends to reinforce established prejudices.

The second of the aforementioned factors is a popular hobby horse of observers and critics of media: the steady substitution of news by gossip; the increasingly porous boundary between fact and fiction. The first, however, has specific application to the IPL. Modi has sought at every stage to constrain, control and direct coverage of his brainchild. The IPL provides its own feed to Sony, employing its own commentators, and strives to dominate online coverage, operating its own website; it imposes significant restrictions on those journalists and photographers it does accredit.

This is part of an overall effort to fit the packaging to the product, for T20 cricket is above all a product—and a fabulous one at that, for all the reasons Test cricket is an unsatisfactory one. Consider: if I want to see Sachin Tendulkar bat, should I attend the first day of a Test, or should I turn on the TV to watch the Mumbai Indians? At the Test, I might see him bat all day, but I might not see him at all; when I change the channel to watch the Mumbai Indians, I not only know I'll see him bat but that he'll be playing shots, and when he gets out I can switch back to a soap opera. Test cricket can be slow, but it is from an entertainment point of view completely unpredictable; T20 is fast, but in entertainment terms perfectly generic. And generic games, or so it is felt, require generic coverage.

Respected writers and broadcasters have run that generic gauntlet with varying degrees of success. In general, however, the coverage often looks suspiciously like propaganda, full of contrived sensation but ultimately as controversial as milk. In the short term, this makes for a readily digestible product; in the long term, it engenders cynicism, even contempt, if not for cricket, certainly for those who report it. *Fake IPL Player* prospered from the attention of two groups of readers on the same continuum: a first group who, bored with the sanitised pap of the mainstream *authorised* media, hankered for a well-connected but non-partisan *unauthorised* alternative; a second group indifferent to whether it was bullshit providing it was fun. If we let the former down, we forfeit the right to complain about the proliferation of the latter.

Seriously Cricket Chronicles, June 2010

CRICKET AND THE MEDIA

The Pantomime Horse

Cricket and the media ... the topic has haunted me since Boria Majumdar suggested it, for all sorts of reasons, but chiefly this—that it's often hard to think of one without the other. Unless we happen to play cricket at the very highest level, the bulk of the cricket we experience will be mediated, accompanied with a ready-made expert narrative; we will recollect it in terms of the voices of the commentators, the words of the writers, the immediate explications of the replays, the lasting imagery of photography, and more recently the competing, clamouring voices of the chat room, the blog and Twitter, each informing and influencing the other. Our conversations about the game are composites of abiding views, received opinions, instant impressions, borrowed prejudices—all of which, nonetheless, have a capacity to endure.

The best example of that endurance is on show this English summer of 2009, the Ashes originating in a jeu d'esprit of the *Sporting Times* 127 years ago. Technology has played its part from the first, too. The first great five-Test series, 1894–95, was partly so because of the *Pall Mall Gazette's* decision to take advantage of the new telegraphic cable from Australia, allowing the English public to partake of events within a day of their occurring—an extraordinary novelty. Of course, it was originally words that had power. It was on the basis of words that Englishmen dug in to defend Bodyline seventy-seven years ago, on the basis of words that Australians complained of their team being dudded at Old Trafford in 1956. Now it is images that matter, and television's economics have become cricket's—cricket must be sold in order to be played.

That changing relationship between cricket and the media, indeed, now puts me in mind of two theatrical images. Once the relationship was that between a ham and his dresser, cricket being costumed and made up for the stage by a media that maintained fairly obsequious and deferential relations in return for a privileged acquaintance. Now cricket and the media seem more like the front and back halves of a pantomime horse—one, furthermore, where the actual division of responsibilities is unclear: that is, which of cricket and the media is the half that gets to stand up straight and peer out, and which half has to spend its time bent over with its nose in its partner's backside. Whatever the case, it's a relationship of some delicacy and mutual dependence.

The relationships between the different parts of the media are also evolving. When I began writing about cricket about twenty years ago, I recall the very decided demarcation between the print and electronic spheres. Ink-stained wretches were crammed together like steerage passengers on the *Titanic*; the radio and television boys, meanwhile, dressed for dinner in the first-class saloon. There's now a bloody great tear along the waterline, and everyone is flooding into one another's areas. Cricket can be watched on free-to-air television, cable, the internet, the phone. Newspaper and agency websites are running video; cable has invested in the Web. Television entrepreneurs have taken to promoting their own independent cricket enterprises; national cricket boards are producing their own online content. Bloggers link to YouTube; intellectual property lawyers run after everyone with a big litigation stick. There's an air of excitement, leavened with *Titanic*-style panic, because of a feeling, particularly among my print colleagues, that there may not be quite enough lifeboats.

Media, moreover, spends only part of the time with its eye on the cricket. Much of its exertion is expended reporting on what has already been reported, which way the journalistic herd is stampeding, whether it is to a press conference announcing a sudden outbreak of unity in the Indian team, or to decrypting the enciphered utterances of *Fake IPL Player*. Lately, too, the commentary box has been swept up directly in the sales and marketing tsunami, with DLF Maximums and Citi Moments of Success bound to lead on to the Google googly, the PlayStation Play-and-Miss, the Dillards Dilscoop and the Three 3.

I could discuss many aspects of this, but it's this increasing coalescence of cricket and media that intrigues me—the sense that, as Eric Morecambe used to say of Ernie Wise's toupee, 'You can't see the join'. That is, the tendency over time for those involved in the description and interpretation of the game to become simply the handmaidens of corporate interests.

This is not, of course, a new challenge. Perhaps you can date it to 1977, when Kerry Packer launched his World Series Cricket venture. At the time of Packer's irruption, of course, the coverage of cricket was generally the preserve of public broadcasters—the BBC, ABC, Doordarshan and others—watching cricket from a suitably discreet distance and stationary aspect. Packer's broadcasting package was unprecedentedly lavish and spectacular: it involved both the *coverage* of the game *and* its promotion. It made ordinary players into stars, and stars into gods, so the limelight they reflected might also impart a shimmer to the goods and services being advertised between overs.

Commentators went from being impartial imparters of cricket's eternal verities to commercial courtiers of an entrepreneur promoting the game as a media property. But the key figure in that change was the one who belied that there was a change taking place at all. Richie Benaud was the face of cricket at the BBC, *primus inter pares* among public broadcasters; to what might at Channel Nine have been a crass and raucous affair, he brought a deft and discriminating touch, an air of rectitude, a sense of being above it all.

Historians have been apt to celebrate the contributions to Packer's progress of Ian Chappell and Tony Greig, or Austin Robertson and John Cornell, but Richie Benaud is the man who *really* made it credible. You bought what he was selling almost before you knew it was for sale; and, as with the best salesmen, the transaction left you feeling enriched.

Benaud had played cricket, we all of us knew, yet his commentary seldom betrayed this directly. The general but unspecific cognisance of his playing career acted instead as a form of quality certification: his was a warming but weightless past. Instead of banging on about how things were better in his day, he endorsed the present and blessed the future; he was the Pangloss of the pitch, who assured us, over and over again, that all was for the best in this best of possible cricket worlds.

Over time, of course, cricket lurched from disaster to disaster: rebel tours, illegal actions, ball tampering, match-fixing, racial squabbles, aggression that trembled on the brink of cheating, commercial chicanery that skirted the bounds of legality. Yet nothing threatened the serene majesty of Benaud's commentary, as interested and engaged by his hundredth one-day international as by his first. Over the years, one waited for Benaud to take a firm position on any of the game's major issues, while knowing also that nothing would ever endanger that stance of magisterial disinterest, and that unstated but unswerving commitment to the product.

Benaud still commentates—what purports to be his last summer lies ahead in Australia later this year. But we're starting to see the strains underlying his position that Benaud's silky skills so successfully disguised—strains laid entirely bare during the IPL in South Africa, where commentary was reduced to the level of infomercial.

The subtle thrall exerted by the commentary voice, in fact, has been integral to the diffusion of Twenty20. Because so much money rides on its success, there has been a competition in who can praise it and its participants more lavishly—every game is thrilling, every player a star, the whole concept the most exciting innovation since the incandescent lightbulb, and, of course, Lalit Modi a modern-day Moses, to the extent that the commentators have almost drowned themselves out, becoming indistinguishable from the advertisements between overs. But great rewards and honours await those who can endear themselves to the right people.

One of my most vivid recollections of the Twenty20 revolution is the game in Melbourne in February 2008 between Australia and India—quite possibly the worst international cricket match I have ever seen, over in two hours and twenty-eight overs, India capitulating for 74. Yet afterwards, Channel Nine's finest prowled the outfield for almost as long as Australia batted, interviewing players about the non-stop excitement that nobody had just seen. It was as credible as a Chinese government press release that the tanks in Tiananmen Square were simply participating in a segment of *Top Gear*. Who did these commentators think they were fooling?

The print media has always occupied a subtly different niche to the electronic. The television is there because cricket is entertainment on the basis of money spent on acquiring rights; newspapers are there because cricket is regarded as news, and enjoy access on a grace and favour basis, while the roles of those who straddle both forms are confused and confusing, like Ian Botham, an aura-for-hire, whether by Sky, the *Mirror* or Allen Stanford. But, as I said earlier, the fissuring boundaries between technologies are further collapsing news into entertainment and vice versa, with inevitable implications for what we say in the print media and how freely we can say it.

My trade has always been a mixture of the superficially sensational and squalid and the thoroughly tame and incurious. 'We do not need censorship *of* the press', noted Chesterton. 'We have censorship *by* the press.' Yet how is it that, in a period of such convulsive change, change that will define the direction of the game for decades to come, there is such limited interest in the relevant institutions: the BCCI, ICC, ECB, Cricket Australia, Sony, ESPN? How was it, for example, that Stanford had to go broke before anyone sussed that he was a fraud? Why the rapt fascination with the prices paid for players at the IPL auction, and such indifference to whom else cricket is making hugely wealthier?

I wonder *now* if we are not, consciously and unconsciously, avoiding evidences of corruption in cricket, as indeed we did in the 1990s, so heavily implicated have we become in this sports–industrial complex. I'm not sure I can offer a definitive answer to that, and there will certainly always be exceptions. But I do know that a lot of the toughest, cleverest, funniest and best informed writing about cricket these days is to be found in the blogosphere, where the writers are without fear or favour, and also, of course, money. Avid viewers, curious readers, discriminating consumers—they are out there in vast numbers, and it is up to cricket *and* the media to deserve them.

ICC History Conference, July 2009

Part VI
The Black Spot

SPOT-FIXING

The Fix is (Back) in

The no-ball is traditionally the most anti-climactic of cricket events, like a fault in tennis, or a false start in a sprint. It usually passes without notice or comment—and so did three bowled last week at Lord's by Pakistan's opening bowlers, Mohammad Amir and Mohammad Asif. As of Sunday morning in London, they took on a chillingly different meaning, when the tabloid *News of the World* presented them as exhibits A, B and C in a case that the national team in question was a plaything in the hands of illegal betting interests based in the sub-continent.

News of the World—the *Screws*, as it is known in the trade— would not normally be regarded as an unimpeachable cricket source. But its print punch came in a one-two with an internet haymaker: footage of thirty-five-year-old property developer Mazhar Majeed, *soi-disant* 'agent' to the Pakistan team, fastidiously counting out £140000 in cash as he enumerated when the three no-balls would be bowled, how most of the team were in on the secret, and how gamblers with the inside dope could clean up.

The paper's reporter, it was explained, had then watched as, precisely on cue, the no-balls were delivered, the eighteen-year-old Amir overstepping, like a clumsy dancer, by a foot. If the allegations were true, you had almost to salute the perpetrators' audacity. This had not happened in some faraway country on a tiny ground with an unfamiliar name; it had occurred in front of a packed house in a

Lord's Test, in the presence of scores of journalists, under the gaze of millions of television watchers around the world.

Cricket had come this way before. From the mid-1990s, every cricket team was at least brushed by the dark presence of match-fixing: essentially playing to lose for money. Pakistan were again deeply implicated; likewise India and South Africa. The Australians Shane Warne and Mark Waugh were fined simply for talking to a bookmaker. The countries involved all undertook inquisitions of differing qualities: the Qayyum inquiry, the Chandrachud inquiry, the King Commission, the O'Regan report. Finally, the Condon report, compiled for the International Cricket Council by the former head of London's Metropolitan Police, presented a manifesto for a new Anti-Corruption Unit, introducing additional security at grounds, imposing more inhibitions on player communication with the outside world.

Betting at the time was crude, primitive, indiscriminate. People thought in terms of fixing results—bribing people to bowl badly, or to bat slowly, in order that games might run away from them. In fact, this was in step with history. In its primordial days, cricket had had a long and intimate acquaintance with gambling: with so many independent variables and events, it was the perfect ecosystem for non-stop wagering. Two hundred years ago in England, betting, and clandestine inducements to fail, were part and parcel of the game.

Doses of Victorian rectitude, and a dawning economic aware-ness that the game was worth more if played fairly, had finally fixed that. But for those with a fondness for luck and chance, cricket never stopped presenting a target-rich environment. Thus, in England and Australia, a huge apparatus for legal gambling; thus, on the sub-continent, an even larger world of illegal bookmaking, hard to trace, nigh impossible to counteract, mixed with organised crime and money laundering, with huge sums changing hands per game on everything from the number of leg-byes to the order in which overs are bowled.

In the aftermath of the revelations, Mazhar Majeed was arrested and released on bail. The Pakistanis stumbled to defeat in front of tens of thousands of accusing eyes; their captain Salman Butt and manager Yawaz Saeed stumbled through a press conference in which every word rattled falsely. More *News of the World* accusations followed, enlarged on by Asif's estranged former girlfriend, casting doubts on the authenticity of Pakistan's capitulation in January's Sydney Test. Just for once, the longer-term implications of a scandal were easier to foresee than the short-term effects. For years after the first match-fixing scandal, every result had a false ring. Did we win? Or did the other team lose? Prepare for similar sensation, on a magnified scale, in which every incident, however minor, seems to contain some possibility of contrivance. No-ball, eh? Wonder how much that was worth...

Tehelka, September 2010

THE SPOT-FIXING SCANDAL

Moral Hazard

The sorriest aspect of the spot-fixing allegations against the Pakistan cricket team is not how appalling they are but how believable. When Hansie Cronje was caught by the short and curlies ten years ago and fessed up to fixing, there was genuine horror and disillusionment. Tough-as-tungsten Hansie on the take: Whoda thunk it? At the sight of a soft-spoken man in a hoodie behind a growing pile of cash explaining the whys and wherefores of no-balls in a Lord's Test, one's first reaction is: yep, that'd be right. Cricket is so filthy rich, ethically disoriented and atrociously administered that nothing comes as a surprise anymore.

Insert boilerplate here: the evidence against Mohammads Amir and Asif is damning but not proven: it scratches the surface of a complicated issue; it involves the boasts of a man with reason to boast. But somewhere along the line, cricket has gone beyond satire. Suraj Randiv bowls a no-ball on the spur of a moment's pique, and is vilified. When players are accused of cashing in on deliberate no-balls, there's no scale left on the moral outrage-o-meter.

This inherent believability of the charges should give us all pause. After all, on what grounds were we entitled to believe that the Pakistan cricket team was secure from corruption? President Asif Ali Zardari is a multibillionaire known as Mr Ten Per Cent for his sticky commercial fingers. Pakistan's institutions are being overwhelmed by multiple, overlapping crises, now exacerbated by a natural disaster of horrifying proportions; a general sense of every man for himself prevails. The country's hopes of hosting an inbound cricket tour do little but dwindle, thanks partly to the intractable security situation, and partly to a board of control that could dissolve into factions over the flavour of the cordial at a drinks break. Poorly paid, poorly led, chronically insecure Pakistani players surrounded by paranoia, cynicism and nepotism would seem absolutely ripe for the plucking, especially when the IPL, from which they are barred, is making such a mockery of relative rewards. To some players, going flat out in a Test match must seem kinda daggy and uncool, given the instant riches obtainable from Twenty20 mediocrity.

Fixing results is rightly viewed as the most heinous of sporting offences. Fundamental to any game, observed the sociologist Anatol Rapoport, is the 'assumption of similarity'—the idea that 'one's opponent intends to win if he can', and that, in attempting this, he will be influenced by 'similar considerations' and the 'same kinds of strategies'. Spot fixing, at least on the face of it, is qualitatively different to the actual doctoring of outcomes, closer on the continuum of malpractice to insider trading than outright fraud and/or embezzlement. And just as some in the securities industry are known to regard insider trading as a 'victimless crime', spot-fixing is not so obviously a blot on honour as playing dead for dollars. After all, the losers if a spot is fixed are illegal gamblers punting with illegal bookmakers—and who cares about them?

The problem is that, as Lady Macbeth found out, spots don't rinse easily. Spot-fixing is a calculated deception; in order to work, it has to be. But when sensed to be a factor, it casts doubt on the integrity of every surrounding event. And once a player has known sin, as it were, he makes himself a target for more elaborate malfeasance. The players compromised in the 1990s were usually sucked in quite casually, then implicated in scenarios from which extrication became more and more difficult. If *News of the World* is to believed—and there is admittedly a certain novelty involved in using that expression—results were not beyond the fixers' ken.

In the comparison of the first fixing wave a decade ago with this latest version, one should not ignore the changed context: the climate of 'easy money' and unquestioned entitlement in which cricketers are now brought up. No sooner has a modern player emerged these days than he is being plied with commercial 'opportunities', to promote this product or that, to endorse this little program or accept that itty-bitty payola—opportunities, however commercially defensible and sanctioned by custom, to effectively lie for money. This car is great! This drink is cool! In such schemings, of course, there will invariably be involved a so-called 'agent', taking a cut for at least purporting to 'look after' the player's interests. One of the distinguishing characteristics of the Pakistanis' travails is that that the inducements are alleged to have come through a trusted intermediary, Mazhar Majeed, also responsible for the team's various commercial arrangements: a lazy, naive or debauched mind might well have failed to distinguish between the different categories of 'sponsorship'.

The sad reality is that a certain kind of personality will always be susceptible to illegal inducement, especially if such inducements fall into the category of 'easy money', in which nobody *really* gets hurt, and not much harm *seems* to have been done. And from this it can be inferred that the security measures the ICC first took to quarantine international teams from potential corrupters, however well-intentioned, were bound to fall short of fixing fixing. They bought cricket a decade to clean itself up, which was valuable in the short term; by acting cosmetically, lending the appearance of integrity rather than achieving its actuality, they might prove to have been counterproductive in the longer term. Because it remains the case that a player willing to sell his services will find buyers whether he's allowed to use a mobile phone in the dressing room or not. Where cricket really needed to act in the last decade, by inculcating a culture protective of the game's welfare, it failed abjectly; if anything, the fast buck mentality and constant moral improvisations of administrators have conduced to the opposite.

The maladministration in Pakistan that leaves not just financial holes in balance sheets but bullet holes in team buses is just the beginning. In the last two years, two member boards of the ICC (the West Indies and England) have gone guilelessly into partnership with a businessman whom the US Securities and Exchange Commission has since called 'a fraud of colossal proportions'. Two other member boards (Zimbabwe and South Africa) have had forensic accountants called in to examine their financial irregularities, the findings in neither case seeing the light of day. Sri Lanka's former captain Arjuna Ranatunga claimed last month that 'the money ... from TV rights deals' in his country had been flowing 'into the pockets of some individuals'; nobody bothered denying it.

The BCCI can claim at least to have taken action against an administrator for the dubiousness of his dealings, the irony being that Lalit Modi, for all his sins, real and imagined, was arguably its ablest officer. The ICC's idea of a good day's work, meanwhile, is mooning John Howard. Corruption has become cricket's gravest challenge, and it neither begins nor ends with Pakistan's benighted cricket team.

Cricinfo, September 2010

SPOT-FIXING

Class Consciousness

The voices are soft, well-spoken. The tone is matter-of-fact. But for the piles of cash accumulating on the coffee table, the exchange could be the negotiation of an everyday investment opportunity.

Yet the *News of the World* video of Mazhar Majeed apparently accepting cash on behalf of Pakistan's cricketers to bowl no-balls on demand deserves to become a motif of cricket in the 21st century, as West Indian pace was to the 1980s and Warne wizardry was to the 1990s.

It's the normality of the transaction that actually makes it so disturbing. It gives an ordinary, even a pleasant face to cricket corruption, like that of the polite, inconspicuous Meyer Wolfsheim in *The Great Gatsby*, whom Gatsby then explains is the infamous World Series fixer. 'It never occurred to me,' muses Nick Carraway, 'that one man could start to play with the faith of fifty million people—with the single-mindedness of a burglar blowing a safe.'

What the video proves exactly will ultimately be for lawyers to decide. But what it and the other footage of Majeed excitedly expositing his schemes show in general is cricket struggling, haplessly and helplessly, with its Asian economic miracle. In the last three years, an ancient pastoral English game has become the biggest wealth engine in sport on the Indian sub-continent. With the breakneck expansion of the Indian economy, massive television rights fees and a herd of corporate investors have promoted a tournament, the Indian Premier League, which has monetised cricket as never before. Short, sharp, exuberant, noisy games of Twenty20 cricket played between privately-owned clubs based in India's main cities fill grounds and cram airwaves—part sport, part soap opera, part Bollywood movie.

The IPL's growth into a brand valued at $US4 billion has not just split cricket but shivered it to fragments. The game's old multi-lateral governance system is in disarray, its nominal administration, the International Cricket Council, having been superceded in influence by the Board of Control for Cricket in India, a round table of self-interested politicians, bureaucrats and businessmen.

Cricket's old hierarchy of values has also been set at nought. Players can now earn millions of dollars in a few weeks of three-hour cricket games. The rewards for traditional five-day cricket are in most countries paltry by comparison—in Pakistan they are downright derisory.

Cricketers have been divided as never before into haves and have-nots, those inside the gilded circle and outside. The world's best-paid player, a very good although not great wicketkeeper-batsman called MS Dhoni who nonetheless looks a treat and sprinkles gold dust on those products he endorses, is estimated by *Forbes* to pull down more than $11 million annually. Pakistan's teen speed sensation Mohammad Amir, meanwhile, earns less than $30 000 a year on his national contract, topped up with Test fees less than half those enjoyed by Australian and English players.

The effects of this disequilibrium are being felt even in Australia. In his new diary, *The Captain's Year*, a chagrined Ricky Ponting describes an Australian team meeting in February to discuss the advisability of players taking up IPL invitation in light of doubts about security arrangements. Ponting, anxious for a collective decision, found that the 'one-in, all-in' ways of yesteryear no longer applied. 'A few of the guys who are involved solely in the IPL put it pretty bluntly they … want to go their own way,' he reports euphemistically. Australian cricketers are at least amply-rewarded, and tend to shrink from the sight of unfamiliar men with bulging chequebooks. Where cricket's new order has placed the gravest strain is on those countries and cricketers deprived of recent bounties.

For there is an underside to mass Asian prosperity: a black economy that accounts for nearly a fifth of India's GDP, and perhaps as much as half of Pakistan's. It is money, almost always cash, in headlong pursuit of superior returns, and the best are often available through illegal gambling. It's estimated that Asian gamblers wager as much as $US500 million on games of cricket which, thanks to the power of satellite television, can come from anywhere: it could be a Test, an IPL fixture, a one-day international in Australia or a T20 game between English counties. The betting need not concern results. The new scourge is spot-fixing—the practice of gambling on specific incidents and variables, like the running total at the end of each over. If this seems akin to betting on flies on a wall, the rewards, and thus the value of inside information, are potentially huge. Bookmakers on the sub-continent are myriad and mistrustful of one another. Plunges—colossal bets spread across multiple bookies—are therefore easy to engineer.

Pakistan had much to offer cricket's exciting, rich, T20-centric new world. Its cricketers are skilful, aggressive, flamboyant. They starred in the first IPL. They won last year's World Twenty20 with cricket of glorious abandon. Their country, however, is at the war on terror's ravaged frontline, dogged by collapsing institutions and accumulating hatreds. President Asif Ali Zardari was rattling around his French chateau while twenty million of his countrymen were recently displaced by a natural disaster, foreign relief for which was grudging because of the conviction most would be corruptly rerouted.

Zardari is also patron of the Pakistan Cricket Board, a nest of cronies chaired by the brother-in-law of the country's defence minister, which metes out life bans as flippantly as a teacher giving detentions, but which protects to the point of impunity those it favours. It is probably no coincidence that one of the bowlers allegedly in Majeed's pay was Mohammad Asif, who has twice tested positive for banned substances but escaped without punishment.

Unsurprisingly given the interpenetration of politics and cricket, Pakistan's cricket fortunes have been a faithful index of its collapse into chaos. As the security situation has worsened, opportunities to play have dried up. The country's only attempt to host an inbound tour in the last three years ended in a hail of bullets; its team played no Tests at all in 2008. This isolation was exacerbated at the end of that year by the Mumbai attacks, which in causing the collapse in Pakistan's relations with India not only deprived its cricketers of their marquee Test series, but led to their exclusion from the IPL. The scenario fits the evidence now presented by *News of the World*—that, deprived of a share in cricket's legitimate economic miracle, the players sought solace in its illegitimate parallel.

Some efforts have been made in the last year to rehabilitate Pakistan cricket: they have been hosted in England these last ten weeks for three Tests against Australia and four against the home team. The rehab has run the same course as that of Ben Cousins, with some great days, some mediocre, and a few nightmarish.

Pakistan's pace attack may be the world's most exciting. Ironically just a day before the *News of the World*'s revelations, former England captain Nasser Hussain was arguing that Amir and Asif had revived the electric thrill of high-quality new-ball bowling: 'I've heard a lot of chat this summer from some of the more experienced players about how much the ball is doing and how hard it has been for batting. To which I'd say: welcome to proper Test cricket.' The day after, however, looked less like proper Test cricket than a play by Nobel laureate cum opening batsman Harold Pinter, all menacing pauses and mumble insinuations. The expressions of the home team as Pakistan's batsmen resumed can best be described as of cold fury. As he handed Amir the man of the series award, the England Cricket Board chairman resembled a lofty diner served a rotting fish.

The worst outcome—and cricket exhibits a rare talent for finding these—will now not be the substantiation of the allegations, but the opposite. The difficulty in making a case based on the *News of World*'s sting is that the evidence is powerful but largely circumstantial, unless it can be demonstrated that at least some of the cash found its way from Majeed to the players. Even then, for an offence to have been committed under English law, a party must be proven to have been defrauded—and illegal gamblers are hardly about to assert their legal rights.

If no prosecutions occur, cricket will be left with a kind of Typhoid Mary in its midst—a participating team nobody will wish contact. Avaricious spot-fixers and venal players will be further emboldened. If a case cannot be made in England, with its sophisticated police force and centuries of jurisprudence, what chance that overtaxed and under-resourced Asian authorities will ever catch up? That will leave the ICC to clean up the mess—a matter of expecting a solution from part of the problem. On it will then depend our chances of again looking at a game of cricket without wondering whether it is not simply the front on a crooked casino.

The Australian, September 2010

CONSPIRACY IN CRICKET

All the Conspirators

We're waiting. Doubly so. We've been waiting almost a month to see what the International Cricket Council's anti-corruption and security unit makes of plausible prima-facie allegations of venality against three cricketers from Pakistan. And as of last week, we're now also waiting for the promise by Pakistan Cricket Board chairman Ejaz Butt to substantiate his claims of 'a conspiracy to defraud Pakistan and Pakistan cricket' by naming 'the names of the people, the parties and the bodies involved'.

The former wait will now be lengthened by the latter, because if it was not obvious before it is clear now that the ICC can expect no assistance from the PCB – on the contrary, its investigations will be resisted at every turn. And although the tendency is to think that nothing is happening, or at least will happen until some form of announcement, the wait has itself become a story, indicative firstly of cricket's sheer administrative dysfunctionality, and now of its collapse into lurid conspiracy theorizing.

The first is no news to anybody; the second less surprising than it ought to be. It's common to say that we are in a vintage era of conspiracism, except that it never really goes away; only the demonologies change. It used to be rosucrucians, freemasons and fluoridation; now it's the Illuminati, the Bilderberg Group and 9/11.

Cricket has a low-level but abiding affection for conspiracies. It reserves a special place for men in smoke-filled rooms – they are called selectors. It used to be said that a good 'un from the north of England might play Test cricket, but a good 'un from the south certainly would. It's still said, in Victoria anyway, that playing for New South Wales is a prerequisite of Australian selection. Umpiring decisions are always a fertile area for speculations.

In Pakistan at the moment, however, the scenario is closer to that delineated by Richard Hofstader in his famous essay 'The Paranoid Style in American Politics'. The paranoid style, he argued, was distinguished not by the seeing of 'plots here and there in history' but the perception of 'a "vast" or "gigantic" conspiracy as the motive force in historical events'. In most countries, conspiracy theorizing comes from outside the mainstream, and government does its best to damp it down. In Pakistan, the government is perhaps the chief propagator. In the matter of spot-fixing, it wasn't long before the first dark hintings from the country's interior minister Rehman Malik. 'We want to ascertain if there is any conspiracy against the team or to defame Pakistan,' said Malik. 'There have been conspiracies against Pakistan in the past. We want to get the facts and get them exonerated.'

Nobody could accuse Malik of prejudging the evidence; he wasn't interested in evidence at all. But, then, nor was he interested last year after the attack on the Sri Lankan team bus en route to Gaddafi Stadium: 'We suspect a foreign hand behind this incident. The democracy of the country has been undermined, and foreigners are repeatedly attacked to harm the country's image.'

In the last month, numerous stories about Indian perfidy have appeared in the Pakistani press, notably Lahore's *Nation* ('Is There an Indian Connection?') and Islamabad's *Daily Mail* ('The Lord's Accusation Another RAW ploy'). Corroborating Churchill's maxim that a lie can be half way round the world before the truth can get its pants on, the *Daily Mail*'s report that 'the *News of the World* and [the] notorious Indian intelligence agency RAW were the mastermind[s] behind all this planned mess' was actually picked up and run on India's *Aaj TV*.

Not that the media has needed to stretch its imagination too far, thanks to Ejaz Butt, who if he holds a position more than a few days it can only be because he has forgotten to contradict himself. 'I don't believe in any conspiracy theory,' said Butt first, after meeting ICC president Sharad Pawar in New Delhi on 15 September. 'I am a simple businessman and a cricket administrator. I am also a part of the ICC and will stick to its Code of Conduct.'

Not for long. Four days later, he was on-message: 'There is loud and clear talk in bookie circles that some English players have taken enormous amounts of money to lose the match. No wonder there was such a collapse.' Even Shahid Afridi trended in the same direction, moving from saying 'sorry to all cricket lovers and all the cricketing nations' to insisting that 'the way so many people are joining the bashing of Pakistan cricket shows that a conspiracy is on to finish our cricket'.

Yet the first hints of corruption among Pakistan's cricketers this year emerged not in the English media, but among PCB officers during the in-camera inquiry into the team's disastrous tour of Australia. Thanks to the video of proceedings screened by Geo Super, we know that the team's leadership was deeply concerned about player underperformance. Coach Intikhab Alam said he had 'heard many stories about match-fixing'; likewise Intikhab's deputy Aaqib Javed: 'I can't say 100 per cent that there is match-fixing, but I have my strong suspicions.' Commenting on his keeper's performance in Sydney, captain Mohammad Yousuf said simply: 'Some things are obviously clear. What shall I say?'

By the same token, Butt hardly has the field of conspiracy-theorizing to himself at the moment. Even in England and Australia, hackles rise in a split second. Counties truckling to Lalit Modi? Countries objecting to John Howard? Both were denounced as conspiracies, even if they were more straightforwardly instances of toadying, opportunism and self-admiration.

Race is an issue fertile with possible fulminations and accusations. A couple of weeks ago, London's *Daily Mail* reported that Tillakaratne Dilshan had, apparently by chance, encountered an illegal bookmaker in a nightclub, while also making amply clear in its story that there was 'no suggestion of any wrongdoing', and that CSL had 'followed the ICC's protocol to the letter'? Sri Lanka Cricket's florid response made Butt look like the acme of restraint: 'It is a foolish attempt to malign a Sri Lankan cricketer without a shred of evidence. It smacks of a white conspiracy ... These allegations are indicative of a deep racist bias, besides plain ignorance of the truth.'

Scratch the surface of south Asian cricket, in fact, and one intriguing low-level conspiracy theory does not take long to emerge: that of 'the veto', of which non-white countries complain of having been helpless victims at the ICC until twenty years ago. It refers to the status of England and Australia as Foundation Members at the ICC for the purposes of rule 4 © of the body's old constitution: 'Recommendations to member countries are to be made by a majority of full members present and voting and one of which in such a majority should be a Foundation member.' It is flourished now as evidence of the existence of a kind of *Protocols of the Elders of Lord's*. Yet the vast majority of those who do so seem quite unencumbered by any knowledge of the ICC's history.

The real reason for rule 4 © was not to exercise power, but to prevent power accumulating, something which for most of the twentieth century suited every ICC member, preserving their sovereignty in matters like fixturing, revenue distribution, player discipline and umpire appointments. At some stages, furthermore, England and Australia were as mistrustful of one another as they were of other countries; indeed, after Kerry Packer's irruption on the scene, their administrators were profoundly divided.

The ICC's structure as an adjunct of the Marylebone Cricket Club with concurrent senior officers remained quaintly archaic, but the majority generally ruled, and rational argument usually prevailed. Despite the sympathies of English and Australian administrators, firm agreement on the sub-continent and in the West Indies kept South Africa in deserved isolation; thanks mainly to Pakistan, an elite umpiring panel came into being; thanks to the arguments chiefly of Sri Lanka, the cause of video adjudication advanced.

The only attempt that England and Australia made to invoke Rule 4 © seems to have been in July 1984, when India argued for moving the next World Cup to the sub-continent. The invocation failed: the ICC chairman, Marylebone president Arthur Dibbs, despite being a rock-ribbed member of the British establishment, agreed with India that only a simple majority was needed. Perhaps he wasn't in on the conspiracy.

What is fascinating about this conspiracy theory is that it has emerged only quite recently as a thick-headed *tu quoque* justification for Indian supremacy: you ran cricket; now we run it, and it's payback time. 'India has been subservient for 100 years,' claimed Lalit Modi, appealing to Indian victimhood. 'People are used to dictating terms to us. We're just evening the playing field. And if it's our turn to have some glory, so much the better.'

Yet the more one looks back on the ICC of the 1980s, the more impressive it seems, because of how productively members collaborated on a host of difficult issues, how reasonably they disagreed, and the overall calibre of administrators like Nur Khan, Allan Rae and NKP Salve. Members certainly coexisted then on terms far more equal than they do now. Today the ICC can't even elect a vice-president without coming apart at the seams. Furthermore, it's not even a necessary argument. There are a great many sound economic and cultural reasons for India to be the dominant voice in world cricket; the previous existence of rule 4 © isn't among them. Its deployment as a rhetorical ploy proves nothing except the comfort of conspiracies, even those one can claim to have routed.

Because conspiracies are a splendid consolation to the vanquished and diminished. As David Aaronovitch explains in his excellent guidebook *Voodoo Histories*: 'If it can be proved that there has been a conspiracy which has transformed politics and society, then their defeat is not the product of their own inherent weakness or popularity, let alone their mistakes; it is due to the almost demonic ruthlessness of their enemy.' Thus their present popularity in cricket, increasingly divided between haves and have-nots, between the big four countries and the rest, between those inside the gilded T20 circle and those excluded. There is a lot of failure to go round, a lot of blame to be apportioned – and also avoided.

If it is to survive its most recent drift into malpractice, cricket badly needs to break the growing attraction of conspiracism, which

The Black Spot

tends always to stand in the way of change by perpetuating the status quo, by thwarting the trust and honesty integral to reform. Conspiracy theories are fundamentally disempowering: they pardon bad behaviour, with their insistence that invisible forces elsewhere are always indulging in worse; they penalize good behaviour, depicting it as futile in the face of clandestine oppressors.

What can cricket do? One reason for the trend is that cricket's administration has always been too incestuous, too secretive and insufficiently accountable. How cricket reaches crucial decisions of policy is to most fans a mystery, when it is not a matter of indifference – the impression conveyed therefore is often of shoddy politicking, diplomatic expediency and cynical self-interest. Transparency of governance and seriousness about conflicts of interest have therefore never been more imperative.

What the situation also calls for is magnanimity. Psychoanalyst Stephen Grosz has explained conspiracies as defence weapons against indifference, against 'the terrible thought that nobody cares about you'. Fans in Pakistan have had a great many reasons to brood on that thought in the last three years, as doors to international cricket then the Indian Premier League have been closed to them. Even now – perhaps especially now – cricket must find ways of keeping faith with Pakistan's benighted and innocent public. They especially cannot wait indefinitely.

CORRUPTION

Who Guards the Guards?

A tenth World Cup. A fourth Indian Premier League. England then Australia hosting India. For cricket, the year of 2011 holds golden promise. That gold, though, is proving more difficult to handle than it should.

Is cricket corrupt? One finding on this question will be returned on 5 February when the judges who last month heard charges of spot-fixing against three Pakistani cricketers publish their deliberations. Whatever the result, it won't be pretty. Even assuming the charges stick, there is precious little for cricket to congratulate itself on: it took a tabloid newspaper then a parallel police investigation to make most of the case.

There is, moreover, a disturbing inattention among cricket's governing classes to the matter of corruption in their own ranks. Players at least are bound by a code of conduct. By what are administrators bound? A classic definition of corruption is 'authority plus monopoly minus transparency'. What form of words could better describe your average member board of the International Cricket Council?

The risk of administrative corruption is something cricket tacitly acknowledges. Last October, after an ICC executive board in Dubai discussed corruption as a general issue, chief executive Haroon Lorgat followed up with a letter to each member organization in which it sought to 'remind all registered players, support personnel and Member Board officials about their responsibilities, our clear stance on corruption, the need to abide by the ICC Anti-Corruption Code and that failure to do so could result in severe penalties'. One paragraph is worth citing in full:

> The Board was also determined to ensure that any other form of corrupt activities in the administration of the game (i.e. outside of the international players and support personnel group who are covered by various rules and regulations) should be rigorously dealt with to protect the integrity of the game. In this regard the Board agreed that any substantive allegations against any individual involved in the administration of the game should be thoroughly and independently investigated, unless there are disciplinary processes contained within the constitution of a Member Board for a credible review to be held internally.

In one respect, it put the boards concerned on notice, that houses not in order should be made so. It also, however, exhibited some of the ICC's limitations. The word 'substantive' looks innocuous enough in this context – after all, who would be expected to investigate something 'insubstantive'? But what about when there is disagreement about 'substantivity', as there evidently is between Mtutuzeli Nyoka and Gerald Majola, respectively president and CEO of Cricket South Africa, in the matter of the bonuses rained on that body's executive after the second Indian Premier League? And what about when there is disagreement about the adequacy of internal disciplinary processes, as there is between the Board of Control for Cricket in India and its erstwhile wunderkind Lalit Modi in respect of the many and varied allegations against the latter? So what starts on the right rhetorical track – 'determined to ensure', 'rigorously dealt with', 'protect the integrity' – wanders off in such a way as to afford ample wriggle room.

And exactly what 'severe penalties' did the ICC really have to brandish? The ultimate sanction, one supposes, would be suspension, which was mooted in some punitive circles last year for the perennially dysfunctional Pakistan Cricket Board. Yet it is a surely only a very last resort, because the sufferers would chiefly be blameless fans, mainly those in Pakistan, but also those who recognize the team as cricket's most exorbitantly talented and mercurial.

So what does the ICC have to hand where enforcing any sort of minimally acceptable behaviour on its members? The answer is: not much. Bear in mind that it has taken a decade for the ICC's member boards to recognize it as an appropriate forum for the policing of match-fixing, following the failure of their individual whitewashings. The only concerted attempt to get to the bottom of the activities of a member was the insertion of forensic accountants into the Augean stable of Zimbabwe Cricket which three years ago cost Lorgat's predecessor his job; around even the PCB in the last six months, the ICC has trodden warily, anxious not to look too doctrinaire.

There is, however, more and more reason for concern. In South Asia, where so much of cricket's wealth is located, corruption is a daily, deep-rooted fact of life. On the annual corruption index published by Transparency International, an NGO, India (87th), Sri Lanka (91st), Bangladesh (134th) and Pakistan (143rd) all rank in the bottom half of the table. The PCB in particular does nothing to discourage the view that the bribery and graft endemic in Pakistan civil society pervades cricket also. Nobody batted an eyelid last year when Lt.-Gen. Tauqir Zia recounted a conversation with a 'gentleman' who rang him during his four-year PCB chairmanship:

> So he said, 'So-and-so player should be included in the team, because he fixes matches and we get money. You know, that's our livelihood.' So I said, 'Ah, I can give you appointment and a job in Pakistan Cricket Board. Why do you have to earn money, you know, in a wrong manner?'

The caller declined the job – apparently he was making enough money where he was, thanks. But welcome to a country where a match-fixer can apparently ring the board president and be offered a gig.

Sri Lanka Cricket, meanwhile, was last year dubbed Sri Lanka's third most corrupt institution by the country's own sports minister Chandara Ratnayake, who then promptly broke his promise of reform. Capable of the instant constitution of a star chamber to punish Suraj Randiv for bowling a no-ball, Sri Lanka Cricket has somehow proven incapable of organizing an election of office bearers since its so-called 'interim committee' was appointed in March 2005, or of doing anything about last year's allegations by former captain (and former ICC executive board member) Arjuna Ranatunga that 'the money that comes from TV rights deals has gone into the pockets of some individuals'.

As for India, where last year's headlines were all of the Radia Tapes and the 2G Scandal, and where one estimate is the country has been illegally bilked of as much as forty per cent of gross domestic product since independence, the strategy of the Board of Control for Cricket in India of simply heaping blame on Modi has worn thin. When they appeared recently before the Parliamentary Standing Committee on Finance, the BCCI's three senior officials simply disclaimed all responsibility for their organization's breaches of the Foreign Exchange Management Act during the second IPL, sidestepped the funding of IPL franchises through tax shelters like the Bahamas, Mauritius and the British Virgin Islands, and otherwise impressed as accountable to nobody. With a year to move on from Modi, the BCCI has made slow progress on restoring faith in its processes: approximately nobody who watches the IPL, for instance, believes that the salary cap is other than cosmetic and that player retention has not been engineered to benefit vested interests.

Treating corruption in cricket as a south Asian problem, however, is unjust. The cricket economy is global, and the challenges affect everyone, a pursuit used to counting its pennies having abruptly become wealthy beyond the dreams of avarice. In some respects, cricket is like a poor but happy soul suddenly in receipt of news about a vast inheritance, and as a result surrounded by a host of new 'friends' who want to 'help' him – although, of course, they also expect to be rewarded for it. The game contains too many people living too comfortably who find it expedient to look the other way, and not just in its administrative echelons, but players, agents and media too.

Cricket administration is also experiencing a cultural shift from residual claims to a philanthropic status, for which it enjoys in many countries an exemption from tax, to something resembling more closely a publicly listed company, but for which it is yet to accept proper degrees of commercial oversight, continuing to arrogate to itself the respect due a charity ('We are doing this for the good of the game!') while doing nothing to disguise its profit motive ('We've got to maximize stakeholder value!').

Direction in that climacteric will have to come from the ICC which, for all the BCCI's status as financial bellwether, is still a major distributor of revenue to the world's far-flung cricket community. This year, containing as it does a World Cup, the ICC will distribute hundreds of millions of dollars among its members – yet it will lose all oversight over those monies the minute they are disgorged. How sure can the ICC be that these funds will actually enrich the game, given the involvement of often small local organizations with few financial controls and essentially no probity checks? Will the ICC be able to enumerate the constructive playing, organizational and infrastructural ends to which these payments have been put?

The answer is that it can't, but that arguably it should, that a system essentially of self-regulation is coming to a point where it is inadequate to guard cricket against the influence of those who are chiefly parasitic on it, and that a system where the difference in the standards of behaviour expected of those who play the game and those who run it now gapes too wide. It should be an exciting year for cricket, but excitement passes; of abiding public respect and trust does the game also have a need.

Cricinfo, January 2011

SPOT-FIXING

Now What?

In 1936–7, Australia, led by Donald Bradman, staged one of cricket's greatest comebacks, fighting back from a 0–2 deficit to overcome England 3–2. There was joy – and some scepticism. Bradman's father put it to him that the first two Tests *must* have been rigged, to guarantee interest in the last three. 'I told him you can't rig a game of cricket,' Bradman recalled, 'but I can't say I convinced him.'

Pace the Don, his father was right. You *can* rig a game of cricket, lucratively, and you need attempt nothing so ambitious as meddling with the result: reach a score at a pre-determined point, yield a certain number of runs in a spell of bowling, and you can take a cut when others clean up.

Cricket is particularly susceptible to manipulation. Its myriad variables and long duration make for plentiful betting opportunites. It is most popular in Asia where gambling is either very restricted or illegal, beyond the reach of supervision and regulation. It has grown rich comparatively quickly – in the last generation – so that its attitudes and institutional structures have struggled to adapt.

In India, cricket's candy mountain, the attitude to corruption is cavalier, even light-hearted. Indian cricketers, it is argued, are so extravagantly rewarded that they would do nothing to endanger their careers. Yet being rich beyond the dreams of avarice did nothing to stop Wall Street financiers driving the world's economy into a ditch. Money does not lead naturally to a state of satiety; more often it instils a yen for more.

Attitudes to fitting reward, moreover, have been debauched by the advent of Twenty20 leagues, which make overnight millionaires of ordinary players who happen to hit a long ball even if they have no other faculty. Cricket, then, is becoming a decidedly unequal society, of haves with a sense of entitlement, and have-nots with a sense of grievance. You could not engineer an environment more conducive to corruption if you tried.

In the last decade, cricket has gotten extremely lucky twice. Indian police tapping a gangster's phone overheard his conversations with Hansie Cronje; a British tabloid caught an intermediary selling the services of Salman Butt, Mohammad Amir and Mohammad Asif. Cricket's authorities can derive no satisfaction from these isolated prosecutions, which they themselves did nothing to initiate. The game will languish under the pall of corruption a while yet – and, frankly, it deserves to.

Sydney Morning Herald March 2011

Index

406 *Index*

BCCI attitude to, 74, 100, 170–1, 197
city-based companies use template of, 23
inaugural games in, 28, 30
IPL and, 149, 165, 170, 197, 333
teams in Pakistan, Bangladesh and Sri Lanka, 100
Twenty20 and, 30, 197
Indian Express, 23
Indian People's League, 207
Indian Premier League (IPL), 29, 34–7, 40–1, 45–7, 49–61 *passim*, 67, 248, 249, 314
as autocracy, 222
BCCI cedes control of, to ICC, 171
as best of the best, 197
brand value of, 50, 208, 209, 210, 223, 387
breathtaking hitting during early games of, 35–6
brings national pride, 198
broadcasting rights to, 30
brought to YouTube, 202
as 'clash of civilisations', 199
commentators and, 35
concept of, introduced to international associations, 29
conflict-of-interest principle ignored by, 35
corruption scandal, 203–12
as cricket's proverbial melting pot, 195–6
'cricketainment' and, 215
entrepreneurship in, 201
fluctuating ratings for, 67
franchises and, *see* franchises/franchisees
as free-standing entity, 220
free enterprise system and, 196
governing council of, 41, 55, 56, 66, 215, 217, 218, 221
imperialism and, ix, 135–7
impetus for, 197
innovation in, 201
IPL: Cricket & Commerce and, 36
'mess', 217
model of, 60, 213–16
Modi forgoes salary from, 41
Modi suspended as chairman of

council of, 59
Modi's alleged misconduct concerning, 56–9, 217–18
and Modi's plans for a 50-over city-based, 26, 28
Modi's equity in teams of, 56
monopoly of official cricket challenged by, 47
naming rights of, 30
Pakistan channel declines to show, 47
player auctions of, 32–3, 44, 47, 50, 62, 249
popularity, compared to Tests, 181
reputation of, 208
and security, during Indian elections, 40–1
skills second to entertainment in, 34
skills seen as secondary to entertainment in, 34
Sony Entertainment/WSG acquire rights to, 30
South Africa offers to stage, 41
Tests and ODIs, 215
transparency within the, 203–7
TV ratings boosted by, 36
2011, 248–52
valued, 50
Viagra-like qualities of, 158
wealth generation through, 386
see also IPL2
Indian Summers (Wright), 14–16
Indian tours, lucrative nature of, 80
Indraprastha Stadium, Delhi, 4
infomercial, 374
intellectual property (IP), 122–3, 163, 372
International Champions League, 172
international cricket, 26, 49, 145, 197, 221, 265, 267, 290, 300, 301, 321, 337, 354, 375
BCCI claims Twenty20 'dilutes', 20
Bodyline and, 199
branding and, 251
Champions Trophy and, 152–6
changing face of, xi, 71, 87, 129, 187, 192, 195, 256, 341, 346, 396
commerce and, 146, 150
'freelance players' and, 47